INSIGHT GUIDES

COSTA RICA

APA PUBLICATIONS

Part of the Langenscheidt Publishing Group

INSIGHT GUIDE
COSTA RICA

Editorial
Project Editor
Paul Murphy
Managing Editor
Huw Hennessy
Series Editor
Dorothy Stannard

Distribution

United States
Langenscheidt Publishers, Inc.
36–36 33rd Street 4th Floor
Long Island City, NY 11106
Fax: 1 (718) 784 0640

UK & Ireland
GeoCenter International Ltd
Meridian House, Churchill Way West
Basingstoke, Hampshire RG21 6YR
Fax: (44) 1256 817988

Australia
Universal Publishers
1 Waterloo Road
Macquarie Park, NSW 2113
Fax: (61) 2 9888 9074

New Zealand
Hema Maps New Zealand Ltd (HNZ)
Unit 2, 10 Cryers Road
East Tamaki, Auckland 2013
Fax: (64) 9 273 6479

Worldwide
Apa Publications GmbH & Co.
Verlag KG (Singapore branch)
38 Joo Koon Road, Singapore 628990
Tel: (65) 6865 1600. Fax: (65) 6861 6438

Printing

Insight Print Services (Pte) Ltd
38 Joo Koon Road, Singapore 628990
Tel: (65) 6865 1600. Fax: (65) 6861 6438

©2009 Apa Publications GmbH & Co.
Verlag KG (Singapore branch)
All Rights Reserved
First Edition 1995
Third Edition (updated) 2004
Updated 2007, Revised 2008

CONTACTING THE EDITORS
We would appreciate it if readers
would alert us to errors or out-
dated information by writing to:
Insight Guides, P.O. Box 7910,
London SE1 1WE, England.
Fax: (44) 20 7403 0290.
insight@apaguide.co.uk
NO part of this book may be reproduced,
stored in a retrieval system or transmitted
in any form or means electronic, mech-
anical, photocopying, recording or otherwise, without prior written permission of
Apa Publications. Brief text quotations
with use of photographs are exempted
for book review purposes only. Information has been obtained from sources
believed to be reliable, but its accuracy
and completeness, and the opinions
based thereon, are not guaranteed.

www.insightguides.com

ABOUT THIS BOOK

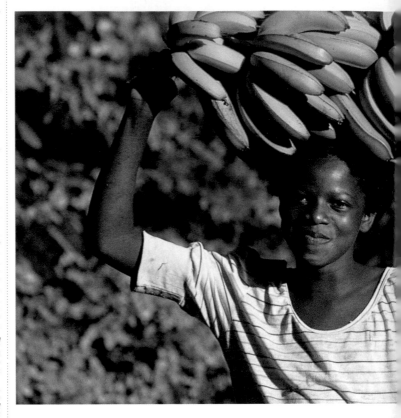

The first Insight Guide pioneered the use of creative full-color photography in travel guides in 1970. Since then, we have expanded our range to cater for our readers' need not only for reliable information about their chosen destination but also for a real understanding of the culture and workings of that destination. Now, when the internet can supply inexhaustible (but not always reliable) facts, our books marry text and pictures to provide those much more elusive qualities: knowledge and discernment. To achieve this, they rely heavily on the authority of locally based writers and photographers.

How to use this book
The book has been carefully structured both to convey an understanding of Costa Rica and its culture and to guide readers through its many sights and natural attractions:

The **Features** section, with a yellow color bar, covers the country's **history** and **culture** in lively authoritative essays written by specialists.

The **Places** section, with a blue bar, provides full details of all the sights and areas worth seeing. The chief places of interest are coordinated by number with specially drawn maps.

The **Travel Tips** listings section, with an orange bar at the back of the book, offers a convenient point of reference for information on travel, accommodation, restaurants and other practical aspects of the country. Information may be located quickly by using the index printed on the back cover flap, which is also designed to serve as a handy bookmark.

The contributors

This new edition, which builds on the earlier edition edited by **Harvey** and **Dona Haber**, was edited by **Paul Murphy**, assisted by managing editor **Huw Hennessy**. Harvey and Dona contributed most of the book's historical pieces, with the feature on the Nicaraguan influx by **Carol Weir**. Carol also did much valuable updating work on many other parts of the book.

Marine biologist and long-time Central America expert **Henry Genthe** wrote the Sports article and several of the Places chapters. **Cindy Hilbrink** wrote on rural aspects of Costa Rica. **David Burnie**, a biologist and natural history writer, wrote features on the flora and fauna.

Other writers whose expert text has been adapted and updated from earlier editions include **Moisés Leon**, **John McPhaul**, **Juan Bernal Ponce**, **Tony Avirgan**, **Martha Honey**, **Marjorie Ross-Cerdas**, **Mary Sheldon**, and **Alexander Skutch**. **John Leach** indexed the book.

Glyn Genin provided many of the photographs, as did Henry Genthe. In San José, **John Skiffingham** also delved deep into his vast picture library. Other photographers who contributed were **Michael** and **Patricia Fogden**, **André Bärtschi**, **Chip** and **Jill Isenhart**, and **Buddy Mays**.

The Features and Places sections have been updated by **Dorothy MacKinnon**, a Canadian who lives in Costa Rica and writes for *The Tico Times*. Costa Rica-based freelance writer and translator, **Suzanna Starcevic**, thoroughly revised and expanded the Travel Tips.

Map Legend

— ·· —	International Boundary
— — —	Province Boundary
⊖	Border Crossing
— · —	National Park/Reserve
— — —	Ferry Route
✈ ✈	Airport: International/Regional
🚌	Bus Station
P	Parking
❶	Tourist Information
✉	Post Office
✝ ✝ ✝	Church/Ruins
☾	Mosque
✡	Synagogue
🏰	Castle/Ruins
∴	Archaeological Site
∩	Cave
⚊	Statue/Monument
★	Place of Interest

The main places of interest in the Places section are coordinated by number with a full-color map (e.g. ❶), and a symbol at the top of every right-hand page tells you where to find the map.

CONTENTS

Maps

A map of Costa Rica can be found on the inside front cover, and a map of National Parks and Reserves can be found on the inside back cover.

Introduction

History

Features

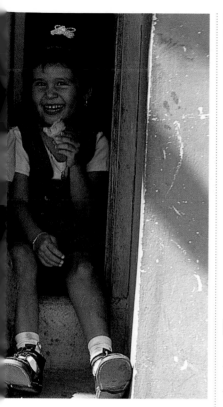

Keeping
cool in the
shade

THE BEST OF COSTA RICA

From paradise beaches and magical rainforests to volcanoes and amazing wildlife, here, at a glance, are our top recommendations for your visit.

BEST BEACHES

- **Playa Carillo** This white-sand beach is south of Sámara. *See page 204.*
- **Playa Tamarindo** A surfer's dream, with up to eight prime spots to catch a wave. *See page 198.*
- **Playa Nosara** Lively playas Pelada and Guiones offer surfing, swimming, or even yoga-on-the-beach. *See page 202.*
- **Playa Uvita** Warm water and a sandy seabed make this a great swimming beach. Part of Ballena National Marine Park, Uvita is also great for dolphin- and whale-watching. *See page 247.*
- **Manuel Antonio** Three long arcs of powdery white sand, backed by a jungle park bursting with birds and monkeys. *See page 172.*
- **Montezuma** Funky retreat, with crashing surf on wide sandy beaches and refreshing waterfalls. *See page 186.*
- **Punta Uva** With crystal-clear waters and droopy palms, ideal for hanging out in a hammock, sipping a cocktail. *See page 237.*
- **Playa Sámara** White-sand beach, ideal for swimming, kayaking, and snorkeling. *See page 203.*

ACTION & ADVENTURE THRILLS

- **Rafting** From idyllic rides to explosive whitewater rapids, rafting companies operate in the Talamanca range, the Cordillera Central and the Río Reventazón.
- **Surfing** Costa Rica is one of the world's top four surfing venues, with the best waves at Playa Jacó, Guanacaste, Nicoya and Puerto Viejo.
- **Diving** Clear waters and exotic marine life offer ideal conditions for diving, particularly in the west side of the Osa Peninsula, the southern Caribbean and northern Guanacaste.
- **Windsurfing** Lakes Arenal and Coter and Bahia Salinas offer world-class waters for experienced surfers from January to April.
- **Sea Kayaking** Ocean kayaking is a great way to tour the coast; kayaks also permit sea access to slow-moving jungle rivers where other boats can't go. An ideal river for beginners is the Corobicí in Guanacaste.
- **Canopy Tours** Get a bird's-eye view of life at the top. Swing from platform to platform high in the rainforest's tree canopy.

LEFT: the idyllic Playa Carillo.
ABOVE: scuba diving with green turtles.

ABOVE: Volcan Poás.
BELOW: Sarchí's wedding-cake church.

BEST CHURCHES

●**Basílica de Nuestra Señora de los Angeles** This enormous church is the main attraction in Cartago. An annual pilgrimage here takes place on August 2. *See page 152.*

●**Sarchí** The elaborate pastel-colored church in the small town of Sarchí reflects Costa Rica's early 20th century prosperity. *See page 162.*

●**Cathedral de las Mercedes** This rusty-red church in Grecia is made from individual sections of metal, imported from Belgium in the 1890s. *See page 162.*

●**San José de Orosí** This colonial church is Costa Rica's oldest. The small adobe structure with finely carved altar was erected by monks in 1743. *See page 154.*

TOP VOLCANOES

●**Volcán Arenal** Majestic conical peak, one of the most active in the country. The molten lava flowing down its side has a temperature of 926°C. View from a safe distance. *See page 217.*

●**Volcán Poás** A more placid volcano, near San José, with a huge crater and nature trails through its national park landscape. *See page 147.*

●**Volcán Irazú** The country's highest volcano, with trails to its brim from where you can see both the Atlantic and Pacific coasts. *See page 157.*

●**Volcán Barva** On the western side of Braulio Carrillo National Park; a hike leads through the cloud forest to a glowing green lake in its crater. *See page 151.*

BEST HIKES

●**Chirripó National Park** The ultimate hike to Costa Rica's highest peak, through pastures, oak forests, and alpine landscape. *See page 262.*

●**The Pacific Coastal Path** Starting from the village of Drake, you can follow this sandy track south to Punta Marenco, it's about a two-hour walk through a tropical paradise.

●**Rincón de la Vieja National Park** A range of hikes: from easy trails past fumaroles, boiling mud pots and sulfurous hot rocks; or a moderate two-hour walk through bird-filled forests and meadows to La Cangreja waterfall with a cool swimming hole and warm springs; or the toughest challenge: to climb to the volcano's

windswept crater. *See page 189.*

●**Corcovado National Park** Many superb jungle hikes between the park stations, with the possible reward of spotting peccary and even the extremely rare jaguar, or at least its footprints. *See page 251.*

●**Barra Honda caves** An expert guide is vital to lead you through this magical network of over 40 limestone caves. *See page 204.*

SCENIC DRIVES & BLISSFUL BOAT RIDES

- **Braulio Carrillo Highway** The main highway to the Caribbean tunnels through a mountain and emerges in the primeval wilderness.
- **La Fortuna to Lake Arenal** Heading west from the sun-baked plains around La Fortuna, one object fills the horizon – the perfect cone of Arenal Volcano.
- **The Costanera** One of the best-maintained roads in the country, the Costanera from Dominical to Cortés provides unparalleled views of the Pacific and jungle-covered mountain ridges.
- **Tortuguero canals** Drift in a boat through the network of waterways near Limón, with heady tropical aromas to soothe your senses.

- **San José to Monteverde** Climbing up to the Continental Divide, along an increasingly potholed road, rewards you with scenic views of dripping cloud forest.
- **Isla del Caño** A one-hour boat ride from the Osa Peninsula to this 304-hectare (750-acre) biological reserve, may be rewarded with views of spotted dolphins, and even humpback whales, down here from chilly Alaska for the breeding season.
- **The Old Pacific Highway** Winding down to the sea from the west of San José, via Puriscal, a stunning route through coffee, sugarcane and banana plantations, this is untouched Costa Rica at its best.

ABOVE: luxurious vegetation in the Monteverde Cloud Forest.
RIGHT: the striking quetzal bird.
BELOW: a boat ride through the waterways.

WILDLIFE VIEWING

- **The Ostional Wildlife Refuge** Nothing beats the *arribadas* (mass arrivals) of Olive Ridley sea turtles at this protected beach north of Nosara. *See page 203.*
- **Tortuguero National Park** With a sharp-eyed guide, you'll see myriad birds, mammals, and reptiles in this labyrinth of canals. *See page 231.*
- **Rainforest Aerial Tram** See eye to eye with an iguana, 35 meters (100 ft) above the forest floor. *See page 159.*
- **Monteverde Cloud Forest** One of the country's most popular parks, brimming with wildlife, from butterflies to hummingbirds, and of course, the quetzal. *See page 205.*

- **Manuel Antonio National Park**. Hard-to-beat combination of gorgeous beaches fringed by jungle teeming with wildlife, from sloths to iguanas. *See page 173.*

RARE ANIMALS

- **The Resplendant Quetzal** The most reliable place for spotting Costa Rica's star bird is **San Gerardo de Dota**, Cerro de la Muerte, in the Costa Rican highlands. *See page 261.*
- **Tapir and Jaguar** Costa Rica's largest mammal, the shy Baird's tapir, might be glimpsed at **Corcovado National Park** (40,5000 hectares/ 100,000 acres), the most remote and pristine park in the country. On very rare occasions a jaguar is sighted here. *See page 251.*
- **Great Green Macaw** Along with almost 400 other species of birds, insects and mammals inhabit the wet lowland forests of **La Selva Biological Station**, to the north of **Braulio Carrillo National Park**. *See page 158.*

ABOVE RIGHT: topiary with a twist in the gardens of Zarcero's church.
BELOW: the rarely spotted jaguar.

ONLY IN COSTA RICA

- **Gallo Pinto** Rice and beans served up with a Tico touch is the nation's favorite staple dish.
- **Sarchí's ox carts** Vividly colored wooden ox-carts are still in use around the country. Sarchí is the center for the carving of wooden crafts of all designs and sizes. *See page 162.*
- **Stone spheres** Huge, mysterious, and perfectly round boulders dot the countryside, still defying scientific explanation. *See page 251.*

- **Turtle** *arribadas* Costa Rica is considered the best place in the world to see the spectacle of sea turtles coming ashore to lay their eggs. *See page 202.*
- **Zarcero** Not all nature's splendors are wild–vegetation is tamed into bizarre formations in the topiary gardens of Zarcero's church. *See page 163.*

MONEY-SAVING TIPS

Go by bus Long-distance buses are very cheap, comfortable, and usually air-conditioned. Take a bus to the town nearest your final destination, and then hire a car locally if you need to get somewhere off the beaten track. *See Transport, page 270.*

Car hire You can avoid a hefty 12 percent airport tax if you hire a car downtown instead of at the airport when you arrive. *See Transport, page 271.*

Cheap sleep You can sometimes camp on private land in rural areas, if you ask the owner first; small countryside hotels may also let you pitch your tent in their grounds for a small fee. Cheap cabins *(cabinas)* are an inexpensive and popular alternative to youth hostels, which are not so widespread. *See Accommodations, page 282.*

Think small Avoid the major attractions and famous national parks if you're traveling in high season. They're very crowded, facilities are much more expensive, and you probably won't come away with such a memorable experience. Instead, look for small, family-run lodges, homestays, and private reserves, where you're likely to find something special. *See Conservation, page 295.*

THE HAPPY MEDIUM

Amid the turmoil that often characterizes Central America
Costa Rica is a land at peace with itself and nature

Nestled between Nicaragua and Panamá on the Central American isthmus, Costa Rica is a small, democratic and peaceful country, with a level of social development that always surprises first-time visitors and belies its definition as a Third-World nation. Lacking the clichéd images and iconographic characteristics of other Latin American countries, such as Mexico, Peru or Brazil, it has become famous for its natural environment and for its efforts in helping bring lasting peace to a troubled region.

Since Don Pepe Figueres abolished Costa Rica's armed forces in 1949, the government has been able to devote a large percentage of its resources to education, health and conservation. Currently about a quarter of the country is protected in national parks, biological reserves, wildlife refuges and private reserves. With more than 850 species of birds, 250 mammals, and some 6 percent of the world's total identified species, Costa Rica is a paradise for anyone who delights in the unspoiled natural world.

A land of dense jungles, active volcanoes and pristine beaches, this is a tiny country but it is full of geophysical contrasts that make it seem much bigger. A third of the country's population (total 4.3 million) live in the temperate Central Valley that houses the modern capital of San José. But as any *Tico* (Costa Rican) will tell you, the "real" Costa Rica will only be found in the *campo*, or rural areas.

It was an official at the World Bank who termed Costa Rica the Land of the Happy Medium. And while its economy is far from perfect, the standard of living is high and the climate temperate. In outlook it is often more European than Latino, and predominantly middle-class. With a per capita income of around US$4,300, Costa Rica's people rely on the state to provide quality health care, schools and other affordable services such as electricity and clean water, while its neighbors lavish equal amounts of money on national defense and putting down military coups.

Since 1994, tourism has been the country's leading industry, along with computer-chip exports, with bananas, pineapples and coffee lagging behind. More than 1.5 million visitors now arrive every year, the vast majority of them coming from North America and Europe. A sophisticated tourism industry is in place, with accommodations ranging from luxury lodges to homey bed-and-breakfasts. Eco- and adventure tourism are the buzzwords that encompass activities as diverse as birdwatching and whitewater rafting. Costa Rica has come a long way from the sleepy, agricultural land it once was, but it retains essential charm, especially in the wilder, more remote areas. ❑

PRECEDING PAGES: cloud forest of Cerro de la Muerte; black-sand beach in Limón province.
LEFT: poison-dart frogs, formerly used by indigenous peoples for tipping arrows.

COAST TO COAST

Costa Rica may be small in area but it is big in diversity, with two oceans, rushing rivers, fiery volcanoes, and chilly peaks touching nearly 4,000 meters

Costa Rica lies at the heart of the Central American isthmus and these days few people mistake it for an island in the Caribbean. Traveling around the countryside gives you the sense of being in a large country; geophysically there are so many things going on. There is the feeling that it would take months to really explore it all. Yet, in reality, it is quite small. From northwest to southwest it measures 460 km (285 miles) and at its narrowest point it is only 120 km (74 miles). In total, Costa Rica's land area is just 51,000 sq km (20,000 sq miles).

Neighbors

Costa Rica is bounded on the north by Nicaragua, and to the south by Panamá; two countries often in the international news, for the wrong reasons, and profoundly different from this usually benevolent and peaceful land. To the east is the tranquil Caribbean Sea and the stormier Atlantic, and to the west is the tumultuous Pacific Ocean. Costa Rica is as complex and perhaps more diverse than any place of its size on earth; divided into several distinct regions, each of them looks like an entirely separate place.

A fertile land

Perhaps it is the hot coastal plains in the tropical zones, with their plantations of palm and banana, or the thickly forested valleys and coastlines, fringed with beaches of every description, that drew many of the early travelers here.

Or perhaps it is the fertile central plateau in the temperate zone, at 975–1,980 meters (3,200–6,500 ft), with its rich, fecund cloud forests and magical tropical jungles, which has attracted a large international community of conservationists, biologists, birdwatchers, environmentalists, naturalists, and the ecologically attuned.

LEFT: a prehistoric-looking mature green iguana.
RIGHT: shy but curious *Tica* welcome.

Many a Northern European or *gringo* hailing from the midwestern or northern United States or Canada has found Costa Rica to be an ideal new home, with its cool highlands of gently rolling, wooded pastureland reminiscent more of Switzerland than of a tropical country.

Running as veins of a precious ore through the body of the country is an intricate network of waterways. They rise and fall through the mountains, flow to the sea and provide a steady source of fresh water and hydraulic power.

The soil of the Central Valley is exceptionally fertile, owing primarily to the volcanic ash that has fallen through the centuries. This rich, drainable soil is ideal for producing Costa Rica's coffee. Traveling through the high country, you can view seemingly endless coffee *fincas* (estates), the bushes with their deep green, jewel-like foliage flowing up impossibly steep ridges and across the floor of great alluvial valleys.

The coast

Never far away is the coastline. Indeed, there are many accessible points throughout this country from where you can simultaneously view both the Caribbean Sea and the Pacific Ocean. The Caribbean coast measures only 220 km (135 miles) in length, while the Pacific coast of Costa Rica, with its deep gulfs and indentations, is several times that length. On the Pacific there is the Nicoya peninsula to the north, and the Osa peninsula to the south. And, remote and mysterious, many miles off the Pacific coast, is the exceptionally beautiful, still pristine Coco Island.

Peaks of delight

Although most of Costa Rica's volcanoes are extinct, some are still active. Poás Volcano, at 2,700 meters (8,900 ft), is near the town of Alajuela, and has one of the world's largest craters, measuring more than a mile in diameter; and Irazú Volcano, at 3,440 meters (11,320 ft), not far from the city of Cartago, is occasionally active, and can be viewed at relatively close range.

At 1,630 meters (5,350 ft) in height, Arenal is the most consistently active of Costa Rica's

ABOVE: birders on Tortuguero's tree-lined canals.
RIGHT: Volcán Arenal letting off steam.

volcanoes. The rumbling, explosive spectacle of Arenal Volcano is the single most impressive pyrotechnic display in the whole country.

The highland mountains traverse Costa Rica, from the northwest to the southeast, in three ranges, rising to more than 3,800 meters (12,500 ft). These are the magnificent Guanacaste, Central, and Talamanca ranges. Chirripó Grande, at 3,820 meters (12,500 ft), is the highest elevation point in the country.

Climate

Although geographically situated in what earlier travelers used to call the "torrid zone," the great majority of Costa Rica never really feel torrid at any time of year. The population lives for the most part on the Central Plateau, at elevations between around 450 meters (1,500 ft) and 1,400 meters (4,500 ft), in "perennial springtime" temperatures of between 20–26°C (68–78°F), day and night.

However, near the coasts the temperatures are indeed tropical and there are distinct alternating wet and dry seasons, at different times of year, for both the Atlantic and Pacific. There are certain times here when even the local residents are overwhelmed by the too-sensuous hot and humid midday air and are driven into the shade to cool down.

Tropical downpours usually arrive with great predictability in the afternoons during the wet seasons along the coasts and are undeniably awesome. If you are caught out in one, you will never forget the experience. Over the years, millions of words have been written about these extraordinary dramas of lightning, thunder, and torrential rains.

Away from the tropical coasts, the climate is greatly determined by the altitude above sea level. At each level, daytime temperatures remain fairly constant regardless of the time of year. At night, however, the heat of the coastal plains cools very slightly, while high up on the mountains and volcano slopes, pleasant sun-warmed temperatures plunge dramatically at night, sometimes to just above the freezing mark.

From the edge of the almost tideless Caribbean Sea and the pounding Pacific coast, up and across the slopes of the volcanic *cordilleras*, and finally up to the highest peak of cold and brittle Chirripó, the Republic of Costa Rica is gloriously invigorating. ❑

Decisive Dates

12,000–4000 BC First signs of human habitation in Central America: hunter-gatherers migrating southward settle in small chiefdoms, developing diverse languages and cultures.

4000–1000 BC Establishment of earliest settlements based on crop cultivation (including maize, yucca and cotton).

1000 BC–AD 1500 Growth and expansion of organized, sedentary farming communities, who form trade and communication links with each other and as far afield as the Chibcha people of South America. By the time of

A WARRIOR OF NICOYA.

the arrival of the Spaniards, five major cultural groups of natives predominate; the Spanish name them the Carib; the Boruca; the Nahua; the Corobici, who were the oldest native group; and the most advanced group of all, the Chorotega, who inhabit the Nicoya Peninsula.

1502 Christopher Columbus drops anchor for two weeks off the island of Uvita (near Puerto Limón), where he encounters the Cariari tribe.

1510–70 The Spanish conquest.

1561 An expedition from the Pacific coast finally manages to reach the Valle Central. Juan Cavallón founds the first town, Castillo de Garcimuñoz, which is relocated several times until it becomes established as present-day Cartago.

1562 Juan Vazquez de Coronado explores the Valle

Central and employs peaceful means to try to convert the *indígenas* (indigenous people).

1572 Beginning of Colonial Period, characterized by an almost continuous absence of labor. Costa Rica remains a poor colony for the next 250 years, largely ignored by Spain because of its lack of mineral resources.

1660–70 Caribbean coast cacao plantations bring the colony its first revenue, but they are constantly raided by pirates.

1723 The tiny fledgling capital of Cartago is wiped out by erupting Irazú Volcano.

1787 Costa Rica is the only colony in the Audiencia de Guatemala allowed to cultivate tobacco.

1821 Guatemala announces independence from Spain.

1823 Civil war breaks out between the conservative imperialists in Cartago and Heredía, who want to join the Mexican Empire, and the republicans *(liberalistas)* who are in the majority in San José and Alajuela. The republicans finally secure Costa Rica's acceptance into the short-lived United Provinces of Central America, led by Guatemala. San José replaces Cartago as the national capital.

1824 Juan Mora Fernández becomes Costa Rica's first head of state (until 1833). The inhabitants of the "Partido de Nicoya" (a region governed until then by Nicaragua, and roughly corresponding to today's Guanacaste) vote to join Costa Rica.

1825 The first constitution of the free state of Costa Rica is promulgated, and the cession of Guanacaste is made official by Congress.

1832 First coffee exports to Europe, via Chile.

1835 Braulio Carrillo becomes president and uses dictatorial methods to introduce liberal reforms. Heredia, Cartago, and Alajuela all oppose these; they form a "league" and declare war on San José, eventually winning the capital.

1838–42 Dictatorship of Braulio Carrillo.

1848 Declaration of the Republic of Costa Rica.

1849 Juan Rafael Mora becomes president and is re-elected in 1853 and 1859. During his presidency coffee exports experience a sharp upswing.

1858 During the war against freebooter William Walker, who wants to turn Central America into a colony of the southern American states and introduce slavery, a decisive battle is fought near Santa Rosa. Walker is finally defeated by Costa Rica's troops in Rivas (Nicaragua).

1870 Tomás Guardia Gutiérrez takes over power after a military coup, introduces a new liberal constitution, and remains in office until 1882.

1871 Railroad construction begins.

1880 First banana exports.

1882 The death penalty is abolished.

1886 Introduction of compulsory education.

1890 First free and honest democratic elections in Central America bring José Joaquin Rodriguez to presidency. The Atlantic Railroad, from Cartago to Limón, is completed.

1914–18 Costa Rica loses export markets because of World War I. Economic recession.

1917 Federico A. Tinoco takes power in a coup supported by the coffee barons. A popular uprising ends his dictatorship two years later.

1932 World economic recession.

1934 A strike among banana workers in response to adverse working conditions at United Fruit Company leads to a series of concessions (including the right to strike and the minimum wage).

1939–45 World War II – coffee exports stagnate. Costa Rica declares war on Germany, Japan and Italy. German and Italian residents are dispossessed and deported.

1940–44 President Rafael Calderón successfully implements a series of social reforms.

1945 The Social Democratic Party (PSD) is founded, later to become the Partido Liberación Nacional (PLN), under (Don Pepe) José Figueres.

1948 Calderón Guardia declares election results to be annulled and reassumes the presidency. Civil war ensues. The victorious junta led by Figueres takes over government.

1949 Under the terms of the new constitution the army is disbanded and replaced by a Civil Guard. Figueres hands over power to elected president Otilio Ulate, but governs the country again from 1953 to 1958 and 1970 to 1974. Blacks and women enfranchised (1949).

1979 The Sandinistas in Nicaragua topple the Somoza dictatorship. During the ensuing civil war, Costa Rica becomes a fallback area for guerilla groups and anti-Sandinistas. As a result of the war, hundreds of thousands of Nicaraguans seek refuge in Costa Rica.

1980 Slump in coffee and banana markets causes the onset of severe economic recession.

1983 President Luis Alberto Monge declares a state of "unarmed neutrality," leading to tensions with the United States.

1986 Oscar Arias Sánchez is elected president and prepares to restore peace to the region. For his efforts in instigating the Central American Peace Plan, "Esquipulas II", he is awarded the Nobel Peace Prize in 1987.

1990 The Social Christian Unity Party (PUSC) wins the

elections. Rafael Angel Calderón Fournier, the son of Calderón Guardia, becomes the country's president. Costa Rica sends a national team to the soccer World Cup for the first time, and reaches the second round.

1991 An earthquake strikes Limón province, killing over 60 and causing extensive damage which remains today.

1994 José M. Figueres becomes Costa Rica's youngest ever president. However, his term is dogged by scandals, including the bankruptcy and closure of Banco Anglo-Costarricense, the nation's oldest bank.

1996 Hurricane César strikes, killing dozens of Costa Ricans and causing over US$100 million of damage.

1998 The Social Christian Unity Party (PUSC) wins general elections and Miguel Angel Rodríguez is sworn

in as president. During his term he encourages foreign investment and privatizes state companies but many criticize the government's lack of transparency.

2000 Nationwide protests against proposed privatization of ICE, the government-run electricity and telecommunications monopoly.

2002 Abel Pacheco of the PUSC wins the first ever presidential run-off vote. Costa Rican astronaut Franklin Chang, crew member of US space shuttle Endeavour, goes for a walk in space.

2006 In the closest election ever run, Oscar Arias Sánchez is elected to an unprecedented second term as president.

2007 Central American Free Trade Agreement (CAFTA) is ratified following a very close public referendum. ❑

PRECEDING PAGES: pre-Columbian ceramics from the National Museum, San José.

LEFT: a Nicoyan warrior, set for battle.

RIGHT: a portrait of idyllic early Amerindian life by the chronologer Figueroa.

BEFORE COLUMBUS

The Amerindians' early culture was largely agrarian. Influenced by their
Mesoamerican neighbors, they learned to fashion goods from stone, jade and gold

On September 8, 1502, Cristóbal Colón (Christopher Columbus) arrived on the Atlantic Coast of Costa Rica and took refuge in the calm waters just off the coast, between tiny Uvita Island and what is now the Port of Limón.

The native population greeted the Spaniards with interest and brought out goods to trade with them. They swam out to the ship carrying cotton cloth, shirts, tumbaga pendants (an alloy made of copper and gold) and weapons such as clubs, bows and arrows.

Golden dreams

Dreaming of gold, Columbus had charted the coastal area from Honduras to Panamá and named it Veragua. He was so enamored by the golden mirrors that the Amerindians of Costa Rica wore about their necks, and by their many stories of gold and gold mines along the coast to the south, that he named the area the Rich Coast of Veragua.

Rich though it seemed to Columbus at the time, the newly discovered area was not to be a great, rich jewel in Spain's crown. In fact, the "Rich Coast" turned out to be one of the poorest of Spain's American colonies. Impassable mountains, impenetrable forests, raging rivers, unbearable heat, floods, disease, swamps, shortages of food, internal rivalries, lack of natural resources and a way to generate wealth all oppressed the settlers. They were often reduced to living like the "savages" they had come to conquer: wearing goat-hair garments or cloth ing made of bark; using cacao (chocolate beans) for currency; eking out a bare subsistence in the fields, using native methods to cultivate native crops.

This bleak reality was yet to come. Columbus naively returned to Spain with dreams of great riches and grandeur, to the point of asking the king to confer on him the title of Duke of Veragua.

LEFT: a ceremonial polychrome vessel.
RIGHT: gold ornament and battlewear.

Natural riches

Unrealistic visions of gold aside, what was life in the newly discovered territory really like? It was a rich land, if not in gold, then in natural resources, with forests, mountains, rivers, grasslands and abundant animal and plant life. In the Atlantic watershed area, where much of

the land is flat, navigable rivers and their tributaries were swelled in some areas by more than 400 cm (160 inches) of rain a year. In the heavy tropical vegetation grew wild rubber trees, orchids and ferns. Fish, alligators and an occasional shark lived in the rivers. Waterfowl, turkeys, iguanas, red monkeys, howler monkeys, peccaries (wild pigs) and jaguars inhabited the forests.

To the north, in the Nicoya region, were tropical dry forests, also abundant in plant and animal life: on the broad, seasonally dry plains grew the beautiful wide, green guanacaste tree; the javillo with its poisonous sap and thorny trunk; the cenicero with its flesh-colored flowers; the guapinol with its characteristic seed pods, referred to as "stinky toes;" and many varieties of cacti and spiny shrubs. White-faced monkeys, howler monkeys, red squirrels with grey tails, tapirs, coatis, deer, jaguars, mountain lions, coyotes and other small animals lived in the forests. In the trees, scarlet macaws and colorful parrots squawked and roosted. Avocados, papayas, guavas and countless other fruits grew wild.

And the grasslands and swamps of the southern Pacific region, also called the Diquis region, were lush with life, as were the often misty green hills and valleys of the Central High-

At the time of Columbus's arrival, the people of the Guanacaste/Nicoya region lived in well-developed settlements, some with populations as large as 20,000. These settlements, supported by the cultivation of corn, were constructed around central plazas, marketplaces and religious centers.

Guayabo city

In the Atlantic Watershed/Central Highlands area, located in the mountains near the present-day city of Turrialba, was a city with wide, cobblestoned walkways, freshwater springs bubbling out of stone-lined pools, and a stone

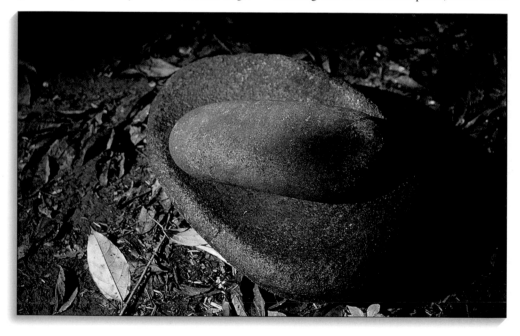

lands, where broadleaf evergreen forests, palms and white oaks grew on the luxuriant hillsides, harboring innumerable species of birds, animals and plants.

Native settlers

Groups of indigenous peoples with diverse languages and cultures lived throughout these areas in small chiefdoms called *cacicazgos*. They were agricultural people, cultivating crops of yucca, corn, *pejibaye* (the bright orange fruit of palm) and numerous other plants. They supplemented their diets with wild fruits and game from the forests, fish and shrimp from the rivers, and crustacea and small oysters from the ocean.

WHAT'S IN A NAME?

The Spanish colonists gave the Amerindians the names by which we know them today (often the name of the chief at the time): the Chorotega, Bribri, Cacebar, Coctu, Corobicí, to name a few. We do not know the names they called themselves. Since some groups were completely wiped out before the Spanish came, we do not have names for them, or know what languages they spoke. Because of this, archeologists usually refer to Amerindian groups by the areas in which they lived: Guanacaste/Nicoya region, the Atlantic Watershed/Central Highlands region and the Diquis, or Southern Pacific region.

aqueduct system carrying fresh water to some of the stone mounds on which houses were built. This ancient ceremonial or administrative center, called Guayabo, flourished and disappeared (approximately 1000 BC to AD 1400) before the arrival of the Spaniards. From Guayabo, ancient roads of stone led to towns and may have even reached the ocean.

Other groups within the Atlantic Watershed/ Central Highlands region were less settled. They cultivated root crops and hunted what small game was available, and then moved on to new lands when the soil or supply of game became depleted.

In the Diquis region, people also hunted, cultivated root crops and lived in well-fortified villages that were strategically laid out to protect villagers from enemy attack.

Crossroads of the Americas

Influenced by some of the other great indigenous cultures of the Americas, the native peoples of Costa Rica had become skilled in the arts of ceramics, gold and metalwork, fine weaving and stone carving. Costa Rica, it

LEFT: a *mano*, or *metate* prehistoric corn grinder.
ABOVE: *conquistador* statue, San José.
ABOVE RIGHT: stone figure found at Guayabo.

seems, was a kind of mercantile and cultural crossroads of the Americas. Linguistic and cultural influences, not to mention a wealth of artifacts and materials, were being exchanged within the country and without, from as far north as Mexico and as far south as Ecuador. The native Costa Ricans were enthusiastic traders and prized jade pieces, ceramic ware, gold and stone carvings from Mesoamerica and South America.

The Nicoya area, with its quiet Pacific bays and safe anchorages, provided pre-Columbian commercial ports. Merchant marines from ancient Ecuador, making ports of call all along the Pacific coast of Mexico, Central and South America, frequently stopped at sites in Nicoya, bringing with them the crafts and arts of those places they have visited. Perhaps it was they who introduced Olmec influences to the area – or perhaps the Olmecs (and others) came themselves. Regardless, the influence of the Olmecs was evident in the Pacific Northwest in the impressive range of pottery styles; utilitarian articles such as grinding stones; and the practice of certain customs, such as filing human teeth into points.

Over the years, the pottery of Nicoya developed into a vigorous hybrid style that for centuries would be traded around Central America and southern Mexico. A collection of such work is on view at the National Museum. It is lively, bold, colorful work: large globular jars and vessels; figures of men and women, some with oversized genitals and physical deformities; animals of all kinds; mysterious effigies of man-birds; haunting funerary masks; and some quieter pieces, almost luminously beautiful.

Mystery of the spheres

The Diquis region is the site of one of the great pre-Columbian riddles. Spheres made of granite, andesite and sedimentary stone have been found in their thousands along river beds and arranged in cemetery sites. Some are as small as oranges while others weigh up to 14 metric tons (16 tons), and measure up to 2 meters (7 ft) in diameter. They are perfectly spherical to within a centimeter or two and are perhaps the finest example of precision stone carving in the ancient world.

The stone spheres are unique – none has been discovered anywhere else in the world. How were they made? How were they shaped to be so perfectly spherical? How were they transported more than 30 km (20 miles) from the source of the stone to the ceremonial sites where they were arranged? And what do they

THE RIDDLE OF JADE

In addition to the enigma of the country's lithic spheres (see above), there is another pre-Columbian riddle in Costa Rica that perplexes historians and archeologists: it is the source of jade for the many pieces found throughout the country. No jade quarries have ever been found in Costa Rica. Guatemala is believed to be the principal source, although some jade may have come from Mexico.

Many of the objects appear to have been treasured for years, passed down as heirlooms; others appear to have arrived in one form and to have been re-sculpted to the tastes of their new owners.

One interesting theory holds that some of the jade was brought to Costa Rica by pre-Columbian looters of Mayan burial sites, thus explaining the presence of Mayan hieroglyphs inscribed on the jade – which apparently had no value or significance to the Costa Ricans.

The Jade Museum in San José (see page 138) has the largest display of jade in the Americas, with over 6,000 pieces. The exhibits are of great variety; notable oddities include a tooth with jade inset and jade breast supports, thought to have been worn by high-ranking women.

mean? Today, they stand mute in their new locations, at the National Museum and in the gardens of expensive homes throughout the Central Valley. You can also see them, undisturbed, in their original habitat, on Isla del Caño, near Corcovado National Park.

Gold and cotton

The Diquis region also abounded with gold, which the Amerindians washed out of rivers, or obtained from shallow digs in the savannahs, under groves of trees on hilltops or in the plains. They became experts in the art of goldworking and employed different techniques, including the "lost wax" method, to craft all manner of items: gold headbands, arm and leg bands, collars, bracelets, beads, bells; golden ornaments sewn on clothes; gold tweezers for plucking away unwanted facial hair; gold awls, fish-hooks and needles; gold sheathing for teeth; gold to use on decorative masks.

The people of the Diquis region also wove fine, white cotton cloth, which was used to wrap the dead. Although no archeological evidence has been uncovered since cotton clothing does not survive for millennia, the cloth may also have been sewn into shirts to be worn by both men and women for ceremonial occasions.

Wars, rituals and religion

Taken in isolation, archeological evidence on village life, diet and the arts and commerce of the early Costa Rican people might suggest that life was plentiful, complete and quite idyllic. In fact it was anything but – war was almost continuous.

In the Guanacaste/Nicoya region, wars were unceasingly fought between rival groups to obtain captives, who were perhaps for human sacrifice (and even consumption). Throughout Costa Rica there were wars to capture women and youths for slaves; to obtain the heads of enemies, which were carried as trophies; and to obtain access to new land. Sometimes, as in the Diquis region, men and women warred together. Artifacts and skeletons found in unearthed graves suggest that the dead were honored. Funerals and burials of high-ranking people were elaborate affairs: people of rank were buried with riches – and their slaves were sacrificed in order to serve their masters once again in the other world.

Spiritual life

Of their spiritual beliefs little is actually known, although much has been speculated. Phallic images and figures in pottery and stone, emphasizing male and female genitalia, suggest a religion focused on fertility. Fertility rites probably included the music of pottery drums, bone and clay flutes, trumpets, ocarinas, and rattles made of clay or gourds. Large vessels for the fermentation of corn, yucca or

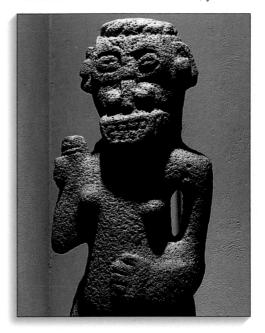

palm fruit suggest ritual inebriation. And there were medicine men – shamans – with vast knowledge of the flora of the forests, who cured illness, forecast the future and dealt with supernatural matters.

The pre-Columbian lineages disintegrated with the arrival of the Europeans, who captured their leaders, disrupted their communities, enslaved their people and destroyed their ceremonial and religious articles. Spirited artistry gave way to a lackluster mediocrity, and dynamic spiritual beliefs were replaced by a half-hearted hybrid religion. Little by little, Costa Rica's rich pre-Columbian traditions were all but extinguished. ❏

LEFT: an elated Nicoya figure.
RIGHT: stone carving of a female, found at Guayabo.

CONQUEST

The conquest of Costa Rica followed the sad pattern of much of Central America,
bringing disease, death and slavery in the largely fruitless quest for gold

When Christopher Columbus set sail from Spain in 1492 on his first voyage to the New World, he was planning to find a group of islands near Japan, which he conceived to be about 2,400 nautical miles to the west of Spain. There, he determined, he would build a great city and trade gold, gems

fort and left 40 men behind to search for gold. He returned to Spain in triumph, with several captive locals.

Columbus was given a grand reception. He was named Admiral of the Ocean Sea and was ordered to organize a second voyage to further explore Hispaniola.

and spices from the Indies with the cities of Europe. He imagined himself as a rich governor, lord of it all.

His ambitions coincided with the interests of the Spanish Crown. The wars to oust the Moors from Spain had depleted the royal treasury. The promise of the wealth of the Indies was attractive indeed.

The voyages of Columbus

The first of his four voyages took Columbus to the Bahamas, where he established the first Spanish settlement in the New World, at Hispaniola, where present-day Haiti and the Dominican Republic are situated. He built a

The second expedition reached Hispaniola only to discover that the 40 settlers had been killed after mistreating the locals. Undeterred, Columbus sailed to the north coast of Hispaniola, where he attempted to establish another settlement.

Leaving his brother, Diego, in charge, he went off to explore for gold. But the settlers fought among themselves and with the Amerindians. Frustrated gold hunters returned to Spain angry; they grumbled about the disappointingly small amounts of gold and the cruelties of Columbus, who, according to historic accounts, was indeed an arrogant commander.

Nevertheless, a third voyage saw Columbus exploring the Atlantic coast of South America and claiming it for Spain. Meanwhile, Hispaniola was seething with discontent. "Not enough gold!" was the cry, and "We can't eat this Indian food!" Columbus tried to placate the rebels, as would his successors throughout Central America, by permitting them to enslave the indigenous population.

But even that measure failed to satisfy many. Large numbers of men returned to Spain demanding back pay and Columbus's head. Columbus was sent back to Spain in chains. Through the intercession of Isabella and

Limón, in a place he called Cariari. There, the local people sent out two girls to welcome the party. In a letter to King Ferdinand, Columbus wrote: "As soon as I got there they sent right out two girls, all dressed up; the elder was hardly eleven, the other seven, both behaving with such lack of modesty as to be no better than whores. As soon as they arrived, I gave orders that they be presented with some of our trading truck and sent them directly ashore."

While in Cariari, Columbus made repairs to his damaged ships – the *Capitania*, *Gallega*, *Viscaína*, and *Santiago de Palos* – as the near tideless ocean lapped on beautiful white- and

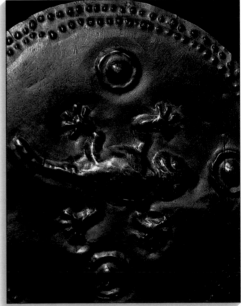

Ferdinand, he managed to secure his release and set out on his fourth voyage.

The "discovery" of Costa Rica

It was on this voyage, in 1502, sailing up and down the Atlantic Coast looking for a passage to what would later be called the Pacific, that Columbus discovered in Central America the Rich Coast of Veragua.

He spent 18 days in what was later to be called Costa Rica, near the present-day port of

black-sand beaches and coconut trees swayed in the gentle breezes. The respite was sorely needed: a violent storm off the coast of Honduras had caused considerable damage to his ships, and his men, one-third of whom were between the ages of 13 and 18, were sick and exhausted. Columbus himself, at 51 years of age, was almost crippled with the pains of arthritis.

A difficult passage home

The return voyage was difficult. Columbus's ships had been attacked by worms and were battered by foul weather: they were leaking badly. He made it only as far as Santa Gloria,

LEFT: ritual drinking vessel.
ABOVE: Nicoyan phallic figure.
ABOVE RIGHT: gold breastplate, Diquis region.

Jamaica and spent a year there, marooned, unable to get help from the governor of Hispaniola, who was worried that Columbus might usurp his position. There were food shortages and an attempted mutiny, but eventually Columbus and 100 of the original 135 men did return to Spain in 1504, shortly after the death of Queen Isabella.

Columbus spent his final years in increasingly failing health, attempting to secure for himself the governorship, trade and other benefits that had been promised to him by the queen. But the king refused even to see him, and the struggle to attain title, territory and wealth fell to his sons and in turn their sons (Columbus' grandson was finally named Duke of Veragua in 1546), and to the *conquistadores* who followed him to the Americas. As for his spiritual and material heirs, they too were to encounter hardships.

The *conquistadores*

It is tempting to characterize the conquest of South America as a brutal cartoon: greedy, ruthless *conquistadores* bungling explorations, slitting each other's throats for gold, territory or titles; murdering, stealing from and enslaving the peoples of the land.

It took 60 years from the time of Columbus's arrival at Limón until the first European settlement in Costa Rica was established. The rough terrain, the unfriendly oceans, the extreme weather and a feisty local population all played a large part in the delay. But the continuous, jealous feuding among the *conquistadores* themselves was also a major factor in the failure of the many colonization attempts.

Gold was consistently the big theme. When the *conquistadores* asked the Amerindians about the location of gold mines, they simply pointed south to the fabled mines of Veragua. It gave the Spaniards gold fever. But if the indigenous population really knew where the mines were, they never revealed their location, and to this day the great, legendary mines remain undiscovered. The *conquistadores*, spurning the gold to be found in rivers, had to content themselves with taking the locals' gold, which they did – until there was no more. Then they had to determine how to survive, let alone get rich.

More expeditions

In 1506, two years after Columbus returned to Spain, King Ferdinand sent Governor Diego de Nicuesa and a group of settlers to establish a colony at Veragua. It was the first of many ill-fated attempts to establish settlements.

dian slaves and sending them to work in the mines of Hispaniola, stealing their gold and furiously searching for a passage across the continent to the other ocean. Finally, in 1513, Vasco Nuñez de Balboa, a young stowaway escaping debts on Hispaniola, led an expedition across the isthmus and discovered the Pacific Ocean. It wasn't long before rudimentary shipyards appeared on the Pacific coast to accommodate would-be explorers who had sailed into Atlantic ports then walked across the isthmus, ready to set sail on the Pacific and continue their explorations. The unexplored Pacific had better anchorages, and was thought to have more gold.

Nicuesa's ship ran aground in Panamá and he and his group set about walking up the coast to their destination. Food shortages and tropical diseases were acute; the terrain was devastating. Indigenous peoples along the way burned their own crops rather than yield their food. By the time the settlers finally arrived, their numbers had been halved.

Around this time, expeditions from Spain were landing throughout the Atlantic coast of Central America. They were capturing Amerin-

The adventures of Gil González

The second inland expedition to Costa Rica was led by Captain Gil González in 1522, and it, too, ended without establishing a settlement. Faulty ships hastily constructed on the Pacific coast of Panamá took on water and forced González and his men to abandon the sea and move forward on foot.

The expeditions of González, which included a walk of 224 leagues (over 1,000 km/600 miles) from the south Pacific coast of Costa Rica to the north, and into Nicaragua, have a mythic quality. At the age of 65 – and suffering from arthritis aggravated by the unceasing rain – González sometimes had to

LEFT: Columbus and *conquistadores*.
ABOVE: the *Pinta* founders in a storm.
ABOVE RIGHT: the Virgin of the Navigators.

be carried on a litter, but he insisted on completing the arduous trip. González rested for 15 days in the home of the Térraba chief near Boruca. According to his accounts, he baptized some 32,000 of the indigenous people here, collecting golden items of vast value.

He also encountered Chief Diríagen, who appeared out of the blue one day along with 500 Amerindians, each carrying one or two turkeys; 17 women covered from head to foot in gold disks; 10 men carrying standards; five trumpeters and other attendants bringing 200 golden hatchets. The party stopped in front of the house where González was staying, the

was aroused by the enormous amounts of gold González had collected and by González's refusal to give up his claim on Nicaragua. The affair ended with González fleeing Panamá with his treasure.

Pestilence and slavery

The people of Nicoya and Nicaragua were not so fortunate as González, who got away with his life and his treasure. His expedition had brought smallpox, influenza and plague to the area, and tens of thousands of Amerindians died. Survivors of the epidemics faced another danger: enslavement. Indigenous peoples from

trumpeters played and then the chiefs, women and lords entered. When González asked their business, Chief Diríagen replied that they had come to see the men with beards who rode upon strange beasts. Probably Diríagen had come to ascertain the strength of the Spaniards, because three days after his visit, he returned and attacked the Spaniards. It was an attack that González and less than 20 men, at least according to the legend, easily repelled.

González ran into trouble later on with the greedy Pedrarias, governor of Panamá, who was responsible for the deaths of many Spanish *conquistadores*, including Balboa, his own son-in-law, whom he had beheaded. Pedrarias's ire

the Nicoya region, who then lived in large population centers and were vulnerable to such attacks, were captured, branded with hot irons and shipped off to Panamá and Peru to be sold as slaves.

The second attempted Costa Rican settlement was at Villa Bruselas, near present-day Orotina, not far from the large port city of Puntarenas. It lasted only three years and succumbed to feuding among the settlers and Amerindian attacks.

During this period, the *conquistadores* who arrived in Central America were free to exploit the indigenous population in virtually any way they wished. The Spanish policy of *requerimiento*, which went into effect in 1510, permitted settlers to make war on those who did not become baptized, a convenient justification for killing Amerindians and plundering their gold.

Later, *encomienda*, a royal grant from the Crown, gave settlers in Central America the right to force indigenous peoples to labor without compensation – or to demand goods as tribute. It was, in effect, slavery. The Amerindians were re-located to live on the land where they worked, and were considered the property of the grant holder. Without the system of *encomienda*, the *conquistadores* could not realize their aspirations of becoming landed aristocracy. All of the rights and assumed privileges of title had no real value without Amerindians to work the land.

Encomienda was not as widely practiced in Costa Rica as it was in other Central American colonies for a variety of reasons: the Amerindian labor force in Costa Rica was smaller; the Costa Rican Amerindians, outside of the Nicoya area, were not living in as large population centers as were, for example, the Maya of Guatemala. Instead, they lived in smaller, autonomous groups spread throughout the country. Thus the Spaniards weren't able simply to move in and conquer large numbers in a single effort as they had in Mexico.

Moreover, the Costa Rican Amerindians did not adapt well to slavery and fiercely resisted its imposition. Many fought and died avoiding enslavement, and many others fled to the mountains where they could not be followed. Finally, the practice of *encomienda* was abolished well before large numbers of Spanish settlers arrived in Costa Rica.

Church intervention

The Church proved to have an uneasy time with the *encomienda* system. After forceful campaigning by many churchmen, including Friar Bartolmé de las Casas, a former *conquistador*, *encomienda* was abolished in 1542.

This set off violent protests among the settlers, who believed they could not survive without slave labor. In Nicaragua, feelings ran so high that an armed uprising of colonists murdered the bishop who had supported *encomienda*'s repeal. Settlers petitioned the

king, arguing that they had invested their lives and possessions, and the Crown had derived much benefit from their sacrifices. To his credit, the king refused.

Repartimiento

Still, the Crown had to support the colonists' need for labor. *Encomienda* was replaced by a system called *repartimiento*, (meaning to divide up) which required all Amerindian men between the ages of 16 and 60 to labor one week of each month for private individuals, religious institutions, municipalities and government offices.

On paper, the system was supposed to provide indigenous peoples with compensation for their labor and leave them free to work their own fields for the remaining three or so weeks of the month. But, in practice, things were very different, and abuses became commonplace.

Locals were required to devote considerably more than a week's labor to the Spaniards, since they had to walk very long distances, sometimes for days on end, from their villages to their places of work. And they were charged for the food and any other goods they consumed – thus using up their miserably small amount of pay.

LEFT: converting the Amerindians with the cross.
RIGHT: Catholic missionaries among the locals.

Years passed and the search continued for the fabled great gold mines of Veragua. But the mines were never found. Spanish *conquistadores* plundered the coastlines, laying claim to whatever booty they could find, capturing local people and enslaving them, and fighting all the while among themselves for claims to the new lands. English pirates appeared on the scene, also competing for gold and slaves.

Spain's Central American colonies were

DUKE OF VERAGUA

In 1546, Luis, the grandson of Christopher Columbus, was finally named Duke of Veragua. He set out with an expedition of 130 men to claim his legacy, but he was attacked by Amerindians, lost most of his men and retreated in failure.

conquistadores, since they scarcely ever attempted to escape and return to their homes.

Cavallón also brought along livestock, including horses, cows, goats, pigs, chickens and ducks, to improve the community's chances of success. It was a well-planned and well-financed expedition. Finally, 60 years after Columbus had arrived in Veragua, the first inland settlement in Costa Rica was established. It was christened Garcimuñoz, after Cavallón's place of birth.

developing, with administrative centers springing up in Panamá, Nicaragua and Guatemala. In 1539, officials in Panamá used the name Costa Rica for the first time to distinguish the territory between Panamá and Nicaragua. But still there were no permanent settlements.

In 1559, Phillip II of Spain insisted that Costa Rica be populated, this time well inland. In 1561, Juan de Cavallón arrived with a group of 90 Spaniards recruited from Guatemala and Nicaragua, along with a team of black slaves and auxiliary Amerindians from Nicaragua.

Bringing indigenous peoples from one area to another was a common practice among the

Juan Vásquez de Coronado

Hailed by some historians as the true conqueror of Costa Rica, Coronado moved the Garcimunōz settlement to the Cartago Valley and thence to El Guarco, and it was there, for the first time, that a permanent community took root. Coronado's tactics with the Amerindians of Costa Rica were different from those of his predecessors. While he fully intended to settle their lands and take what gold he could lay his hands on, he was friendly toward them, he treated them with respect and he requested, rather than demanded, labor and tribute.

Coronado was pressured by his soldiers and the settlers, who weren't particularly interested in peace, to be more aggressive with the indigenous population. The settlers wanted food, gold and labor, or at least the promise of wealth and an easier life. During this time, they were continuously threatening to desert Costa Rica, claiming life was too difficult. Coronado's peaceful strategies were effective, however, and the colony flourished.

Pacification and punishment

Among Coronado's successes was the surrender (pacification, it was called) of a local chief named Quitao. At a meeting of all the chiefs in the area, Quitao announced that he was tired of hiding in the jungles and was ready to submit to the Spaniards. He told the other chiefs they were free to decide for themselves what they would do. The chiefs asked Quitao to decide for them and he replied that they would have to serve the king and his representative. Those who did not go along would be severely punished. Then, as a token of his submission, he sent 150 locals to serve the Spanish, an act that was "cause for great admiration among the Spaniards."

Coronado's chronicles of his explorations through Costa Rica include keen, almost affectionate observations of the Amerindians. In the Diquis region, visiting the Coctu, he wrote of the well-organized and well-developed villages, unlike any he had previously seen. He noted that the people had a lot of gold, which they acquired from tribes on the Atlantic coast and scooped from the rivers, and fine cotton clothing as well. He described them as a very good-looking people, bellicose, skillful in their manners, and very honest, "a thing rarely seen in indians."

It was among the Coctu that Coronado met the "most good-looking indian" he had ever seen, Chief Corrohore, who asked his assistance in recovering his sister, Dulcehe, who had been kidnapped by a neighboring chief. Coronado succeeded and Dulcehe was returned.

The situation was not always peaceful, however. Coronado, known for making peace among some of the warring tribes of Costa Rica, joined them in their wars against one another. There were also Amerindian uprisings in the colony. Returning after an exploration,

Coronado found that all the Amerindians of the area, including Quitao, were at war with the Spanish. (The Spanish had been stealing the locals' corn.) Amerindians in Orosi had killed eight Spaniards and their horses. His old friends, the chiefs Aserrí, Currirabá, Yurustí, Quircó and Purirsí, had been made prisoners. In an attempt to calm the situation, Coronado went to speak to the Amerindians and, in a fit of temper, ordered two of them to be dismembered.

The lack of gold, food shortages and indigenous revolts imposed continuous hardships on the settlers. Supplies and new settlers were brought in from Nicaragua, but life was almost

unendurable for the Spaniards. In 1569, settlers demanded indigenous slaves, threatening to abandon the colony if their demands weren't met. Perafán de Ribera, Coronado's successor, a man of 74 years and in frail health, defied Spanish law and permitted the settlers to enslave the locals.

The late 1560s marked the end of the conquest of Costa Rica. By then the majority of the indigenous population of the new colony had been killed, had died of diseases, had submitted to the Spaniards or had fled to the forested mountains of Talamanca. The land was now available to the settlers from Spain to come and make a new life. ❑

LEFT: the return of Dulcehe by Coronado.
RIGHT: Don Juan de Cavallón.

COLONIALISM AND INDEPENDENCE

After years as a forgotten penurious colony that received news of its independence by mail, Costa Rica discovered coffee and launched a fledgling democracy

The Costa Rican colony grew slowly. In 1573, there was a total of 50 families in Cartago, and a fledgling community that would later become San José. Spanish immigrants arrived from Extremadura, in the west of Spain; from Andalucia, in the south, with its strong Moorish influences; and from Castile, the heart of old Spain. The Spanish had also founded colonies on the Pacific coast, at Espiritú Santo de Esparza and Nicoya. Although the population of Costa Rica was slowly growing, life was anything but easy.

Riches to rags

During the conquest, *conquistadores* had loaded their ships and lined their pockets with gold and had sent their obligatory percentages off to the royal treasury, which had swelled with their contributions. But by the end of the 16th century, what little gold there was in Costa Rica was gone. There was little Spanish currency available and it appeared as though there was no way to generate wealth. Cacao beans were used as money and barter became common. Even the few goods the colonists "bought" from Spain were traded for wheat flour, pigs, lard, chickens, tobacco and liquor produced on their farms. Most families lived on isolated farms in the Central Valley, using primitive methods of agriculture. Social and even church life was non-existent, and the populace lived in a state of grim impoverishment.

The forgotten colony

By now Spain was paying scant attention to its far-off colony and even the colonial governor in Guatemala made little effort to acquaint himself with the colony's concerns. It was, after all, a three-month trip from Guatemala by horse, and there was little reason to travel to Costa Rica.

Official neglect had a positive side effect, however. Without large landholdings or plentiful peon labor to work plantations, even Costa Rica's

governor and the aristocratic Spanish settlers were forced to work their own fields. Despite the gruelling labor, the land at least was fertile, enriched by volcanic ash and irrigated by rivers. Colonists grew wheat, vegetables and sugar, and raised livestock and poultry. Slowly but surely, the seeds of an economy began to take root.

GENERAL PETER SLAM.

The birth of commerce

The first export of the Costa Rican colony was mules. They were walked along the Mule Road to Panamá, where they were sold to hardy souls who needed beasts to bear goods from the Atlantic to the Pacific coast. Later came cacao production on the Atlantic coast, and then tobacco, in the Central Plateau. In an attempt to give Costa Rica a product to export and a dependable income that could be taxed, the Crown set up tobacco-processing plants and granted to Costa Rica sole rights within the colonies to grow tobacco. But Costa Rican tobacco was never of good quality, and there was not a large market for it.

LEFT: the infamous English pirate Henry Morgan.
RIGHT: Miskito bandits, scourge of the colonists.

On the Atlantic coast, piracy and slave-trading were the business of the day. The Atlantic waters were continually plundered by English pirates, including Drake, Mansfield, Morgan and Owens; and by French, Dutch and Portuguese buccaneers. They were all attempting to control the territory so they could cross the isthmus, from the Atlantic to the Pacific, and thus avoid the Spaniards in Panamá.

The *Miskitos*

In 1641 a slave ship was wrecked off the coast of Nicaragua/Honduras. The black slaves on board escaped onto the Atlantic coast. Well-

the British-controlled Jamaican governor. (The British and the Spanish were then at war.)

Protection money

By 1779 the pirate situation had gotten so out of hand that the government started paying tribute to the *Miskitos* and leaving them "gifts" of coats made of fine fabric, shiny buttons, or three-cornered French hats, to collect at Matina.

Many years later, in 1841, President Braulio Carrillo refused to continue paying tribute to, or bestow gifts upon the *Miskitos* and threatened to bring the resources of the country to war against them. Probably because cacao produc-

liked by the Amerindians, they intermarried and, over the years, developed an identity and language of their own, named *Miskito*. British pirates joined forces with the *Miskitos*, and together they wreaked havoc along the Atlantic coast of Costa Rica and in the cacao plantations. For the *Miskitos*, the undefended plantations offered little resistance. They sailed in for their biannual raids, took the cacao, captured the black slaves and set off again.

In 1742, after many years of such devastation, the government built Fort San Fernando in Matina, north of present-day Limón. Only five years later, the fort was destroyed by the pirate Owens and the *Miskitos*, under orders of

tion had dwindled greatly by then, the *Miskitos* stopped raiding Matina. Traces of their influence remain in the Atlantic coast area, however, and many of the place names there come from the *Miskito* language, including Talamanca (Talamalka), Sixaola and Cahuita.

Amerindian resettlement

Owing to its mountainous terrain and inaccessibility, the Talamanca region of Costa Rica had escaped the conquest. Groups of indigenous people, some of them refugees fleeing oppressive conditions elsewhere in the country, lived there, undisturbed by the invading Spaniards. However, as more colonists arrived in Costa Rica to clear land, build roads and farm, the paltry size of the available Amerindian labor force became a serious problem. The solution was to begin raids on the Talamanca region. After numerous raids, attempts to conquer Talamanca proved unsuccessful. There were counter attacks and cruel revenges on both sides. Ultimately, hundreds of Amerindians were "re-located" to the Central Valley by the Indian Resettlement Policies of 1747.

Meanwhile, in the Central Valley, growing communities were being established. In 1706, the village of Cubujuqui, which later became

Independence – by mail

Costa Ricans like to tell the story of how they received their independence from Spain by mail. In fact, a courier aboard a mule arrived in the Central Valley of Costa Rica with the news on October 13, 1821, nearly a month after colonial officials in Guatemala City had declared independence for Costa Rica from the Spanish Empire.

The news aroused ambivalence, confusion and conflict over what independence meant for the backwater region of Costa Rica. Being the province farthest removed from the colonial capital, Costa Rica came under the least influence of

Heredia, was founded; in 1737, Villa Nueva de la Boca del Monte, now San José, was born; and in 1782, Villa Hermosa, now Alajuela, was settled.

Costa Ricans, living at subsistence levels, were too busy trying to survive to be much affected by the currents of thought and the conflicts that led to Central America's struggle for independence from Spain. The discord that was brewing elsewhere in Central America, fueled by class distinctions and onerous trade restrictions, largely passed them by.

LEFT: English pirates sack a village near the Pacific.
ABOVE: a public beheading in Talamanca.

the Spanish Crown, the Catholic Church, the colonial bureaucracy and the monopolistic Guatemalan traders who dominated colonial life in the rest of Central America. Tucked away in the recesses of the country's central highlands, leaders of the four small communities of San José, Cartago, Heredia and Alajuela began a lengthy debate over what to do next.

Which way now?

Taking their cues from the 1812 Spanish Constitution, written with the participation of distinguished liberal Costa Rican Florencio de Castillo, local leaders drafted their first Constitution, the *Pacto de Concordia,* on December 1,

1821. A split quickly developed over whether or not to follow the lead of other Central American countries in joining Mexican nationalist and emperor Agustín de Itúrbide's Empire, or to opt for total independence.

Leaders of the towns of San José and Alajuela, inspired by the revolutionary ideas that were then sweeping the world, argued for independence, while those of Cartago and Heredia leaned toward the Mexican Empire. There were even those who argued passionately that Costa Rica should become a part of Colombia, at the time ruled by Simón Bolívar.

The disagreements reflected the basic dispar-

ity in the respective characters of the cities. Cartago and Heredia had been founded to create Catholic congregations out of the early settlers: these towns evolved into centers of conservative thought and were more closely linked to the Church and the old colonial bureaucracy. By contrast, San José was founded by settlers who were banished from Cartago for defying the strict colonial trading laws on smuggling. Alajuela, too, developed into a fringe agricultural center where the smuggling of tobacco flourished. Both towns developed more free-wheeling, commercially based liberal attitudes than those of their strait-laced neighbors.

los Varones Ilustres en Costa Rica

THE OLD CAPITAL

The country's first capital of Cartago was founded in 1561 by Juan de Cavallón as Castillo de Garcimuñoz. The site and name were abandoned when Coronado moved all the inhabitants to El Guarco in the Cartago Valley. Then Perafán de Ribera moved it again, to Mata Redonda, near present-day Sabana. Later, the peripatetic city returned to the Cartago Valley, to its present location.

In 1723, Irazú Volcano erupted, covering Cartago in layers of ash. At that time, Costa Rica's capital comprised just 70 houses, a parish church and two shrines. It had no shops, no drug store, not even a resident doctor.

The issue of whether or not Costa Rica would join the Mexican Empire was settled on April 5, 1823. Two armies from the rival cities met in battle on the Continental Divide between San José and Cartago in a skirmish that left 20 men dead. The victorious independence forces, led by a former merchant seaman named Gregorio José Ramírez, took the town of Cartago.

Independence from the Mexican Empire was assured. As it turned out, they need not have bothered: the Costa Ricans belatedly learned that Itúrbide had been declared a traitor several days before the battle, and had been captured and executed. And with him had gone the Mexican Empire.

Farmers and teachers

Gregorio Ramírez set a precedent by relinquishing power in order to return to his farm, an example that would be followed by other victorious Costa Rican leaders. He later returned to put down an army coup, establishing civilian dominance over the military at a very early stage in the country's development.

Statehood was conferred upon a rather ambivalent Costa Rica by the Federal Republic of Central America. This confederation was a noble effort to create a "United States of Central America" out of the five provinces, with a capital in Guatemala City. But it was doomed to

dez distinguished himself by conducting the affairs of state with prudence and humility.

The first printing presses arrived in Costa Rica under Mora Fernández's tenure. By the time his successor, another elementary school teacher named José Rafael Gallegos, was elected, (against his will) in 1833, several newspapers were in print. One of them, *La Tertulia*, published humiliating attacks on Gallegas. Not much interested in the office to begin with, Gallegas resigned as Head of State. One of *La Tertulia*'s major complaints was the social disintegration that had befallen the community as a result of the first modest signs of prosperity

failure because of class disparities and the tenacity with which the elite class clung to the local colonial social order in other parts of Central America.

Costa Rica, on the other hand, was largely a nation of family farmers. It lacked both an elite class and a well-defined social order, so it offered neither great resistance to, nor enthusiasm for, the confederation. As a sovereign federal state, the country elected its first Head of State, Juan Mora Fernández, in 1824. An elementary school teacher, Fernán-

brought on by the planting of coffee, near San José. That limited prosperity brought with it prostitution, gambling and property theft at levels unknown during the more austere colonial era. A strong, no-nonsense authoritarian hand seemed called for, and a San José lawyer, named Braulio Carrillo, was the right man in the right place at the right time.

Braulio Carrillo

Carrillo imposed vagrancy laws, withdrew Costa Rica from the faltering Central American Federal Republic and enacted liberal reforms such as a civil and penal code. He also outlawed the church's right to tithe and earned the enmity

LEFT: 19th century heads of state.
ABOVE: early 20th-century Nicoya group.

of Central Valley townships by imposing a tax on rural land, using the revenues to build roads and ports. Braulio Carrillo also settled Costa Rica's share of a debt to British bankers that had been incurred by the founders of the Central American Federation. Other Central American countries would have that debt hanging over them until well into the 20th century. The payback of the "English debt" eventually paid dividends in the form of good credit with which to invest in the country's new-found source of wealth: coffee.

ROTATING CAPITALS

To minimize the rivalries between the four main population centers of the day, the honor of being capital was rotated among them every four years.

The economic power that coffee gave to the citizens of San José, added to Carrillo's reorganizing of the country's institutions around the new source of wealth, caused resentment from the other townships. In 1837, Cartago, Alajuela and Heredia challenged Carrillo and San José in the *Guerra de la Liga*. Emerging victorious from the battle, Carrillo moved the capital permanently to San José.

When his term was up in 1837, Braulio Carrillo left office, only to return in a military

Coffee power

Carrillo had, with unabashed autocracy, reorganized public administration to support the demands of the coffee economy. Serendipitously, in 1843 William Le Lacheuron, an English seaman on his way back home with a cargo of pelts, put in to Puntarenas in Costa Rica in search of ballast for his ship, which had been battered by storms off the Mexican coast. He loaded some 500,000 pounds of coffee into his hold and the Costa Rica–Liverpool connection was established. Thus were the British Isles and, ultimately, the European continent, opened up as an important new market for Costa Rican coffee.

coup the following year, after his successor tried to roll back some of his reforms. Continuing to force the country down the road to a coffee-fueled progress, he proclaimed himself president-in-perpetuity.

General Morazán

By 1842, the new social order created by Carrillo rose up to overwhelm him. Members of the budding coffee oligarchy called on General Francisco Morazán, a hero of the Central American Federal Republic, to free them from what they perceived as Carrillo's despotism. Morazán was welcomed as a liberator when he arrived in Costa Rica, in April of 1842, with an army of 500 mostly Salvadoran volunteers. The head of Carrillo's army, Vicente Villaseñor, met up with Morazán just as the general and his men neared Alajuela on their march from the Pacific port of Caldera, and offered to join forces with him. The *Pacto de Jocote* sealed, Carrillo fell and was forced into exile in El Salvador.

A special assembly named Morazán Provisional Head of the State of Costa Rica. The General received a hero's welcome in Heredia and Alajuela, but received a somewhat restrained and cooler reception in San José.

Morazán wore out his welcome when he attempted to use Costa Rica as a base to revive his moribund Confederation. The General sent missives to the other Central American countries calling for a National Constituent Assembly to revive his dream of a unified Central American nation. He threatened to impose compliance by force of arms. When Morazán tried to conscript Costa Ricans to enforce his ultimatum, the people of San José revolted. After three days of fierce fighting, Morazán was captured and, on September 15, 1842, he was executed in San José's Central Park.

Less than three years later, Braulio Carrillo, too, was to meet a violent end, assassinated in El Salvador. Today, Costa Ricans have mixed feelings about Braulio Carrillo. He is remembered as both a despot and as a strong, sometimes benevolent leader who, perhaps, was the right man at the right time. He forced Costa Rica to break with its colonial past, placing the country firmly, if hesitatingly, on the path to nationhood.

William Walker

In 1855, a Tennessee adventurer named William Walker took control of Nicaragua. One of his aims was to institutionalize slavery there and in neighboring countries so that he could sell slaves to the United States. Certain US industrialists liked the plan and gave support to Walker. The following year, with an army of 300 mercenaries, called *filibusteros*, he invaded Costa Rica, advancing as far as the site of the present Santa Rosa National Park. Walker and his men entrenched themselves in the fortified Santa Rosa *casona* (mansion). Costa Rican

President Juan Rafael Mora, a member of the coffee oligarchy, had been monitoring the threat and had already mustered a force of *campesinos* (farm workers) to repel Walker. The Costa Ricans were numerically superior, though many were poorly armed with little more than farming implements and rusty rifles. On May 20, 1856, they engaged Walker in a 14-minute-long battle and forced him to retreat back toward the Nicaraguan border.

The Costa Rican army pursued them and, at Rivas in Nicaragua, trapped Walker in a wooden fort. A young drummer boy named Juan Santamaría volunteered to torch the fort,

but was shot dead in the process. With the fort in flames, Walker's men were routed and his Costa Rican adventure was over. Three years later, he met his end in front of a firing squad in Honduras. The name of Juan Santamaría lives on in Costa Rican folklore as a youthful hero and symbol of national freedom, and in the country's main international airport, which is named after him.

President Mora was not such a hero. Despite his victory, his domestic policies were not popular. He rigged the elections of 1859, however, to win another term in office. He was deposed, attempted an unsuccessful coup d'état, and was executed. ❑

LEFT: a 19th-century mud-and-wattle home.
RIGHT: statue of Juan Santamaría, Alajuela.

MODERN TIMES

Economic difficulties and the rising tide of reform came to a head in civil war,
but 21st-century Costa Rica became Central America's peace broker

In 1889, with the drafting of the country's liberal constitution and the institution of a reliable, quadrennial electoral process, Costa Rica entered an era of bucolic prosperity and political stability. Affairs of state were left in the hands of so-called "Olympian" political plutocrats who administered public affairs with a laissez-faire assurance.

The coffee coup

It was not all plain sailing, however. The presumed downward trickle of profits in the coffee economy failed to reach enough people, especially in the neglected urban centers. Faced with the closing of European coffee markets during World War I, Costa Rica's first reformist president, Alfredo Gonzáles Flores, instituted a tax on coffee. This incurred the wrath of the coffee establishment, which backed the president's own army chief, Federico Tinoco, in a successful coup on January 27, 1917. Tinoco assumed the presidency and named his brother, Joaquín, to head the army.

The warrior priest

Popular reaction to the repressive Tinoco dictatorship brought Jorge Volio Jiménez onto the country's political stage with a dramatic flourish. The pious scion of a Cartago coffee family, which bred Costa Rica several presidents, Volio began studying for the priesthood at Belgium's Leuven University in 1903. Heavily influenced by Belgian social Christian thinking, Volio returned to Costa Rica in 1910 to become pastor of the parish of Carmen de Heredia. No simple parish priest, in 1912 Volio denounced the silence of the Costa Rican government over the intervention of US marines in Nicaragua and backed up his words by leading a group of Nicaraguan revolutionaries into battle. He was seriously wounded in the battle of Paz Centro, which took place in southern Nicaragua.

PRECEDING PAGES: volunteer militiamen.
LEFT: young soldiers in a border dispute with Panamá.
RIGHT: animal trophies were once the fashion.

For his military adventure Volio was suspended from the Church, but was later reinstated and assigned to the Santa Ana parish. His passion for social justice led him to more clashes with the conservative local hierarchy, and, in 1915, he left the priesthood to devote himself full-time to working for social change.

As the Tinoco dictatorship became even more repressive, Volio and a handful of other Costa Ricans left the country and formed an armed resistance. The revolutionary forces were defeated by government troops led by army chief Joaquín Tinoco in battles near the Nicaraguan border in early 1919. The Tinoco dictatorship was brought down not by this armed resistance nor by a military one, but rather by school teachers and students who rioted after soldiers marched on them, during a demonstration, in July of 1919. On August 9, 1919, Federico Tinoco resigned the presidency. The next day, Joaquín Tinoco was gunned down. The gunman was never identified.

¡Viva Volio!

His military defeat notwithstanding, Volio received a hero's welcome on his arrival in San José and the ready cry "¡Viva Volio!" expressed the hope for change in the country's stodgy political status quo. The title of General was conferred on Volio by Congress. But much to Volio's consternation, the fall of Tinoco meant a return to business as usual in Costa Rica. Volio established the Reformist Party in 1923, which set an agenda for agrarian reform, decent housing, job security and social protections. During the same year he ran for president on the Reformist ticket against Ricardo Jiménez and

fight that left two government soldiers and Volio himself wounded, he was apprehended. Volio was taken back to San José where he was examined by doctors. They diagnosed him as suffering from "nervous hypersensitivity." Rather than imprisoning the patriot, Jiménez, in consultation with Volio's family, allowed the General to be taken to Belgium for psychiatric care. Volio's promising political career came to an ignominious end.

The growth of reform

Volio's brand of reformism collapsed with his party, but the reformist movement was

Alberto Echandi. Volio came in a close third in a vote that gave none of the candidates a majority. He agreed to join forces with Jiménez, accepting the vice-presidency and a seat in Congress. But Volio did not see his pact with Jiménez as one of compromise. Instead, he used his seat to bewilder his fellow congressmen with forceful attacks on the country's upper classes.

When the government once again showed indifference to strife in neighboring Nicaragua, Volio commanded a force across the border to intervene. Concerned as to what an increasingly belligerent Volio might do with his force upon return, Jiménez ordered the General to be intercepted when he arrived in Liberia. After a gun-

important in giving voice to the aspirations of sectors of society on the margins of the agro-export economy. It also inspired young intellectuals to action. One of those intellectuals was Manuel Mora, who, in his own words, "used to follow Volio around like a puppy dog." Disillusioned with Volio's political flirtation with Jiménez, Mora split with the Reformist Party to eventually form the Communist Party in 1931.

The Communists immediately made their presence felt in the lowland banana zones. In a strike in the banana zones in 1934, immortalized in the novel *Mamita Yunai* by labor organizer Carlos Luis Fallas, the Communists won wage guarantees and the right to unionize, but only after a heated battle with both government troops and the United Fruit Company.

Meanwhile, plummeting coffee prices during the Great Depression had created additional hardship for a great many Costa Ricans.

Calderón Guardia

The rising tide of reform finally found its champion when, as the economic crisis reached its breaking point, Costa Ricans elected Dr Rafael Angel Calderón Guardia to the presidency in 1939. Inheritor of his father's humanitarian legacy and backed by the coffee establishment, Calderón Guardia seemed the perfect choice.

Calderón Guardia, also steeped in social Christian doctrine at medical school in Belgium, carried out reforms beyond the hopes of even the most fervent reformers and the fears of the most entrenched liberal, creating a social-security system, a labor code and various other social guarantees.

Costa Rica declared war on Germany and Japan following the attack on Pearl Harbor – a day before the United States. But Calderón Guardia added insult to injury for the coffee barons by using his wartime emergency powers

ABOVE: mural in Costa Rica's Museum of Art: *Cultivating the Wild New Country.*

to confiscate the lands of German families, some of whom had been in Costa Rica for generations and who had intermarried with the oligarchy.

Having alienated himself from the traditional source of political power, Calderón Guardia made common cause with Manual Mora and his Communist Party, and with the Catholic Church, led by the socially minded Archbishop Victor Sanabria. Together they defied the coffee barons and the economic liberals who had dominated Costa Rica since the end of the 19th century and set about expanding the role of the state in providing for people's needs. The nascent bureaucracies would invariably be headed by a member of the Communist Party. Manuel Mora would be named head of the country's army.

When the worldwide anti-Nazi alliances – which made this peculiar church-state-party pact feasible – vanished, so too did the wide-based, popular support for Calderón's leadership. As the government clung to power, a disillusioned Mora was paid a visit by an old friend who offered his support. It was the elderly and ailing General Jorge Volio Jiménez.

History has shown that the winners of the ensuing 1948 civil war, led by José (Don Pepe) Figueres, had no intention of rolling back the social guarantees. Instead, they further institutionalized the legacy of nearly 30 years of reformist struggle. It was a legacy summed up by the immortal cry: "¡Viva Volio!"

The grandfather of Costa Rica

José Figueres is best known abroad for abolishing the army, but Costa Ricans remember him for the way in which he lived his life, and for the heritage of democracy that he created and solidified. Don Pepe was born of Catalán parents, and for many, that somehow explained his ego, his opinionated, self-righteous, impossibly principled, obstinate, courageous, unyielding, unpredictable self. He was self-educated, and as a young man, he virtually lived in the Boston Public Library, where he became infected with the new and exciting spirit of North American liberalism. He returned to Costa Rica from Boston and New York City in the 1920s with a romantic vision and deeply held belief in the nobility of the human spirit, and hope for social justice for the people of his country.

Until 1942, Don Pepe had no real political experience. Then, on July 2, the *San Pablo*, a United Fruit Company vessel, was sunk by a

German submarine in the Port of Limón. All of the Costa Ricans aboard were killed. President Calderón responded by imprisoning German and Italian citizens of the Atlantic region. Two days later, 20,000 people began to riot after a German-educated medical doctor's window was smashed. Looting followed, and the government not only did nothing to control the mob, but also allegedly encouraged it.

In the aftermath of the riots a climate of fear and suspicion grew. Businessmen who had been looted were afraid to seek redress. Don Pepe Figueres blamed Calderón for failing to maintain public order and safety.

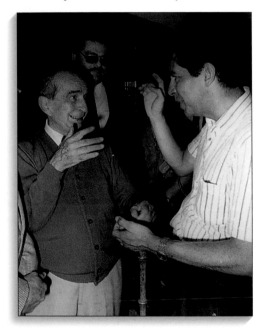

Figueres decided to express "what everyone felt but was afraid to say," and purchased radio air time on "America Latina." In strident mocking tones he accused the administration of an inability to govern. His acid denunciation of the government was interrupted mid-sentence as the director-general of the police arrived and hauled him away. The result was, perhaps all too predictably, the making of a martyr and national hero out of the imprisoned Don Pepe Figueres.

The seeds of revolution

Figueres spent the next two years in exile in Mexico. Force, he was convinced, was the only way to overthrow the government of Rafael An-

gel Calderón. Figueres formed mutual-help relationships and forged agreements with exiles, intellectuals and revolutionaries from other countries, and he began stockpiling arms.

In 1944, after a particularly violent and discreditable election, Teodoro Picado, Calderón's political successor, was elected president. The fraudulent election, the faltering economy, the Communist presence and widespread official corruption were just too much for Figueres. He returned to Costa Rica in May 1944. Determined to do something about Calderón, he jumped into opposition politics, but felt that only a violent revolution would bring about real change.

In the fateful 1948 presidential elections, Otilio Ulate, publisher of the San José newspaper, *Diario de Costa Rica*, ran against Calderón. Ulate won by a substantial margin, but the *calderonistas* maintained control of congress. There were charges and counter-charges of fraud. And, in the midst of all the violent confrontations, a large number of ballots were set ablaze. The Electoral Tribunal, which had been entrusted to oversee fair elections, and to which the nation was looking for an electoral verdict, failed to issue one.

With no action forthcoming from the Electoral Tribunal and no compromise possible between the candidates, the *calderonista*-controlled Congress, in an unprecedented act, annulled the presidential election. Ulate was arrested by Picado's police colonel, and his closest advisor, Dr. Carlos Luis Valverde, was shot and died the following day. In San José, businesses were closed and storefronts were boarded up. It felt as though a bomb were ready to go off.

LA LUCHA SIN FIN

Don Pepe founded a farm high in the mountains, to the south of San José, and called it *La Lucha Sin Fin* (The Endless Struggle). It was a success and he used the profits to open schools, libraries, stores, movie houses, soccer fields and medical clinics for local people.

At *La Lucha*, Don Pepe worked at liberating the *campesino* (farm laborer) from ignorance and poverty and attempting to turn some of the Utopian theories he had studied into a workable reality.

The day-to-day way of life on the farm provided lessons that in many ways Don Pepe Figueres was later to apply to all of Costa Rica.

Meanwhile, Figueres was in the mountains near his ranch, *La Lucha Sin Fin* (the Endless Struggle), planning for the coming war.

Civil war

The War of National Liberation began on March 11, 1948. It consisted of a well-planned offensive carried out by men with no formal military backgrounds, who were trained by guerrilla fighters from the Dominican Republic and Honduras, and armed with guns flown in from Guatemala. Forty-four days later, 2,000 men, one in every 300 Costa Ricans, had been killed during the violent, sad war of liberation. Figueres' forces were victorious, despite the efforts of the Nicaraguan dictator Anastasio Somoza, and his invasion of the north of Costa Rica. President Picado, who had never really believed an armed insurrection would occur, and who had no heart for conflict, saw that a swiftly negotiated peace was essential; he announced his surrender.

The Second Republic

Don Pepe Figueres, as both the acknowledged winner of the battle and head of the victorious junta, entered San José five days after the cease-fire and led a triumphant parade. His National Liberation Army marched up Avenida Central to the airport at La Sabana. Figueres addressed the people, outlining his goals and fundamental concepts, which he referred to as "the greatest good for the greatest number." More precisely, he described the four main objectives of what he called his Second Republic: the re-establishment of civic ethics, elimination of the spoils system in public administration, social progress without communism, and a greater sense of solidarity with other nations.

One of Figueres' first acts was to place a 10 percent tax on wealth, a law that was resented, badly administered and, in most cases, evaded by the affluent. He expanded the social-security system, enacted full voting rights for all women, created a minimum wage, established low-cost national health care services for all, passed legislation on child support, and proposed nationalizing every bank in the country. The firing of large numbers of bureaucrats and

LEFT: Don Pepe, the country's grandfather *(left)*, and Oscar Arias, Costa Rica's president and the Nobel Laureate *(right)*. **RIGHT:** a pensive Don Pepe.

schoolteachers, in an attempt to reorganize government agencies, exacerbated his declining popularity. And then the assets of individuals connected with the Calderón-Picado governments were frozen. Don Pepe's extreme and, to some, arbitrary politics, alienated many. Even the press became hostile to him.

The constitution of 1949 did reflect many of the goals of the Second Republic. It included political and individual freedoms, and added new social guarantees. It established the principle of public regulation of private property and enterprise, and empowered the state to take actions assuring the widest distribution of wealth

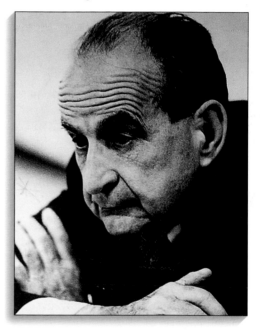

possible. But arguably its finest social guarantee was to extend citizenship to everyone born in Costa Rica. This was an important issue to Afro-Caribbean people, who until that time, had been treated as second-class persons.

The end of the military

The new constitution also abolished the military. This was perhaps Figueres' most celebrated and memorable achievement, and one that he would point to over and over again. As he liked to explain, if a member of the family is ill, you should call the doctor. But that doesn't mean that the doctor has to continue to live with you for the rest of your life.

In a public ceremony, Figueres delivered the keys of the Bella Vista military fortress to the Minister of Public Education, and told him to convert the old fort into a national museum. Don Pepe knew how to exploit the moment: with photographers standing by, he raised a sledgehammer and symbolically smashed at the wall of the fortress.

Figueres's supporters considered that dramatic act as a final blow to militarism. His enemies regarded the abolition of the military as a clever move, since lacking the full backing of the military, he simply decided to get rid of it.

out the decade, debt continued to mount and by 1989 Costa Rica was in the red to the tune of a massive US$5 billion.

The silver lining on the cloud hanging over the nation was provided by its president, Oscar Arias, who was trying to mediate a peace settlement in the escalating regional conflicts. By now El Salvador, Honduras and Guatamala were also embroiled in various types of war or disputes. Costa Rica, for all its economic problems, was at least an oasis of peace. In 1987, Arias was awarded the Nobel Peace Prize for his efforts to bring peace to Central America. He also managed to accept millions of dollars

Calm before storm

The 1960s and 1970s were essentially peaceful and prosperous decades for Costa Rica. The development of a welfare state and rights bills protecting indigenous peoples were just two of the highlights of a progressive regime. But in 1979, the anti-government Sandinista forces in neighboring Nicaragua toppled the Somoza dictatorship. Costa Rica became a fallback area for guerilla groups and anti-Sandinistas, largely at the behest of the United States, to whom Costa Rica was financially indebted.

Equally bad news, if not worse, was the collapse of both the banana and coffee markets, reaching its peak in the early 1980s. Through-

THE PRAGMATIC REVOLUTIONARY

The junta of Don Pepe was not universally popular and he suffered criticism from all quarters. He was accused of being a Communist by the right and a Nazi by the left. Indeed, his revolution had received funding from very conservative Costa Ricans; he had accepted military aid from the United States; he had also received armaments from a group called the Caribbean Legion, who had supplied him on the understanding that this revolution was to be the first of a series that would re-create the Central American region and oust many of the dictatorial regimes that had risen to power with the aid of the United States.

of aid for his country from the United States but not without compromising Costa Rica's neutral position.

A family affair

Despite the success of Oscar Arias abroad, he was voted out in 1990 in favor of Rafael Calderón Fournier, the son of post-war president Dr Rafael Calderón Guardia. Following a lackluster term, he was succeeded by José Maria Figueres, son of Don Pepe, who was, of course, Calderón Guardia senior's arch rival.

An unpleasant legacy of the Calderón era was the Banco Anglo Costariccense affair. In 1994, just after the president left office, the nation's oldest government-owned bank went bankrupt, to the tune of more than US$100 million. The legal battles continue to this day.

Sadly, the young Figueres was unable to repeat his father's success or even improve much on the previous miserable administration, and proved to be one of Costa Rica's most unpopular presidents. In 1998 the Social Christian Unity Party (PUSC) won the election under conservative economist Miguel Angel Rodríguez, who pledged to liberalize certain key economic sectors and slash government spending. Despite attracting foreign investment such as the Intel silicon-chip plant, and signing free-trade deals with Canada and Mexico, many Costa Ricans suspected that his privatization plans for the state-run telecommunication and energy monopolies pointed to corruption. Critics accused his government of lack of transparency, triggering the largest street demonstrations since the 1948 revolution.

In April 2002, PUSC retained power with the election of Abel Pacheco, who placed much emphasis on tourism as the country's greatest economic priority. His tenure was plagued by incompetence, lack of leadership, an intransigent, uncooperative congress and a plethora of political, financial and environmental scandals. In 2004 two ex-presidents were arrested on corruption charges, including Rodriguez, who had to ignominiously step down from his post as the first-ever Central American Secretary General of the Organization of American States.

Financial scandals included the collapse of

LEFT: national flag-waving politicos.
RIGHT: twice-elected president Oscar Arias, winner of the Nobel Peace Prize.

half a dozen unregulated tax shelters and mutual funds, in which the expat community was heavily invested and hard hit. Pacheco's environmental reforms were never passed and the country's national-park system deteriorated, with uncontrolled poaching and logging thanks to lack of funding for park guards.

A political phoenix

The 2006 election was a prolonged showdown between Citizen Action Party (PAC) leader Ottón Solís and the National Liberation Party's Oscar Arias, who had managed to constitutionally overturn the country's ban on presi-

dential re-election. After a recount, Arias won with the slimmest of margins. Some 20 years after his first term started in 1986, Arias returned to the Casa Presidencial to face a nation polarized by CAFTA, the US-Central American Free Trade Agreement, marked by huge pro- and anti-CAFTA demonstrations. An increase in violent crime and a growing gap between rich and poor are threatening the Costa Rica's image as a peaceful, safe country. The child-sex industry has also cast a pall over tourism. At this writing, Costa Rica is the last hold-out on signing the CAFTA agreement and the ex-presidents are still under investigation, awaiting formal charges. ❏

WHERE THE WORLD's CHOICEST COFFEE GROWS.

 MATION APPLY TO

JOSÉ, COSTA RICA, (CENTRAL AMERICA)

CY OR COSTA RICAN CONSULATE.

SAN JOSÉ – THE WAY IT WAS

Thanks to coffee, San José enjoyed a golden age in the early 1900s. It became the
toast of Central America, a bourgeois paradise. But, sadly, it was not to last

In 1737, the authorities ordered the construction of a thatch-covered hermitage on the flatlands of the Boca del Monte. It was to be the centerpoint of a new village to bring together the residents of the area, whose small homes were scattered over the valley. From this humble beginning began the city of San José.

For its first 39 years, it was still just a village, with mud-covered streets and miserable little houses. Then an official ordered the construction of a tobacco factory, and it was from here that the country's tobacco industry monopoly was administered. It proved to be an activity that brought a certain degree of prosperity.

The coffee boom

Tobacco was a short-lived success, as was cacao. But then came experimentation with a new crop: coffee. It grew with such ease and it bore fruit with such abundance that this once-small Central American colony very quickly left behind the squalor that it had known.

England was interested in not only buying this coffee, but also in loaning funds, on account, against the next harvest. The surrounding areas filled quickly with orderly rows of coffee plantations and the people, with their new wealth, sought the life of San José, transforming it into a prosperous coffee-growing center.

Beside the town square there was at first only the Church of Mercy and the Town Council building. But other conveniences, created to serve the foreigners who were beginning to arrive, were soon set up. At the end of the 18th century, the Education Building was erected, as was a cathedral, at the front of which stood a beautiful central park, where both Amerindians and farmers of Spanish extraction held their weekly fairs. Money was minted at the Currency House, and, to support the nascent militia, military quarters were erected.

Social and cultural life

In 1821, Costa Rica gained its independence from the Spanish Empire and became a republic. The small village-town of San José soon grew into a city, then a capital city, and its newly installed authorities struggled to improve the streets, build bridges and open roads to the ports. Guards, armed with rusty muskets, patrolled the brick-layered streets, illuminated at night by kerosene lamps.

In the dance parlors of the bourgeoisie, the quadrille was in vogue. An actor would recite poetry and a young lady would play Chopin ballads amidst conversations concerning the price of coffee in London.

Social and economic life was rigidly defined. The indigenous population was severely depleted; the black community was excluded from the Central Valley and consigned to manual labor. Meanwhile the descendants of the Spanish lived in the central part of town where they built their large adobe houses with corridors opening onto enclosed vegetable gardens.

Cultural life centered around the Mora Theater, where fourth-rate companies would perform, along with jugglers and an occasional virtuoso musician. The ladies would sit and listen, dressed in their regal dresses, while the gentlemen stood around, robed in their Spanish capes, smoking and engaging in small-talk concerning politics.

Foreign visitors would stay in a rooming house and venture forth to see the town's sights. Some considered the possibility of entering the coffee-export business and others idly took notes for their travel diaries.

The European influence

Earnings from the export of coffee engendered an illustrious bourgeoisie. The members of this

Ever grander plantations were created in an effort to stay ahead of their competitors.

Costa Rican architects visited the Universal Exposition of Paris in 1900 and, along with other new and imported ideas, brought back metal buildings for schools. They imported finely wrought metal plates for walls, steel columns, building crests, and Italian mosaics. The homes of the coffee growers soon began to look like the mansions of the wealthy in New Orleans and Jamaica: French adobe walls; wide, inclined roofs; ornate verandahs with white balustrades and woodwork cut in the style of gingerbread. Jalousies and shades pro-

class traveled to France to have their children educated in Europe. When home in San José, the children missed the theaters, the boulevards, the cafés and the fine architecture of Europe. As they grew up, they insisted on improving the appearance of their native capital city. As coffee production engendered greater prosperity, the leading planter families increased their investments, which led to rivalries among them.

PRECEDING PAGES: an early attempt to lure tourists.
LEFT: downtown San José was conceived as a handsome place of fine buildings and grand statues.
ABOVE: First Avenue, San José, during the early years of the 20th century.

EARLY IMPRESSIONS

A German scientist, visiting during the mid-19th century, wrote: "There is not a building that calls attention for its beauty. The government buildings, the garrison and its gallery, the university and the theater are insignificant structures. The cathedral has an air of negligence and economy. There aren't even any chairs. The president of the republic has to sit with his followers on a wooden bench." By contrast a French journalist noted: "The presidential palace is an enchanting square building with an internal half-Spanish, half-Arab patio. A circular stair led to the congressional room where a ball was staged for me."

tected the windows made of colored glass through which the brilliant tropical sun shone.

The city's golden age

Toward the end of the 19th century, Monsieur Amon Faiseleau Duplantier, who received the concession to establish the streetcar system, divided his farm on the sunny slopes of the Torres River and there began the business of real-estate sales. The best of San José society fought for the urban lots, building mansions, a few of which still survive in Barrio Amón. Soon the coffee plantations were replaced with tree-shaded streets and stately residences with large

the shape of a horseshoe was financed from the national budget and by a tax paid by the rich coffee growers.

By the early 1900s, the village had given way to a glowing city, which, even if it did not attain the elegant, urbane layout to which it aspired, developed a comfortable lifestyle permitted by its growing prosperity.

If the early European critics of Costa Rica had looked in the crystal ball and foreseen the amenities of San José at the turn of the 20th-century, they would surely have remained. In front of the theater was the elegant Hotel Français. Nearby, the Petite Trianon was a coffee

gardens. Meanwhile, Minor Keith, who was occupied with developing The United Fruit Company and the railroad system to the Atlantic coast, finished the Atlantic Railroad station in San José. At the same time, Mother Superior Barthelemy Rich was opening her prestigious girls' high school, *Colegio de Sión*, where the daughters of the bourgeoisie received their education.

On October 19, 1897, the president and a select audience entered the wide doors of the National Theater to inaugurate the building. That opening night featured a magnificent presentation of the opera *Faust*. The sumptuous building with its four levels and a floor plan in

house favored by high society, artists and diplomats; a little beyond, the windows of the Golden Eagle were filled with French wine and liquors and Spanish preserves and fine oils. *Talabarteria Inglesa* and *La Tiendita* satisfied the most demanding tastes in matters of decoration and leatherwork.

The Ford agency exhibited its 1912 model, which was priced at US$975. It competed with a number of other import agencies, along with booming real-estate businesses that offered farms, lots, beaches and Victorian residences. The streetcar ran to the limits of the city carrying great numbers of merchants, their employees and office workers.

The other side of the tracks

Not all members of San José society enjoyed a rose-colored lifestyle. The city had expanded too rapidly, with vast, obscure and sad suburbs encircling older areas. World War I and the accompanying fall in coffee demand and prices brought wide-scale unemployment to those who had previously been able to live relatively well, along with salaries that fell below the poverty level. The Society of Casas Baratas began the construction of workers' housing units of the type known as *puerta ventana*, where several families would cram in narrow and poorly ventilated rooms.

End of an era

Under the pick and sledgehammer, the magnificent National Palace, the Garrison, the National Library, the Union Club and many lovely residences disappeared. The inner city lost its sense of identity and was invaded by mediocre commercial constructions. Fast highways opened up and North American influence began to replace elegant European ideals.

San José spilled over and outward in a random fashion. Cars permitted the wealthy classes to move their residences from what had now become the depressed inner city to the desirable suburbs of Escalante, Los Yoses, Cur-

To the south and near the railroad station to the Pacific, there soon appeared barracks, warehouses and factories, where soap and candles were made. An industrial zone with beer factories, ice-making factories, printing presses, mechanics' shops and lumber mills slowly began to surround and envelop the elegant urban center. With the advent of cement structures, the arrival of the new rich, and the industrialization of the city, there also came the desire to modernize, to create new statements and to destroy the past.

ridabat, Paseo Colon, Sabana and Rohrmoser. By the 1960s, several satellite town centers evolved, resembling the style of suburban North America.

Certainly San José would no longer win a prize as the most beautiful Central American city. Traffic pollution and congestion are constant irritants. But it still possesses a certain charm. You won't find the monumental scale of Guatemala City nor the cosmopolitan quality of Panamá City; yet there is a vital quality to the hustle and sheer movement of the place, along with tangible remains of the coffee-growing bourgeoisie and their neo-classical architecture and whimsical Caribbean-colonial style. ❑

LEFT: San José, around 1928.
ABOVE: the leisured class at home.

THE PEOPLE OF COSTA RICA

Costa Ricans, or Ticos, *come in all shapes, sizes and colors.*

"We are all Ticos," is the proud claim, though some Ticos *fare better than others*

Racially and ethnically, Costa Rica is not a simple place. Along with the overwhelming majority of Spanish-heritage *Ticos*, there are four other distinct ethnic groups. The people of Guanacaste have dark skin, resembling their Nicaraguan neighbors in manner and accent. In the southern, mountainous regions of the country, the Amerindians of Costa Rica, who were here long before the Spanish, belong to six discrete linguistic groups. Though they increasingly speak Spanish, they still debate whether it is more important to retain their indigenous cultural identity or to assimilate more into mainstream Costa Rican culture.

The blacks of the Atlantic Coast are the country's largest immigrant minority; they speak Caribbean-accented English and talk with pride of their Jamaican heritage. Sino-Costa Ricans are called *Chinos*. Descendents of indentured laborers, they own many of the bars, restaurants and stores, especially in small towns.

All these different races are *Costarricenses*.

Indigenous people

Archeologists, using very different methods of calculating populations, estimate that anywhere from 30,000 to 400,000 native people lived in Costa Rica when Columbus arrived. Today, about 63,000 native people remain, although it is hard to establish an accurate figure since many indigenous people have had mixed marriages.

The history of the Amerindians of Costa Rica is much like that of other indigenous peoples of the American continent. The Europeans brought diseases to which the native populations had no immunity. Entire tribes were obliterated before they had even seen a white man.

In pre-Columbian times, the Chorotegas, cousins of the Nicaro, inhabited Guanacaste and the Nicoya Peninsula. They lived in patrimonial groups, grew corn and were culturally similar to groups from southern Mexico. These peoples were devastated during the Spanish Conquest by disease and by slave traders who shipped them off to Panamá and Peru. Their surviving descendants are today mostly integrated into contemporary Costa Rican life.

Other native groups spoke dialects originating in Colombia. They were divided into clans,

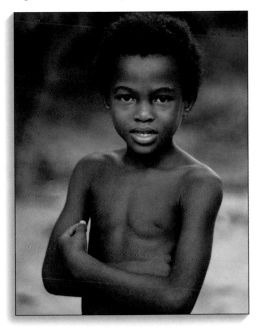

PRECEDING PAGES: Carnival time; ox-cart painter.
LEFT: *campesino* cultivating onions.
RIGHT: a forthright Afro-Caribbean boy.

A PROUD PEOPLE

"The blood that flows in the veins of the people of this Republic is too generous. The Costa Ricans are a people of such excellent mettle; ardently patriotic, they are very proud of their independence, their autonomy, and of a prosperity due almost wholly to industry. The country is one of flourishing villages. There it is that the population of Costa Rica dwells, since it is there that are found the hardy toilers who wrest from the earth the products which form the wealth of the land. An air of ease combined with antique simplicity characterizes these villages."

A.S. Calvert, *A Year of Costa Rica,* 1901

which the Spanish gave names to, and their original names are mostly lost to history: the Guaymí, for example, call themselves Ngabe, pronounced Nobe. The other clans were named the Terraba, the Boruca and, in the Talamanca mountains, the Bribri and Cabecar. These people lived in matrilineal societies in clearings in the jungles. With the coming of the Europeans, many of them fled to the almost inaccessible jungle regions of the southern mountains. Much of their culture has been preserved by their descendants, who still speak their original languages and live in the remote regions of the Talamanca mountains.

these people who live without electricity and running water. The cultural imperialism of the airwaves is persistently penetrating the world of people who have resisted the *conquistadores* for 500 years. Among the young, the temptations of this high-tech world are enticing and the desire to assimilate strong.

Today, indigenous peoples live on reserves designated for their use in 1971. By law, non-native people cannot own land inside these areas, but this has been difficult to enforce and non-Amerindians have moved into these territories, which happen to contain a significant proportion of the country's mineral wealth.

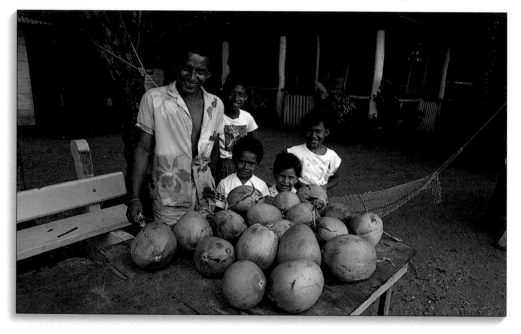

Despite the influence of Christian missionaries, many native people have not forsaken their animistic religious traditions. The Bribri call their deity Sibu and use shamans, with their vast knowledge of the rainforest's medicinal herbs, to cure a range of illnesses. Farther south, along the Panamá border, the Guaymí live in their traditional areas, which span political boundaries.

Modern temptations

No matter how remote their jungle reserves, the Amerindians are still not insulated from contemporary culture. Battery-powered televisions bring pressure to consume soft drinks and junk food, as well as images of the First World to

THE *TICO* SPIRIT

Costa Ricans call themselves *Ticos* in a reference to their common use of the diminutive ending: "*Un momentico, por favor.*" There is a sweetness to the way in which they speak Spanish.

Ticos are politically temperate, shy and unaggressive, yet, today more than ever, they are actively democratic. Once it was only a game; more of a pretense, a love of the rules and trappings of democracy. "Hey, look at me, I voted!" Today, it is stronger, more involved, more functional, more passionate. Demonstrations, protests, strikes, rallies and caucuses are common. Yet the people remain mostly prudent, respectful and discreet.

Encroaching contemporary society threatens indigenous peoples' language, cultural identity and way of life. Caught in time between two worlds, slowly relinquishing the old, but not yet embracing the new, native peoples are extremely vulnerable. In the 500 years since the European conquest, little has changed for the aboriginal Costa Rican people.

Black settlers

As early as 1825, Afro-Caribbeans came to Costa Rica to fish, hunt turtles and market coconuts. These immigrants were part of a migration from the West Indies to the Central

railroad. They proved more successful than previous laborers imported by Keith in their ability to tolerate the working conditions, which included exposure to yellow fever, malaria and poisonous snakes, as well as severe physical labor and oppressive management. The maltreatment of workers in the banana fields of the Caribbean United Fruit Company is well-documented. But the blacks were certainly not invulnerable and they, too, died in their thousands while building the tracks, the endless numbers of bridges, the docks and the wide, rectangular streets of the port city of Limón.

Other Afro-Caribbeans came to the

American Caribbean coast. From Panamá to Honduras, they came looking for ways to support themselves. Many were transient. One man might harvest cacao in Limón, then find employment on the barges in Nicaragua and next labor on the construction of the Panamá Canal; they went where there was work.

In 1872, under contract from Minor C. Keith, who was later to become the founder of the United Fruit Company, blacks from the West Indies came to work on building the Atlantic

Caribbean coast on their own, looking for any kind of work to escape the poverty of their native islands. Some ultimately were given land along the railroad right-of-way and others, thanks to their command of English, rose from the ranks of laborers to become managers in the banana business and on the railways. Most originally planned to earn whatever they could and then return to their islands.

When United Fruit left the Caribbean region and moved to the Pacific coast, the blacks were left behind, unemployed. Many emigrated for the same reason that had motivated their parents to immigrate to the country in the first place: they were again seeking work. Those

LEFT: *pipas* – drinking coconuts for sale at a roadside stand in Limón province.
ABOVE: Puntarenas schoolboys.

who stayed behind lived for the most part at subsistence level, producing what they could from small plots of land. They retained their English language and their Protestant religion, remaining proudly separate from the Hispanic Costa Ricans and enriching these coastal communities with a distinct Afro-Caribbean flavor. At the same time, they endured racist immigration and residency laws that restricted their movement until the middle of the 20th century.

When the Constitution of 1949 declared that anyone born in Costa Rica had automatic citizenship, doors finally opened for blacks. They were allowed to travel outside Limón province

two-sided racism that exists. Blacks usually consider themselves more civilized and superior to Hispanic Costa Ricans, while Hispanic Costa Ricans sometimes insist that blacks are racially inferior.

Today, less than 5 percent of the total Costa Rican population is black, and less than 25 percent of the population of the Caribbean coast is of black ancestry.

The construction of the railroad to the Caribbean coast brought other waves of immigrants during the late 19th century. Among the builders, managers and technicians of the Northern Railway Company were English, Irish

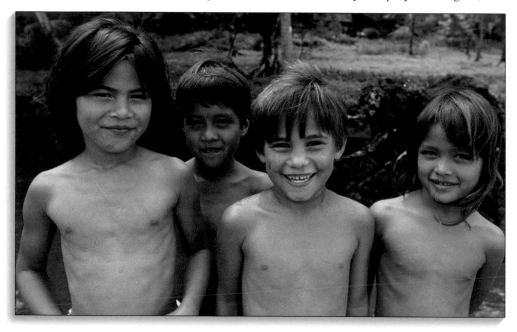

and they began to attend public schools and enter politics. When, in the 1950s, the value of cacao soared on the international market, many of the squatter-farmers were able to achieve a certain prosperity. And, in an ironic reversal of historical patterns, they hired Hispanics to work their fields.

Many members of the subsequent generation of blacks were well educated and, preferring professions to farming, left the Limón area. Indeed, many left Costa Rica entirely to find jobs elsewhere. Some middle-class, educated blacks who remained in Costa Rica married Hispanics, but their assimilation into Costa Rican society is not total, owing to the curious,

ORIGIN OF THE SPECIES

Tradition holds that most Costa Ricans descended from hard-working rural Spanish farmers; that they came from good, simple, unpretentious, egalitarian stock.

Yet among colonial immigrants to Costa Rica from the Iberian peninsula there were also Spanish Jews and Arabs, Catalans and Basques, as well as a great many people from the Middle East.

Then in the 19th century, lured by the promise of coffee prosperity, German and English settlers set up import-export trades, while Lebanese, Turks and Polish Jews became powerful local merchants. Clearly these were no simple agrarian folk.

and North Americans. But the largest group of immigrants, apart from the Afro-Caribbean workers, were laborers from southern China, who joined the blacks on the railroad, essentially as slaves, but euphemistically referred to as "indentured workers."

Chinese immigrants

The first Chinese to set foot in Costa Rica were 77 indentured servants, in 1855. Almost 20 years later, despite the existence of a law against the permanent settlement in Costa Rica of African and Asian

BLOOD ON THE TRACKS

After 4,000 West Indians died during the laying of the first 32 km (20 miles) of the Atlantic Railroad, businessman Minor C. Keith simply imported another 10,000 laborers.

lowed the first railroad workers benefited from those who were already established. Through work contracts and credit assistance from other Chinese, they set up commercial ventures along the railroad, in the port cities and in growing rural communities throughout the country. Their small-scale businesses required little capital investment, only a minimal acquaintance with the language, and allowed all members of the growing family network to become involved in tending the business. Chinese family traditions upheld

races, contractors for the Atlantic railroad imported "one thousand healthy, robust Chinese of good customs and addicted to work." These two groups were to become the founding fathers of the Chinese colony of Costa Rica.

Those contracted by the railroad left as quickly as they could escape, to work as cooks and domestic servants. As their fortunes improved, Chinese immigrants set up small eateries, groceries and liquor stores. The steady trickle of Chinese immigrant laborers that fol-

LEFT: the younger generation.
ABOVE: the ubiquitous Costa Rican *pulpería* (neighborhood store) and its proud owner.

the authority of elders and reinforced an already strong generational hierarchy. Well-defined divisions of labor, plus a strong work ethic, ensured that their businesses flourished.

Chinese colonies, headed by businessmen's associations, evolved into strong business groups in the cities and towns of Costa Rica. By the beginning of the 20th century, a number of Chinese immigrants had become wealthy, and were then able to sponsor the immigration of other family members and acquaintances.

Among the first generations of Chinese to settle in Costa Rica, many men lived with local Costa Rican white women, while retaining marriages established in China with childhood brides. The money they sent to China was often used to finance family enterprises back home.

In the last century, the successful Sino-Costa Rican businessman traveled to China to oversee his holdings, raise a family and invest toward retirement in the home of his ancestors. During his absence from Costa Rica, his business was managed by close younger kin.

With the Communist takeover of mainland China in 1949, return to their ancestral homeland became less attractive, and most Sino-Costa Ricans forsook any hopes of a permanent return to China.

Many among them have married Hispanics, and faced opposition from their parents and ostracism by the Chinese community. Nevertheless, they have retained venerable family traditions that express Chinese values of ancestral wisdom and family solidarity.

Many young Sino-Costa Ricans have now joined the ranks of the professionally educated; although they are doctors, lawyers, engineers, business administrators and university professors, many still continue to also oversee the family businesses that allowed their ancestors to achieve economic success in Costa Rica.

More recent events also reinforced this influx from the East. The prospect of the British colony of Hong Kong being transferred to Chinese hands caused a steady flow of Asian immigrants from Hong Kong as long ago as the 1970s. Today, 1 percent of the total population in Costa Rica is Chinese, and there are more than 250 Chinese restaurants in the San José area alone.

Those Chinese born of mixed Costa Rican-Chinese families consider themselves full members of Costa Rican society, identifying heartily with its ways and traditions, while, at the same time, expressing a strong sense of devotion to their immigrant forefathers.

The Italians

The Atlantic railroad had serious difficulties retaining Chinese laborers. In an attempt to find an alternative working force, in 1888 it imported 1,500 "good, humble, thrifty Italians of a superior race". The disagreeable working conditions soon led the Italians to leave the railroad project. Many remained in Costa Rica, and in the 1950s they were joined by an influx of Italian farmers who settled in a government-sponsored colony, San Vito, in the southern Pacific region of Costa Rica.

Today, San Vito still has a distinctive Italian flavor: there is a Dante Alighieri Society; there are a dozen shoe stores in town, as well as *pas-*

ticcerias serving Italian *gelato* and pastries. More recently, entrepreneurial Italians have come to Costa Rica to open restaurants and hotels all over the country, bringing a dash of style and culinary gusto.

The *gringo*

They are unmistakable in San José, their heads sticking out above the throng of people crowding the chaotic city sidewalks. *Gringos*, fairer and usually taller than the locals, easily catch the eye. A pejorative term in much of Latin America, *gringo* is a much milder moniker here, applied not only to US citizens but also

In the 1950s, Quakers from the United States came to Costa Rica looking for peace. They found it in the cloud forest of Monteverde, where they formed a community dedicated to a life of harmony with the land. They created a successful dairy and cheese industry, which today supplies much of Costa Rica's specialty cheese market.

Since the 1960s, Costa Rican laws favoring North American and European retirees have led to the establishment of a large number of comparatively wealthy *gringos* in the Central Valley area. These retirees, recently estimated at more than 35,000, are officially called *pensionados*,

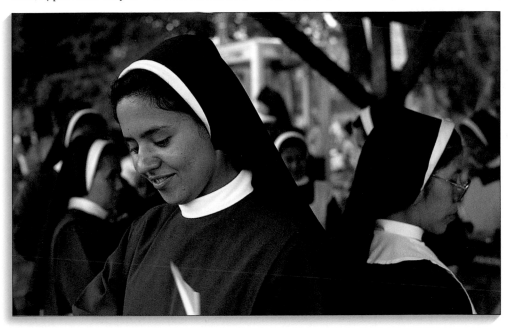

to Canadians and Europeans. They have been coming to Costa Rica for a long time. Early in the 19th century, attracted by the promise of wealth from coffee, French, German and British entrepreneurs, along with teachers, scientists and professionals came to Costa Rica. Many married Costa Rican women, and most became thoroughly assimilated into the aggregate of *Tico* culture. Today, many powerful families in the arts and politics bear British or German surnames.

LEFT: growing old in Costa Rica.
ABOVE: shining sisters of devotion at a town fair in Guanacaste province.

non-nationals living in Costa Rica with a guaranteed monthly income. They come to Costa Rica for the warm climate and for the higher standard of living their dollar affords them.

Effects of tourism

The most dramatic influx of people today is the result of the country's flourishing tourism industry. Environmentally concerned young people come to carry out ecological work. For them the country is a laboratory, a place where the viability of living in harmony with the environment can be demonstrated to the world at large. Their arrival has stimulated major changes in the country's environmental awareness.

A large cadre of biologists, botanists and scientific researchers has had a huge impact on both the academic world in Costa Rica, and on research efforts into conservation.

While Costa Ricans are proud to show off their beautiful land, tourism often has a downside: the small landowner may lose his land for a biological reserve; dairy farmers can't afford to buy fresh pasture because property speculation has driven prices sky high; cattle ranchers without enough water

LIMÓN CARNIVAL

Chinese participation in the social life of the towns they settled is nowhere more in evidence than at the Limón Carnival, when the traditional Chinese dragon snakes its way alongside flamboyantly costumed Caribbean dancers.

Latin American newcomers

More recently, Costa Rica has become a haven for those fleeing violence, wars and economic problems: during the past couple of decades, onerous political conditions and deteriorating economic circumstances in their home countries have brought significant numbers of South Americans to settle in Costa Rica, including educated Chileans, Argentinians, Uruguayans and Colombians. These different groups of people have greatly

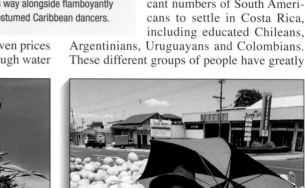

for their livestock in the dry season watch as huge resorts build water-hungry golf courses. Profits often flow abroad to large hotel groups, and promised local benefits often amount to little more than the modest wages of waiters, hotel maids, gardeners and pool attendants.

Sustainable tourism, which benefits the local community, has become the watchword of both international conservation organizations active in Costa Rica and the Ministry of Tourism. A program that awards "green-leaf" status, according to the eco-friendliness of hotels, has been successful, along with the Bandera Azul (Blue Flag) program that promotes clean beaches around the country.

enhanced Costa Rica's cultural sensibilities over the past 20 years or so.

Absorbing poorer, more desperate illegal immigrants, especially from Nicaragua, has caused undeniable difficulties. Drug trafficking has also increased, employing both newcomers and *Ticos*. In general the country has accepted newcomers with a mix of grace and tolerance *(see box on Ticos and Nicas, page 77)*.

Ticos today

A Latin American writer recently observed: "The problem is that the Costa Rican looks too much to the North. He should be looking to the South." But even if he did, the *Tico* would insist that he is different from most Latinos because of what he sees as his "whiteness," (fair skin, light hair and light-colored eyes) or European heritage.

Just go to Guatemala, Panamá or El Salvador, and observe the differences. These countries are only short distances away but the Costa Rican is as different from these other Latin people as, say, the Swiss is to the Italian, or the German to the Dane. Costa Ricans revel in the difference and are unabashedly proud of it.

INVASION OF THE ANTS

Even today, the native tribes refer disparagingly to the white man as *"hormiga"* (ant), a creature that wipes out everything in its path.

from people in other Central and South American countries, yet they notice it in subtle ways. Perhaps it's because Costa Ricans have acquired the curious and skillful art of being poor and not showing it. Cardboard shanty towns that dominate the cityscape of other developing countries are less evident here. People seen on the streets of the towns and cities are, more often than not, well-dressed. Homeless people are not omnipresent as they are in other Latin and Asian countries, and, indeed, in many large US cities.

Grace under pressure

Costa Ricans have a graceful sense of the universal corruption that surrounds them. They shake their heads, lamentably acknowledging it. They know that almost endless problems beyond easy resolution abound. But despite some skeptical complaining they express confidence that their government is the most honest in Latin America.

Travelers to Costa Rica find it difficult to identify just how different Costa Ricans are

LEFT: heady blossoms off to market; melon seller at the 10th Avenue open-air market in San José.
ABOVE: *boyero* ("cowboy") with his Brahman oxen.

Small-town family life

To fly to Costa Rica, leaving behind the numbing babble of Los Angeles or the crowded bustle of western European cities, and to head for a small town here is like leaping backwards to an earlier time. But it is not an earlier time by North American or even European standards; it is somewhere more idealized and more precious.

In the villages and small towns of Costa Rica there is a connectedness, a familial unity. The family is still the main focus here. Young people live at home well into their twenties and thirties, and some even stay home after marrying. The pressure of life in the cities is essentially at odds with this national character. San José can feel unreal at times, as though it is out of place and time, because it represents a basic contradiction to Costa Rican ideals. So many *Ticos* live in and around San José, yet Costa Ricans are much happier living and working in a village or a small town surrounded by a familiar community.

US influence

Because the United States is by far the richest neighbor in the hemisphere, and the most powerful broadcaster of image and ideology, Costa Rica knows a great deal more about the United

States than the United States knows about Costa Rica. *Ticos* know the names of sports figures, actors and actresses, television personalities, musicians and politicians from the USA. And they know the strange collection of fact and fallacy that viewers derive from watching satellite-relayed North American television shows and subtitled Hollywood movies.

Increasingly, a bilingual education is the key to success for young *Ticos*, many of whom will have careers working for branches of foreign companies.

Costa Rica welcomes foreign investors. There are duty-free zones, tax-free incentives to foreigners setting up industry, and other incentives to build tourist facilities. Several government institutions exist to encourage people to come and view the marvels of the country and to invest here.

A fragile world

Costa Rica is fragile, book-ended by politically volatile Nicaragua and Americanized Panamá. Foreign investors buy whatever appears profitable; political and economic refugees come in from other parts of Central America; and drug dealers infiltrate the shores and ports of this relatively violence-free country.

Yet somehow you feel that Costa Rica will endure. Though Costa Ricans may not be perfect, they are essentially a democratic, benevolent and peaceful nation. There is a kind of strength in their fragility. After coming to visit, many people from all over the world are inspired to do whatever they can to ensure the survival and intelligent growth of this vulnerable country and its peaceable people. ❑

HEALTH AND EDUCATION

The standards of health and education in Costa Rica are anything but Third World. In 1920, infant mortality was nearly 26 percent. Today it is less than 10 percent. A century ago the annual mortality rate was 41 per thousand. By 1944 it had dropped to 18 and today it is less than five. According to a a recent survey by *The Economist*, the average Costa Rican man lives to be over 78 years old, on a par with the average US citizen and several European nations.

This is not sheer luck, or just the quality of the air they breathe; without the burden of supporting any armed forces, Costa Rica is able to invest around 10 percent of its GNP on health care. The public system, accessible to all, is showing lots of wear and tear. But the quality of care is high enough, especially in the private sector, that it is said even Beverly Hills residents come here for their plastic surgery and dental work.

Costa Rica is also an exceptionally literate nation, which claims 96 percent literacy across the population aged 10 and over. Again, this is a figure that compares favorably with the US and many European nations.

The country has always been progressive in electing teachers to high political posts and, in 1869, it was the first country in the world to make education both mandatory and free of charge.

Ticos and Nicas

Costa Rica's poor stepsister, Nicaragua, reminds *Ticos* of what their country's fortune could have been, given slightly different geographical and political conditions.

An estimated 500,000 Nicaraguans (although some action groups suggest up to a million) fleeing nearly 70 percent unemployment and harsh living conditions in their home country, work in Costa Rica, many of them illegally. Most form part of the country's growing informal sector, with low wages, under-the-table payments and no access to the country's socialized health service. Many work as maids, gardeners or construction workers, or sell snacks or trinkets in the streets. The sugar cane and coffee industries depend on Nicaraguan workers for their harvests. Perhaps it is not surprising that they are prepared to work for such low wages when you consider that the average per capita income in their own country is just US$900 per year, one of the lowest in the Western hemisphere.

Not all Nicaraguan refugees are poor, however. Middle- and upper-class supporters of the Somoza regime came in the 1980s seeking refuge from Nicaragua's civil war. Many run successful businesses.

When former president Figueres signed an accord in mid-1997 allowing all Nicaraguans in the country a five-month window to apply for work permits, thus obtaining health and other benefits, lines of applicants at the Nicaraguan embassy stretched around the block.

Always a troubling issue in Central America, the immigration debate became more polemic when the US adopted a harsh immigration law in early 1997. Though the law was later toned down and mass deportations avoided, thousands of Nicaraguans chose Costa Rica instead of the US as their destination in the search of a better life.

In March 1998, 29 Nicaraguans drowned when their overladen boat *El Cairo* overturned on the choppy waters of Lake Nicaragua, many of them on their way to Costa Rica to seek employment. Later that year Nicaragua suffered two terrible blows – after drought caused the loss of 40 percent of its crop, Hurricane Mitch hit Central America and approximately 3,000 Nicaraguans perished. The government estimated that 870,000 people were directly affected and it cost the country US$1.5 billion. A huge number of illegal immigrants fled to Costa Rica, which, although hit badly by the hurri-

LEFT: cellist of the National Symphony Orchestra, San José. **RIGHT:** Nicaraguan mother and child.

cane, had not suffered such catastrophic losses.

Immigration officials of the southern Nicaraguan port of San Carlos estimate some 5,000 people enter Costa Rica illegally each month. The two countries share a 320-km (200-mile) border and the Costa Rican authorities have tried to stem the flow by tightening migration controls in the north.

Shanty towns full of Nicaraguan immigrants ring the capital, and many squat, rent or own farms in the Northern Zone. *Ticos* are often prejudiced against their northern neighbors, who are stereotyped as "dirty," "violent" and are unjustly accused of committing crimes. Further, "Nicas" are often blamed for the perceived social decline of the country and for putting a burden on the

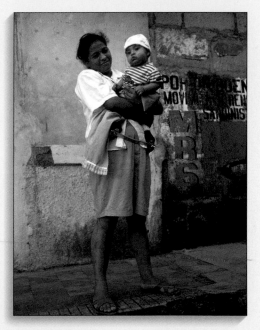

health service, schools and the workplace, when in reality the immigrants are doing the work many *Ticos* refuse to do, and without them coffee, banana and sugar production would be devastated.

Thick-accented and darker-skinned than most Costa Ricans, who like to forget that the province of Guanacaste was once part of Nicaragua, *Nicas* are generally quieter and less educated than *Ticos*. They tend to be hard workers and many people prefer to hire Nicaraguans as domestic help. Nicaraguans also bring with them a love of poetry and music, and a tradition of camaraderie. Often it is desperation that drives so many Nicaraguans to leave their homeland and their loved ones, and they risk everything to come to a land where they are not wanted. ❑

NATIONAL PARKS

With so much of its land under protected status, Costa Rica is the flag bearer for the forces of conservation. But, while many battles have been won, the war goes on

An astonishing 26 percent of Costa Rica is designated as national park, biological reserve, wildlife refuge or some other category of protected area, both private and public. Increasingly, individuals and groups are purchasing tracts of Costa Rican wilderness in order to preserve it. And so, more than a quarter of the country has been set aside in some capacity or other by human beings to protect it from the potential exploitation and ravages of other human beings.

Heroes and villains

The story of the creation of Costa Rica's parks and protected areas is one of drama, ideals, and sacrifice. One of the earliest in an international lineage of protectors was Nils Olaf Wessberg, who, with his wife, Karen Mogensen Fischer, came to Costa Rica from Sweden in 1955 and bought a farm in Nicoya near Montezuma. Fervent naturalists, they built a home of palm leaves, determined to live in harmony with the land.

Yet even in this removed corner of the world they did not escape what many call progress, and they watched, dismayed, as the destruction of virgin forest took place at Cabo Blanco, on the Nicoya peninsula. Nils became an activist, working ardently to raise money to purchase the property and thereby preserve it.

After three years and 1,000 pages of letters, he raised the US$30,000 he needed to buy the 1,200 hectares (3,000 acres) that constitute the Cabo Blanco Strict Nature Reserve. Today, a plaque inside the park is a memorial to Nils, who, while trying to establish another park in the Osa Peninsula, was murdered by those who had vested interests in preventing his work. In 2004, a new reserve near Montezuma was established and named after Karen Mogensen Fischer.

Another individual, Mario Boza, a student of Costa Rican forestry, was able to put his con-

servation ideas to work in the creation of Santa Rosa, the country's first national park. In 1969, the Forestry Law trumpeted the creation of the Santa Rosa National Monument and established the National Parks Department. But with little funding and personnel to enforce it, the new law went unrecognized and the land continued

NATURAL WONDERLAND

There are many astounding statistics concerning Costa Rica's natural abundance. In a space that occupies less than 0.03 percent of the earth's surface are 4 percent of all of the scientifically identified plant and animal species on the planet. In total this numbers somewhere around 500,000 species of flora and fauna including: 50,000 species of insects (some the size of small mammals!); over 1,000 species of orchids; 800 ferns (more than in all North America and Mexico); 208 species of mammals; 850 species of birds; 200 species of reptiles (half of which are snakes), and thousands of species of moths and butterflies.

PRECEDING PAGES: dusk at Braulio Carrillo; heliconias on the jungle floor; iguanas at La Orotina.
LEFT: jaguars. **RIGHT:** the *bejuquillo* vine snake.

to be used as it had been in the past, as grazing pasture for the cattle of nearby ranchers and as the homesteads of squatters who cleared the land by using the slash and burn technique.

Unable to halt the destruction through bureaucratic channels, Boza went to the people through the press. "Santa Rosa in Flames; National Park Being Ruined" read the headlines. The public was outraged and park authorities were duly authorized to move out the squatters and protect the land from the encroachment of livestock and agriculture.

Rodrigo Carazo, president of Costa Rica from 1978 to 1982, described the national parks as

country's population in the most fertile area of the country, the Central Valley – covers the land with concrete and asphalt, and it continues at a frenzied pace. Extensive soil erosion, an effect of the rapid deforestation of the country by the destructive use of land for cattle grazing, causes a phenomenal loss of topsoil.

Threats to the watershed, as well as the nation's extensive hydroelectric system, also result. Uncontrolled dumping of toxic waste from the banana, coffee, and fertilizer industries has contaminated coastal and inland waters. Agricultural chemicals used in pesticides, once employed only on the traditional export crops of

"splendid natural laboratories which we offer to the international scientific community and also to children, young people and adults who should not be denied the joy of direct contact with nature in its pristine state. All of this represents the contribution of the Costa Rican people to peace among men and goodwill among nations."

The economy versus the ecology

As admirable as Costa Rica's conservation initiatives may be, the environmental efforts of this Third World country are counter to its economic development. Parks are, after all, expensive. Urban sprawl – resulting from the concentration of more than 60 percent of the

bananas and sugar, are now being used by vegetable and flower growers; pesticide poisoning has resulted in, among other things, the virtual elimination of large species such as armadillos and crocodiles along the Tempisque River. The crazed rush to feed the demands for exotic plywood by the First World is resulting in the deforestation of the land surrounding the magnificent Tortuguero canals. And so it goes on.

In its attempts to imitate much of North America and the First World, the country experiences the inevitable conflict between consumption and conservation. Trying to balance these forces are armies of international naturalists. Environmentalists and ecologists from all over the world come to Costa Rica to join the side of "the good guys." Today, Costa Rica has environmental experts in abundance, and dozens of international conservation organizations work on behalf of the country's ecological efforts.

Conservation by education

Believing that true conservation can only be accomplished by the will of the people, the national parks system has made a great effort to educate the *Ticos* most affected by the transfer of land into parks. The co-operation of these people is necessary for the parks' survival. For example, the custom of hunting species for whom the

through their work and contributions to the many foundations working in Costa Rica.

Sometimes eco-projects even cross Costa Rica's borders. Current projects include the extension of La Amistad International Park, which spans the border of Panamá, and is considered one of the first Bi-National reserves; and also the proposed Peace Park, known as Sía Paz, a joint effort with Nicaragua along the San Juan River, which forms the border between the two nations. These are just two examples of the potential for national parks to engender co-operative international relations.

parks are a refuge must be changed. Large animals, such as pumas and jaguars, require an extensive amount of free territory in order to survive. Convincing people not to kill them, despite the fact that the cats are a constant threat to livestock, is an enormous and often thankless task.

Eco-tourists and traditional travelers to Costa Rica support the national parks system by coming to visit, by staying at the private reserves, by viewing and understanding some of the workings of the national parks, and

LEFT: the arboreal fruit-eating kinkajou (martilla).
ABOVE: sometimes you have to look very carefully to penetrate the jungle's camouflage.

Future perfect?

Yet is this good news enough? The fact that Costa Rica is thought of as a safe, quiet democratic place is perhaps both the nation's great blessing and problem. Ironically the world will not be sufficiently moved to donate aid, attention and media coverage to such a gentle democratic place.

It is not clear yet as to which side will prevail, the conservationists or the economic development-at-all-costs forces; it is not predictable whether Costa Rica will become a successful environmental model for the nations of the world or just another failed experiment in ecological idealism. ❑

A Tropical Forest Watcher's Guide

Don't be disappointed if, on your first few visits to the tropical rainforest, you fail to see any of the hundreds of bird species and spectacular large cats, monkeys and sloths that are listed as living there. In fact, your first impression of the forest will probably be of a great green wall of vegetation, not the spectacular variety of colorful animals you had hoped to see. However, be assured a great diversity of organisms do inhabit the tropical forest and their very sur-

vival, which may span millennia, depends not least on how successful they are in avoiding the attention of predators, which include humans.

Before setting off into the forest, do your homework. Study specialist guidebooks that describe animals living in the area and familiarize yourself with the characteristics that are used to identify them, such as color, shape and behavior.

Determine the time of day or night when they are most active. A good pair of binoculars is essential; they can also be used backwards as a powerful magnifying glass. Take every opportunity to charter a boat for lake or river trips; they are always worth the investment.

Observe safety tips before proceeding. Remem-

ber that even though it may look like Disneyland, it isn't. Here snakes slither, insects bite and animals may (in very rare cases) become aggressive. Notify someone of your intentions: where you are going, when you plan to arrive, when to expect you back. Take water, insect repellent, flashlight, sunscreen, umbrella or rain poncho and hat.

Look before you touch, step, sit or lean. Scan the trail for slippery rocks, mud, downed trees, ants and snakes. Then move ahead while you search the canopy for animals. Continually shift your gaze. Don't wander off into the woods following a bird without carefully looking where you step. Snakes are rare but potentially lethal. *Antivenin serum is available throughout the country. Try not to panic and try to remember the snake's colors.

A general guideline: forest wildlife-viewing is easiest in the early morning and late afternoon, and most productive along habitat "edges" next to rivers, beaches, open fields, roads and trail heads. Look for shapes, colors and behaviors that stand out and do not appear to "fit" the design of the forest vegetation.

In the dry season deciduous forests lose their leaves, opening the canopy for viewing; and water sources are frequented by thirsty animals.

Seasoned forest-watchers, like legendary animal trackers, are alert to certain small and easily overlooked clues that indicate the presence of animals or birds present in the forest. Things rustling or dropping from the forest canopy (especially on a windless day) and unexplained noises are often a sign that an animal is nearby. Seeds or leaves dropping from above are probably caused by parrots, monkeys or sloths in the canopy. Fruits, nuts, seed husks or leaf fragments in the trail mean a food tree is nearby and perhaps sustaining feeding animals or birds.

Large, dark shapes in tree crevices might be sleeping sloths, anteaters or monkeys. A hanging green tail may indicate an iguana. Logs on river banks could be crocodiles. Rotten tree sections are often home to amphibians, insects, fungi and mosses. Holes in trees might contain precious birds' nests.

When you've developed skills in seeing and identifying some of the plants and animals, think about what they eat and why they live where they do. Soon you will begin to understand the complexity that makes the forest so mesmerising. ❏

LEFT: a small colorful forest dweller.
RIGHT: birdwatchers at Monteverde.

Ecosystems of Costa Rica

For its size, this country contains a remarkable variety of natural ecosystems. A journey of a few miles is often enough to take you from one to another, each with quite different plants and animals. Much of this variety is due to the country's mountains, which create a range of "life zones" at different altitudes and rainfall patterns. Some species of plants and animals live in several zones, but many are confined to just one.

Dry tropical forest

In some parts of Costa Rica – particularly the lowlands of Guanacaste – little rain falls for four or five months of the year. Here, the natural vegetation is dry tropical forest, with most of the trees shedding their leaves soon after the dry season begins. The trees are rarely more than 30 meters (100 ft) high, and there is usually a tangled understory of spiny and thorny shrubs.

Although the trees are leafless during the dry season, few of them are fully dormant, and many burst into flower soon after their leaves have been shed. Among the most conspicuous of these dry-season flowerers is the *guayacan* or *corteza amarilla* tree, which puts on a particularly spectacular display of waxy yellow blooms. Dry tropical forest abounds with reptiles, including rattlesnakes and large lizards called ctenosaurs, which often feed on the fallen *guayacan* flowers and fruit.

Rainforest

Across most of the Costa Rican lowlands, the climate is wet and warm enough for trees to keep growing for much of the year. The result of this non-stop growth is generally called rainforest. Strictly speaking, though, botanists restrict this term for the wettest forests of all. Unlike the trees in tropical dry forests, rainforest trees are evergreen, and their dense crowns form a continuous canopy that casts a deep and almost unbroken shade.

In lowland rainforest, the canopy trees generally reach up to 50 meters (165 ft), and many have buttress roots called *gambas*. Scattered among them are emergents – giant trees that rise above the canopy, and which may reach 60 meters (200 ft) or more. With increasing altitude, the canopy height starts to drop, while rainfall levels usually rise, typically reaching a maximum at about 1,000 meters (3,300 ft). Above this height, rainfall begins to decline again. But on slopes facing the prevailing wind, the forest is often enveloped by cloud. At mid- and higher altitudes, the trees are often laden with such epiphytic plants as bromeliads, orchids and ferns.

Epiphytes use trees as living perches in their quest for light, and they generally do their hosts little harm. However, where high rainfall allows them to grow unchecked, their combined weight sometimes brings branches crashing to the ground.

Costa Rica's rainforests – both on low ground and at high altitude – harbor an immense variety of life. But actually seeing wild animals is not as easy as it sounds. With the exception of monkeys and agoutis, most forest mammals are nocturnal. Some birds feed on or near the forest floor, and a number specialize in following columns of army ants, snapping up small insects that flee the ants' advancing front. However, the full richness of rainforest wildlife is in the canopy overhead, where a complex community of species lives with minimal contact with the ground.

Páramo

On Costa Rica's highest peaks, the forest gives way to a treeless landscape known as *páramo*. Cold and frequently swathed in cloud, *páramo* seems a world away from the warmth and lushness of lower altitudes. This ecosystem is dominated by tough, low-growing shrubs that can withstand strong winds. *Páramo* is also found in the Andes, and Costa Rica's scattered patches of it – for example, in the Talamanca Mountains – are the northernmost in the Americas.

Freshwater wetlands

Costa Rica's topography means that its rivers are generally short and fast-flowing, quickly completing their journey from the interior to the sea. Sudden fluctuations in water level – brought on by tropical downpours – are a common event, and freshwater animals are experts at taking cover when flow levels abruptly increase. On lower ground, where the flow is more sluggish, river wildlife is more varied. Animals of particular note include caimans, which often bask on the banks. One of the world's few bipedal lizards, the basilisk, escapes danger by running across the water on its back legs, thus earning its nickname, the Jesus Christ lizard.

Small forest streams usually flow beneath a continuous overhead canopy, but most rivers are broad enough to allow light to reach the forest floor. The result is a linear "light gap," and a profusion of plant growth of the kind rarely seen inside forests themselves. Some of the most eye-catching species are heliconias, or lobster-claws, which are pollinated by hummingbirds. They often spring up on mudbanks and sandbars, but rarely grow in deep shade.

Costa Rica's largest body of freshwater – manmade Lake Arenal – has a distinctly highland feel, and while it teems with fish, its bird life is unexceptional. By contrast, the shallow lakes and marshes of Palo Verde National Park and Caño Negro are much more productive ecosystems. These seasonal wetlands attract a wide variety of wading birds, particularly when water levels are low, and prey is easier to catch.

Mangrove swamps

Mangroves are the natural vegetation of muddy, low-lying coasts throughout the tropics. In Costa Rica, there are five species of mangrove, and they form extensive forests on both the Caribbean and Pacific shores. None of the five species is closely related to each other, but they have all evolved a collection of adaptations for surviving in seawater and saline silt. Known to botanists as halophytes, these trees have mechanisms for getting rid of excess salt and elaborate roots that anchor them in the shifting mud.

Although they are often inaccessible, smelly and hot, Costa Rican mangrove swamps abound with life. Crabs are a particular specialty, including hordes of fiddler crabs, which pick over the mud for

particles of food, fist-sized land crabs and the mangrove tree crab, which feeds on mangrove leaves and leaps acrobatically from branch to branch. Even mangrove mud makes an important contribution to the marine food chain for the nutrient-rich algae and other small organisms it produces.

Coasts and coral reefs

Apart from mangrove swamps, Costa Rica's coastline consists largely of extensive beaches – often of dark volcanic sand – low-lying rocks and a small number of offshore islands. Although the two coasts are never far apart, their marine life is quite different, and their physical differences also affect other animals. Brown

pelicans, for example, feed on both coasts, but they only breed on the Pacific, where the rocky islands give them the protection that they need. The spectacular frigatebird is also a much more common sight in the Pacific Ocean than in the waters of the Caribbean.

Costa Rica has a number of small coral reefs on its Pacific coast, but only one significant area on the Caribbean, at Cahuita. Reef-building corals need sunlight to grow, and they can only survive in clear water. This limits them to areas well away from the mouths of silt-laden rivers, but it also makes them vulnerable to any increase in silt run-off. Unfortunately, in recent years the Cahuita reef has been affected by deforestation, which has increased silt levels in the surrounding water. ❑

LEFT: the density of the rainforest, seen from above.
RIGHT: malachite butterfly in Braulio Carillo Park.

A PASSION FOR PLANTS

From the beautiful to the bizarre, Costa Rica's many species of flora offer a vibrant introduction to the kaleidoscopic plant wealth of the tropics

For many visitors to Costa Rica, first contact with the country's spectacular plant life comes at the hotel reception desk. As likely as not, the desk will be adorned by a vase of heliconias – strikingly angular red or orange flowers, also known as lobster claws, which grow in the country's forests.

Heliconias are typical of the outsize blooms that flourish in Costa Rica's warm and humid climate. As a rule of thumb, the biggest and most robust flowers – including heliconias – are pollinated by birds or bats, while more delicate flowers are pollinated by insects. This second category includes most of the country's orchids – another group of plants for which Costa Rica is justly famous.

INTRODUCED PLANTS

Costa Rica has a vast number of native plants, including about a thousand different species of trees. To add to this botanical richness, many other species have been introduced from different parts of the tropics, either for food or for ornament. The food plants include bananas, which arrived in the Americas in the early 1500s, coffee, mangoes and sugar cane, and also the African oil palm, first cultivated on a large scale in the 1960s. Many of the showiest garden and roadside plants are from distant parts of the world. Among the most eye-catching are jacarandas, South American trees that produce a mass of purplish-blue flowers.

▷ GIANT LEAVES
Elephant ear takes its name from its enormous leaves, over 1.2m (4ft) long. Originally from southern and southeast Asia, they are common on marshy ground by streams. Also known as giant taro, these plants have edible roots and stems.

◁ LANDING PLATFORM
Popular garden plants throughout Costa Rica, bird-of-paradise flowers are pollinated by birds. The flower has a built-in perch.

◁ NATIONAL FLOWER

Like most orchids, *Guarianthe skinnerii*, the national flower (*Guaria morada* in Spanish) lives high up on trees, and is very difficult to spot from the ground. Visiting an orchid garden is the easiest way to see it.

▷ PRIZED ORNAMENTALS

Named after a 19th-century German naturalist, kohlerias have hanging tubular flowers and live in damp, shady places on the forest floor. The family that they belong to is widespread throughout the tropics, and includes many popular indoor plants, such as African violets and gloxinias.

◁ YELLOW BLOOMS

The Tabebui tree bursts into a mass of bright yellow blossom for brief periods during the dry season. It's a spectacular sight as the trees can reach a height of up to 90 feet (27 meters).

▷ SYMBOLIC FLOWERS

Legend has it that Spanish missionaries named the red passionflower after Christ's crucifixion: the flower's three stigmas, for example, represent the three nails.

THE PLANTS THAT GROW ON PLANTS

Costa Rica's forests are home to an immense variety of epiphytes, or plants that grow on the shoulders of other plants, often far above the ground. Epiphytes manage this remarkable feat by collecting rainwater and by scavenging nutrients from any organic debris that is washed or blown their way.

Of all the country's epiphytes, bromeliads are the most conspicuous. Tank bromeliads, like the one shown above, collect water by funneling it into a central reservoir formed by their leaves. These plants can be over 1 meter (3 ft) across, and their tanks can hold several liters of water. Other epiphytes, including most orchids, have specialized roots that absorb water and nutrients before they have a chance to drain away.

In forests, a different collection of plants – including philodendrons and the Swiss-cheese plant (*Monstera deliciosa*) – start life rooted in the ground, but soon head for the sunlit treetops. In the wild, the cheese plant and its relatives have a bizarre growth pattern. If the plant climbs up a tree that turns out to be too short, it simply drops back to the forest floor and searches for another one.

△ LOBSTER CLAWS

The flowers of heliconias, or lobster claws, are clasped by brilliantly coloured flaps. In some species, the flower head stays upright, but in others it gradually topples over as it grows.

▽ NECTAR STATION

The nectar-rich flowers of ginger lilies have a magnetic effect on butterflies and on nectar-drinking birds. These shoulder-high relatives of edible ginger come from India and southeast Asia and are widely grown in Costa Rica as garden plants.

THE SPORTS SCENE

Activity holidays are booming in Costa Rica. Getting wet – whether
by spilling out of a raft or falling off a board – is usually part of the game

Sport is a much-loved pastime in Cost Rica, and *Ticos* are always happy to have visiting foreigners join them in watching an important game of soccer. In the past decade a fitness craze has swept the country – joggers and cyclists are a common sight puffing up the hills of the Central Valley in the early morning. On weekends, the enormous La Sabana Park, on the west side of San José, is filled with thousands of athletes: soccer teams, basketball players, swimmers, volleyball players, roller-blade teams and baseball enthusiasts. On the Central Valley plateau, private golf and tennis clubs with complete health spas cater for wealthy suburbanites.

The country's burgeoning watersports, however, are the main attractions for the increasing number of visitors who are coming to Costa Rica to surf isolated beaches, to windsurf on magnificent Lake Arenal, and to enjoy some of the best whitewater rafting in the world.

Whitewater rafting

The brightly colored inflatable raft rushes down a chute of cascading white water, then plunges over and through waves that are nearly 2 meters (6 ft) high. Those in the raft gleefully dig their paddles into the frothing water, and then shriek with delight as they maneuver the raft between boulders the size of small cars. After a while, a calm spot on the river is reached, an eddy, and from there the raft passengers pause and look up from the roaring river course to inhale and appreciate the beauty of the Reventazón Gorge. The scenery includes the colossally broad panorama of the canyon, rolling fields of coffee, sugar-cane, wild grasses and radiant flowers blooming unexpectedly in the canopy of trees that lean over the river.

Costa Rica has more accessible whitewater rivers and rapids than any other place in the world. It is, of course, the unique geography of

the country that makes it one of the world's great destinations for whitewater rafting. To have the right kind of rapids, you need a river that descends in a fairly steep gradient. The four mountain chains that wind down the axis of Costa Rica provide the perfect conditions. The Talamanca range and the Cordillera Central

---

PRECEDING PAGES: rafting on the Reventazón River.
LEFT: surf's up at Playa Dominical.
RIGHT: a windsurfer enjoys a breezy, late-afternoon sail on Lake Arenal.

MAKING A SPLASH

Sadly, every year whitewater accidents do happen and even the most experienced rafters, caught in a powerful river eddy, can drown. So choose your trip according to your level of expertise and find an outfitter that sticks to all the safety precautions: life vest, helmets and accompanying safety/rescue kayaks. Before you enter the water in the raft you should have a practice drill to ensure everyone understands the instructions (often shouted over the thundering water!). You should also check your travel insurance policy that you are covered for rafting. River water is unsafe to drink, so if you do tumble in, keep your mouth closed!

have many steep, wide, perennial rivers that are regularly supplied with bounteous rainfall.

The variety of these rivers provides an enormous range of wilderness experiences. Some offer idyllic float trips through luscious landscapes with abundant wildlife, while others contain explosive whitewater and raging rapids that challenge the most experienced rafter.

The Sarapiquí

The Sarapiquí River flows through the lowlands of Heredia, providing stunning scenery and exceptional whitewater. About a two-hour drive from San José, the upper portion of the Sarapiquí contains moderate rapids that are suitable for novice paddlers. On the calm, lower section of the river, the jungle closes in and gives rafters the opportunity to relax for a while and view the monkeys, otters and abundant water fowl of the area.

The Reventazón

The head of the Reventazón River is a 90-minute drive from San José and offers some of Costa Rica's most turbulent whitewater and spectacular scenery. Rafting companies run four sections of the river. The first, which is just below the hydro-electric power plant of

WHITEWATER RAFTING – THE MAJOR PLAYERS

Whitewater rafting, also known as river running offers anyone in moderately good health an exhilarating way to observe the scenery and wildlife of the country. Several professional outfitters provide all of the necessities: life preservers, helmets and rafts.

Guides have been through training in the classroom and on the rivers. Most Costa Rican head guides have been trained at whitewater schools in the USA and many have worked with the world's best.

The first whitewater exploration of Costa Rican rivers was made by Costa Rica Expeditions on the Reventazón River in 1978.

The following year the same company pioneered commercial whitewater rafting in Central America. Ríos Tropicales, founded in 1985, started rafting on the Sarapiquí and Sucio rivers, and local graduates of their kayaking school have represented Costa Rica at the World Championships of Whitewater Racing. Aventuras Naturales is the third major company in this field. Others of varying expertise have also sprung up in San José, Turrialba, and elsewhere.

Many offer day-trip packages from San José, including transportation, breakfast and lunch, at very reasonable rates.

Cachí, is steep and contains continuous rapids of moderate to high difficulty. The second section, from Tucurrique to Angostura, is suited to novice paddlers and provides splendid views of the surrounding volcanoes.

The final two sections of the Reventazón, from Angostura to Siquirres, have some of the most challenging whitewater in the world.

The Pacuare

Many consider Costa Rica's most famous white water river to be the Pacuare. Accessible from the Central Valley via Turrialba, it passes through a deep gorge in dense jungle that con-

been observed and many can be seen from rafts on the Corobicí. Because the river's perennial flow is controlled by a dam on Lake Arenal, it becomes an oasis that attracts birds, monkeys and lizards during the dry season in Guanacaste.

Surfing

During the past few years, Costa Rica's unending beaches have been discovered by surfers from North America, Australia and Europe. They generally concur that the quality of Costa Rica's surf is firmly in the top four – along with California, Hawaii and Australia.

tains rich flora and wildlife. Most groups spend two or more days descending this river from Tres Equis to Siquirres, and camping in riverside sites within view of thundering waterfalls and great flocks of birds.

The Corobicí

This is the gentlest of Costa Rica's rafting rivers and is ideal for rafters who are also birdwatchers. In the adjacent Palo Verde National Park, over 300 species of birds have

LEFT: surfers appreciate the beautifully shaped waves on the Pacific seaboard.
ABOVE: wave jumping on Lake Arenal.

Moreover, they find that the surf here is plentiful and relatively uncrowded, the water temperature is a comfortable 27°C (80°F) throughout the year, and there is still the rare experience of having a wave all to yourself, just offshore a pristine and empty beach.

Costa Rica is blessed with masses of beaches: there are some 200 km (120 miles) of Caribbean coast and 1,000 km (630 miles) of Pacific shore, sculpted with sandy beaches, rocky headlands, offshore reefs and river mouths near coastal jungles.

There is also a great number of open beaches that are exposed to ocean swells coming from many directions. Much of the coastline is removed from civilization, so there may be no facilities, food or emergency services within many miles. A four-wheel drive vehicle is often essential, especially during the rainy season.

Popular surf spots

With hundreds of miles of coastline, there are many undiscovered, nameless surfing beaches. But among the favorites are the following:

Jacó, a Pacific beach town southeast of the Gulf of Nicoya, is less than two hours by car or bus from San José. It is a long, silty beach trapped between two jungle-covered rocky points, with waves that are particularly good for body surfing or boogie boarding. The surf is easily accessible, just beyond the patios of many of the hotels and *cabinas*. For non-surfers, however, the beach is unattractive and the currents and riptides are strong.

Just under 3 km (2 miles) to the south of Jacó is Playa Hermosa. It is possible to hitchhike, rent a bike or take a bus with a surfboard around the point south of Jacó to this beach. South from Jacó to Playa Panamá are many superb unexploited surfing spots. North of Jacó, near Puntarenas, the sandspit at the mouth of the Barranca River produces what is reputed to be one of the world's longest left-breaking waves.

SWELLS AND BREAKS

Wave-making conditions are complex in Costa Rica. On the Pacific coast, swells originating from storms in the north and central Pacific Ocean occur frequently from November through March. South swells from distant storms prevail for the remainder of the year.

Pacific beaches are shaped by sediment carried to the sea by major rivers. The silt migrates up and down the coast on strong onshore currents. Sandbars produce beach breaks with long and fast right and left rides along much of the coast. Sandspits form at the river mouths, and create long, and often clean, point breaks. But because the sand floor is unstable, bars and sandspits change with the season. Tides and winds also strongly influence wave shape.

From December to April, large swells caused by winds and storms originating in the Caribbean arrive at Costa Rica's east-coast beaches. The steep, fast-moving waves break over shallow coral reefs, often in shapes and sizes that rival those of the north shore of Oahu in Hawaii. Smaller west swells from tradewinds originating in the West Indies prevail from June through August. The only time when there is generally little or no surf on the east coast is September through November.

To check on conditions visit www.surfingcr.com

Far to the north, the beaches of Guanacaste province have some of the best surf anywhere, particularly during the dry season when steady offshore winds help to create the waves. The break near Roca de la Bruja (*see page 194*) at Playa Naranjo, in the Santa Rosa National Park, is one of the most spectacular waves; the number of surfers is officially limited. Surfers need to book ahead with one of the many local surf shops and travel by boats to this surfing spot.

The Nicoya Peninsula to the south of Guanacaste is scalloped with beaches, notably Playa Avellanas and Playa Negra; many of them have rideable waves. Some of the best surfing in the country is found in remote Pavones on the Golfo Dulce coast.

Near Limón, 2½ hours east of San José, Playa Bonita is a good, popular surfing beach. About 1 hour south of Limón, Puerto Viejo, a tranquil Caribbean village, is the site of the sometimes awesome Salsa Brava, a surf break that has acquired an international reputation; from December through March, consistent, large north swells hit the coral reef with tremendous force.

Windsurfing

Since Costa Rica held its first windsurfing contest on Lake Arenal more than 15 years ago, the country has been recognized as an outstanding destination for international windsurfers. With strong tradewinds whipping the picturesque lake into a sea of whitewater and waves, it compares favorably with the world's best windsurfing locations, such as the Columbia River Gorge in Oregon and Maui in the Hawaiian Islands (with the only caveat that the waves are sometimes rather choppy).

Almost every other day between January and April, consistent winds of around 20 knots whip the waves to a metre-high swell along the length of Arenal, creating excellent short-board sailing conditions. For the rest of the season, lighter winds predominate and are ideal for longboard sailing. Lake Arenal is not a suitable place for beginners. Sideshore winds are consistent and blow across the full width of the lake. During high winds, steep swells provide the right conditions to practice acrobatic speed runs, jumps, and loops. The water is a comfortable 18–21°C

(64–70°F) year-round. Hotel Tilawa and River Rock Lodge are good places to hire equipment.

If you are looking for the "funnel effect," try windswept Bahía Salinas, near La Cruz, in the far north west of the country.

Golf

Golf is growing in popularity in Costa Rica. The Hotel Cariari and Country Club, northwest of San José, was the country's first championship course. A less pricey option is the Valle del Sol public golf course in Santa Ana, a western suburb of San José. Since the 1990s, famous golf architects have been designing new courses in

Costa Rica. There are excellent courses on the Nicoya Peninsula, including the par-72 Garra de León, designed by Robert Trent Jones Jr in the Paradisus Meliá Playa Conchal Hotel, and the par-72 courses at Hacienda Pinilla, designed by Mike Young. The newest course opened in 2004 at the new Four Seasons Papagayo Resort at the north end of the peninsula. There is also a Ted Robinson-designed course at the Marriott Los Sueños Hotel in the Central Pacific zone.

There are fairly good nine-hole courses at Tango Mar, which overlooks the Gulf of Nicoya; Costa Rica Country Club in Escazú; the Los Reyes Country Club, La Guácima; and the El Castillo Country Club, above Heredia. ❑

LEFT: divers explore Isla del Caño's beautiful coral reef.
RIGHT: bougainvillea frames the fairways at Cariari Country Club golf course.

BIG FINS AND FRESH FISH

Costa Rica is a paradise for both fresh and saltwater fishing. It's quiet, too:
you'll run into other fishing folk only if you really want to

The king of game fish swims calmly toward Costa Rica's Caribbean coast. At around 70 kilos (150 lbs), he fears no predators, except sharks, as he cruises toward the mouth of the Colorado River.

Where the tarpon has come from is a mystery. He could have been off the coasts of Flor-ida, South America or West Africa. Or he might have been in local waters the entire time.

But now he is with an ocean school of 100 fish of the same size. Suddenly they spot a school of titi, a small sardine-like fish, and chase them to the surface. The tarpon cause an acre of the Caribbean to explode as they churn

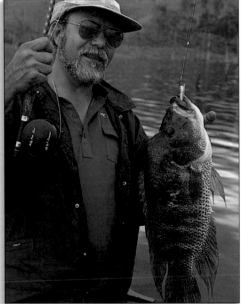

RULES OF ENGAGEMENT

In tarpon fishing, the rules of angling must be suspended or reversed. Otherwise there's no chance of success. The first trick that goes against all that you've ever learned is to retrieve the lure with the rod tip low – at water level or, better yet, in the water. That way, when it's time to set the hook, the rod tip can be brought up and backwards in a long arc. The maneuver must be repeated rapidly at least three times with a force that would tear the hook out of the mouth of almost any other fish.

Tarpon sometimes strike like a rocket, hurtling 5 meters (16 ft) straight up as they hit the plug. At other times it is hard to tell whether or not one of these giant fish is even on your hook. If you react fast enough, and if you're lucky, the tarpon will be hooked before it makes its first jump. If you're not so lucky, you'll see your lure thrown into the air as the great silver fish seems to explode out of the water and reach for the clouds. A tarpon's jump is like no other in fishing. They reach incredibly high; twist right, twist left, flip over, fall back on the line and do everything possible to get free.

Usually the tarpon succeeds and you lose. The success rate of experts is to land about one out of every 10 hooked. though try telling that to your friends when you go back after a day's tarpon fishing empty-handed.

the water and devour the titi. If you are lucky enough to witness this scene, it's simply a matter of casting into the chaos to get into contact with what many consider the most exciting aquatic quarry on earth.

Tarpon enter the river mouths all along the Caribbean coast of Costa Rica, from the Colorado River in the north to the Sixaola River, which forms the border with Panamá. In most rivers, they swim a few hundred meters upstream in search of food and then return to the sea.

Only in the Río Colorado do they keep going upriver, following the titi, in an incredible journey of more than 200 km (124 miles) to Lake Nicaragua, close to the Pacific Ocean.

Freshwater "lakes"

As the tarpon begin their long swim, they pass a series of thin fingers of water stretching northward almost to the border with Nicaragua. These freshwater "lakes" are full of a variety of exotic fish that make great sport on light tackle. One of the most fascinating is the alligator gar, known in Costa Rica as *gaspar*. Looking like a throwback to prehistoric times, this fish has a long, narrow snout as full of sharp teeth as an alligator's. Its coffee-colored body is covered with tough skin and large scales. Its tail is broad and powerful. The meat of the *gaspar* is firm and sweet, not unlike that of shrimps. But the eggs should never be eaten as they are highly toxic to humans.

The tarpon is not alone in his upriver swims. Snook also make the long journey following the titi. And following them all are bull sharks.

The sharks, like the tarpon, continue all the way to Lake Nicaragua. Their presence has led many people to believe that there are "freshwater sharks" in the lake. Actually, they are just visitors from the faraway Caribbean.

Snook are the mainstay of sport fishing in Costa Rica. Large snook are plentiful along all parts of the Caribbean and Pacific coasts, as well as in rivers throughout the country.

All along the Río San Juan there are lesser rivers flowing into it from Costa Rica. At the confluence of the San Juan with the Colorado,

Sarapiquí, San Carlos, Infernito, Pocosol, Medio Queso and Frío rivers there is some excellent angling for tarpon and snook. None of these rivers is heavily fished and all require a bit of enterprise to reach. But those who make the effort are usually well rewarded.

The Río Frío

An exception to this rule of relative inaccessibility is the Río Frío, which passes right through "downtown" Los Chiles – an approximate three-hour drive, on paved roads, from San José.

The Río Frío is full of tarpon, snook, white drum, gar and other exotic species. Some

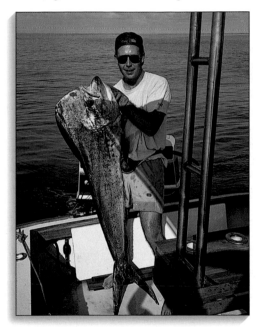

ROLLING FOR AIR

Tarpon are one of the few fish that are capable of taking in air directly through the mouth rather than by filtering water through their gills. This ability is necessary because these big active fish need more oxygen than they can get from the waters that they sometimes inhabit.

This method of direct breathing accounts for the phenomenon known as "rolling," when they come to the surface and flop on their side while gulping air. This unusual adaptation also makes it possible for tarpon to swim freely between saltwater and freshwater and even in oxygen-depleted water.

LEFT: gone fishing; searching for the catch of the day.
RIGHT: a proud fisherman with his freshly caught *mahi-mahi* (dolphin fish), off the Nicoya coast.

people fish right from the municipal landing in Los Chiles; others with boats launch them there and venture north or south. For those who don't have a boat, it is possible to rent a *panga* (barge), driven by a knowledgeable local person who also acts as a guide. These *pangas* can be found at the municipal landing.

Some tarpon, as they swim up the Río San Juan, apparently take diversions far into the side rivers. This is the case with the Río Frío. Thirty minutes by boat south of Los Chiles is the convergence of the Río Frío and the Río Sabogal. Here tarpon up to 45 kg (100 lbs) seem to be present at all times.

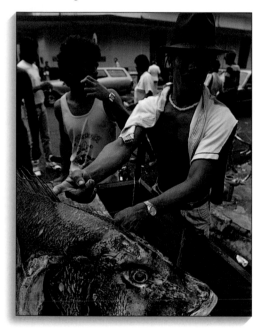

Every morning and every evening the giant fish, too big to be in a narrow river, leap high into the air, re-entering the water with a thundering splash. It is a sight every fishing enthusiast would love to see. It can also be one of the most frustrating experiences imaginable, because there are days when these fish just won't take a lure. However, just the sight is well worth the trip – and there's always a good chance of hooking into one of them.

More river fish

The Río Frío, as well as most of the other rivers of Costa Rica, is full of a fish often overlooked by anglers. The *machacha,* a silvery speedster,

is an unusual fish in that it is primarily a vegetarian. *Machacha* can often be found under the overhang of *chilemate* trees waiting for ripe fruit to fall into the water. Costa Ricans fish for them using pieces of banana or tomato, but *machacha* will also take small lures or flies running, changing directions, diving and leaping into the air. They can grow up to 9 kg (20 lbs) and 1–2 kg (2–5 pounders) are common and offer great sport. Their flesh is bony but tasty.

Up a few of the rivers that feed into the San Juan, particularly the Sarapiquí, you can find the *bobo*, a difficult but rewarding quarry. These fish, which weigh up to 14 kg (30 lbs), feed in shallow, fast-moving water. They are relatives of the saltwater mullet and are pure vegetarians. But they can be taken on small spinners and they offer great sport as they fight hard through the rapids.

In these Atlantic-slope rivers you can also find other exotic species including the *mojarra*, a strong, sharp-toothed, brightly colored pan fish resembling a perch on steroids, and related to the sun fish.

Sea angling

For most people, fishing off the Pacific coast of Costa Rica means angling for sailfish, marlin and tuna. All along the Pacific coast there are sport fishing operations springing up and all are finding success.

Operators in the Gulf of Papagayo were the first, and the area was often shown to have the most productive sailfishing in the world. Sails here are not the scrawny Atlantic variety. They are hefty, healthy Pacific sailfish averaging over 45 kg (100 lbs). Fought on a 7-kg (15-lb) line or less, they offer fantastic sport and a spectacular show full of graceful jumps. Laws require that all sails (except record catches) are released and this is generally respected by fishermen.

In recent years, marlin have been discovered along most of the Pacific coast. Offshore, dolphin, tuna, and rainbow runner are plentiful. Offshore reefs also offer great fishing for snapper, including the prized *cubbera*.

Often overlooked are the fishing possibilities straight from the Pacific beaches. Every beach on the Pacific coast offers the chance to take various types of jack and drum, as well as trophy-sized snook from the surf. Mouths of rivers and streams often attract congregations of snook. Casting from rocks often locates snapper and rooster fish.

Roosters abound on Costa Rica's Pacific coast. The colorful, wide-bodied and powerful fish with the long, spiky dorsal fin that gives it its name, is particularly plentiful in the water surrounding the rocks in Puntarenas or the nearby Pacific port of Caldera. Once hooked, the rooster fish raises its "comb" and speeds away across the surface, offering a unique show and fight.

LICENSED TO FISH

You can buy a fishing license from Deportes Keko, Ca 20 and Av 4–6 in San José (tel: 223 4142, closed noon-2 pm).

of a rhinoceros and if it gets there it will almost certainly cut the line on underbrush.

The *guapote* is a spectacular fish. A breeding male has large bulbous protrusions above the eyes that "light up", displaying many colors on its flank. *Guapote* in Lake Arenal, the main place where they are fished, weigh up to 9 kg (20 lbs) or more, although a 7-kg (15-lb) fish is about as much as most can handle. The *guapote pinto*, or painted guapote, can be found in rivers that flow into the San Juan. ❏

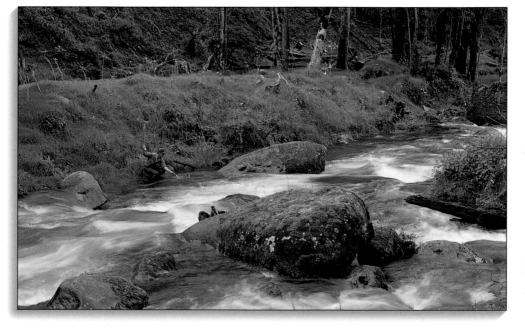

The *guapote*

The star of Costa Rica's few lakes is the *guapote*. Some people call this fish the "rainbow bass," although taxonomically it has nothing to do with bass. The main similarity to bass is in the way it is fished: casting or flipping plugs or spinner baits.

Once hooked, the resemblance is soon forgotten. The *guapote* is to a bass what a diesel is to a model train; it is not a light tackle fish. Once hooked, it heads for cover with the force

TROUT AND MACHÍN

Wild trout have never done well in Costa Rica (although farmed trout do very well). Despite numerous attempts to stock them in high mountain streams, they have never really thrived. Trout fishing is possible in the breathtaking mountains between San José and San Isidro del General, such as the Río Savegre in the San Gerardo de Dota valley area, and, even if the fish are somewhat small, the scenery alone makes a day spent here worthwhile.

If you cannot find any trout then a good substitute is the *machín*, a fish which is found in rivers where trout would be expected. It puts up a vigorous fight, very similar to that of a trout.

LEFT: unfamiliar faces in the fish market.
ABOVE: fishing for trout and *machín* in the breathtaking mountains north of San Isidro del General.

TICO COOKING

When you can try Painted Rooster and Married Man on the menu in Costa Rica's

sodas, why spend time at fast-food or international restaurants?

While it is possible in Costa Rica to order anything from sushi to *huevos rancheros* (Mexican-style eggs), part of the joy of traveling is sampling local cuisine. The Ticos' basic diet is simple, low in fat and rich in protein and carbohydrate. Fruit, fresh vegetables, rice and beans, beef and abundant salads

these contain cornflour, salt, garlic, black pepper, onion, cilantro, paprika and a small amount of hot chili. "English sauce," the native version of Worcestershire sauce, is also used, albeit sparingly, by most cooks. Jalapeño peppers, from the mountain towns of Zarcero and Cervantes, are very good and not as hot as the Mexican vari-

are the trademarks of Costa Rican cooking. *Picadillos* are found in every Tico home: diced potatoes, *chayotes* (water squash or vegetable pears) or string beans are mixed with finely chopped meat, tomatoes, onions, cilantro (fresh coriander), bell peppers and whatever the cook feels may add flavor to the pot. Leftover *picadillos*, fried with rice, are served for breakfast, usually with hot *tortillas* (a kind of pancake), and are called *amanecido*.

Costa Ricans season their food with a mixture of dry spices called *condimentos mixtos*, which is readily available at the markets. There are many different brands of liquid sauces as well, the most famous being *Salsa Lizano*. Most often

eties. Most Costa Ricans do not like very spicy food, although tabasco and chili sauce are always on the table in inexpensive restaurants.

Gallo pinto and casado

The classic Costa Rican dish of *gallo pinto* (literally, painted rooster) is rice and black or red beans mixed with seasonings including onion, cilantro, garlic and finely chopped bell pepper. While predominantly a breakfast dish in the city, rural Costa Ricans eat *gallo pinto* three times daily, accompanied by homemade corn *tortillas*. For breakfast they order it with scrambled or fried eggs and sour cream, or *natilla*.

For lunch, businesspeople, professionals,

students and farmers alike usually have a *casado* (meaning husband)– a hearty combination including rice, beans, cabbage salad, fried plantains and chicken, fish or beef. An example of Tico macho humor, the name *casado* derives from the ordinary daily fare a man supposedly receives after he is married.

More Tico favorites

Another typical dish is the hearty *olla de carne* (literally, meat stew), which includes a small amount of beef and many vegetables common to the region: often *ñampi* and *camote* (both relatives of the sweet potato), *chayote* (water squash), carrots and potatoes. It is usually served with white rice – something Ticos feel no meal is complete without. This dish can be traced back to Cervantes' novel *Don Quixote*.

The *olla podrida* is the great-grandparent of the soup the people in Costa Rica love the most. What gives the distinct flavor to the Costa Rican version is the mixture of vegetables cooked in it: yucca, green plantain, sweet potato, *tannia*, *tacacos*, taro, pumpkin, carrot, *cho-cho*, onion, cabbage and whatever else comes to hand.

Another interesting soup that is available at neighborhood restaurants throught the country is *sopa negra,* made with black beans, onions, cilantro and hard-boiled eggs.

For lunch or dinner, *arroz con pollo* (rice with chicken) or *arroz con mariscos* (rice with seafood) are filling, inexpensive meals served in *sodas* and hotel restaurants.

Other local favorites include *lengua* (cow's tongue), and *mondongo* (cow's stomach lining). While tongue is tender and often deliciously prepared, *mondongo* has a strong taste and odd texture (think tripe), and is not appreciated by most foreigners.

The ubiquitous accompaniment to most meals is plantains – a relative of the banana. It can be sweet (maduro) or green, but it must be cooked before eating and is usually cut into strips and fried in oil or lard (called *manteca*).

Bocas and *bebidas*

Some bars still serve *bocas* ("mouthfuls") with drinks in the same tradition as Spanish *tapas*. Traditionally they were complimentary but these days are increasingly sold separately.

Favorite *bocas* include *ceviche* (raw fish marinated in lemon juice), *carne en salsa* (meat stewed in a tomato sauce), fried cassava, and fried chicken. Beer, rum and *guaro* (a sugarcane alcoholic drink) are favorite local tipples.

Special occasions

On weekends, Costa Ricans love to eat two versions of *chicharrones* – either deep-fried pig skin (including the layer of fat just below the skin) or tender chunks of lean pork that has been simmered slowly. *Chicharrones* are served with *tortillas* and wedges of lemon.

PRECEDING PAGES: an astonishing tropical harvest.
ABOVE LEFT AND RIGHT: the joy of eating in Costa Rica.
RIGHT: succulent *gambas* (shrimps).

COSTA RICAN NOUVELLE CUISINE

The concept of Costa Rican nouvelle cuisine may sound like a contradiction in terms, but increasing exportation of food has stirred new interest in the country's vegetables and fruits. New recipes and traditional ones alike have been imaginatively rewritten.

Pejibaye soup, a delicate orange creamy broth, features at banquets. The common, but never ordinary, mashed black beans *(frijoles)*, well-seasoned with onions, sweet peppers and cilantro, are now served at formal dinners as *hors d'oeuvres*. Posh restaurants offer native cooking nights, starring such delicacies as plantain soufflé and pork-filled cassava pastries.

At Christmas, everyone eats *tamales*, which are made with *masa*, a corn dough, stuffed with different fillings, then wrapped in banana leaves and steamed. The dish is of Aztec origin and is eaten throughout Central America. It is very rarely the same in any two countries. In Costa Rica, *tamales* are traditionally filled with tender bits of pork, rice, carrots, olives, and sometimes dried plums.

Easter fare

Since colonial times, the Easter meal has been an important and traditional celebration. The Catholic Church's prohibition on eating red

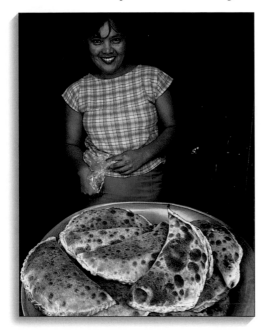

meat during Lent explains why fish, pastries and sweets are popular for the Easter celebration. Since the 19th century, *bacalao con papas* (salt cod and potatoes) has been traditionally prepared for Easter. Huge quantities of salt cod are imported from Europe especially for this occasion.

Just before Easter week, particularly in and around the Cartago area, a type of fruit similar to the pumpkin, but oval and quite large, is sold in the streets. These are *chiverres*, and a sweet preserve made with them, called *cabellito de angel* (angel's hair), is eaten during Easter throughout the Central Valley.

Costa Rican *ceviche* is an Easter speciality,

but is available all year round at any neighborhood *cevichería*. It is prepared by marinating small cubes of fresh white fish or shellfish in a sauce made with lime juice, olive oil, fresh cilantro, onions and bell peppers, for at least 12 hours. Most Costa Rican cooks believe in keeping the lime juice to a minimum and using cilantro freely to perfume the fish. It is similar to the Peruvian dish of the same name, and both show the influence of the Aztecs. *Patacones* – slices of green plantain mashed, then crisply fried – often accompany *ceviche*.

Fresh *palmito* (palm hearts) are also traditionally eaten during Lent, but can be bought any time pickled in vinegar. *Palmitos* and rice is an elegant, festive dish served with grated cheese on top. *Flor de itabo* is the flower of a plant often used in the fences of the coffee farms. The plants have a very white bunch of lily-like flowers, which are also eaten for Easter, stewed in butter with eggs and tomato.

Regional cooking

Costa Rica may only be a small country, but it still maintains several clearly differentiated regional cuisines.

The foods of Limón are exotically tropical and flavorsome. The area offers a wide diversity of dishes influenced by African and West Indian cooking. The names of the ingredients *(haki, yokotaw, bami, calaloo)* have the beat of Calypso and reggae, as do the names of the dishes themselves *(tie-a-leave, dokunu, johnny cake)*. You will also find strong traces of Chinese cuisine, as there are many Chinese living in the area.

The trademark of the cooking of Limón is coconut. Coconut oil and milk are used generously in most recipes, including the traditional rice and beans. For this popular dish, rice is cooked in a pot filled with red beans, coconut milk and aromatic herbs. It is the regional variation of the traditional *gallo pinto*, but in Limón it is usually served on Sundays and on festive occasions. Another local dish is *rondon*, a slow-cooked spicy fish and root-vegetable stew, but it is getting hard to find amongst the fast-food pizza and fried chicken.

From their African background the *Limonenses* have kept the original names of many ingredients; the use of tubers, such as the yam; and maintain the using of green leaves in soups and stews. Their African heritage also shows in their use of herbal teas made with an infinite variety of plants. From their ancestors' hard lives in the sugar plantations of the West Indies, the *Limonenses* have inherited many products that were included in the daily rations of the slaves: breadfruit, salt cod, mangoes, cassava, plantains and a great variety of tropical fruits. And from the demands and preferences of their British masters, they have retained several recipes for cakes, pastries and breads.

In Guanacaste, pre-Columbian traditions in cooking are very much alive. A larger variety of corn dishes are cooked there than in the rest of the country, including delicious pastries. *Tam-*

fast, eaten with hot *tortillas guanacastecas*, which are larger than the ones eaten in the rest of the country. African slave women were brought to the region during colonial times to work in the kitchens of the *haciendas*. They also left their mark on many exotic recipes still cooked in that province. *Ajiaco* and *bajo*, stews made with a mixture of meats and vegetables, maintain their African origins.

On the Pacific coast, Puntarenas presents recipes using ingredients from the sea, including *guiso de cambute* (conch stew) and dishes featuring different combinations of fresh shrimp, lobster and squid. ❑

ales, *chorreadas*, *tanelas* and many other regional delicacies can still be found throughout Guanacaste. Some beach hotels there are starting to include them on their menus.

Since cattle farming is one of Guanacaste's main resources, milk products are often very good. *Bagaces* (a hard, salted cheese, used grated and added to other recipes) has been, since the 19th century, an important part of the salary of the *peones* (farmhands). *Cuajadas* (fresh cheese balls) are usually served at break-

---

LEFT: *empanadas* (meat or vegetable patties) are a typical country fair food.
ABOVE: *gallo pinto*, the national dish.

THE CHOROTEGA LEGACY

Long before the white man arrived, the indigenous Chorotega tribe prepared a very thin unleavened cornmeal pancake called the *tortilla*. It is the main ingredient of Costa Rican *gallitos*, an hors d'oeuvre made by wrapping *tortillas* around mashed black beans, spicy meat, vegetable stew, pork chunks, or whatever else takes the chef's fancy. The best, authentic *tortillas* can be found at Coope-Tortillas in Santa Cruz, cooked over a wood-fire stove. The Chorotega also prepared *tamales*, rectangular pieces of corn dough stuffed with deer or turkey meat and a sauce made from tomatoes, pumpkin seeds and sweet peppers. The sauce, called *pipian*, is still prepared today in a very similar way.

FRUITS OF COSTA RICA

Whether piled high in the market, served up on a plate or whipped into a milkshake,
Costa Rica's rainbow of fruits is a delightful assault on all the senses

F ernández de Oviedo, a Spanish writer who came to Costa Rica in the l6th century, was probably the first European to chronicle the country's astounding variety of tropical fruits. Enthusiastic at every new discovery, he pronounced the pineapple the "best-looking, most wonderful lady in the vegetable world."

De Oviedo probably didn't get to taste all of Costa Rica's different fruits. There are simply too many, and they are available for every possible taste preference throughout the year. Get up early in the morning in San José and visit the Mercado Borbón, or the produce market off 10th Avenue, or the dozens of fruit stalls near the Coca Cola bus station. Or go to the open-air produce and fruit markets on Saturday morning, held in almost every town on the Central Plateau, to see and taste the season's harvest. Along the highways and main roads will be vendors of all kinds of fruit and fruit drinks. In this chapter, we take a look at Costa Rica's A–Z of fruits – from *anona* to *zapote*.

Anona

A strange-looking heart-shaped fruit, also called "the bullock's heart," the *anona* changes from green to a dark reddish-brown as it ripens. The sweet pulp is milk white and contains several large black seeds. After cutting it in half, eat it with a spoon, using the skin as a bowl. The *anona* is related to the custard-apple *(anona chirimoya)* found in the northern part of the country. It has a delicate sweetness and a delightful fragrance like rose-water. Mark Twain described it as "deliciousness itself".

Breadfruit

Breadfruit, like bananas, are grown in the Atlantic region of Costa Rica. This fruit of Polynesian origin was introduced to the West Indies by Captain Bligh, and the Jamaicans planted it in Limón. An attractive, ornamental tree with large leaves, the breadfruit is an ingredient in many savory Caribbean dishes.

Caimitos and other stars

The *caimito* or Costa Rican star apple looks just like a star when cut, similar in taste to the mangosteen (an exotic fruit found in Malaysia and Thailand). This glossy fruit varies in shade from purple to light green. The sweet flesh is usually eaten fresh, but in Limón you can still find it made into a mixture called "matrimony," prepared by scooping out the pulp and adding it to a glass of sour orange juice.

Carambolas, which also look like beautiful stars when cut in thin slices crosswise, are used as garnishes for desserts and for making juice. This shiny, five-sided pinkish-yellow fruit is about 5–8 cm (2–3 in) long.

Cashew fruit

An exotic cousin of the mango, the cashew fruit is best known for the kidney-shaped nut attached to its lower end. The fleshy portion, or apple, varying in color from brilliant yellow to flame-scarlet, is eaten fresh here. Its superb color and penetrating, almost pungent, aroma make this one of the most delectable of all tropical fruits. The flesh is soft, very juicy and zesty. It is also used to make a jam, a wine and a refreshing beverage similar to lemonade, which retains the special aroma and flavor of the unique fruit. In the late 1970s, the government decided to plant many areas with cashews, to be exported abroad. The venture was a failure, but the trees are still there.

There was a wonderful side effect, too: parakeets and parrots adore the fruit, and many species that were almost extinct are now increasing their numbers while dining on abundant cashew apples. Beware, if the seeds are not roasted before eating, they are poisonous.

beverages. Foreigners find the flavor somewhat suggestive of a combination of pineapple and mango, but *Ticos* consider that to be heresy.

Guava

A bestselling book by the acclaimed Colombian writer Gabriel García Marquez has the provocative title *The Fragrance of Guava*. You will better understand how the title elicits the Latin American experience if you visit a home when guava jelly is being cooked. The entire house fills with the aroma of this wonderful fruit. But cooking is not obligatory; you can simply eat the guava raw.

Granadilla

The sweet *granadilla* (passion fruit) is a favorite all over Central America. This fruit is oval and orange to orange-brown. Within the hard, crisp skin, a bundle of seeds is surrounded by an almost liquid, translucent and wonderfully tasty pulp. Use a spoon to eat it.

Guanábana

Related to the *anona*, the *guanábana* is unrivaled for its use in sherbets and refreshing

LEFT: cashew apples; the gray part is the edible nut.
ABOVE: papaya near Turrialba. Squeeze a dash of lemon or lime juice on the flesh to give it a zing.

Another fruit, called in English "Costa Rican guava" *(cas)*, is yellow in color, round, and has soft white flesh. It is acidic, but highly valued for jelly-making and for drinks. If you see it on a menu, under *"naturales"*, try a freshly squeezed *jugo de cas* (*cas* juice).

Loquat

The loquat *(níspero)* is a small, oval-shaped fruit with a large stone, pale-yellow to orange in color. It is also called the Japanese medlar. The flesh, firm and meaty in some varieties, melting in others, is juicy and of a sprightly acid flavor. Although commonly eaten fresh, it can also be used in cooking.

Mango

Alajuela's Central Park is full of mango trees with their tempting fragrance, and that is why the town, second in importance only to San José, is called Mango City. Alajuela's mangoes are sweet, firm and delicate. The ripe mangos are sweeter and spicier, but smaller and softer than the unripe *mangas*. The aroma is spicy and alluring. Few other fruits have a historical background as developed as the mango, and few others are so inextricably connected with religious beliefs. Buddha himself is said to have been presented with a mango grove, so that he might find rest beneath its graceful shade.

fresh, as is its yellow-version cousin. Some refer to the yellow variety as the hogplum because hogs are very fond of them and fatten on the fruit that falls to the ground from wild trees in the forest.

The coco-plum *(icaco)*, on the other hand, is never eaten fresh, but its white flesh is made into a sweet preserve, called *miel de icaco*. Another cousin, the *ambarella (yuplón)*, was brought to Jamaica by Captain Bligh of *Bounty* fame. It came to Costa Rica in the hands of English-speaking Jamaican immigrants to the Port of Limón. It is eaten uncooked, with a little salt, or made into a preserve.

Besides eating them as dessert fruits, Costa Ricans make mangoes into chutney – that spicy sauce well-known to those who enjoy Indian food – as well as preserves, sauces and pies.

Mombín

The Spaniards said the *mombín* (or *jocote*) was a type of plum when they first saw it, but it really has nothing in common with the plum. This fruit is juicy and spicy, unlike any other. The *tronador* is the best variety. Street vendors sell brown paper bags full of *mombínes* from August through October, the color varying from dark green to bright red, depending on ripeness. The *mombín* is usually eaten

Nanzi

You'll recognize a nanzi *(nance)* by its fragrance. This small, round yellow fruit has been popular among Costa Ricans since pre-Columbian times, but foreigners tend to find its smell too strong. It is used for preserves, wines and jellies. *Nances en guaro* (nanzis in liqueur) are very good. Left to ferment in liqueur for nine months, they take on an amber-brown color. Nanzi sherbets are also very popular.

Papaya

Papaya (or paw-paw) grows almost everywhere in the country, and most tourists are particularly enamored of a drink called *papaya en leche*, a sort of papaya milkshake. There are two varieties: the huge local papaya and the smaller, sweeter Hawaiian version. Papaya is also excellent as a meat tenderizer.

Pejibaye

More a vegetable than a fruit, this was a treasured food of the aboriginal peoples. You will surely see it on the fruit stands, with its glossy orange skin and black stripes, resembling a large acorn. Cooked and peeled, its yellow pulp tastes very good when a little mayonnaise is added to it to soften its rather dry texture. It cannot be eaten fresh. *Pejibaye* soup is one of the most exceptional dishes of Costa Rican cuisine.

Rambutan

The most exotic sight in a fruit market in Costa Rica has to be the rambutan *(mamon chino)*. The bunches of red and orange fruits, sometimes called "hairy lychees", look like gooseberries covered in fleshy spines. To eat them, simply cut the leathery rind with a sharp knife and pull it back from the pulp.

Rose-apple and mountain-apple

The fragrance of the guava is only rivaled by that of the rose-apple *(manzana rosa)*, a beautiful round fruit, whitish green to apricot-yellow in color, and perfumed with the scent of the rose. The flesh is crisp, juicy and sweet. As a preserve or crystallized, it is delicious. If you eat it fresh, don't overdo it since the seeds are poisonous when eaten in large quantities.

A relative of the rose-apple, the *ohia* or water-apple *(manzana de agua)* is a beautiful oval fruit, white to crimson in color. Its flesh is apple-like: crisp, white, and juicy but not very flavourful. *Ohia* jam is exquisite.

Sapodilla

One of the best fruits of tropical America from the province of Guanacaste is the *sapodilla* or naseberry, here called *chicozapote* or *níspero*. It is a dessert fruit, rarely cooked or preserved in any way. The French botanist Descourtilz described it as having the "sweet perfumes of honey, jasmine and lily of the valley."

Zapote

A relative of the *sapodilla*, the *mammee-sapota* or marmalade-plum *(zapote)* kept Cortés and his army alive on their famous march from Mexico City to Honduras. The bright salmon-red color of the pulp catches the eyes of tourists walking the Avenida Central in San José. Street vendors, knowing the sales appeal of the beautiful color, cut the marmalade-plums in halves.

Beware, however, if you are not used to the very sweet fruits of the tropics – the flavor of the *zapote* may be rather cloying. Very ripe *zapotes* are used to make the most wonderful ice creams and sherbets. ❏

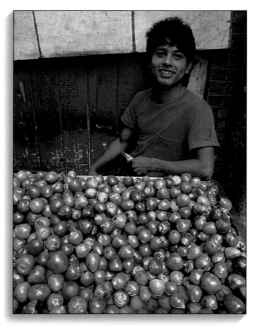

LEFT: a mountain of melons at Cartago.
RIGHT: the humble *pejibaye* has become an unlikely star of modern Costa Rican cuisine.

REFRESCOS & NATURALES

Refreshing fruit drinks or *naturales*, such as *fresco de maracuyá* (passion fruit) accompany every Costa Rican meal. One of the most nourishing is made from strained *moras* (blackberries), in sugar water or milk. *Cas*, a type of guava, is made into a thirst-quenching drink. A *tamarindo refresco* is similar in color and taste to apple juice. It is made from seeds of the tamarind tree, mixed with sugar and water. Tamarind seeds and pulp are available at every market. A bottled fruit drink called Tropical has flooded the market recently. It is acceptable at a pinch but hold out, if you can, for the real thing made with fresh fruit or fruit pulp.

COFFEE

When white coffee blossoms blanket the fields of the Central Valley, filling the air with a sweet jasmine-like fragrance, the Ticos *call it "Costa Rican Snow"*

You might well surmise that coffee is indigenous to Costa Rica, but it's not. The Spanish, French and Portuguese brought coffee beans to the New World from Ethiopia and Arabia. In the early 1800s, when seeds were first planted in Costa Rica, coffee plants were merely ornamental, grown to decorate

much of the land, except for that needed to graze oxen. As the only Costa Rican export, the country's financial resources were organized to support it. By 1840, coffee had become big business, carried by oxcart through mountains to the Pacific port at Puntarenas, and from there by ship to Chile from where it was transported to Europe. By the mid-1800s Costa Rica's oligarchy of coffee barons had risen to positions of power and wealth, for the most part through processing and exporting the golden bean, rather than by actually growing it.

A mixed blessing

Costa Rica was fortunate in its early development of the coffee industry, but at times it has been a mixed blessing. The country incurred a heavy debt borrowing US$3 million from England to finance the Atlantic railroad so coffee could be exported from the Caribbean port of Limón. And when coffee hit bottom on the international market in 1900, the result was a severe shortage of basic foods in Costa Rica that year.

This dependency on an overseas market has left the Costa Ricans vulnerable on many occasions. Throughout the 20th century, coffee prices fluctuated wildly and the health of the nation's economy varied accordingly.

Traditionally, banana, citrus and poro trees were planted in the coffee fields to provide some

patios and courtyards with their glossy green leaves, seasonal white flowers and red berries. Costa Ricans had to be persuaded, even coerced, into growing them so the country might have a national export crop. Every *Tico* family was required by law to have at least a couple of bushes in the yard. The government awarded free plants to the poor and grants of land to anyone who was willing to plant coffee on it.

The Central Valley is the ideal place for the production of coffee. Its altitude, above 1,200 meters (4,000 ft); its temperatures, which average between 15°C and 28°C (59°F and 82°F); and its soil conditions are all perfect for coffee cultivation. Coffee estates quickly occupied

COFFEE TO EUROPE

In 1843, an English sea captain, William Le Lacheur, returning to England from the United States, stopped in at Costa Rica's Pacific port of Puntarenas in search of ballast for his empty ship. As it happened, 1843 was an exceptional year for coffee production and the farmers had more beans than they could sell.

They made a deal with Le Lacheur and loaded up the holds of his ship with coffee, allowing him to use the heavy sacks as ballast. He made the trip to England around the Cape, and two years later he returned to pay the coffee planters their profit. And thus began the Costa Rican-European coffee trade.

shade for the coffee plants. Later, coffee hybrids were developed that did not need shade and tree-less fields allowed more yield per acre. These varieties, however, were found to deplete the soil more rapidly and required fertilizer to enrich it, adding to the cost of production. Today, many coffee-growers have returned to the traditional shade-loving plants, pleasing environmentalists who advocate shade-grown coffee.

The coffee plant itself is grown in nurseries until it's a year old, at which time it is trans-planted to the field. Two years later it bears harvestable berries and, with care, will continue to bear fruit for the next 30 to 40 years.

November to January, during school vacation and Christmas holidays. Traditionally entire families in rural areas picked coffee together, some of the money earned going for Christmas presents and new outfits. But today, most coffee is picked by migrant workers from Panamá and Nicaragua.

Costa Rican coffee has been traditionally mixed with other coffees destined for world-wide export. But today, coffee growers are con-centrating on high-altitude specialty coffees. Coffees from the highland regions around Poás, Barva de Heredia, Tres Ríos and Tarrazú are rated by many aficionados among the best in the world. ❑

Since coffee grows best in a mountainous cli-mate, many of the hillsides in the Central Valley are covered with rows of the bright green bushes, reflecting the sun with their shiny, luxuriant leaves. Some of the fields seem almost vertical and it is difficult to see how pickers keep from tumbling down the slopes as they collect the berries. The answer lies in the ingenious solution of planting the trees directly behind one another so that the trunk of the downhill tree serves as a foothold for the pickers. Coffee is harvested from

LEFT: fast hands; most coffee is picked today by migrant workers. **ABOVE:** coffee pickers *circa* 1920, when every Costa Rican joined in the harvest.

CAFE BRITT

The best way to get a taste of Costa Rica's coffee culture is to take Cafe Britt's Coffee Tour. Located almost 1 km (²/₃ mile) north of Heredia in Barva (signposted from Heredia center), this theatrical, highly entertaining experience takes visitors through the entire coffee process, from growing the coffee cherry to correctly tasting the final product. Combining ele-ments of professional theater, a multimedia show, a farm visit, plant tour and tasting session, Cafe Britt whirls the visitor through the world of coffee in about two hours. You must reserve your tour in advance by telephoning 260-2748 or visit www.coffeetour.com.

PLACES

*A detailed guide to the entire country, with principal sites
cross-referenced by number to the maps*

Costa Rica may be a relatively small country, but don't think that means there's little to see or do here. Some of its beaches rival the best of the Caribbean for their crystal waters and white sand. Inland, lush forests and towering volcanoes attract walkers and nature lovers from all over the world. With 27 national parks, eight biological reserves and 60-plus wildlife refuges, Costa Rica deserves its reputation as the home of eco-tourism.

We begin the places section in the capital, San José, the small but bustling metropolis that acts as the international gateway to Costa Rica. It is not a beautiful city, but like most capitals it has a buzz. It's worth staying a day or so to visit some fascinating museums, from the underground Gold Museum to the Jade Museum atop a skyscraper. It is also a good base for exploring the country, and there are some excellent lodges in the nearby mountains offering activities from horseback riding to whitewater rafting.

Next we focus on the Central Valley. This is the country's green and fertile heartland. It is an area of agricultural towns, coffee farms and many cultural treasures. From here it's a short hop to the beaches of the Central Pacific; these are some of the best in the country. Particularly famous is Manuel Antonio whose perfect white sands are the stuff of tropical dreams.

Many visitors regard the north as the true Costa Rica. This is almost a country in itself with the wonderful beaches of the Nicoya Peninsula, the great cattlelands of Guanacaste and the natural riches of Monteverde and the Sarapiquí. By night, Arenal Volcano, belching sulfurous smoke and oozing red lava, is an unforgettable sight.

By contrast, the Caribbean Coast presents Costa Rica's laid-back face: its tall palms, radiant sunshine and aquamarine waters beckoning visitors to share in its indolent lifestyle.

Our tour ends in the south, off the beaten track, amid a wild and wonderful region of vast tropical forests and Central America's highest peak. The Osa Peninsula and the Golfo Dulce are truly a world apart, often accessible only by boat, small plane or on foot. And in special picture features we'll tell you more about Costa Rica's volcanoes, its traditional handicrafts, its abundant flora, and its spectacular birdlife including its proudest natural treasure, the aptly and exotically named resplendent quetzal.

All the sites of interest are numbered on specially drawn maps to help you find your way around. Don't worry about getting lost – everyone does. But then, just getting there is half the fun of enjoying this remarkable country. ❑

PRECEDING PAGES: Caribbean coastline; *páramo*, an unusual ecosystem seen on the summit of Mount Chirripó; Basílica de Nuestra Señora de los Angeles in Cartago.
LEFT: a *campesino* ponders the origin and significance of this giant stone sphere.

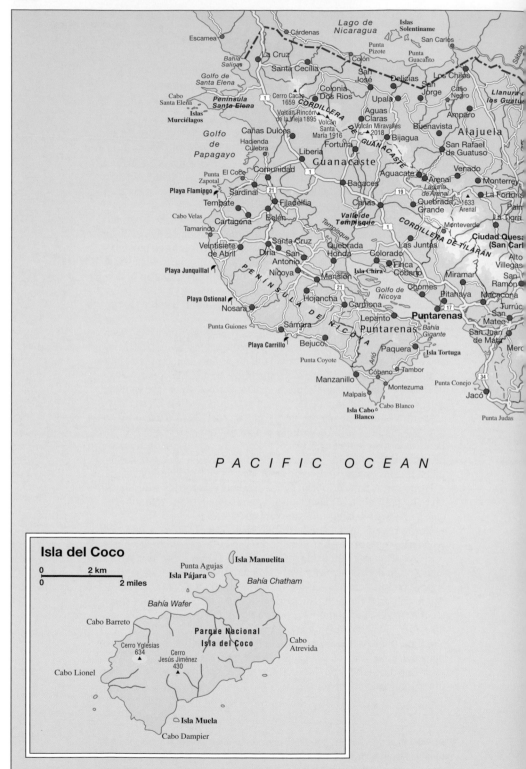

Escamea
Cárdenas
Lago de
Nicaragua
Islas
Solentiname
San Carlos
Bahía
Salinas
La Cruz
Punta
Pizote
Punta
Guacafito
Sabalo
Santa Cecilia
Colón
San
José
Delicias
Los Chiles
San
Jorge
Caño
Negro
Golfo de
Santa Elena
Cabo
Santa Elena
Península
Santa Elena
Cerro Cacao
1659
Colonia
Dos Rios
Upala
Amparo
Llanura
los Guatu
Islas
Murciélagos
CORDILLERA
Volcán Rincón
de la Vieja 1895
Aguas
Claras
Buenavista
Alajuela
Golfo
de
Papagayo
Cañas Dulces
Volcán
Santa
María 1916
Volcán Miravalles
2018
Bijagua
San Rafael
de Guatuso
Hacienda
Culebra
Fortuna
DE
GUANACASTE
Venado
Monterrey
Liberia
Guanacaste
Aguacate
Arenal
Punta
Zapotal
El Coco
Comunidad
Bagaces
Laguna
de Arenal
La Fortu
Pair
Playa Flamingo
Sardinal
Cañas
19
1633
Arenal
La Tigra
Tempate
Filadelfia
Quebrada
Grande
Cabo Velas
Belén
Valle de
Tempisque
CORDILLERA DE TILARÁN
Monteverde
Cartagéna
Tamarindo
Ciudad Quesa
(San Carl
Veintisiete
de Abril
Santa Cruz
Quebrada
Honda
Las Juntas
Alto
Villegas
Playa Junquillal
Diria
San
Antonio
Colorado
Isla Chira
Finca
Cóbano
Miramar
San
Ramón
Nicoya
Mansión
Golfo de
Nicoya
Chomes
Pitahaya
Macacona
Playa Ostional
Hojancha
Carmona
Puntarenas
17
Turrúc
San
Mateo
Nosara
PENÍNSULA DE NICOYA
Lepanto
Puntarenas
Bahía
Gigante
San Juan
de Mata
Merc
Punta Guiones
Sámara
Playa Carrillo
Bejuco
Paquera
Isla Tortuga
Punta Coyote
Aró
Cóbano
Tambor
Punta Conejo
34
Jacó
Manzanillo
Montezuma
Malpaís
Cabo Blanco
Isla Cabo
Blanco
Cabo Blanco
Punta Judas

PACIFIC OCEAN

Isla del Coco

0   2 km
0   2 miles

Punta Agujas
Isla Pájara
Isla Manuelita
Bahía Chatham
Bahía Wafer
Cabo Barreto
Parque Nacional
Isla del Coco
Cabo
Atrevida
Cerro Yglesias
634
Cerro
Jesús Jiménez
430
Cabo Lionel
Isla Muela
Cabo Dampier

Costa Rica

0   20 km
0   20 miles

N

CARIBBEAN SEA

NICARAGUA

Indío
Caño Negro
Deseado
San Juan
del Norte
Punta
Castilla

itas

San Juan

Boca
Sahino

Trinidad

HEREDIA

Las
Medias

Puerto Viejo
de Sarapiquí

Llanura de
Tortuguero

Tortuguero
Suerte

La Virgen
Venecia

Las
Horquetas

Cariari

Limón
Parismina

chona

Volcán
Cacho Negro
2150

Rita
Roxana

Río Jiménez

CORDILLERA CENTRAL

Guápiles

Jiménez
Florida
Batán
Siquirres
Matina
Puerto
Limón
Isla Uvita

a
Charrizal

San José
de la Montaña

Volcán Irazú
3452

Santa
Cruz
Peralta

ajuela

Heredia
Pavas

San José

Turrialba

Pavones

Petróleo

Limón

36

Desamparados
Cartago
Tucurrique
Platanillo

Finca
Banaga

scazú
Tabarcia

Aserrí

San Gabriel
Orosi

Pejibaye

Cahuita

Chirripó

Vesta

Punta Cahuita
Pto.
Viejo

Punta Uva

ngrejal

San Andrés

Empalme

Cartago

CORDILLERA

Valle de la Estrella

Bibrí

Punta Mona
Manzanillo

an José

Parrita
rrenas
de Parrita
rrita

Santa María
de Dota

San
Lorenzo

San Gerardo
de Dota

Cerro Urán
3333

DE

Telire

Shiroles

Valle de
Talamanca

Bratsi

Sixaola

I. Colón

epos

Naranjito

Río Nuevo

Rivas

Cerro Chirripó
3819

Coén

Teribé

Changuinola

I. Cristóbal

Manuel
Antonio

34

Savegre

General Viejo

San Isidro

Cerro Eli
3097

TALAMANCA

Almirante

Matapalo

Barú

22

Cajón
San Pedro

2

General

Volcán

Dominical

Cerro Kamuk
3549

Uvita

Punta
Uvita

Pejibaye

Valle de
El General

Buenos
Aires

Cerro Fábegra
3336

PANAMÁ

Colinas

Boruca

Potrero
Grande

Valle de
Coto Brus

Santa
Elena

Bahía
de
Coronado

Cortés

Palmar
Sur

Valle de
Diquís

2

Chánguena

Puntarenas

San
Vito

Alturas

Río Sereno

Sierpe

Chacarita

Limoncito

Sabalito

Hato del
Volcán

Boquete

Isla del Caño

Bahía
Drake

Drake

Rincón

Agua Buena

16

Agujitas

Punta San
Pedrillo

Golfo
Dulce

Golfito

Neily

Pueblo
Nuevo

Gualaca

Punta Llorona

Península de Osa

Puerto
Jiménez

14

Zancudo

Perrón

La Concepción

Canoas

Punta
Salsipuedes

Carate

Bahía
Pavón

Punta
Banco

La Cuesta

David

Cabo
Matapalo

Banco

Puerto Armuelles

I. Sevilla

Península
de Burica

Bahía de
Charco Azul

I. Boca
Brava

Yerbazales

Punta Burica

Isla Burica

Heredia

MONTSERRAT

LOMAS
DE PINAR

Torres

Autopista General Cañas

Calle 28
Calle 26
Calle 22

Calle Las Américas

ROHRMOSER

AMÉRICAS

Instituto de
Electricidad
ICE

CLARET

RINCÓN DE
CUBILLOS

JUAREZ

Ave
Av.7

Avenida 7

Avenida 5

Avenida Las Américas

PARQUE METROPOLITANA

LA SABANA   PADRE CHAPUI

Estadio
Nacional

Laguito

Calle 40
Calle 38
Calle 36
Calle 34
Calle 32

PITAHAJA

Avenida 3

Calle 30

Avenida 1

CENTRO COLÓN

Calle 26
Calle 24
Calle 22

Calle 20

Mercado
Coca Cola

Avenida Central

Paseo Colón

Museo de Arte
Costarricense

Hungría Libre

Avenida 2

Calle 42
Calle 40
Calle 38
Calle 36
Calle 34
Calle 32

Avenida 4

Hospital
Nacional
de Niños

Avenida 6

Castro Madriz

Calle 26
Calle 24

C. 22
Calle 20

Ministe
de Sal

Pueblo Antiguo

Calle Lang

LAS VEGAS

Calle Alvarez

Calle Morenos

Calle del Golf

TOVAR

Avenida 10

Avenida 8

Calle 36

San Martín

Calle 28

Hospital
Antituberculoso

Simón Bolívar

Calle 20
Calle 18 bis
Calle 18

Cruz

Avenida 10

Museo de
Ciencias Naturales,
Colegio La Salle

PERPUETUO
SOCORRO

SABANA SUR

PASEO
COLÓN

CEMENTERIO
CALVO

CEMENTERIO
ISRAELITA

CEMENTERIO
DE OBREROS

CEMENTERIO
GENERAL

Calle 22

BOLÍVAR

PINO

Av. 24

CORAZÓN
DE JESÚS

Av. 26

Juan Santamaría

ALMENDARES

HATILLO NO. 8

Avenida Nosara

María Aguila

Calle 24

CUBA

Calle 20

Calle 18 bis
Calle 18

Escazú

Avenida Tiribí

Avenida Nosara

PINOS

Avenida 28

HATILLO
NO. 7

Calle C

Calle B

Avenida 30

Avenida 28

Avenida Vilania

HATILLO NO. 6

Calle A

Calle Tempisque

HATILLO
NO. 1

Sixaola

Calle 21
C. 22 bis
C. 22

Avenida 32

HATILLONAZ

Av. Panamá

Av. Nicaragua

Calle Costa Rica

Avenida Tempisque

SAGRADA FAMILIA

Avenida Central

Calle Brasil

Calle Argentina

Calle Tempisque

Hatillo

110

39

HATILLO
NO. 3

Calle Bolívar

Calle Colombia

HATILLO
NO. 5

N

Dinamarca

25 DE JULIO

CAÑA
DEL S

Calle Pipianes

San José

Avenida

Av. España

HATILLO
NO. 4

Calle Ecuador

Alajuelita

0   500 m
0   500 yds

SAN JOSÉ

*With modern high-rises ranked alongside tile-roofed, faded
colonial villas, Costa Rica's capital may seem a jumble at first.
Yet it possesses a certain Tico charm*

Map
on page
130–31

T he growth, some might say the flowering, of San José, began on that day,
sometime during the first half of the 19th century, when Europe decided to
have its daily cup of coffee.

By the 1850s, San José had been transformed from a humble village to a
boom town. Everything had to be the best, the most modern, the most European.
With every bag of coffee that was exported, there was a proportionate enrich-
ment of the economic, social and cultural life of the *Josefinos*, as the people of
San José are called. And as the city became wealthy, so its inhabitants became
more refined, more sophisticated, and more worldly.

The golden age

By the end of the 19th century, San José was booming from the profits of its coffee exports. It was the third city in the world to have public electric lighting; one
of the first to have public telephones; the first in Central America, perhaps in all
of Latin America, to initiate free and compulsory public education to all of its
citizens; and the first to allow girls to attend high school. Admittedly, the roads
were unpaved, but most upper-class homes had pianos.

Through much of the first part of the 20th century, San José continued to
prosper and build: a national library, schools, banks,
parks and plazas, ministries, numerous hotels, theaters, a sumptuous post office, bookstores, hospitals,
churches, a magnificent Palace of Justice, and an
international airport.

And then, in 1956, Costa Rica's population passed
the one million mark. The international focus of influence had shifted and the people ceased coveting things
European and became heavily influenced by North
American standards and sensibilities.

The modern city

Cars and trucks began to appear where there had only
been the gentle horse and buggy, ox carts, pedestrians
and bicycles. The population doubled over the following two decades.

By the mid-1970s, the air in San José had become
noticeably dirty and the once civilized, narrow streets
had become overwhelmed with a relentless rush of
cars and people, all seemingly in a big hurry to get
somewhere. Graceful, ornate old buildings were torn
down and replaced with harsh, ugly copies of North
American modern architecture. San José, the civilized
19th-century city, could not adapt its physical
limitations to meet the demands of its consumerist
20th-century people. And today, in the early 21st century, this conflict has engendered a city that, by most
standards, is traffic-clogged and unattractive.

PRECEDING PAGES: a
section of ceiling in
the National Theater.
LEFT: carnival time
in the streets of
San José.
BELOW: the National
Youth Symphonic
Orchestra.

Oases of calm

Fortunately, amid the miasma of diesel fumes, and the hordes of people, there are still some islands of repose where you can rest and refresh yourself as you search to find the heart of this city. The National Theater is probably the most beautiful building in the country and its coffee shop is a favorite place; quiet, elegant, yet alive. And to relax, sipping a *refresco natural* on the veranda of the Grand Hotel, while listening to marimba bands and the burble of 20 different languages as other people rush around the plaza, should not be missed.

The National Museum and the Gold Museum are worth seeking out, along with the world-class Jade Museum; there are souvenir shops, good theaters, many good restaurants, an abundance of cabarets and nightclubs, and a few interesting art galleries. There are also some extraordinary remnants of old San José, hints of what a handsome, delightful place this used to be, not so long ago.

Getting your bearings

Before you embark on the following tour of the city, or indeed go looking for any address within San José, sit down with our map *(see pages 130–131)* and familiarize yourself with the way it is laid out. The city is organized on a grid system of numbered streets *(calles)*, which run north to south, and avenues *(avenidas)*, which run east to west. The northern avenues and eastern streets have odd numbers; the southern avenues and western streets have even numbers. Confusingly, however, buildings are not numbered and, for the most part, only in downtown San José do any streets have names. Addresses are often given in the following format: Metropolitan Cathedral, Calle Central, Avenida 2–4, meaning that it is on the Calle Central between Avenida 2 and Avenida 4. Alter-

BELOW: busy Parque Central.

natively and more commonly, addresses are given in terms of distance in meters *(metros)*, north, south, east or west from known landmarks. It's as well to know, however, that *Ticos* often equate a city block with 100 meters (no matter how long or short it is). The end result is that *Ticos* and visitors alike can be seen wandering the city streets perpetually stopping one another to ask for directions. The good news is that people are generally happy to help.

The best time to walk in San José is on a Sunday morning, when there is less traffic on the streets. Or, during the week, go early, before the rush and roar of the city has yet to begin.

The heart of the city

The Plaza de la Cultura marks the heart of the city. The area around this large square is a popular meeting point for traders, artisans, street musicians, painters, actors, in fact just about anybody and everybody. The pride of the square is the **Teatro Nacional** , without doubt the finest building in San José, if not all Costa Rica. Its construction was financed by 19th-century coffee barons, who, embarrassed that there was no appropriate venue here for the world-renowned opera star, Adelina Patti to perform (she had snubbed San José on her 1890 tour of Central America), offered to pay a tax on every bag of coffee exported.

Modeled after the Paris Opera House and neoclassical in style, the theater was opened in 1897 with a production of *Faust*. It is on four levels, with a well-equipped stage system and a main audience seating floor that is adjustable to different heights. The floor plan is in the form of a horseshoe, and the acoustics are excellent. The detailing was done by Spanish and Italian artisans. Ironically, Adelina Patti never did come to Costa Rica, but Costa Rica's top-quality

ABOVE: mountains of fruit for sale at the Central Market.
BELOW: a night in San José.

City Buses

Buses are ubiquitous in San José. They go everywhere throughout the city and its surrounding areas. Some downtown streets are clogged with them: shiny new Mercedes models, freshly washed and festively painted with murals on their rear windows; sooty, rusty wrecks emitting thick black smoke; recycled school buses from the US, scrupulously cared for and graced with fanciful names to give them new life.

Whether new and slick or decrepit and smoky, the buses have a common trait. They are wonderful windows into Costa Rican life. Most everyone uses them: students on their way to classes; women in heels, dressy clothes and impeccable make-up on their way to work; country folk coming into town to do business of one kind or another; young mothers taking children to doctors' appointments at the social security hospital; men with briefcases and neat pants and shirts. They're all on the bus, heading this way or that.

And for a fistful of colones, you can climb aboard and join in the great comings and goings of life on the Central Valley. A bus ride in San José is not particularly comfortable, especially during peak hours, but there's no better or more enjoyable way to make quick and often delicious observations on *Tico* life and characteristics.

For one thing, chivalry is still alive. Or is it a simple sense of decency, of caring for others? Young men will assist older men or women with children in tow up the steps, a seated passenger will offer to hold your packages while you stand, someone will always offer his or her seat to an older person or a pregnant woman. The bus driver will wait for someone making a last-minute dash. A young boy, known to the bus driver by name, boards on Paseo Colón and, for a few stops, becomes the bus's official door-opener.

A wizened old *campesino* (peasant), returning from a trip to the city, takes a long time to board. He carries with him a heavy burlap bag, redolent of coffee beans and *pejibaye*.

A small girl in a rumpled pink dress enters the parked bus, waiting for its scheduled departure at the Coca Cola bus stop. She speaks to the driver, then stands at the front of the bus, singing a mournful song about love. When she finishes, she moves down the aisle with an open hand, into which we drop our small change.

Take at least one bus ride in San José. Board near the beginning of the line, when you can still get a seat, and watch the rush of humanity come aboard, pausing to place their fare in the driver's hand, pushing past the turnstile, greeting friends and neighbors as they make their way down the aisle, more passengers stop after stop, until it isn't possible to squeeze another body on.

Buses marked Sabana-Cementerio take you on a loop around downtown, past the Central Post Office, the central Market, Sabana Park and the vast city cemetery. It's a good idea to take a ride outside the city too. The bus ride to Heredia, via Santo Domingo, gives you a glimpse of San José's prosperous suburbs as well as some of the shabbier parts of town. ❏

LEFT: traveling "a la Tica" is a quick way to get an insight into local life.

National Symphony Orchestra performs here with illustrious international guest artists; their season begins in March. There are also daily tours where you can admire the marble, gold, bronze, tropical woods, crystal chandeliers, velvet drapes and statuary. The ceiling fresco is famous and features an idyllic, if improbable, scene of coffee and banana pickers *(see pages 128–9)*.

The **Cafe del Teatro Nacional** features changing art exhibits and is a very popular place, serving excellent salads, snacks, desserts and specialty coffees. Adjacent to the National Theater is the **Gran Hotel Costa Rica** , renowned as a meeting place for tourists who gather in its outdoor cafe where musicians often entertain with marimbas. The hotel was renovated to mark its 75th birthday.

Beneath the Plaza de la Cultura is the **Museo de Oro** ◉ (Gold Museum). On the east side of the square in cool, darkened, cavernous rooms, the collection features more than 2,000 brilliant pre-Columbian artifacts made by the indigenous peoples from the southwestern part of the country. Highlights include tiny half-man, half-bird figures, and erotic statuettes (open Tues–Sun 9.30am–5pm; entrance fee). The museum also contains the national coin collection and occasional exhibitions of modern art. Before leaving the Plaza de la Cultura pay a visit to the Costa Rica Tourist Office (ICT) at the entrance to the Gold Museum for news of what's on in town and to pick up a free bus schedule.

More museums

A short walk west of the Plaza de la Cultura along Avenida 2 is the **Parque Central** ◉ (Central Park), another great place for people-watching. The Gaudí-like kiosk in the center of the park was donated by the Somoza family of Nicaragua and sometimes hosts open-air concerts on weekends.

Map on page 130–31

TIP

On the Avenida Central side of the Plaza de la Cultura is a branch of Pop's Ice-Cream Parlor, generally agreed to be the best in Costa Rica. It is always crowded.

BELOW: the National Theater.

TIP

At the northern end of the Parque Central, look out for the recently restored neoclassical facade of the Teatro Popular Melico Salazar.

Directly in front of the park is the huge **Catedral Metropolitana** (Metropolitan Cathedral). It is of little architectural merit, but do notice the finely carved wood ceiling of the Chapel of the Holy Sacrament; also its walls, so carefully adorned with flower motifs that it almost looks as if they have been tiled. Look for a new monumental white statue of Pope John Paul II in the cathedral garden. The cathedral provides a refuge of peace from the hot bustling city, and microphone-amplified midday Masses are well attended by local people.

Due north of Parque Central, along Calle 2, is the **Correos** (central post office) in a grand old building that also houses the **Museo Postal** (Post Office Museum, open Mon–Fri 8am–5pm, Sat 8am–noon) and a pleasant café. Three blocks west of the post office on Avenida 1 you'll find the **Mercado Central** (Central Market), the city's best market, dating from 1881. There are over 200 stalls selling everything from old kitchen utensils to saddle bags, fresh fish, coffee and spices by the kilo, to religious icons. The prices are some of the cheapest in the city. At the center of the hall are the snack stands, a good place to find real *Tico* food at real *Tico* prices. Keep your hand on your wallet as pickpockets operate here (and just love tourists), but don't be deterred from diving into this den to witness gritty *Tico* life at first hand (open Mon–Sat 6.30am–6.30pm).

If you have children in tow, you might at this point like to make a diversion a few blocks north to the former Penitenciaria Central (city jail), now the **Museo de los Niños** (Children's Museum; tel: 258 4929), which has lots of interesting interactive exhibits that are entertaining for adults, too. There is a good summary of *Ticos*' historical developments, with models of Amerindian huts, Caribbean wooden shacks and modern housing (open Tues–Fri 8am–4.30pm, Sat–Sun 10am–5pm; entrance fee). It is in a rough part of town, however, so take a cab, rather than walking there.

BELOW: the Central Market is one of the most colorful and dynamic places in the city.

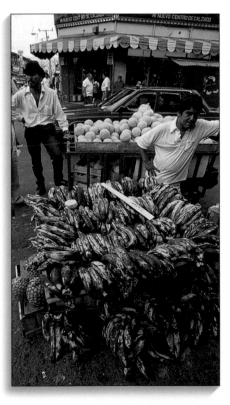

On Avenida 7, on the north side of the Parque España, is the not-to-be-missed **Museo de Jade** (Jade Museum; open Mon–Fri 8.30am–3.30pm, Sat 9am–1pm; entrance fee). It can be found on the 11th floor of the National Insurance Institute, better known as the INS **Building**, a useful landmark that also offers great views over the city. Alongside the museum's carefully crafted jade pieces *(see page 28)*, most of which are *colgantes* (amulets or pendants), are masterpieces of pre-Hispanic sculpture from all regions of the country.

Opposite the Jade Museum is one of the capital's most interesting old buildings, the **Edificio Metalico** (Metal Building school), shipped here in 1892 from Belgium to house 1,000 students. Next door to the museum under the shade of a magnificent ceibo tree is the **Casa Amarilla** (Yellow House), the home of the Foreign Ministry, but constructed in 1816 as the Court of Justice. You can take a look inside its foyer and take a peek at a piece of the Berlin Wall, made into a fountain in the garden.

Nature in the city

A block north of the Jade Museum is the **Parque Zoológico Simón Bolívar** (Simón Bolívar Zoo), with a small collection of African, Asian, and Costa Rican animals. Although the zoo has received some much-needed renovation in recent years, it is still a very sad place for the ill-housed animals, especially the larger ones. Geared primarily toward locals and school groups, nevertheless the park makes for a pleasant stroll especially on a weekday morning, when you may have it all to yourself (open Mon–Fri 8am–4.30pm, Sat–Sun 9am–4.30pm; entrance fee).

Map on page 130–31

Immediately north, at the back of the park, is the enchanting **Spyrogyra Jardín de Mariposas Ⓚ** (Spyrogyra Butterfly Garden). It's not far, as the butterfly flies, but the entrance is a long way off on foot, so you will need to take a cab from the zoo to get to this secret city garden. One of the main aims of Spyrogyra is to help rural women find alternative sources of income from laboring in the fields by exporting butterfly cocoons to Europe and the US instead (open daily 8am–4pm; entrance fee). In addition to the many colorful butterflies, there are gardens and hummingbirds to enjoy. Go on a sunny day when the butterflies are most active.

Arts, history and culture

Also close to the INS building is the **Fábrica Nacional de Licores Ⓛ** (National Liquor Factory), also known as FANAL. Founded in 1856, the complex, which takes up a whole city block, has been turned into an arts and cultural center, somewhat confusingly also known as the Centro Nacional de la Cultura y la Ciencia or CENAC (National Center of Culture and Science). Pop into the pretty courtyard and amphitheater, which lead to another part of the complex: the **Museum of Contemporary Art and Design** (open Mon–Sat 10.30am–5.30pm; museum free on Mon), with changing exhibitions of art, sculpture and photography. FANAL is open Tues–Sat; free except for some special exhibits; check the *Tico Times* for what's on. One block southeast of here is the **Parque Nacional**

ABOVE: crested iguana at the zoo. **BELOW:** central post office *(Correos)* and Post Office Museum.

Map on page 130–31

ABOVE: gold plate, Museo de Oro.
BELOW: potatoes make a change from rice and beans.
RIGHT: national identity.

M (National Park). This is the largest of San José's parks, where lovers drape themselves over park benches and bureaucrats eat their lunches under the shade of the 50 or so native tree species. It's a very pleasant place by day, and well-lit by night, but probably not advisable to stroll in alone after dark. In the center of the park is a monument depicting victory in the war against the hated *filibustero*, William Walker *(see page 45)*.

Two blocks south of here, on Calle 17, is the **Museo Nacional N** (open Tues–Fri 8.30am–4.30pm, Sat and Sun 9am–4.30pm; entrance fee) housed in the old Bellavista fortress, which still bears the bullet marks from the 1948 Civil War. Constructed in 1870, the building served as a barracks until the abolition of the army in 1949. The collections provide an overview of Costa Rica's history and culture, and include displays on burial ceremonies, a treasury of gold pieces and rustic furniture from the colonial period. In the courtyard are cannons and some of the mysterious stone spheres found in the south of the country *(see pages 28 and 251)*. From the terrace of the building there are fine views down onto the city and the amphitheater-like Plaza de la Democracia, where open-air concerts are sometimes held. Artisans congregate to sell handicrafts and souvenirs in a roofed-over corridor of market stalls.

Sabana Park and Pueblo Antiguo

The large grassy area of **Parque La Sabana** occupies what was Costa Rica's first international airport. The Spanish-style building has been converted into the **Museo de Arte Costarricense O** (Museum of Costa Rican Art). This features revolving exhibitions of works by the country's finest 19th- and 20th-century painters and sculptors as well as works by international artists (open Tues–Sun when there is an exhibition mounted; entrance fee, Sunday free). In the *Salón Dorado* (Golden Room, upper story), French artist Luis Ferrón has immortalized Costa Rican history in a striking-looking stucco and bronze mural.

Across from the southwest corner of the park is the Museum of Natural Sciences, also known as the **Museo La Salle**. The main attraction is a huge collection of stuffed animals. With pickled snakes, toads and fish; a stuffed swan suspended from the ceiling; and a scale model of a US space shuttle, the place has a faintly eccentric air (open daily, entrance fee).

Sabana Park is a popular weekend retreat for families who come to picnic, ride their bikes, skate, play and feed the ducks in the many lakes. Kite vendors also do a brisk trade on breezy days. Sporting facilities include soccer fields, tennis courts, a swimming pool (only occasionally open), and jogging trails. The park should be avoided after dark, however.

A short bus ride northwest of Sabana Park in the district of La Uruca is the **Pueblo Antiguo P** (literally "Old Village"), an idyllic re-creation of old Costa Rica set in the Parque de Diversiones. Actors demonstrate traditional craft skills and bygone agricultural techniques, and there are other shows plus restaurants serving local food (open Wed–Thurs 9am–5pm, Fri–Sat 9am–9pm, Sun 9am–6pm; entrance fee). Sunday is the best day to visit, when a carnival is always enacted in an authentic setting. ❏

THE CENTRAL VALLEY

Map on page 146

The heartland of Costa Rica is home to 60 percent of the nation's people. It is the center of government, agriculture and commerce, and has the oldest cities and many cultural treasures

The Central Valley *(Valle Central)*, or Central Plateau *(Meseta Central)*, as it is often called, is strictly speaking neither a valley nor a plateau since it contains both kinds of landscape. The Central Highlands might be a more apt name for this area, only 24 km by 64 km (15 miles by 40 miles), where two mountain ranges meet. You'll find rich, volcanic hills and river-filled valleys, with altitudes reaching up to 1,500 meters (4,500 ft).

The good life

The countryside is beautiful and variable. The climate is salubrious. The air is sweet and soft. The people are generally friendly, dignified and independent. Volcanoes, some still active, others dormant or extinct, rise up above the hills around the valley. Above them, a big sky is constantly changing – dark, charcoal rain clouds; intense, searing patches of blue; fluffy white cumulus; and occasional rainbows. All come and go in quick succession.

There are misty, almost enchanted places such as the Orosí Valley; adobe villages that sing of old Costa Rica, such as Barva; and crowded, noisy, relentlessly vital cities, such as Heredia or Cartago. And they're all easily accessible. Daytrips by bus or car, or with tour groups can easily be arranged.

PRECEDING PAGES: grazing in the hills above Heredia. **LEFT:** Central Valley coffee plantation. **BELOW:** the parish church is the focus of every Costa Rican village.

Passing through the small, highland towns and villages, you see what in Central America is the unusual and impressive sight of people living in houses on plots of land that they themselves own and farm. Neighborhoods are often a hodgepodge of larger, fancy homes and smaller, humble ones. Housewives in aprons chat in front yards as they watch their babies. Children in school uniforms walk up the road for lunch at home. Produce from backyard fruit trees is for sale on little tables or stands in front of houses: soft-fruit preserves, homemade cheese and sour cream, oranges, candy-stuffed grapefruit, mangoes, tomatoes. Visitors are accepted with a mild, easy curiosity; no one seems especially surprised to have a *gringo* walk into the local *soda* and order *arroz con pollo* (chicken and rice).

San José, Alajuela, Cartago and Heredia are the largest and most important cities of the Central Valley. Radiating out from San José are towns and suburbs, each with its own flavor and identity: Americanized Escazú; residential, upscale Rohrmoser; exclusive Los Yoses with its lovely old residences; San Pedro, home to many good restaurants, the University of Costa Rica, and one of the largest shopping malls in Central America. There are also four national parks to explore, several volcanoes to climb and Guayabo National Monument, the country's most important archeological site.

Central Valley

N

0   5 km
0   5 miles

Though most travelers visit the Central Valley between December and March to escape the winter chill of North America and Europe, these months are Costa Rica's dry season, its "summer." Frequent travelers to the area know that it is the rainy season in Costa Rica, with its afternoon downpours and dramatic displays of lightning, when the Central Valley is at its magnificent best: lush and colorful. Best of all, the air and San José itself are cleansed by a daily bath.

Map on page 146

Poás Volcano National Park

The most developed of all the parks is **Parque Nacional Volcán Poás ❶**, a popular attraction. It is only 37 km (25 miles) from San José on good roads leading through the city of Alajuela. Poás can become crowded and cloudy, so it's best to visit early in the day when views are better and before the throngs arrive. The cool freshness of the air as you ascend the mountain is invigorating, but it can get chilly and rainy, so dress appropriately.

A map of the nature trails is available at the Visitors' Center, where there is an insect exhibition and a cafe. From a lookout point above the crater, there is an overview of the volcano, which in 1989 shot ash a mile into the air. The main crater, which is 1.5 km (1 mile) wide and 300 meters (1,000 ft) deep, is one of the largest in the world. Poás rarely has violent eruptions and is one of the more accessible active volcanoes on the continent. It is active in 40-year cycles and is currently producing acid-like rain and sulfurous gases. It is therefore not advisable to stay for more than 20 minutes near the active crater. Just a 20-minute hike away is another crater filled with a jewel-colored lake.

ABOVE: mangoes in Alajuela. **BELOW:** a streambed in Braulio Carrillo National Park.

Well-maintained trails lead through a landscape rich with wildflowers and a multitude of mosses, bromeliads and ferns. The resplendent quetzal *(see page 206)* can be seen here at certain times of the year.

Descend from the park to one of the nearby restaurants and enjoy the local specialty of *fresas en leche*, strawberry milkshake, or stop at one of the roadside stands to buy strawberry preserves and cookies made by local women. Alternatively, continue to the nearby La Paz Waterfall Gardens and set off on 4 km (2 miles) of trails past hummingbird and orchid gardens and the largest butterfly observatory in the world en route to five impressive waterfalls. To spend more time in the mountain air consider an overnight stay at cozy Poás Volcano Lodge, furnished with fireplaces.

Alajuela and environs

As you descend by some 200 meters (660 ft) into **Alajuela ❷** (pop. 248,000) it becomes noticeably warmer. To relax, you can join the old-timers in the central park, amid an orchard of mango trees. Each April work crews use high-pressure hoses to fell the ripe mangos so they don't fall on people's heads.

Alajuela is the birthplace of Juan Santamaría, the young Costa Rican whose courage was responsible for the routing of William Walker and his *filibusteros* from Costa Rica in 1856 *(see page 45)*. **The Museo Juan Santamaría** in the former jail, one block from the central park, tells his story (open Tues–Sun 10am–6pm; free). A week-long festival of parades, concerts and dances centers around his April 11 birthday.

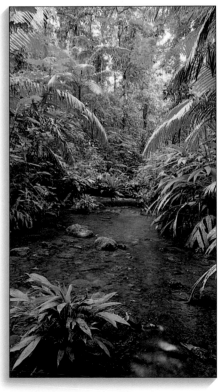

From Alajuela take the old highway toward the Pacific–La Garita. En route is **Zoo-Ave ❸**, which has more than 80 species of Costa Rican birds, as well as - monkeys, deer, crocodiles, giant tortoises and the occasional puma or ocelot (open daily 9am–5pm; entrance fee). **La Garita ❹** is expansive and green, filled with lovely gardens, fields of shiny green coffee bushes and plant nurseries *(viveros)*. La Fiesta del Máiz restaurant, open on weekends, features the near-endless variety of tasty dishes that *Ticos* make from corn. A few kilometers southeast near Guacima is **The Butterfly Farm ❺**, a breeding farm for more than 57 kinds of exotic butterflies, which are exported by the tens of thousands to Europe. The Butterfly Farm has waterfalls and extensive tropical plantings (open daily 8.30am–5pm; tours 8.30am, 11am, 1pm and 3pm; entrance fee).

The most spectacular of all Costa Rica's butterflies is the Blue Morpho, a veritable giant that grows up to 13–20 cm (5–8 inches) long.

Water holes

If it is a warm day and you feel like cooling down and splashing around, then stop on the way back to San José (6 km/4 miles before town) at the **Balneario Ojo de Agua ❻** (open daily 8am–4pm; entrance fee). Thousands of gallons of water pump out of this natural spring every hour of the day and around it has been created three swimming pools. The wet season is the best time to visit, when the spring is in full flood. At weekends, however, Ojo de Agua is very busy with locals. The water isn't just used for recreational purposes, it is also pumped to Puntarenas *(see page 181)* to use as a major part of its water supply.

Coffee country

A day trip to the province of Heredia, the center of Costa Rica's coffee production, quickly takes you away from the heat and clatter of San José. Just 24 km

BELOW:
Volcán Poás in an active phase; signs warn visitors not to linger too long near the summit.

Map on page 146

(15 miles) from the city, you can walk in an evergreen forest or cloud forest reserve rivaling those of much more remote and inaccessible areas.

En route to Heredia from San José is Santo Domingo, which retains an historical charm with low, white stucco houses trimmed in traditional royal-blue paint. Just to the southwest of the town center is **BioPark/INBioparque ❼**, a 5.5-hectare (13½-acre) coffee estate turned naturalist center that provides an entertaining introduction to Costa Rica's biodiversity. Trails lead through three representative eco-systems, passing a serpentarium, an ant farm and tarantula and frog exhibits. There are guided tours by naturalists, excellent videos on biodiversity, exhibition halls that give an overview of the national parks' system, a pleasant restaurant, a lakeside cafe and an excellent shop with unusual gifts for naturalists aged nine to 90 (open Tues–Sun 8am–4pm; entrance fee; tel: 244 4730).

Heredia ❽ (pop. 115,000) lies 9 km (6 miles) north of San José, and is known as *La Ciudad de las Flores* (The City of Flowers). The city was first settled in 1706 by Spaniards. Many fully stocked stores suggest that this coffee-rich area is affluent, and, indeed, by Costa Rican standards, it is. **The National University** is located in Heredia; it turns out the nation's teachers and has one of the best veterinarian schools in Latin America. The old town center, with its colonial Casa de Cultura, pitted fort and lovely church, is a pleasant place to stroll. The **Immaculada Concepción**, constructed in 1796, is adorned with bells brought from Cuzco, Peru and its "seismic baroque" construction has enabled it to survive many earth tremors.

The newer section of Heredia is rapidly gentrifying, with lots of trendy new stores reflecting the global spread of North American brands.

ABOVE: the lovely church of Sarchí.
BELOW: after church on Sunday; spectators at a soccer match.

TIP

After a hike in Laguna Barva, pay a visit to the Hotel Chalet Tirol, where top-quality French cooking refreshes weary walkers.

BELOW: the coffee crop, all picked by hand, earns Costa Rica about US$30 million in exports each year.

Alpine scenery

Take the road to **San Rafael** and begin the ascent into the mountains. Some villas above the town are architecturally alpine, often down to Tyrolean paintings on the shutters. Driving through here, you get the feeling of having suddenly entered into an Austrian watercolor landscape. Wealthy *Ticos* of earlier generations were educated in Europe and returned to their country with a great appreciation for the architecture of Northern Europe, which is evident in this cool, mountain area. Now, many young *Ticos* go to North American universities, and with this shift in academic background, cultural affinities are changing.

Above San Rafael the temperature drops dramatically. Six km (4 miles) above the town, in wonderfully fresh mountain air, Hotel and Villas La Condesa offers horseback riding in the surrounding hills, hiking, a swimming pool, luxury rooms, and a conference center (tel: 267 6000). Next you will pass a sign to El Castillo Country Club (some facilities available to non-members for a fee). The road beyond El Castillo continues to **Monte de la Cruz** ❾ where a huge, illuminated cross sits in a cloud forest-reserve. For Sunday hikers from San Rafael, far below, this is a favorite destination.

Proceed downhill to the fork and turn back uphill to El Tirol. Costa Ricans like to stroll the roads, especially on Sundays, the traditional day for visiting with family; bus services are reduced on Sundays, further necessitating walking. *Tico* drivers are used to sharing the shoulder-less roads with pedestrians, but some foreigners in rental cars can find such driving conditions unnerving. Before El Castillo, look for a sign indicating **Bosque de la Hoja**. Here, you can hike along a lovely road bordered by graceful trees, for a mile or so, to the Heredia Water Works. From there, you can walk to other areas that are perfect for hiking, but you'll need a guide to find the trails. Rich Tandlich (tel: 267 6325), a local resident and guide, knows them all.

Tell the guard at El Tirol gatehouse that you are going to Hotel Chalet Tirol (tel: 267 6222) and drive through a residential area of weekend cottages and retirement homes set in alpine fields. A good road leads through a cypress forest where sun filters warmly through branches and dapples meadow wildflowers.

Hotel Chalet Tirol sits in the middle of a cloud forest reserve bordering Braulio Carrillo National Park. A fern-choked trail winding under orchid and bromeliad-laden old trees allows visitors to hike several hours through the cloud reserve to the border of the national park. A grove of A-frame wooden cottages awaits those who choose to spend the night.

As you descend, the warmth of the valley below is welcome. The road to San José de la Montaña is lined with flowers grown for export in wonderfully fresh, cool mountain air.

Barva and environs

In **Barva de Heredia** ❿, founded in 1561, colonial-era adobe houses surrounding the central park are being restored, giving the entire area the atmosphere of a colonial town. If you stand on the steps in front of the adobe **Basílica de Barva**, which dates back to 1767, and look out over the red tile-roofed adobe houses to the mountains beyond, you will get a sense of what the Central Valley probably looked like in the 18th century. The Basílica de Barva was built on an ancient Amerindian burial ground. Close by is the small grotto of the **Virgen de Lourdes** (1913).

In the hills just outside Barva is the lively and entertaining Aventura de Café tour at the **Cafe Britt ⓫** coffee farm, which takes you from raw bean to hot, steaming final product, using a multimedia, theatrical approach (open June–Nov daily 11am; Dec–May daily 9am, 11am and 3pm; entrance fee; transport to and from San José available; tel: 260 2748; www.coffeetours.com.) Ask to taste the ripe, red fruit that surrounds the coffee bean. It is surprisingly sweet and good, though beware eating too many at once as they act as a mild laxative.

In **Santa Lucía de Barva**, 4 km (2½ miles) north of Heredia, the **Museo de Cultura Popular** has renovated the charming and graceful González house, a 19th-century home, built just around the time that coffee cultivation was beginning to change Costa Rican life forever (open Mon–Fri 8am–5pm, Sat–Sun 10am–5pm; entrance fee).

Barva Volcano

There is a steep road to **Volcán Barva ⓬** that runs just above the town of Barva de Heredia, through San José de la Montaña and on toward Sacramento. The volcano is on the western side of Parque Nacional Braulio Carrillo; the approach road is in terrible condition and cars without four-wheel drive must be left 4 km (2½ miles) from the park entrance. From the ranger station it's an enjoyable hike through pasture land and cloud forest dripping with moss and epiphytes to the crater lake. An alternative one-hour hike will take you to **Laguna Barva** (2,900 meters/9,514 ft), a green lake in an extinct crater rimmed with trees.

ABOVE: Spanish fort, Heredia.
BELOW: Lankester Gardens.

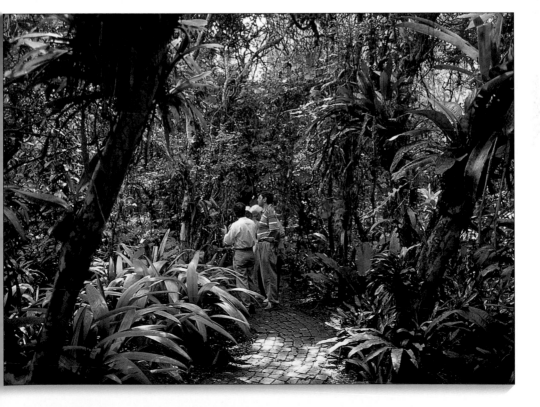

If you are still feeling energetic, there is the smaller Laguna Copey to explore, another 40-minute walk away. You may be rewarded by sighting a quetzal there – but don't bank on it. Wherever you hike on Volcán Barva, bring raingear, a compass and waterproof shoes or boots – even in the dry season – and be sure to keep to the designated paths. The roads in this area criss-cross one another and are not at all well-marked. Even *Josefinos* taking Sunday drives have to stop passersby and ask for directions.

Cartago and south

Cartago ⓲ (pop. 110,000) is 23 km (14 miles) south of San José. It was the capital of Costa Rica until 1823, when it lost its status to San José. Its illustrious colonial past is obscured, however, since repeated earthquakes and eruptions of Volcán Irazú have destroyed most of the colonial buildings. Throughout their history, Cartagans have attempted to build a temple to Saint James the Apostle, patron saint of Spain. The first church, begun in 1562, was finished in 1570, and was one of only two in the entire country. When it was destroyed, a stronger building was erected in 1580 on the same site. This, too, was leveled by the trembling earth. Subsequent churches met the same fate and when Cartago's massive cathedral, begun early in the 20th century, was toppled by the 1910 earthquake, all efforts to rebuild were abandoned. The roofless cathedral walls with their empty Gothic windows still stand. The site, called **Las Ruinas** (The Ruins), is now a garden with a small pond and is a popular and romantic spot.

Cartago, once the center of Costa Rican culture, is still her religious center. The enormous **Basílica de Nuestra Señora de los Angeles** (Basilica of Our

Vásquez de Coronado wrote to the Spanish king of Cartago:"I have never seen a more beautiful valley, and I have laid out a city between [its] two rivers."

BELOW: flowering bougainvillea in front of the 17th-century ruins of Costa Rica's oldest church at Ujarrás.

Map on page 146

Lady of the Angels), a Byzantine structure that dominates the landscape for miles, was built in honor of Costa Rica's patron saint, *La Negrita*.

From Cartago it is a short trip to the **Jardines Lankester** ⑭ in Paraíso de Cartago. It is said that Paraíso (Paradise) was named by weary Spaniards moving inland from the Atlantic coast who found its cooler weather and lack of malarial mosquitoes paradisical. English botanist Charles Lankester, sent to Costa Rica by a British company to work on coffee planting, arrived in 1900 at the age of 21. The coffee venture failed, but he decided to stay and bought 15 hectares (37 acres) of land to preserve local flora, especially orchids and bromeliads, and to regenerate a natural forest. Today, Lankester Gardens is run by the University of Costa Rica. Hundreds of species of orchids attract orchid fanciers from all over the world, particularly in the peak flowering months of January through April (open daily 8.30am–4.30pm; entrance fee). The garden is also a great bird-watching spot.

The Sanchiri Mirador, 2 km (1 mile) south of Paraíso, not far from Lankester Gardens, is a good place to stop for a light snack. The open dining room offers guests stunning views across the Orosí valley.

Ujarrás

South of Cartago the landscape becomes green, misty and almost magical, especially during the verdant rainy season. At **Ujarrás** ⑮, on a beautiful site in a sea of *chayote* vines, are the ruins of Costa Rica's oldest church, Nuestra Señora de la Limpia, dating from the 17th century.

The first place of worship constructed in this region was not the church, but a shrine in honor of La Virgen del Rescate de Ujarrás, who, in 1565, appeared to an Amerindian fishing on the banks of the Reventazón River. The apparition came from inside a small tree. The man carried the trunk to the center of Ujarrás, but by the time he got there, it had become so heavy that even a dozen men could not lift it. The phenomenon was interpreted by the Franciscan fathers as a sign that the Virgin wanted them to construct a shrine on that spot to be used by both the indigenous population and the Spanish, and so it was constructed.

A hundred years later, in 1666, so the story goes, a band of pirates led by the notorious Mansfield and Henry Morgan landed on the Atlantic coast of Costa Rica with the intention of sacking the country. The Spanish governor, Juan López de la Flor, assembled all available fighting men and sent everyone else to the mission to pray. The pirates came inland as far as Turrialba and then, mysteriously, abruptly turned back. Some say the pirates were tricked by de la Flor, who had posted the few men and guns he had at strategic points in the hills and then leaked the word that there was an ambush awaiting the pirates. A few gunshots from different points convinced the pirates to retreat. Other accounts say their retreat was a miracle worked by the Virgin. The grateful townspeople built the church of Ujarrás to commemorate the miracle, though it was destroyed 100 years later by an earthquake. Its remains stand among gardens and trees draped with Spanish moss.

BELOW: raging torrents flood the spillway of the dam at Cachí.

Near Orosí is La Casona del Cafetal, a restaurant set in the *hacienda* of a large coffee plantation overlooking Lake Cachí. The weekend buffets are extremely popular and lavish, with a whole table of coffee-flavored desserts.

BELOW: the Basilica of Our Lady of the Angels is one of the country's most sacred sites.

The Orosí River Valley

A few kilometers beyond Orosí, the **Cachí Hydroelectric Dam** channels waters from a reservoir on the Reventazón and Orosí rivers into an immense spillway. The concrete-dam structure contrasts sharply with the lush natural terrain surrounding it, as does the power of the rushing water with the peace of the river.

Just west of the dam is **La Casa del Soñador** (the House of the Dreamer), a simple two-story cane structure embellished with primitive wood sculptures. Here Macedonio Quesada, a famous Costa Rican primitivist artist lived and worked until his death in 1995. His work can be seen in galleries around San José, but it is best viewed in this charming cane building where his sons now work, producing melancholy *campesino* (peasant) and religious figures from coffee wood. Visitors are welcome.

The town of **Orosí 🔟** is untouched by the earthquakes that have leveled the colonial structures of Cartago, and it retains the look of an earlier Costa Rica, with wide streets and wooden houses with painted verandahs. Make your first stop Orosí Turismo, in the center, where you can pick up useful information on the town. Visit the colonial church of San José de Orosí (the oldest church in use in Costa Rica) and the former Franciscan monastery, now the **Museo de Arte Religioso** (Museum of Religious Art), just north of the church, which features artifacts from the colonial era (open Tues–Sat 1–5pm, Sun 9am–5pm; entrance fee). Take a walk around town and have a snack at one of the *sodas* or take a dip in the spacious heated *balneario* (pool). Just above the valley there is a lookout site *(mirador)* and park, maintained by the ICT (Costan Rican Institute of Tourism). Its large area of sloping, well-trimmed lawns provides spec-

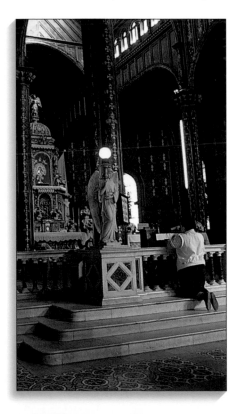

LA NEGRITA

The origins of Cartago's Basílica de Nuestra Señora de los Angeles are rooted in the miraculous. In 1635, a young girl walking through the forest that once grew on the site of the basilica discovered a dark-skinned statue of the Virgin Mary. A priest carried the statue, called La Negrita, to the parish church, but it mysteriously returned, twice, to its location in the forest.

In 1926, the Catholic Church built a basilica on the spot to house the statue. Today, in the shrine room, cases full of abandoned crutches, plaster casts and votive offerings (some made of gold) representing various parts of the body testify to the cures effected by La Negrita, Costa Rica's patron saint. Water from the spring behind the church is also said to have healing powers and the faithful fill their bottles from there.

On the patron saint's feast day, August 2, thousands of pilgrims gather at the basilica. Many walk the 22 km (14 miles) from San José; devoted penitents making the last part of the journey on their knees. Some walk from as far afield as Panamá and Nicaragua. On that day, the image of the black virgin is carried to another church in Cartago and then, in a solemn procession, through the city and back to its shrine in the basilica.

Map on page 146

tacular views over the Reventazón River with Cachí to the left and Orosí to the right. It makes a perfect spot for a picnic and a pleasant walk.

Tapantí National Park

The upper part of the **Orosí Valley** has enormous rainfall, rendering it unsuited for agriculture: thus it still has magnificent virgin rainforest. **Parque Nacional Tapantí ⑰** protects the rivers that supply San José with water and electricity. It also offers great birdwatching, fishing and river swimming. Birdwatchers will want to get an early start and arrive in Tapantí when the park opens at 7am. The drive from San José is especially beautiful at dawn. Past misty valleys and lush coffee farms, the last 10 km (6 miles) is over a rough road.

Trails are well-marked in the lower part of the refuge. Oropendolas – black, raven-sized birds with golden tail feathers and stout ivory-colored bills – nest in colonies within the park. Clusters of 30 or more pendulous nests hang from branches high in the trees. Two eggs are laid by the oropendola females, but parasitic giant cowbirds steal a spot in the nest for their own eggs, letting oropendola females raise their chicks. An exchange is affected, however, as the baby cowbirds, which feed on botflies, keep the baby oropendolas free from these parasites. Visitors usually hear oropendolas before seeing them. The males let out a gurgling, liquid-like song, then bow and flap their wings to females in unusual courtship displays.

The creek running parallel to Oropendola Trail is filled with smooth, warm boulders and invites hikers to cool their feet in the water, and perhaps lie back for a mid-morning snooze in the sun. However, it is always advisable to take raingear and warm clothes on the trails.

ABOVE: Orosí's colonial-era church.
BELOW: the House of the Dreamer, near Orosí.

Turrialba

Turrialba ⓲ (pop. 25,000) is a busy town bustling with people talking, yelling, buying, selling. The open fruit and vegetable market that lines the sidewalk along the river features some of the freshest and best-looking produce available in Costa Rica, most of it grown in the hills above town. Turrialba's reputation as a whitewater river-rafting center is growing, and rafters and kayakers from all over the world are discovering the Reventazón and Pacuare rivers *(see pages 98–99)*.

Just a few miles beyond the town of Turrialba on the highway is CATIE, the **Centro Agronómico Tropical de Investigación y Enseñanza** ⓳ (Center for Tropical Agronomy Research and Teaching). On this 800-hectare (2,000-acre) research plantation, scientists are experimenting with the introduction of more than 5,000 varieties of 335 species of crops with economic potential. More than 2,500 varieties of coffee and 450 varieties of cacao, as well as many varieties of bananas and pejibaye palms, are part of the seed bank of CATIE.

Work is being done here on the critical problems of deforestation, overgrazing and the sensitive ecology of the river basins. Guides demonstrate the cultivation, processing and care of palms, coffee, cacao and orchids. (If you are not with a group, call ahead to arrange a tour, tel: 556-2700.)

Visitors to CATIE and the surrounding areas can stay at the modest Hotel Wagelia in Turrialba or the more spacious Hotel Geliwa (tel: 556 1029) in a garden setting north of town. About 5 km (3 miles) out of town on the road toward Siquirres is the very luxurious Casa Turire (tel: 531-1111), a lavish plantation-style hotel in the grounds of a sugar cane, coffee, and macadamia nut plantation. In the mountains above the valley, not far away, is the Turrialtico (tel: 538-1111), which has handsome rooms with lovely views of Volcán Irazú.

ABOVE: Turrialba is a popular rafting center. **BELOW:** the symbiosis of water buffalo and egret.

Guayabo National Monument

The **Monumento Nacional Guayabo** ⑳ is the site of a large pre-Columbian center on the slope of Volcán Turrialba, 18 km (11 miles) from Turrialba. Archeologists are still unclear as to whether this was purely a ceremonial site or a combination administrative/ceremonial center. The ancient stone ruins and the remains of imposing stone roads radiating out to surrounding areas date from 1000 BC to AD 1400, when the site was abandoned for some as yet unknown reason, but speculation suggests disease or starvation.

Visitors can take a guided tour along a forest trail to the excavated area, which contains a complex system of stone aqueducts, building foundations, and roadways amid a setting of guava trees, wild impatiens and clusters of oropendola nests. Stone-lined graves, now empty, served as the first indication to archeologists that a cultural site was nearby. In addition, there are several large petroglyphs, the significance of which remains a mystery.

About 20 km (12 miles) north of Guayabo, on the slope of Turrialba volcano, is Volcán Turrialba Lodge, with comfortable wooden cabins and woodburning stoves to ward off the evening chill. Hikes and horseback rides to the volcano's extinct crater are exhilarating in the clear mountain air (tel: 273 4335).

On the way back to Cartago stop for rest and refreshment in the village of Cervantes at La Posada de la Luna (tel: 534 8330).

Irazú Volcano National Park

Easily accessible from Cartago is **Parque Nacional Volcán Irazú** ㉑. From the 3,800-meter (11,000-ft) summit, it is possible on a clear day to see both the Caribbean and the Pacific. Irazú, Costa Rica's highest volcano, also known as

Map on page 146

Around Guayabo grow the best pejibaye in the country. Every end of October there is a Pejibaye Festival in Tucurrique where you can feast on pejibaye, in sweet or savory dishes, and even drink pejibaye chiche (moonshine).

BELOW: volcanic farmlands on the Meseta Central.

TIP

Braulio Carrillo Park and Volcán Irazú Park both suffer from security problems. Don't leave anything of value in a parked car, and if you intend hiking, check first with the park authorities as to the security situation.

BELOW: relaxing at a lookout point over the beautiful Orosí Valley.

El Coloso, broke a 30-year period of silence with a single, noisy eruption on December 8, 1994. The previous eruption, on March 19, 1963, the day of the arrival of President John F. Kennedy in Costa Rica was even more powerful.

For two years Irazú continued to shower ash over much of the Central Valley. People carried umbrellas to protect themselves. Ash piled up on the Reventazón River, causing it to flood and destroy 300 homes. Roofs caved in from the weight of the ash and San José's air was temporarily turned black.

A visit to Irazú is a relatively easy half-day tour from San José. Visitors can go to the top ridge, walk along the rim of the main crater and look across another-worldly landscape consisting of a brilliant green lake and black-and-gray slopes, punctuated with plumes of white steam jetting into the air, escaping from fissures in the rock. There are also wonderful hiking and birding trails in the Prusia sector of the park.

Braulio Carrillo National Park

Only 45 minutes from downtown San José is **Parque Nacional Braulio Carrillo ㉒**. Take the highway to Limón and turn off before the Zurquí tunnel at signs to the Barva section of the park *(see page 151)*. Or alternatively, you can take the entrance 17 km (11 miles) beyond the tunnel to the Quebrada Gonzales station, where La Botella Trail is not so steep and strenuous. This is a great bird-watching trail but you have to get there early. The trails are often muddy and snakes are sometimes sighted; be sure to wear sturdy boots, long pants and mosquito repellent.

Occupying 445 sq. km (170 sq. miles) of mostly primary forest, Braulio Carrillo National Park was founded in 1978 thanks to pressure exerted by envi-

Map on page 146

ronmentalists who feared that the opening of a highway between San José and Guápiles would provide loggers and developers with access to rapidly vanishing virgin forest; deforestation had followed the opening of many other roads throughout the country. A compromise was reached: the road would go through, but the 32,000 hectares (80,000 acres) of virgin forest surrounding the highway would be preserved as a national park. The park thus embodies some ideals of enlightened progress.

Braulio Carrillo contains five distinctly separate forest habitats, dominated by the wet tropical forest. Hundreds of varieties of orchids and ferns, and a majority of the bird species native to Costa Rica are found here. In order to understand the life cycles, to spot the camouflaged wildlife and avoid missing hidden spectacular vistas, it is essential to arrange for a guide through the National Parks Service or an eco-tourism agency. Although the territory is vast, there are few through trails and many solo hikers get lost for days. The lingering impression of Braulio Carrillo is of vastness: huge canyons, misty mountains and the ubiquitous broad-leaf plant, the Poor Man's Umbrella, covering the hillsides.

Rainforests made easy

For a bird's-eye view of the forest canopy adjacent to Braulio Carrillo, take a ride on the **Rainforest Aerial Tram ㉓**, a 90-minute, 1.3-km (1-mile) trip through the forest's treetops, 35 meters (100 ft) above the forest floor. The "tram" allows visitors to experience the forest canopy up close: to breathe the steamy air, to catch the unforgettable tropical smell of damp, mossy tree trunks and, if you are very lucky, to spot the elusive wildlife. It is located about 5 km (3 miles) north of Río Sucio on the road to Puerto Limón, about 50 minutes

ABOVE: Costa Rica's national orchid.
BELOW: all aboard for the Rainforest Aerial Tram.

from San José (open daily, reservations recommended, tel: 257 5961; entrance fee includes tram ride, video and a short hike).

Amphibian-lovers won't want to miss the **Tropical Frog Farm** ㉔, 6 km (4 miles) past the Aerial Tram. On display are more than 200 tiny, colorful poison-dart frogs – easy to miss in the wild – along with their larger, nocturnal cousins, the endearing red-eyed leaf frogs that have become an almost ubiquitous mascot throughout Costa Rica. The frog farm next door to Restaurant Rancho Roberto also has original frog art for sale (entrance fee).

San José suburbs

On the west side of San José are the suburbs of Pavas, Rohrmoser, Escazú and Santa Ana. The rather colorless, modern suburbs of **Rohrmoser** and **Pavas** are chiefly of interest to certain travelers due to the presence of the Embassy of the United States of America. Owing to this, many diplomatic personnel live along the wide, nearly treeless streets of Rohrmoser, in modern houses protected by wrought-iron grillework.

Escazú ㉕ was originally a crossroads of trails between Amerindian villages. Because water was abundant there, the Amerindians found it a good place to spend the night on their journeys, and gave it the name Escazú, which in their language means "resting place."

Spanish settlers were also attracted to Escazú: they settled in the hills and began farming. It was during these early days that Escazú became known as the city of the witches. Today, the legends of witches remain, but the old adobe houses, painted blue and white to ward off witches, are being replaced by luxury condominiums.

TIP

The San José suburb of San Pedro is one of the capital's liveliest areas thanks to the presence of the university. It features several good restaurants, bars and nightspots, all of them noisy.

BELOW: the *Fiesta Dia del Boyero* in San Antonio de Escazú.

Escazú is an interesting if sometimes chaotic blend of old Costa Rica and a modern, international community, with a large contingent of North Americans. It is often jokingly referred to as "Gringolandia." The town center has adobe buildings; an attractive, Ravenna-style church; and, of course, a soccer field. Just outside of town are enclaves of fancy homes owned by North Americans, Europeans and wealthy locals, drawn to Escazú by the agreeable climate and superlative views. Unfortunately, the town's main road is now clogged with traffic and lined with fast-food chains, clothing stores and tall condominium buildings.

Map on page 146

In the hills to the east of the town, in an area called **Bello Horizonte**, are many fine old residences with lovely gardens. It is worth a drive through the hills of Bello Horizonte to visit **Biesanz Woodworks** (tel: 289 4337; www.biesanz. com), the studio/workshop of Barry Biesanz, an accomplished artist who works with Costa Rican hardwoods. Wooden bowls and boxes, remarkable for their grace and fluidity, are on display in his *hacienda*-style showroom, which is surrounded by an interesting herb garden with an ornamental pond.

San Rafael de Escazú is a newer section of town along the highway to Santa Ana. It has several shiny commercial centers where the town's glamorous inhabitants do their shopping, with international stores, supermarkets, a dazzling array of trendy restaurants and glitzy interior-design shops.

On the old road to Santa Ana, across from the new Los Laureles shopping center, there is a large walled compound with lights, guards, and surveillance paraphernalia. It isn't a high-security penitentiary: it's the residence of the United States Ambassador to Costa Rica.

ABOVE: Central Valley adobe house.
BELOW: Escazú celebrates its heritage of witches.

Santa Ana

Although condominiums, luxury villas and shopping centers are rapidly urbanizing the town, a rural atmosphere still survives in **Santa Ana ㉖**, a town once famous for its onions, which hang braided on the lintels and eaves of rustic restaurants along the road. On the west side of town there are still a few stands selling pottery, baskets and locally grown onions.

Above Santa Ana is a reminder of its recent agricultural past. The **Historical Museum of Agriculture** has displays of 19th-century farm implements, along with a traditional sugar mill and live animals (open Mon–Fri 8am–4pm, Sat–Sun 9am–5pm, entrance fee; tel: 282 8434). Lovely Santa Ana church reverberates with the sound of chamber music at the Baroque Music Festival, usually held the second week of November. It's an intimate, evocative setting with excellent acoustics.

Rancho del Macho (tel: 282 9295; closed Mon) is high in the hills above Santa Ana. Sit under the stars, overlooking the city lights, and enjoy the balmy breezes; sip a cold beer and partake of delicious grilled onions and barbecued chicken and beef. Another romantic aerie is the Mirador Valle Azul (tel: 811 8282) high above Escazú.

For a taste of modern luxury, the Hotel Alta (tel: 282 4160), half-way between Escazú and Santa Ana on the old road, has an excellent restaurant and sometimes exhibits local artists' work.

If you are in search of more ordinary pursuits, look for **Multiplaza**, one of the largest shopping malls in all of Central America. It is located just off the freeway on the way to Santa Ana, across the road from El Camino Real Hotel.

Ciudad Colón can be reached by backroads from Santa Ana, through rolling hills, or by way of the freeway. It's best known perhaps to those who have come to inspect the **University for Peace**, which is on a well-marked road not far out of town. The University for Peace, sponsored by the United Nations to study the ways of peace, and to offer a counter to the teachings of war colleges that predominate in many other countries, offers graduate courses to students from all over the world. There are hiking and birding trails throughout the property, as well as popular picnic areas beside a lake populated by geese and ducks.

Returning to Santa Ana via back roads, you will pass **El Rodeo**, a popular weekend restaurant where horses can be hired. The food is nothing special, but the gently rolling hills above it are beautiful and perfect for horseback riding.

Sarchí and surrounding villages

For a half-day excursion of craft shopping and sightseeing around typical Central Valley villages, head north through Alajuela toward Sarchí, stopping en route at **Grecia** ㉗. This tidy little place has been voted the cleanest town in Latin America. It is definitely worth taking a stroll around and is well known for its unusual dark-red, all-metal church. Just a few minutes' walk away is the popular World of Snakes, which has more than 150 snakes from all over the world (open daily 8am–4pm; guided tours; tel: 494 3700).

The approach to the mountain town of **Sarchí** ㉘ is unmistakable. Distinctive and colorful Sarchí decorative designs can be seen on bus stops, bars and bakeries, restaurants and houses.

Sarchí is a crafts center heavily geared toward the tourist trade where you can see artisans painting traditional ox-cart designs *(see pages 164–5)* and creating household furnishings out of tropical hardwoods. Around 1910, as legend has it, a *campesino* (peasant) was crossing the Beneficio la Luisa when it occurred to him to decorate his ox-cart wheels with colorful mandala-like designs inspired by ancient Moorish decoration.

Surprisingly, the art form caught on. Originally, each district in Costa Rica had its own special design and locals could tell just by looking at the cart where the driver lived. It was also said that each cart had its own distinctive "*chirrido*," or song of the wheels, by which people could identify who was passing by, without the listener even glancing upward.

As late as 1960, the most typical mode of transportation was the ox-cart since it was the only vehicle that could transport agricultural products through the rugged Costa Rican terrain. The father of president Oscar Arias Sánchez made his original fortune hauling coffee by ox-cart to Puntarenas. The painted carts are still in use today in villages as close to the capital as San Antonio de Escazú.

There are pleasant little roadside stalls on the outskirts of Sarchí selling homemade candied fruits, honey and fudge. In comparison to the large com-

Near Escazú, at the village of San Antonio de Escazú, an annual ox-cart festival, Día de los Boyeros, *is held the second Sunday of March. It attracts around 100 painted antique carts and the great oxen that pull them, plus thousands of visitors.*

BELOW: Grecia's metal church was imported from Belgium in 1897.

Map on page 146

mercialized furniture shops that predominate in Sarchí, a visit to these small stands is very friendly and personal, as though stepping into a Costa Rican home for a chat.

About 15 km (9 miles) up the road is the town of **Zarcero** ㉙. Should you arrive on a day when the highland clouds are swirling through the town or when a drizzling fog is bathing everything in soft, diffused light, you might feel that you have just walked into a fantasy dreamland.

Unique in Costa Rica, and possibly the world, is the **Parque Central** in Zarcero, a museum of topiary. Evangelisto Blanco, the park gardener, has clipped and pruned cypress bushes and hedges into a whimsical garden of amazing creatures: birds, rabbits, oxen, bulbous elephants with lightbulbs for eyes, a bull ring complete with spectators, matador and charging bull, a cross-bearing Christ, a man wearing a top hat, and a cat with tail flying, riding a motorcycle along the top of a hedge.

Evangelisto has been sculpting the hedges alone for over 40 years, 7 days a week, including holidays. The energetic compulsion of Evangelisto's work has been compared to the creations of Antonio Gaudí, in Barcelona in Spain, and of Simón Rodía, who created the Watts Towers in Los Angeles. Unable to afford marble or stone, Evangelisto works with the plants as his medium of self-expression creating extraordinary sculpted shrubs.

About 8 km (5 miles) after the turn off for Sarchí, along the Pan-American Highway, is the exit for the 200-year-old colonial town of **Palmares**. This lovely area used to be a tobacco-growing center. Unaffected by the vicissitudes of modern tourism, it is a model town through which to stroll and view typical *Tico* life. ❏

BELOW: taking a break from planting new coffee bushes.

POTTERS, SCULPTORS AND GOLDSMITHS

The Amerindians of Costa Rica left behind gold, pottery and stone artifacts. Most of their traditions were destroyed by the conquistadores

Because Costa Rica was a cultural and commercial meeting point for ancient civilizations in the Americas, native Costa Ricans absorbed and modified known techniques in ceramics, gold and jade work, weaving and stone carving. Early inhabitants, especially in the pre-Columbian port of Nicoya (in the province of Guanacaste), traded with travelers from as far away as Ecuador and Mexico. They also developed their own style of decorating pottery: beasts that are half-bird, half-man and people with exaggerated genitals, suggesting a fertility-rite culture. Examples of the pottery, which was widely traded, can be found throughout Central America.

Visitors to the Museum of Gold, the Jade Museum and the National Museum can see early pieces and learn more of their history and uses.

CRAFTSMEN AND ARTISTS

While the Spanish never found the gold deposits that inspired them to name the land "Rich Coast," early Costa Ricans worked with both gold and jade (not found in the country) to make statuettes and other decorative pieces. Although these traditions – along with stone work and the southern Pacific tradition of making fine white cloth – have been all but lost, pottery and the more modern craft of ox-cart decoration have been revived by the tourist dollar. For pottery, visit Guatil and Nicoya, for other crafts try Sarchí.

Other examples of Costa Rica's crafts, less compromised by modern tourism, are found in the south of the country; *molas* (hand-sewn appliqué) pieces are produced around Drake Bay, and both grotesque and beautiful balsawood masks are made by the Boruca people.

▷ **"HOUSE OF THE DREAMER"**
Self-taught sculptor Macedonio Quesada, who died in 1997, whittled charming statues depicting Costa Rican life. His two sons continue the tradition, sculpting in coffee wood in the Orosí Valley. Some of the pieces are for sale.

▽ **COTTAGE INDUSTRY**
Costa Rica's clay-rich soils provide excellent material for pottery, most of which is shaped without the aid of a potter's wheel. Many Guanacaste families have outdoor ovens for baking pots.

◁ **EARLY STONE WORK THE HARD WAY**
Early Costa Ricans used granite andesite and sedimentary stone to fashion stone figures with wooden tools. It is thought that they may have split the rocks by inserting wooden dowels into cracks and soaking them with water. The expanding wooden dowel would then have cracked the stone.

ORNAMENTED OX-CARTS

Used exclusively to transport coffee and other agricultural products until well into the 20th century, wooden ox-carts are unmistakably Costa Rican, and symbolize the self-reliance of the small farmer.

Ideally suited for the country's mountainous conditions and rutted dirt roads, ox-carts are still common in many parts of the country. The carts, which come in all sizes (including a miniature about the size of a toy car), are made in Sarchí, the wooden crafts capital of the country. There, master carvers began painting the carts in the early part of the 20th century. Originally adorned with bright colors and geometric patterns, these days ox-carts are being decorated with jungle scenes, wild animals, flowers and other non-traditional designs.

Visitors to Sarchí can have a go at painting the carts themselves with fine-tipped brushes, or alternatively they can leave it to the experts and order a custom-painted cart; these are often used as home bars or as decorations at hotels and the country estates of the wealthy.

◁ **BRILLIANT BIRDS, MAGNIFICENT MEN**
Reproductions of pre-Columbian gold figures make excellent gifts.

▷ **LIVING TRADITIONS**
Boruca Amerindians make their woven goods and carved gourds according to traditional designs.

◁ **PAINTED POTS APLENTY**
Although the Chorotega culture no longer exists, their descendants use water-based paints to decorate inexpensive pottery with whimsical animals and other pre-Columbian images.

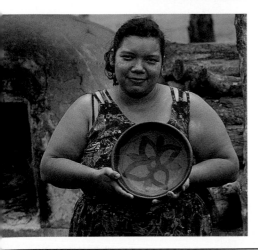

▷ **SONG OF THE WHEELS**
Neighbors can recognize the distinctive sound of each other's ox-cart in motion.

THE CENTRAL PACIFIC

Map
on page
170

*The Central Pacific beaches are among the best in Costa Rica,
and Manuel Antonio National Park is the stuff of tropical dreams.
And there is a host of natural wonders to see en route.*

San José

When the chaos of San José becomes just a bit too much, take a day trip
to the Pacific coast and get away from it all at the beach. The nearest is
Jacó, one of the country's most developed seaside destinations, a little
less than two hours away. Some of the country's finest beaches, at Manuel
Antonio National Park, are just an hour's drive south of Jacó, but if you don't
want to drive, there are inexpensive flights from San José to Quepos (adjacent
to Manuel Antonio). Buy tickets well in advance during the dry season.

The road to the coast

If you go by car, and want to take the fast route to the coast (as opposed to the
old scenic route, *see page 174*), turn off the highway toward Atenas, past the
Juan Santamaría International Airport, then head through La Garita de Alajuela.
One of the first lowland towns that you'll approach is Orotina. The road to
Orotina winds through coffee plantations built on precariously steep slopes.
Driving along the ledges of these mountains, the views are often of rich green
farmland and undulating valleys; and looking up at the almost horizontal estates,
you may find it difficult to imagine how coffee can possibly be harvested here.

PRECEDING PAGES:
Manuel Antonio
National Park.
LEFT: a cascade
waters the plants.
BELOW: scarlet
macaw at Carara
National Park.

As you approach the **Río Tárcoles bridge ❶**, you'll notice tourists clustered
at the railings, cameras and binoculars aimed down.
The fascination here is **crocodiles** – gray, primordial
behemoths, some as long as 7 meters (20 ft) basking
on the muddy banks or stealthily patrolling the brown
river, with only snouts and crenellated spines showing
above the waterline. Most reptilians in Costa Rica are
the smaller cayman species. This is the easiest place to
spot these larger American crocodiles or *crocodylus
acutus*. There can be as many as 20 of them lurking
here at the river's mouth.

The **Parque Nacional Carara ❷** borders the highway between Playa Jacó and Puntarenas just south of
the bridge. Carara lies in a transitional zone between
humid and dry forest, and sustains wildlife from mountainous terrain, primary and secondary forests, lagoons
and marshlands of the Tárcoles River. The vegetation
in Carara covers a similarly broad range: from shady
evergreens to clustering epiphytes and strangling vines.
Among the birds most commonly spotted here are
aracaris, toucans and guans, ducks and scarlet macaws.
Squirrel, howler, white-faced and spider monkeys are
often seen, and, very rarely, wildcats such as margays,
jaguarundis, ocelots and jaguars. There are also sloths,
coatis and agoutis, as well as a variety of reptiles and
lovely, blue morpho butterflies. Guides are invaluable
in interpreting the ecological complexity of this
reserve; available right at the park entrance, or by
advance request (contact the National Parks Service).

More than 200 pairs of scarlet macaws are the great glory of Carara. These enormous red, yellow and blue parrots mate for life and live for over 30 years. They nest in December, and in January the young are still in their nests. They make easy prey at this point for thieves who sell them on the black market. Ornithologists estimate that there are 1,500–2,000 scarlet macaws in Costa Rica, almost double the number there were 10 years ago, thanks to conservation programs. Public-education campaigns to discourage people from buying macaw chicks have had some effect in lowering the number of scarlet macaws in captivity, although it is impossible to estimate how many macaws are kept as pets.

In the evenings, when the lowlands cool, pairs of macaws fly down from their daytime feeding areas in the mountains. At sunset, park your car near the bridge over the Tárcoles River along the highway outside of the park entrance and listen for their raucous squawking as they fly to their roosting areas in the nearby coastal mangroves. Also watch for shorebirds and waders that frequent the estuary. Roseate spoonbills, with their startling pink plumage, are spectacular at sunset. Crocodiles bask on the river banks, apparently comatose, but are waiting for such a prize as one of the spoonbills.

The beaches

If you are anticipating the white-powder beaches washed by gentle, clear waters of tourist brochures, then the beaches of the Central Pacific could be something of a disappointment (Jacó is a dirty gray). The lure of these places is their proximity to San José, their big waves for surfers and their lively nightlife, not their picture-postcard perfection. Still, with a bit of exploration off the main road, and once away from the density and hustle of the central beach scene,

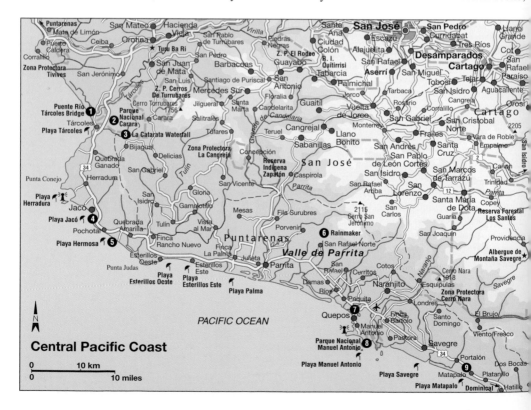

Central Pacific Coast

0   10 km
0   10 miles

PACIFIC OCEAN

you will find some clean and appealing beaches. **Playa Herradura** lies 5 minutes north of Jacó, its waves are gentle, and there is shade and trees for stringing hammocks on the public end of the beach; the other end is dominated by the huge Marriott Los Sueños resort and marina. **Playa Esterillos** is a huge 11-km (7-mile) stretch of mostly deserted beach, about 10 km (6 miles) south of Jacó, but beware strong riptides. Avoid Playa Tárcoles, which is polluted.

Crocodile tours run along the Tárcoles River, but don't use or encourage irresponsible operators who get their clients to feed the crocs with pieces of meat. Once a crocodile associates a person with food, it is one dangerous animal.

Several kilometers from the Jacó-San José highway, 17 km (10½ miles) before Playa Jacó, is **La Catarata Waterfall** ❸, a 200-meter (650-ft) high falls. The hour-long hike to La Catarata is strenuous: hikers must be in good physical shape and should bring plenty of water with them. Alternatively, horseback-riding tours to the waterfall can be arranged from the Complejo Ecológico La Catarata at the top of the falls (tel: 661 8263). Nearby, Hotel Villa Lapas offers hikes along suspension bridges, a canopy tour and comfortable rooms in an all-inclusive resort hotel (tel: 637 0232).

Map on page 170

Jacó Beach

Playa Jacó ❹ has a raucous, party-time, beach town ambience, with hammocks slung between coconut palms, and plenty of cold beer. *Cabinas* are inexpensive to rent and readily available; they are usually clean and often situated right on the beach. There are several hotels, with swimming pools, bars, air conditioning and tour packages to other points of interest in this coastal province. Perhaps the hotel pool is the best place to swim in Jacó since the

ABOVE: Caribbean coast T-shirt.
BELOW: iguanas are a common sight all over Costa Rica.

water is not very clean and there are dangerous undercurrents. Jacó has no shortage of amusements: horses, bikes, scooters and kayaks are available for rent. Chuck's Surf Shop rents surfboards, offers lessons and provides free information on surfing conditions. For dancing, try Club Olé; for billiards, visit the Jungle Bar, above the Subway sandwich shop. Men should be aware that the companionship of a local girl may cost them more than the price of drinks.

A haven of elegance amid the honky-tonk Jacó atmosphere is Hotel Poseidon (tel: 643 1642), in the center of town on a quiet side street. The restaurant serves sophisticated fare with a modern Pacific Rim take. At the far southern end of the beach, Hotel Club del Mar Resort (tel: 643 3194) offers another enclave of sophistication, comfort and tranquility.

Along the coast some 3 km (2 miles) from Playa Jacó is **Playa Hermosa 5**, one of the best surfing spots on the coast with very strong beach breaks. It is an easily accessible place where there is also a variety of wading birds to observe: great white herons and snowy egrets; and great blue, little blue, tricolor and little green herons. You may also see jacanas, walking on lily pads on their huge yellow feet; and black-bellied whistling ducks.

Head east on the coastal highway for 40 km (24 miles) to the small plantation town of **Parrita**, dominated by an enormous African oil-palm development, which was established in 1985. Oil palms do very well here. Palm-oil workers live next to the highway, in plantation villages of two-story, brightly painted homes, set in a "U" around what is the focal point of every *Tico* village: the soccer field.

Around 10 km (6 miles) east of Parrita is the tiny village of Pocares from where you should turn inland and continue for around 6–7 km (4 miles) to reach **Rainmaker 6** (tel: 288 0654), an exciting eco-project. Rainmaker allows visitors to explore the rainforest canopy with the minimum of environmental disturbance. Boardwalks link six suspension bridges; one bridge spans 90 meters (300 ft) and at the highest point of the trail you will be a dizzying 25 stories above the jungle floor. Visits must be booked in advance with operators in Quepos and Manuel Antonio (*see below*).

Manuel Antonio National Park

Once an important banana-shipping port, **Quepos 7** is now something of a dormitory town to Manuel Antonio, 7 km (4 miles) away. There are some good accommodations, restaurants, shops, and nightlife, a regular bus service, and the flavor of an old-time Costa Rican fishing and banana town. Its beaches are polluted, however. Reservations are essential during the vacation season at both Manuel Antonio and Quepos. The first mission in Costa Rica was established near here, in 1570. It was abandoned in 1751 and its ruins are located up the Naranjo River; the cemetery is still visible, as are remnants of the fruit orchard, which has regenerated from the original stumps.

Parque Nacional Manuel Antonio 8 (open Tues–Sun 7am–4pm; tel: 777 5185) is composed of three long strands of magnificent white sand, fringed by jungle and by the Pacific. The beaches are clean and wide. Above them are tall cliffs covered in thick jungle vegetation. This park is one of the few places in the coun-

BELOW: driving in Costa Rica is rarely without interest.

try where the primary forest comes down to the water's edge in places, sometimes allowing bathers to swim in the shade. In order to protect the eco-system of the park, rangers allow a maximum of 600 visitors on weekdays and 800 on weekends. Avoid weekends when the beaches can be crowded; early morning is the best time to visit when tourist groups are fewer and animal sightings easiest. There are always licensed naturalist guides available at the entrance to the park.

Playa Espadilla is the very popular public beach just outside the north end of the park. It is beautiful but has unpredictable riptides. You enter the park across an estuary, which at high tide often requires a boat ride. To get to **Playa Espadilla Sur**, the first beach in the park, follow the jungly path across a long sand spit called a *tombolo*. **Playa Manuel Antonio** and **Playa Puerto Escondido** require more hiking but the latter, accessible only at low tide, is less crowded. All provide relatively safe swimming, but watch out for rocks hidden by high tides.

There are excellent trails for hiking and wildlife sighting. Keep an eye out for all four of Costa Rica's monkey species – the aggressive, white-faced (or capuchin) monkeys that may steal your picnic (or bite you); the larger, acrobatic spider monkeys *(colorados)* that keep their distance; the sedentary leaf-eating howler monkeys *(mono congo)*; and the tiny squirrel monkeys *(titís)* that tumble through the treetops. Bird life includes more than 200 species, including boobies, frigate birds, pelicans and terns. Snakes and iguanas abound, and if you are sharp-eyed, you may be able to distinguish a sloth from a heap of vegetation in a *cecropia* tree. You can sunbathe, body surf, swim and snorkel (if you bring your own gear) and picnic. There are very rudimentary rest rooms and cold-water showers at Playas Espadilla Sur and Manuel Antonio. Outside the park, you can rent horses from Equus Stables (tel: 771-0001) for a jungle ride or go

Map on page 170

TIP

Beware of over-tame monkeys in search of a free lunch at Manuel Antonio. Don't feed them as you not only create a begging colony, but risk catching diseases should they bite you.

BELOW: one of the advantages of flying to Manuel Antonio is the bird's-eye view.

ABOVE AND BELOW:
beachside at
Manuel Antonio and
poolside at the
Costa Verde Hotel in
Quepos.

RIGHT: pavoncillo
flower.

on a four-hour sailing cruise offered by Sunset Sails (tel: 777 1304). Other options in areas outside the national park include mountain biking, whitewater river rafting or sea kayaking tours, available from Ríos Tropicales. For excellent assistance and information on the area, as well as books and papers in English and local handicrafts, go to La Buena Nota at the north end of the village of Manuel Antonio near the beach.

Just outside the park to the north, in the hills that rise up from the beach, there is a garish profusion of signs advertising an ever-growing number of hotels, restaurants and *cabinas*. With rare exceptions, most accommodations on the ocean side of the road are built on the cliffs above the beach and offer views of the ocean rather than direct access to beaches. One of the best views is from Hotel Sí Como No (tel: 777 0777; www.sicomono.com), a luxury eco-hotel that has won international prizes for its sustainability in both design and services.

You can get to Manuel Antonio by car, bus or plane. The road is paved all the way to Quepos, and new bridges have replaced the rickety old wooden ones. You pass through some beautiful countryside, although the flat coastal section runs through endless green corridors of palm plantations, which soon become monotonous. It's about a three-hour trip by car, some four hours by bus and 20 minutes by plane. SANSA and NatureAir fly daily to Quepos. A final word about Quepos/Manuel Antonio: theft is on the increase. Be attentive: don't leave your belongings unattended on the beach and keep valuables in your hotel's safe.

The old highway to the Pacific

The road less-traveled to Manuel Antonio heads west of San José, through Ciudad Colón and Puriscal. It was once *the* highway to the Pacific coast. Today, most traffic heads through Orotina, leaving the old route for those interested in a much more relaxed drive, through unspoiled mountain terrain.

About 6 km (4 miles) west of **Ciudad Colón**, the old highway passes through the Guayabo reserve of the Quitirrisí Amerindians, who sell woven vine baskets and other hand-made goods at roadside stands.

Santiago de Puriscal, a vital farming town with a once-beautiful church, damaged by an earthquake but still standing, is the last outpost of city life before reaching Quepos, on the Pacific coast. Soon after Puriscal the road is unpaved and winds its way through stunning mountains and valleys, carpeted with coffee, sugar cane and banana plantations, and rows of orange groves, populated only by small farms and settlements. This is untouched Costa Rica. Aside from one bumpy stretch just outside of Puriscal, the gravel road is generally in good shape, and there is little traffic. After the village of La Gloria the road quickly descends to sea level, south to Parrita, and onward to Quepos and Manuel Antonio.

Matapalo ❾ is a beach town 25 km (16 miles) south of Manuel Antonio on the Costanera Sur road (15 km/ 9 miles north of Dominical). The beach is long and quiet, the surf is big. To north and south respectively are **Playa Savegre** and **Playa Barú**, with seldom-visited but beautiful beaches. Visit both of these at low tide. ❏

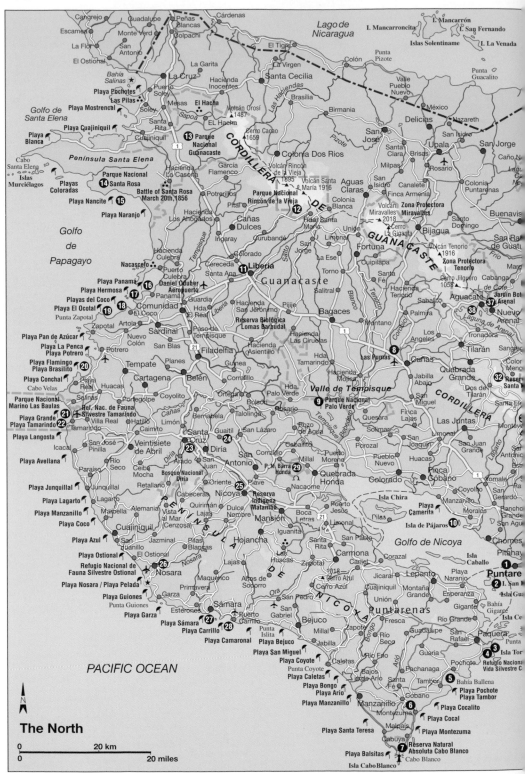

Cangrejo
Guadalupe
Peñas Blancas
Cárdenas
Escamea
Monte Verd
Colpachi
Lago de Nicaragua
I. Mancarroncita
I. Mancarrón
I. San Fernando
La Flor
San Antonio
El Tigre
Islas Solentiname
I. La Venada
El Ostional
La Garita
La Virgen
Colón
Punta Pizote
Punta Guacalito
Bahía Salinas ★
Hacienda Inocentes
Santa Cecilia
Valle Pueblo Nuevo
Playa Pochotes
Las Pilas
Puerto Soley
Las Haciendas
Brasilia
México
Playa Mostrencal
Mesas
El Hacha
Birmania
Delicias
Nazareth
Golfo de Santa Elena
Soley
Volcán Orosí ▲1487
San Isidro
San Jorge
Playa Cuajiniquil
Santa Rita
EL Hacha
Sapoa
San José
Santa Clara
Upala
Caño N
Playa Blanca
Cuajiniquil
13 Parque Nacional Guanacaste
Cerro Cacao ▲1659
Colonia Dos Rios
Brisas
Rosario
Colonia Puntarenas
Cabo Santa Elena
Península Santa Elena
Hacienda La Casona
García Flamenco
Volcán Rincón de la Vieja ▲1895
Aguas Claras
San Isidro
Canalete
Finca Armenia
Islas Murciélagos
Parque Nacional **14** Santa Rosa
Potrerillos
Volcán Santa María 1916
Parque Nacional Rincón de la Vieja **12**
Colonia Blanca
Volcán Miravalles ▲2018
Zona Protectora Miravalles
Santo Domingo
Buenavista
Playas Coloradas
Battle of Santa Rosa March 20th,1856
Pitat
Cañas Dulces
Hda. Santa María
Unión
Cerro La Giganta
Bijagua
San Rte de Guati
Playa Nancite **15**
Hacienda Los Ahogados
Curubandé
Fortuna
Volcán Tenorio ▲1916
San Ja
Playa Naranjo
Ingaray
Colorado
San Jorge
Limonal
La Ese
Quipilapa
Zona Protectora Tenorio
Golfo de Papagayo
Hacienda Culebra
Cereceda
Liberia
La Ese
Santa Fé
Cerro Jilguero 1056
Cabanga
Marg
Nacascalo
Puerto Culebra
Santa Ana
11 Liberia
Torno
Santa Fé
Hacienda Tenorio
Sabalito
Jardín Bot Arenal **37**
Playa Panama **16**
Daniel Oduber Aeropuerto
Guanacaste
Salitral
Palmira
Aguacate
38 Nuevo Arenal
Playa Hermosa **17**
Playas del Coco
Guardia
Pijije
Bagaces
Mántano
Los Angeles
Tronadora
Playa El Ocotal **18** Comunidad
El Coco
Hacienda San Jerónimo
Hda. Santa
19
Liberia
Hda. El Real
Reserva Biológica Lomas Barbudal
Tilarán
Sangare
Punta Zapotal
Zapotal
Artola
Paso de Tempisque
Hacienda Las Ciruelas
1
Color
Playa Pan de Azúcar
Nuevo Colón
San Blas
Las Pumas
Cañas
32 Rese Santa
Playa La Penca Playa Potrero
Sardinal
Filadelfia
Hacienda Asientillo
Hda. Tamarindo
8
Jabilla Abajo
Quebrada Grande
Dos de Tilarán
Playa Flamingo Playa Brasilito **20**
Tempate
Planes
Guinea
Hacienda Mojosa
San Miguel
CORDILLERA
Santa Ba
Playa Conchal
Cabo Velas
Playa Real
Huacas
Belén
Corralillo
Hda. Palo Verde
Valle de Tempisque
Finca Lajas
Las Juntas
Monte
Parque Nacional Marino Las Baulas
Selinas
Portegolpe
Coyolito
Ortega
Boleon
9 Parque Nacional Palo Verde
Quesara
San Joaquin
San Juan Grande
Sant
Anton
Playa Grande **21**
Ref. Nac. de Fauna Silvestre Tamarindo
Cartagena
Bernabela
Talolinga
Pozo de Agua
Porozal
San
Playa Tamarindo **22**
Villa Real
Hatillo
Cañas
Guaitil
San Lázaro
Caballito
Pueblo Nuevo
Huacas
Finca Cóbano
1
omale
Playa Langosta
Tamarindo
Caimito
Limón
Corralillo
Millal
Puerto Moreno
Colorado
Coyolho
San Gerardo
Ra
Icacal
San José Pinilla
Veintisiete de Abril **23**
Santa Cruz
Diría **24**
Nacaome
Isla Chira
Playa Camerita
Manzanillo
Moralco
Rancho Grande
Playa Avellana
Río Seco
Diriá
Arado
San Juan
San Antonio
Quebrada Honda
Puerto Jesús
Pilas
10
San Gerardo
Paraíso
Ceiba Mocha
Bosque Nacional Diriá
Oriente
Piave
P. N. Barra Honda **29**
Boca Letras
Limonal
Isla de Pájaros
Chomes
Pitahay
Playa Junquillal
Retallano
Nicoya **25**
Reserva Indígena Matambú
21
Golfo de Nicoya
Isla Caballo
Playa Lagarto
Junquillal
Lagarto
Cabeceras
Quirimán
Dulce Nombre
Iguanita
San Pablo
Corazal
Isla Tor
Lepanto
Playa Manzanillo
Manpella
Alemania
Vista al Mar (Cenzoa)
Lajas
Mansión
Carmona
Canjel
Jicaral
Montaña Grande
Playa Naranjo
2 I. San
4sla Gu
Playa Coco
Cuajiniquil
Jazminal
Pilas Blancas
Hojancha
Zapotal
Cerro Azul 1018
Esperanza
Gigante
Bahía Gigante
Playa Azul
San Juanillo
El Ostional
Las Huacas
Santa Rita
Cerro Azul
Cuajiniquil
Unión
Isla Ce
Playa Ostional
26 Nosara
Lajas
Maquenco
Altos de Soporro
San Pedro
PENÍNSULA DE NICOYA
Fresca
San Rafael
Paquera
Refugio Nacional de Fauna Silvestre Ostional
Primavera
Garza
Ora
San Gabriel
Bejuco
Puntarenas
Río Grande
Guadalupe
San Rafael
Punta
Playa Nosara / Playa Pelada
Punta Guiones
Estéronees
Sámara
Puerto Carrillo
Millal
Jabilla
Río Seco
Guaria
3 Isla Tor
Refugio Nacional Vida Silvestre C
Playa Guiones
Playa Garza
Playa Sámara **27** **28**
Punta Islita
Playa Bejuco
Zapot
Pachanaga
San Rafael
Playa Santa Sámara
Playa Carrillo
Playa Camaronal
Playa San Miguel
Caletas
Santa Fé
Tambor
5 Bahía Ballena
Playa Pochote Playa Tambor
PACIFIC OCEAN
Playa Coyote
Punta Coyote
Playa Caletas
Bajos de Ario
Cóbano
6
Playa Cocalito
Playa Bongo Playa Arío
Río Frio
Manzanillo
Montezuma
Playa Cocal
Playa Manzanillo
Malpaís
Playa Montezuma
Playa Santa Teresa
Cabuya
Reserva Natural Absoluta Cabo Blanco **7**
The North
Playa Balsitas
Cabo Blanco
Isla Cabo Blanco

N

0   20 km
0   20 miles

THE NORTHWEST

Map on page 178–79

Almost all of Costa Rica's natural attractions are represented in this large and rewarding region: miles of beaches and acres of tropical forests, interspersed with cattle ranges and cowboy towns.

San José

The northwest of the country is split into two provinces. The larger part is Guanacaste, Central America's Big Country, where vast grasslands are punctuated by huge spreading guanacaste trees and bony, white Brahman cattle. During the rainy season, the landscape is a sea of green but in the dry season, the savannahs become sun-baked tracts of gold. Though traditionally cattle country, Guanacaste is nowadays also known for its beaches, many of which have been developed as part of controversially large hotel/resorts. The international airport outside Liberia brings sun-starved tourists directly to their beach destinations.

Puntarenas province, which straddles the Gulf of Nicoya and takes in the South Nicoya Peninsula, is also becoming a vacation paradise of broad sandy beaches, turquoise waters and shady palm trees. Also just within this region (though it actually belongs to Alajuela province) is the very popular Monteverde Cloud Forest.

PRECEDING PAGES: the tabebria tree. **LEFT:** getting down and dirty. **BELOW:** Guanacaste cowboy.

The *Guanacastecos*

The *Guanacastecos*, as the residents of this province are called, are an independent people. Many are descended from the Chorotega Amerindians with skin the color of tortoise shell, eyes a warm brown, black wavy hair and an easy, friendly grace.

In 1787, the Captaincy General of Costa Rica, which then governed the country from Guatemala, decided that Guanacaste should be part of Nicaragua. There it stayed until 1821 when the Captaincy General was dissolved and the people of Guanacaste were asked to decide their own national identity. Opinions were divided: the Northerners around Liberia wanted to be a part of Nicaragua and the Southerners on the Nicoyan peninsula wanted to revert to Costa Rica. A vote was held and the majority elected to be a part of Costa Rica.

Puntarenas

Many people think that **Puntarenas ❶** (pop. 11,000) is simply a place to pass through to get somewhere else: namely, the islands of the Gulf of Nicoya, or the car ferries that cross the Gulf of Nicoya to the southern part of the Nicoya Peninsula.

Puntarenas used to be the country's main port, bustling with longshoremen, sailors on leave, prostitutes, and merchants from San José who traveled by train to escape the city and conduct their import/export businesses. But the growth of the port of Limón and the more recent opening of the deep-water port at nearby **Puerto Caldera** have made Puntarenas somewhat of a commercial anachronism.

Stretched along a narrow spit of sand – *punta de arenas*, or point of sand – Puntarenas is still worth exploring, though. You can even arrive here aboard a vintage diesel train, courtesy of the Tico Train Tour, which travels on weekends, leaving San José's old Pacific railroad station at 6am and arriving in Puntarenas at 11am (reserve ahead, tel: 233 3300).

Today, fishing is the main industry of Puntarenas and a visit to the busy fish market is exciting. Go early in the morning and watch expert shellfish shuckers and fish gutters at work.

Take a trip into the glorious waters of the Gulf of Nicoya aboard the luxurious, 70-ft (21 meters) Manta Ray *catamaran, which sails from the Calypso dock in Puntarenas.*

The tourism industry is small, though there are some recently spruced-up large hotels. There's also the new Puntarenas Marine Park at the east end of town with 28 large aquariums showcasing the marine life of the Gulf of Nicoya (open Tues–Sun 8am–4pm; entrance fee; tel: 661 5275). With its views of the long, arching coastline, the beach along the gulf is beautiful, and the sunsets over Nicoya are spectacular. Though the ocean waters were until quite recently badly polluted, they have now been cleaned up, and Puntarenas town beach now flies the Bandera Azul (blue flag), denoting an eco-friendly, clean beach inspected by government officials. The estuary and rivers, however, should be avoided.

Downtown

The crowded center of Puntarenas, three blocks back from the beach, bustles in the morning as the townfolk conduct business, often getting around town on bicycles. Everyone seems in a hurry, perhaps to accomplish what they need to before the onset of the afternoon heat. Though, like San José, an architectural victim of excessive concrete, Puntarenas still retains many of its older build-

BELOW: beach goers at Puntarenas.

ings: plank structures with latticework below the roof to permit the breeze. The wooden buildings are painted in such color combinations as bright turquoise and red, and together with the few remaining mansions of the merchants and the magnificent stone church, they convey the flavor of a Puntarenas in its prime.

Map on page 178–79

Visit the museum in the **Casa de Cultura** (House of Culture), formerly the city's jail, where exhibits feature the area's history, geography, natural history and indigenous crafts (open Mon–Sat, closed noon–1pm; free), plus the **Museo Histórico Marino** (open Tues–Sun; entrance free), for a look at the city's seafaring history.

Evening is perhaps the best time to catch Puntarenas. Enjoy a late afternoon *refresco* at one of the *sodas* (cafes) on the mile-long, broad **Paseo de Turistas** fronting the beach and watch the sun sink below the mountains of Nicoya across the bay. The *sodas* offer a chance to try some native Costa Rican fruit drinks. This is perhaps the only place in the country to get *maté*, a type of milkshake with a lingering, nostalgic aftertaste. Try a cold, creamy *pinolillo* made with toasted, ground corn, or a "Churchill," a very sweet, cold fruit drink that includes condensed milk.

Seafood restaurants and hotels line the oceanfront. Most are air-conditioned or adjusted to catch the ocean breezes. The hotels along the estuary also offer free mooring and facilities to cruising sailboats. The Yacht Club here is extensive, well protected, professionally managed, and one of the very first stops a trans-oceanic yacht makes on the first leg of a trip from the West Coast of the US to more distant ports of call.

Just to the south, down the coast from Puntarenas, is **Playa Doña Ana**. Here the Tourist Institute (ICT) has developed a beach resort with bar, restaurant,

ABOVE: crushed-ice fruit drinks stand. **BELOW:** paddling a kayak in the Gulf of Nicoya.

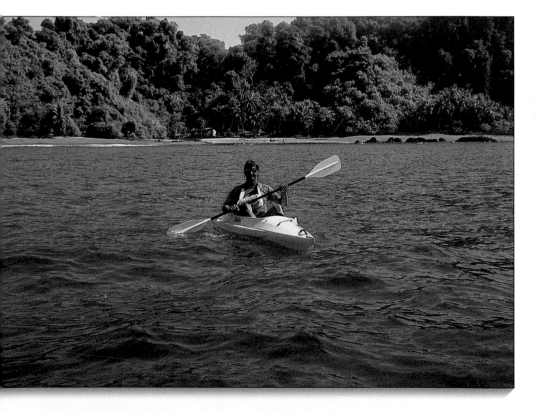

showers and parking, on a cove well situated between two spectacular rock headlands. Costa Rica's second-largest surfing wave is just offshore and there are fantastic facilities for surfers, including rentals and repairs.

The Gulf of Nicoya

Car ferries, as well as a smaller passenger-only *lancha* (launch), cross from Puntarenas to Paquera on the **Nicoya Peninsula**. The two-hour trip across the gulf passes by 40 or so islands, including **Isla San Lucas ❷**, Costa Rica's former prison island. The prison was closed in 1991 and the island deserted, except for the guards posted there to prevent vandalism. There are no restrictions preventing visits to the island, however, and visitors who are so inclined can view disturbing reminders of the life prisoners endured here.

Calypso Tours offers a cruise on its 21-meter (70-ft) catamaran and visits to the islands in the Gulf of Nicoya. It crosses the waters of the Gulf and visits **Isla Tortuga ❸** (Turtle Island), where, in an idyllic setting of white sand and turquoise waters, you can enjoy what is perhaps the best seafood buffet in the country, as well as folk music and entertainment. There is also adequate time for swimming, snorkeling and sunbathing. Calypso, one of the oldest tour operators in Costa Rica, also offers other excellent tours, including fishing trips (tel: 256 2727).

The South Nicoya Peninsula

The ferry ride across the Gulf of Nicoya brings you to a different world. It is one of seasonally dry grasslands, gigantic spreading trees, rolling cattle ranches, memorable bays and beautiful beaches.

TIP

If you like a game of golf or enjoy horseback riding, there are resorts on the Nicoya Peninsula that specialize in both activities.

BELOW: tumbling waters at Catarata de Cangreja, one of the hiking destinations in El Rincón de la Vieja.

From the ferry landing at Paquera, Tambor is just a short drive, and Montezuma is about an hour away. Buses wait to meet the Paquera ferry to head south to Montezuma, but there are no such direct services from Playa Naranjo. If you are driving south from Paquera, the roads are largely unpaved, with few road signs, but the local people are used to giving visitors directions.

The drive along the peninsula, although rough, is rewarding. It traverses miles of pastureland, through small towns and villages, past people on horseback and dwellings of every description – and every now and again reveals views of the blue bays of the Pacific.

Some 7 km (4½ miles) south of the town of Paquera lies the **Refugio Nacional de Vida Silvestre Curú ❹** (Curú National Wildlife Refuge). Although small, the park encompasses five habitats and offers sanctuary to a surprisingly large and diverse number of plants, animals (including the white-faced monkey) and over 220 species of birds. It has three beautiful beaches, ideal for swimming and diving. There are very basic accommodations available, along with horseback tours and sea kayaking to nearby islands. The hiking is also excellent. The refuge is private property, owned by the Schutt family; it's a good idea to call in advance to arrange accommodations and tours (tel: 710 8236).

Bahía Ballena

A large, wide bay, **Bahía Ballena ❺**, which means Whale Bay, is a place of surprising beauty and tranquility. The waters are gentle and warm, with large flocks of pelicans diving for fish. January is an especially good time for sighting whales. The bay shelters two beaches, **Playa Pochote** and **Playa Tambor**. In the 1990s, however, its tranquil face was irrevocably and controversially

Map on page 178–79

BELOW: a Costa Rican bullfight, where only the *toreros* get hurt.

transformed by the construction of the enormous, Spanish-owned resort, Hotel Barceló Playa Tambor. The project inspired a passionate debate about what kind of tourism is best for Costa Rica: mammoth projects such as this, or small businesses that reflect the character of their communities. In the end, big business won. In the village of **Tambor**, inexpensive lodgings and good local-style meals can be found, and you might just get a sense of life as it was before the arrival of big-time tourism. Continuing southeast to the town of Cóbano the road leads to Montezuma.

Montezuma

Montezuma ➏, in many ways, feels like the end of the line. The partially paved road rolls down a hill and ends abruptly in front of a row of funky hotels, trendy new restaurants and bars, and *cantinas* (snack bars) on the beachfront. Here, young North American and European travelers far outnumber the local people, who have accepted them with seeming good grace. Hotel rooms fill up quickly everywhere in Montezuma during the dry season and peak holiday times, so reserve well ahead.

Lodging and dining in Montezuma ranges from the basic to the luxurious, and the beach-going is exceptional. To the north of town there are wide, sandy beaches, with beautiful clear water. A scenic footpath leads north for 6 km (4 miles) to a dramatic waterfall that spills into a pool right on the beach. To the south, the surf crashes against volcanic rock – and, just a short hike away up a river, there is another waterfall with a pool for swimming. The first couple of rocky bays north of Montezuma have strong currents, but Playa Grande is safe for swimming.

BELOW: young *Guanacastecos* get in the saddle at a very early age.

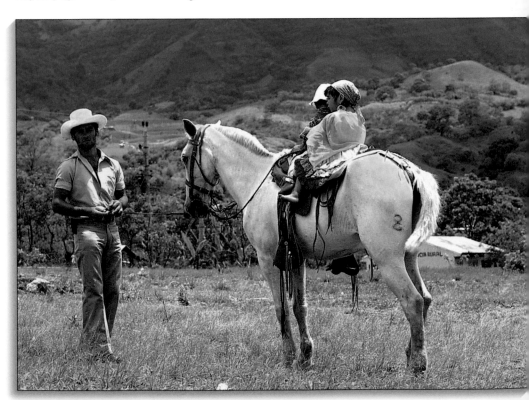

You can rent bikes and boogie boards at agencies in town, and horses through the Finca Los Caballos, outside of town, as well as through in-town tour operators. But most visitors to Montezuma seem to spend their time swimming, sunning or simply hanging out in this laid-back place that seems expressly designed for the youthful, low-budget traveler. Perhaps the most romantic restaurant in all of Costa Rica is tucked away on a rocky cove, a few minutes' walk south of town. Playa de los Artistas specializes in seafood served al fresco at driftwood tables illuminated at night by lanterns and starlight (closed Sun; tel: 642 0920).

Map on page 178–79

Cabo Blanco

It is almost 11 km (7 miles) from Montezuma to the **Cabo Blanco Absolute Wildlife Reserve ❼** (open Wed–Sun 8am–4pm) along a little-used, unpaved road that runs parallel to the beach. There's a cluster of small *cabina*-hotels in the town of Cabuya. The reserve, established in 1963 through the inspiration and tireless efforts of Swedish immigrant Nils Olaf Wessberg, is Costa Rica's oldest protected wildlife region. Sadly, Wessberg was murdered while trying to establish a similar reserve in the Osa Peninsula, and he is fondly recalled as an important pioneer of the parks system in Costa Rica.

Originally, Cabo Blanco allowed no public access: all life there was to be protected, without any interference from humans. Today, however, approximately one-third of the reserve is open to visitors. It encompasses a wet, tropical forest on the tip of the peninsula and is one of the most scenic spots along the whole Pacific coast. It is also one of the hottest, so bring plenty of water. There is a large population of marine and shore birds as well as mammals.

ABOVE: spiky agave in Cabo Blanco.
BELOW: waiting for the tide to turn in the Nicoya Peninsula.

In addition, there is a ranger station with restrooms and picnic tables, well-maintained trails and a lovely remote beach, where you may swim but not snorkel.

Strict rules guide the behavior of all visitors, starting with registration and a briefing at the reserve's administration center. To drive to the reserve you must cross two small streams, for which a four-wheel drive vehicle is recommended. The reserve is closed on Monday and Tuesday to reduce the impact of tourism.

Beyond Cabo Blanco, the road is rough and unpaved. During the rainy season it is muddy and some of the rivers and creeks without bridges are only passable in a four-wheel drive vehicle. During the dry season things don't get any more comfortable as vehicles churn up a fine, brown dust coats travelers and plants along the roadway.

Surfers and nature-lovers have recently discovered Malpais and Santa Teresa, two beaches about 6 km (4 miles) north of Cabo Blanco. A clutter of hotels and restaurants has sprung up almost overnight to cater to an international, young surfing crowd. There are also a few luxury retreats here.

The Interamericana northbound

From San José the Interamericana Highway, route C1, cuts northwest straight through the heart of Guanacaste, via its capital, Liberia, and northward to Nicaragua.

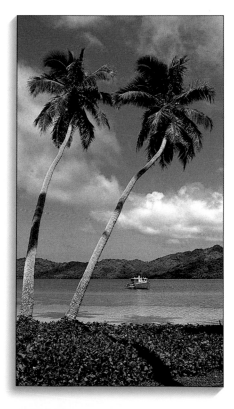

At **Cañas** you first get the sense that immense Guanacaste is more like a separate country, caught somewhere between Costa Rica and Nicaragua, than it is a province of Costa Rica. Cañas, which was named for the fields of white-flowered wild cane that covered the countryside, is a cowboy town, with a frontier feeling, not unlike a village in Mexico.

Four kilometers (2½ miles) north of Cañas on the highway is **Las Pumas** 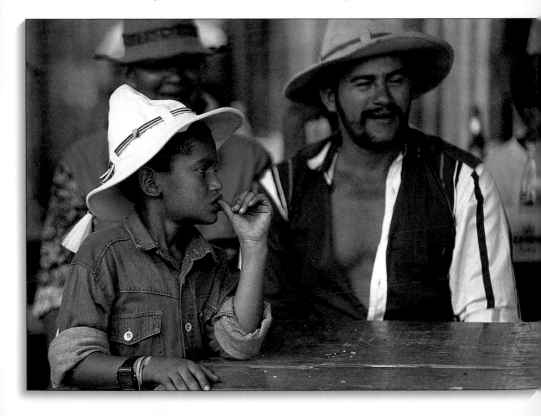, a private wildlife refuge that provides a shelter for some of Costa Rica's large cats that, for various reasons, are not able to live in the wild (open daily 8am–5pm; donations requested).

Nearby, **Safaris Corobicí** offers guided "floats" down the Corobicí River on its 6-meter (17-ft) Avon rafts, a wonderful opportunity to observe the river habitat, especially the birds – laughing falcons, herons, trogons, wood storks, motmots, parrots, osprey, and, of course, egrets. Howler and white-faced monkeys all make their homes along the shores of the Corobicí. Plan for an early-morning trip to enjoy the best birding (tel: 669 6191).

Palo Verde National Park

Parque Nacional Palo Verde ❾ is one of Central America's largest protected wildlife areas, situated near the mouth of the Tempisque River. To get there take the road from Bagaces to the west, off the Interamericana highway. Four-wheel drive is recommended, especially during the rainy season. If you are traveling independently, note that the southern entrance to the park, from Cañas, may be closed; be sure to call the National Parks Service office (tel: 200 0125) to find out which routes are open and which are the most navigable. Alternatively, book a tour with one of the many operators who visit here.

Founded 20 years ago by a Swiss animal-lover, Las Pumas provides a haven for rescued wild cats and other animals. Since the death of its founder, it has been run by the non-profit Hagnauer Foundation; donations are welcome.

BELOW: father and son at a rodeo near Liberia.

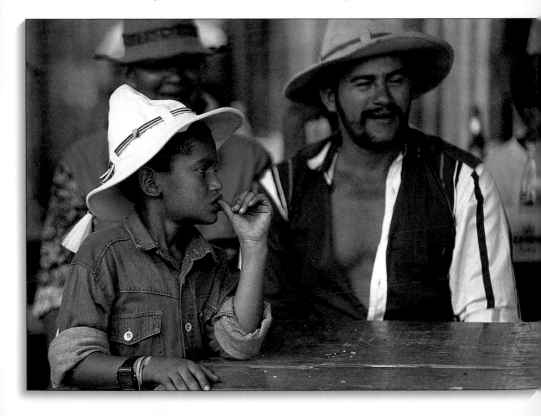

Palo Verde encompasses lakes, swamps, woodlands, grasslands and forest and is a major sanctuary for migrating waterfowl in Central America. Tidal fluctuations and seasonally overflowing rivers attract 300 species of terrestrial and waterbirds, including herons, whistling ducks, ibises and the immense Jabirú stork. Large mammals and reptiles are also abundant and can easily be seen during the dry season when they gather at waterholes. Coatimundis, armadillos, iguanas and crocodiles measuring up to 5 meters (15 ft) long are not uncommon here. You can stay in dormitory-style lodging in the park or in the more comfortable lodge run by the Organization for Tropical Studies (tel: 240-6696).

Only 25 years ago, currents and sediment run-off from Guanacaste formed a sand bar, which then became stabilized as an island in the middle of the Tempisque River near the head of the Gulf of Nicoya. Today, it is known as **Isla de Pájaros ⓾**. From the park, you can charter a boat and guide. This quiet place provides the isolation that is favored by many water birds. While the white ibis and a species of egret are the only birds that regularly nest here, roseate spoonbills, wood storks and anhingas also occasionally make their homes on Isla de Pájaros.

Map on page 178–79

Liberia

The capital city of Guanacaste province, **Liberia ⓫** was established over 200 years ago. It is also known as *Ciudad Blanca*, the White City. Original residents took the white volcanic earth and gravel from the nearby slopes of Rincón de la Vieja and Miravalles volcanoes to construct traditional white adobe homes. In the *Puertas del Sol* – "Doorways of the Sun" – style, these houses were designed to let both morning and afternoon sunlight into north-facing corner houses. Many of these lovely old adobe homes can still be seen, situated off the city's narrow streets, just south of the park. Some of them are in the process of being restored, and the owners may welcome visitors inside to see the work in progress. Many of the houses have classical courtyards and grand rooms with high ceilings and 19th-century murals. The kitchens, to the rear of the house, open onto courtyards, where corn and other grains were once dried.

ABOVE: Sunday-best cowboy tack.
BELOW: bubbling mud pots at Rincón de la Vieja.

Early morning is an ideal time to take a walk through the center of Liberia. Visit **Agonía Church**, (located at the end of the main street) an adobe structure built in 1852 and one of the oldest Catholic churches in the country. Apart from these few colonial-era remnants, Liberia is starting to resemble a giant shopping mall and even has a multiplex cinema now on the outskirts of town.

Rincón de la Vieja National Park

Continuing upcountry from the city of Liberia is the **Parque Nacional Rincón de la Vieja ⓬** with four complete ecosystems contained within its 14,000 hectares (35,000 acres). The name, which applies to both the park and the volcano it protects, derives from the legend of an old woman who once lived on its slopes. Her house was referred to as "the old woman's corner" – hence Rincón de la Vieja.

BELOW: four-wheel drive vehicles are a good option if you can afford it.

Las Pailas

The turn-off for the park from the Interamerican Highway is just 5 km (3 miles) northwest of Liberia. The road to the Las Pailas entrance, via the small community of Curubandé, is very rough, slow-going for 17 km (10 miles). The road appears to be covered in snow but it's actually chalky limestone, the same rock that was used to build the early houses in Liberia, explaining its nickname of the White City. Spectacular views along the way include the green slopes and towering cone of the volcano to the north and, to the west, a verdant valley with grassy coastal plains edging the Pacific Ocean far below.

At the Las Pailas ranger station, you sign in and pick up a map of the park and the hiking trails. Just steps away is the park's most spectacular volcanic area, **Las Pailas**, Spanish for "the kitchen stoves". There is a well-marked self-guided loop tour around 8 hectares (20 acres) of hot springs, boiling mud pots, sulfur lakes and vapor geysers that color the surrounding rocks red, green and vivid yellow. Researchers announced the discovery of a new organism that thrives here in the boiling mud. It may prove useful in helping plants adapt to higher temperatures with global warming. Your nose will also be tingling with the strong aroma of rotten eggs (sulfur) here. The warm mud from the so-called *sala de belleza* (beauty salon) makes an excellent facial mask. Visitors must exercise extreme caution, however, and stay on the trail. Breaking through the brittle surface of the area or getting a face full of steam can result in severe burns.

Cangreja waterfall

From the Las Pailas entrance you can hike about two hours to the **Cangreja Waterfall**. The water fall is 40 meters (132 feet) high and cascades down to

form a blue pool. Take a dip in the refreshing swimming hole edged with pockets of contrasting thermal waters. If you tread softly, the wildlife viewing here is very good. Listen and look for the park's famous resident, the long-tailed manakin, a red, blue and black bird whose song sounds like "toledo" (the bird's name in Spanish).

The two closest lodges to the park are **Rincón de la Vieja Lodge** (tel: 200 0238), a collection of rustic cabins with good hiking trails to nearby hot springs and an excellent canopy tour; and **Hacienda Guachipélin** (tel: 666 8075), a more upscale lodge with good food and lots of it. It's also a working ranch, with first-rate horses and miles of hiking and birding trails and adventure activities, including canopy tours and river tubing.

To the Nicaraguan border

At the end of a day in this region, consider making a short trip east to the village of Santa Cecilia to watch the sun set over **Lake Nicaragua**, or as the Nicaraguans have named it "the Sweet Sea". You may be fortunate enough to see freshwater sharks.

During the civil war in Nicaragua, many of the local young men from this area were drawn into the battle, either for or against the US-backed Contra forces who were trying to overthrow the ruling Sandinistas. Near here, in the northern addition to Santa

Map on page 178–79

Rosa National Park, a clandestine CIA airstrip was constructed to bring in supplies to aid the Contra effort, in violation of Costa Rica's neutrality laws. Built with the blessing of ex-president Alberto Monge, it was torn up under the administration of Oscar Arias in 1986. The Reagan administration took great umbrage to this and drastically decreased US aid money for Costa Rica *(see page 195)*.

A rise in the bumpy road about 8 km (5 miles) beyond the center of Santa Cecilia brings the vast inland sea that is Lake Nicaragua into view. William Walker *(see page 45)* planned to conquer Nicaragua and to use the Nicaraguans as a labor force to build canals from Lake Nicaragua to the Pacific. He envisioned a waterway to transport goods by boat across the isthmus from the Pacific to the Atlantic. Wealthy investors in the United States backed this plan. But the defeat of Walker in Costa Rica, and later in Nicaragua and Honduras, put an end to the venture.

A trip to the bay at **Puerto Soley**, the northernmost Pacific beach of Costa Rica, passes through the small town of La Cruz, a stopping place for those traveling north through Central America, and for migrant laborers from Nicaragua crossing back and forth, seeking work in Costa Rica.

From La Cruz, there are wonderful windswept views of the valley and Salinas Bay situated below. Winding down the hill, you will pass a ranch established by Anastasio Somoza, the ex-dictator of Nicaragua, before reaching Puerto Soley, a windy beach with a new villa complex. The wind is so strong here that the windsurfing conditions rival Lake Arenal. Kite-surfing has also become popular here at Playa Copal where there is a kite-surfing school (tel: 826 5221).

BELOW: bathing in the waterfall at Rincón de la Vieja National Park.

TIP

In Parque Nacional
Santa Rosa there are
fine views from the
look-out point at the
Monumento a los
Héroes – a large
concrete arch that
commemorates those
who fell in battle at
Santa Rosa in 1856.

Guanacaste National Park

Parque Nacional Guanacaste ⑬ was created in 1989 with foreign funds donated to Costa Rica's Neotropica and National Park foundations in order to protect the migratory paths of animals living in the adjacent protected area of Santa Rosa National Park *(see opposite)*.

Parque Nacional Guanacaste encompasses a wide band of largely deforested land that extends from the Orosí and Cacao volcanos to the Pacific coast. Dry tropical forest dominates this vast land, but habitats ranging from mangrove swamps and beaches to rain- and cloud forest are also located within the park's boundaries.

Over the past several hundred years, complex patterns of cutting, grazing, burning and farming have dissected Guanacaste's landscape into a complex mosaic of life zones.

The American visionary ecologist, naturalist and conservationist, Dan Janzen, whose life work has been the preservation and reforestation of Guanacaste, feels that this park will ultimately be restored to its original state. "Dry forests have been destroyed," Janzen says, "but they are tough, able to withstand six months of drought a year and are very regenerable." With the acquisition of Parque Nacional Guanacaste, the large tracts of land necessary for successful forest regeneration are now protected and under national park management. The park sustains large populations of many animal species that are able to find refuge during summer droughts and migrate freely between "islands" of forested areas.

Animals eat and disperse seeds from the trees, and have created these forest islands. Rainforest insects, important for pollinating dry forest plants, are attract-

BELOW: a deserted
Pacific Coast
beach.

ed from nearby mountain slopes. In 20 years, significant canopy forest will have developed. And, in 200 or 300 years, full-grown tropical dry forests may again dominate Guanacaste.

Map on page 178–79

Santa Rosa National Park

Parque Nacional Santa Rosa ⑭ encompasses virtually all of the environmental habitats of the region. A nearly infinite system of trails takes visitors through zones of deciduous tropical hardwoods to arid mountains with deserts of cactus and thorny shrubs, and along rivers lined with forests to mangrove-swamp estuaries near the beach. Two of its remote beaches, Nancite and Naranjo, are important turtle nesting sites. Elsewhere, many mammals, including monkeys and peccaries (wild pigs), plus over 20 species of bats, live in the national park.

During more than 20 years of scientific work at Santa Rosa, Dan Janzen has taught two generations of local people an intelligent appreciation of the forest. Through his work, residents of Guanacaste now have experience and expertise in firefighting, maintaining horses and managing cattle, identifying plants and dealing with "biotic challenges" like ticks, diseases, thirst and wounds. Jobs as research assistants, guides and reserve caretakers provide many with skills and a stable, long-term source of income.

Along Santa Rosa's short **Naked Indian Path**, as with many of the park's trails, you pass through forest that, during the dry season, loses many of its leaves, making wildlife viewing easier for the naturalist. Huge multi-colored iguanas are commonly seen in the trees bordering the trail. Hiking toward Duende Creek and the bat cave, look for them sunning on tree branches.

ABOVE: pestle and mortar, La Casona.
BELOW: a Guaitil potter at work

Santa Rosa's significance as the location of the historic battle against William Walker *(see page 45)* was a primary factor in the government's decision to make it a national park. A decisive battle against Walker took place at **La Casona** ("The Big House") *hacienda*. By coincidence, on the three occasions that Costa Rica has been invaded, it has been here that the invaders were eventually turned back.

Today, a different kind of battle is fought in Santa Rosa. The rangers at the station tell of their encounters with hunters. Though hunting is outlawed in the park, the law is virtually unenforceable due to the inadequate number of rangers. Armed hunters are frequently met by unarmed rangers who often must fight them to remove them from park boundaries. The low-paid rangers often risk their lives in these skirmishes.

The long-running battle between rangers and poachers reached a terrible climax in May 2002, when a pair of disgruntled hunters set fire to La Casona, the historic farm estate *(see above)*, and burned it to the ground. The house, a landmark in Costa Rican history, has since been rebuilt and once again provides a window into the life of Costa Ricans during the colonial period (open 8am–4pm).

A trail leads from the house to a memorial to the heroes and martyrs of the battle. President Juan Rafael Mora's famous speech, in which he exhorted his countrymen to defend Costa Rica against William Walker, is preserved on an historic plaque.

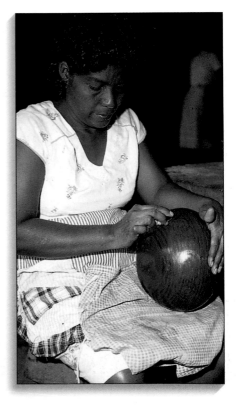

Wartime secrets

The northern section of the national park was expanded to include the ranch of former Nicaraguan dictator Anastasio Somoza, who lived there so he could move easily and clandestinely back and forth across the border. The Costa Rican government was interested in expanding Santa Rosa Park to make possible a stable population for some of the park's species. It also felt that its best interests were not served by the presence of an ousted military dictator near its border. So, in 1979, the **Hacienda Murcíelago**, owned by the Somoza family, was expropriated and made part of the national parks system. The *hacienda*, which lies on **Saint Elena Bay** with access to **Playa Blanca** and its untouched white- sand beach, is now a part of Santa Rosa Park. A recent addition to the park is the land that was occupied by the formerly secret **Santa Elena Airstrip**, used by Oliver North and his cronies in their Iran-Contra activities *(see opposite)*.

Santa Rosa National Park beaches

A rugged 13-km (8-mile) hiking trail, or four-wheel drive road during the dry season (inaccessible during the wet season), leads from the Santa Rosa ranger station to **Playa Naranjo**. White sand and clear water with excellent surf breaking near Roca de la Bruja (Witch's Rock; *see page 100)*, a monolith 2 km (1 mile) offshore, make Naranjo a popular but remote surfing destination. Boats can be chartered from Playas del Coco to Naranjo. Alternatively, there is camping at both playas Naranjo and Nancite (tel: 666 5051).

Playa Nancite ⓯, one of Costa Rica's most pristine beaches, is northwest from Naranjo. Each month, usually on a waxing three-quarter moon, turtles

BELOW: a park ranger cycling to work on Playa Nancite, famous for turtle nesting, from August–December.

come ashore here to nest. Tens of thousands may participate in the event, called an *arribada*, one of Costa Rica's grandest natural spectacles *(see pages 240–41)*. Exact times are unpredictable, as they are with most biological phenomena. Even though a full-scale *arribada* may not be taking place, solitary turtles can usually be seen nesting on Nancite and Naranjo beaches.

Map on page 178–79

Papagayo to Playa Ocotal

And now for something completely different... If you like a beach holiday with lots of action, the Pacific beaches to the southwest of Liberia are extremely popular. In just five years, this coast has become the new hub of tourism in Guanacaste, largely owing to the expansion of the Daniel Oduber International Airport just 45 minutes away. Huge all-inclusive resorts cater to masses of winter-weary tourists arriving in Liberia from the north, in search of heat and sun.

The Papagayo Peninsula project already has an 18-hole golf course and an ultra-expensive flagship hotel, the Four Seasons Costa Rica Resort, with more hotels and private villas planned. Around **Playa Panamá** ⓰, half a dozen all-inclusive resorts are packed in the high season with budget-minded package travelers who rarely leave the manicured hotel grounds.

To the south is **Playa Hermosa** ⓱, a sparkling half-moon cove with gentle surf. Despite some large-scale development at the northern end, this beach still has some charm and some excellent small restaurants and hotels. It's also a major diving center, with the long-established Diving Safaris (tel: 672 0012). Hotel Playa Hermosa (tel: 672 0046), one of the only hotels right on the beach, sits in a lush garden, shaded by mature trees. It's small and as laid-back as a beach hotel can be.

The Santa Elena Airstrip was financed by a bogus Panamanian company set up by Oliver North. Its seizure by the Costa Rican government was a major source of friction between Costa Rica and the United States.

BELOW: an idyllic beach scene on the Nicoya peninsula.

Nearby **Playas del Coco** ⓲ is a working beach town with a large fishing fleet. The beach is neither pretty nor great for swimming but it is the launching point for a wide range of diving, surfing and sport-fishing trips. The town itself has lots of character, albeit a little honky-tonk, with plenty of open-air bars, discos and tacky souvenir stalls. But there are also some excellent seafood restaurants at every price range.

The north end of the beach caters to a more sophisticated crowd with small bed and breakfast establishments and the stylish, Italian-owned Hotel La Puerta del Sol (tel: 670 0195), which also has a romantic, al-fresco Italian restaurant, El Sol y La Luna.

Just a couple of kilometers south of Coco is dramatic **Playa Ocotal** ⓳, a black-sand beach fringed with cliffs. Dominating the highest point is Hotel El Ocotal Beach Resort, overlooking the sandy coves, rocky capes and islands off the Nicoya coast. You can take a boat trip to a nearby island to find great swimming and snorkeling or arrange a diving expedition in local waters or as far away as Isla del Caño.

Hotel El Velero on Playa Hermosa is named for the sailboat that brought its Canadian owners all the way from Canada to Playa Hermosa. Its 12-meter (38-ft) sloop is available for cruises to secluded beaches, and for other trips.

Playa Flamingo

From Comunidad, head south on the highway toward Belén. From there it is a short distance to **Playa Brasilito** and the Playa Flamingo area, which includes **Playa Potrero**. In the dry season, if you feel adventurous and have a four-wheel-drive car, you can negotiate the bumpy Monkey Trail shortcut that starts near Sardinal and emerges near **Playa Pan de Azúcar** (Sugar Loaf Beach). Ask the locals for directions.

Playa Conchal, once a deserted slice of beach composed of bottomless

BELOW: handsome craft at Playa Flamingo marina.

drifts of pink, orange, mauve and sunset-colored sea shells, lies just south of Flamingo. It is an ideal place to snorkel. The huge **Paradisus Playa Conchal Beach & Golf Resort** now looms over the beach, blocking access from the main road. But you can still reach the public beach by walking south for a kilometer (½ mile) along the shore from **Brasilito**, a bustling small town with a few interesting restaurants and the vintage **Hotel Brasilito** (tel: 654 4237), which has modest rooms in an old wooden building close to the beach. The hotel is also home to Gecko's at the Beach, a trendy restaurant with excellent seafood and pasta dishes.

About 7 km (4 miles) north of Brasilito you will find **Playa Flamingo 20**, one of Costa Rica's loveliest, longest, white-sand beaches. The natural harbor formed by Flamingo Bay is home to a huge charter-boat fleet. For the past few years the marina has been closed while the local authorities make up their minds about granting a new concession, but the fishing boats and pleasure sailboats are moored in the bay.

The town itself climbs up a steep hill to the Mar y Sol Restaurant and Bar (tel: 654 5222) with a terrace that has the best view in the area, as well as the best food, a blend of tropical and classic French. You'll feel as though you have stumbled onto the Côte d'Azur (but at half the price).

Flamingo Marina Resort (tel: 654 4141), an upscale, pretty hotel on the bay side, looks out onto a brown-sand beach, rocks and islands dotting the horizon. On the ocean side, **Flamingo Beach Resort** (tel: 654 4444), recently updated, is a more family-oriented hotel, with a huge swimming pool, just steps away from the white-sand beach.

To the north is **Playa Potrero**, a cove of coconut palms and calm water,

ABOVE: the taste of the tropics.
BELOW: shooting green turtles the ecological way.

which is an excellent place for a picnic and a dip in the ocean. A cluster of new hotels, from modestly comfortable to extravagantly luxurious, dot the beach. The views get better, although the roads get worse, as you continue north along this picturesque coastline toward **Playa Pan de Azúcar**.

When you arrive at Pan de Azucar, it is obviously the last resort. Stop in at the **Hotel Sugar Beach** (tel: 654 4242), the only hotel on the beach, for incredible views and enjoy a drink, lunch or a swim in the cove.

Playa Tamarindo area

Go through Brasilito to Huacas and continue for 13 km (8 miles) south, where you will need to make a right turn for **Playa Grande** ㉑ and **Playa Tamarindo** ㉒. Tamarindo has a national wildlife refuge, though you would scarcely realize it. The wildlife seems more concentrated in the town's many bars and clubs than it is in the nearby estuary. The friendly, Swiss-owned Capitán Suizo on the beach is still the most luxurious hotel in town and has the best location, right on the beach. Relatively inexpensive lodging is available in the village of Tamarindo. Over the past five years, Tamarindo has experienced a major growth spurt, with commercial centers and condominium developments popping up everywhere. On the plus side, there is lots more to do in town, including dining at a plethora of international restaurants.

BELOW: away from the beaches and resorts, everyday life trundles on at a slow pace.

Tamarindo is a favorite surfers' haunt and has many surf shops, including the well-run Iguana Surf, where you can rent boards, kayaks and snorkeling equipment. Iguana Surf also offers tours: one of its most popular is a 2-hour guided paddle through the estuary – a great way to see birds and wildlife.

Playa Grande is just a 5-minute boat ride across an estuary, or it is a 1-hour drive over dirt roads, and has excellent surf.

Playa Grande is also a major leatherback turtle nesting habitat, and the site of environmental conflicts between conservationists and developers. The developers appear to be getting the upper hand but the beach itself is still protected.

Parque Nacional Marino Las Baulas, which incorporates Playa Grande, was created in 1991 to protect the world's most important leatherback hatching area, and was expanded in 1995. It was estimated at that time that there were only about 35,000 leatherbacks left in the world and approximately 900 of them came to Playa Grande to lay their eggs each year. Sadly, the population has subsequently fallen into a dramatic decline despite concerted efforts by the National Park Service and scientists to protect them. During the long nesting season from August to February, if you are lucky, you may see one or two turtles struggling up the beach to dig a nest. Visitors must join a guided group since beach access is strictly limited, and flash photography of the wildlife is completely forbidden.

On the beach at Playa Grande is Hotel Las Tortugas (tel: 653 0423), a congenial, turtle-friendly hotel, with low-lighting at night for the turtle's well-being. Catch the Guanacastecan breezes from a comfortable hammock near the turtle-shaped swimming pool, chat with the garrulous owner of the hotel, Lewis Wilson, who was instrumental in establishing the marine park, or take a guided tour of the mangrove estuary in a kayak, ensuring a peaceful trip for riders and the birds they observe.

Playa Langosta, immediately south of Tamarindo beyond a rocky headland that is impassable at high tide, is also frequented by surfers who ride waves just in front of the estuary at the southern end. More sedate than its noisy neighbor, Playa Langosta is home to a few lovely bed and breakfast establishments. Directly south from Tamarindo, along a bumpy road, **Playa Avellanas** and **Playa Negra** are popular surfers' turf. So far, they have escaped the over-development of the Tamarindo area. At Playa Avellanas, there is an idyllic beach café called Lola's on the Beach (tel: 658 8097) where you can lounge under palm trees. Or you can take a nature walk in the mangroves in front of Cabinas Las Olas. Even if you're not a surfer, the Playa Negra Hotel (tel: 658 8034) is a charming place to stay with round, thatched-roof cabins overlooking the ocean and a round pool.

Head inland from Tamarindo for some 18 km (11 miles) and, at the junction of the 27 de Abril school, turn toward the coast and proceed for approximately 12 km (8 miles) to lovely **Playa Junquillal**. Junquillal is a paradisical, wide beach with high surf that gives you the sense of having found a secret place.

Inland to Santa Cruz

Heading inland from the coast at Paraíso, few populated areas disturb the unbroken beauty of the rolling hills and valleys. An occasional cluster of three or four houses indicates a village. Here chickens, ducks and the occasional cyclist claim the road. The kilometers are marked by the infrequent passage of herds

Map on page 178–79

TIP

For more on turtles, see the features on page 202 and pages 240–41.

BELOW: a glorious Nicoya sunset.

The Vampire Bats of Guanacaste

There are more than 100 kinds of bats in Costa Rica. They are everywhere, from the shrilling flutterings of millions that rise up from the deep caves of Barra Honda, to a quiet few hanging in the cool, darkened corners of La Casona in Santa Rosa Park. Most of them are benevolent, curious-looking animals, who feed on nectar, fruit and insects. But within Santa Rosa Park, in Guanacaste, inside a cave near Naked - Indian Path, lives a group of *Desmodex Rotundum*, or vampire bats.

Bats are beneficial, even necessary, as significant pollinators and disseminators of seeds, especially in deforested areas in Costa Rica. Researchers know them to be clean, docile – even friendly. Nectar bats are gregarious and hang from the ceilings of caves in tight clusters. In the evening, they feed on insects along roads or dry river beds.

At night, they search for nectar from white, night-blooming flowers, which they pollinate. Bats do much to control insect populations; it is estimated that a colony of 1 million bats can consume more than 4,500 kg (10,000 lbs) of insects a night.

Only three of the species drink blood. Hollywood and Victorian novelists have done their part in creating the myth of the vampire who lives on the blood of innocent humans. And there are certain other factors that contribute to the legends that surround this creature: the vampire bat has large thumbs that protrude from the wings, appendages used for stealthy crawling toward the prey. A flat, red, pig-like nose; large eyes; prominent front teeth; and relatively small and pointed ears make this one of the least appealing creatures of the night.

The caped and fanged, black-haired fictional figure from Transylvania no doubt rose up, fully formed, in the imagination of early movie makers who had heard of the nocturnal activities of these animals. For it is true that this species feeds mainly during the darkest hours, before the moon is out, quietly alighting upon a sleeping victim and making a painless incision with razor sharp teeth. Contrary to the myth, the blood of the victim is not sucked out, but rather lapped up, much as a cat drinks milk.

A bat does not drink its victim dry. Instead, rabies and other infections, introduced through the wounds, kill the prey. More than a million animals a year die this way. Humans are sometimes prey as well, and sleeping people have been infected by the bat with dreaded rabies.

Cattle ranchers are striking back against the vampire bat. Methods of extermination have included gassing their caves with toxic substances and dynamiting. Such methods, often born of an irrational aversion to the bat, do not specifically target the vampire variety. Unfortunately, anything and everything in the area is harmed or killed. A more precise, but equally extreme, system involves trapping the bats and coating them with poisons. When released, each bat will then fatally infect up to 20 others. ❑

LEFT: vampire bats inflict huge financial damage each year by infecting farm animals.

Map on page 178–79

of noisy Brahman cows, turning traffic into a cattle drive, followed in their leisurely journey by *sabaneros* on horseback. These *Guanacasteco* cowboys don't direct the animals out of the road; they let the automobile wend its way through them. The cattle, with their sensitive faces, seem neither concerned nor particularly curious.

Santa Cruz ㉓ (pop. 20,000) is a bustling market town. In the central plaza, the modern church, built when the old one was destroyed by an earthquake in 1950, stands beside the original colonial clock tower. The central park is a quiet, shady place for sitting and viewing the life of a Guanacaste town.

Hungry visitors to Santa Cruz should not miss the experience of eating indigenous food at the Coopetortillas (tel: 680 0688), 200 meters /220 yards past the church, then turn right. In a huge single-room building of tin and screen, members of a women's cooperative use an open wood fire to prepare the large, handmade *tortillas Guanacastecas*, rice and beans, and other cheap and tasty local dishes. A sign says "*ambiente familiar*," or family atmosphere. For visitors wishing to spend the night in Santa Cruz, the Hotel Diriá (tel: 680 0080) provides air-conditioned rooms and a swimming pool, and many *cabinas* are available around the town offering basic facilities.

One of the main visitor attractions in this part of Guanacaste is the small town of **Guaitil** ㉔, where you will find ceramic pots in the style of the pre-Columbian inhabitants of this part of Costa Rica. After the Conquest, pottery-making died out here, possibly because the images adorning pots were considered pagan by the Catholic Church. The craft has been revived in recent years and today the popularity of these giant, luscious ceramic pots is obvious from their presence in the lobbies and dining rooms of many hotels in Gua-

ABOVE: Guaitil pottery.
BELOW: golden sands and mangroves at Tamarindo.

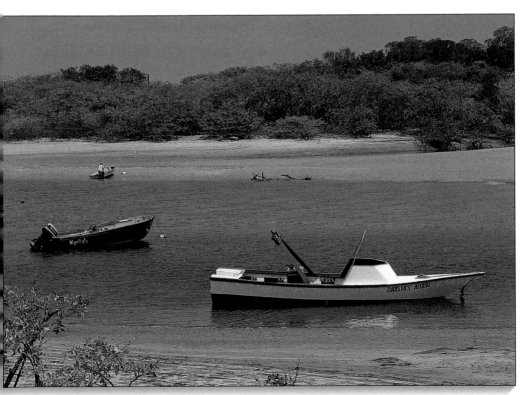

nacaste. It seems as though almost every house in the neighborhood of Guaitil has a kiln and pots for sale in the yard. The widest selection, however, will be found next to the soccer field in front of the church.

Nicoya

From Guaitil it is a scenic, 20-minute drive on a smoothly paved highway to the town of **Nicoya 25**, considered to be the cultural capital of Guanacaste. The pride of Nicoya is its central park and white, adobe colonial church, now a museum (open 8am–noon, 2–6pm, closed Sun and Wed; donation). With the completion of the Friendship Bridge across the **Río Tempisque**, Nicoya is the fastest-growing gateway to the central Nicoya coast beaches.

Playa Nosara

The beaches of Nosara and nearby Sámara are becoming increasingly popular destinations for North American and European vacationers. Playa Nosara is the most remote beach. **Nosara 26** itself is a small, nondescript inland town. The attractions here are Playa Pelada and Playa Guiones, two long white-sand beaches with excellent surfing waves and miles of beach bordered by forest and green sea grape edging the sand. The last 18 km (11 miles) of the road from Nicoya are nearly impassable during the rainy season, and many visitors fly here from San José.

Despite the difficulty getting here by road, the Nosara area is in the midst of a building boom. Private villas, small hotels and restaurants are being built by an international cast of characters, including a large contingent of nature-loving Swiss. Nosara is also a haven for new agers; yoga, alternative therapies and

If you don't already find that Nosara is the sort of place where you can totally unwind, try seeking out the Nosara Retreat, which specializes in physical and spiritual rejuvenation.

BELOW: against mighty odds, a baby turtle makes it to the ocean's edge.

THE *ARRIBADA*

Created to protect the endangered Olive Ridley turtle, the Ostional National Wildlife refuge is witness to the spectacular phenomenon known as the *arribada*, when tens of thousands of turtles come to the beach to lay their eggs. It is estimated that during these brief periods as many as 100,000 Olive Ridleys may come ashore to this isolated beach, and leave behind over ten million eggs. *Arribadas* generally occur at two to four-week intervals between the third quarter and full moon from April to December, peaking during July through September.

Presently, there is a controversial program of egg collecting in operation at Ostional, which gives the people of the nearby village the legal right to gather as many of the Olive Ridley turtle eggs as they can during the first 36 hours of every *arribada* in an attempt to prevent poaching.

If you wish to view the amazing sight of thousands of these creatures laboriously coming ashore to thump the sand with their flippers and dig their incubation holes to lay their eggs, then check in at the guard station on your journey down to the beach. And please remember to watch the activities as unobtrusively as possible.

Map
on page
178–79

vegetarianism abound. A large part of Nosara is still protected as a reserve, and as a result it is more forested and richer in wildlife than other parts of the region. Coatimundis, armadillos, parrots, toucans and monkeys are plentiful. There is also excellent snorkeling, tide pool exploring and camping in the area.

Endangered eggs

At the far northern edge of Nosara, Lagarta Lodge Biological Reserve (tel: 682 0035) occupies an eagle's aerie, high above its own private nature reserve with hiking trails and the **Refugio Nacional de Vida Silvestre Ostional**, an important turtle-nesting site. Sadly, in season, you can still buy the eggs of endangered species of turtles, considered by many to be an aphrodisiac.

Some of the eggs have been excavated by adventurers, others have been purchased at *sodas* near the beach and are the booty of *hueveros* (egg-gatherers), who make an illegal business of raiding the turtles' nests. Others are part of a cache of eggs taken legally by those who are given permits by the government to take the eggs during the first 36 hours of an *arribada (see page 202).*

Playa Sámara and south

Playa Sámara ㉗, nearly an hour south of Nosara along dicey, dirty roads, has a beautiful white-sand beach and a good reef for snorkeling, which also protects the beach from direct waves. Swimming is safe in crystalline, shallow waters with minimal surf. Off season, there is a feeling of dramatic isolation. During the high season, Playa Sámara is popular with Costa Ricans and many *Ticos* have summer homes here.

Diving, snorkeling, fishing, bicycle and horse-back trips, and kayaking can be

ABOVE: statuesque white egret.
BELOW: another lazy day on the Nicoya peninsula.

Rip tides are a danger in Costa Rica and kill several visitors every year. Ask around first whether a beach is safe for swimming. If you are caught by a rip tide, don't panic and do not swim against it. Try to swim parallel to the shore, and eventually the breaking waves will carry you back in.

BELOW: the aptly named elephant's ear plant.

arranged by all the local hotels. On the south side of the beach Hotel Las Brisas del Pacífico has the best beach location in town, with a pool fronting the ocean. To the north of the beach are smaller, basic *cabinas*, small hotels and some excellent restaurants. A block north of the beach, Hotel Giada (tel: 656 0132) has a lot of Italian style and the best food in town. There are regular flights to Sámara, which cut out the long and tiring drive. Driving is particularly difficult during the wet season, as you have to cross many shallow rivers between Nosara and Sámara.

A little way south of Sámara is **Playa Carrillo** ㉘, yet another near-flawless white-sand beach protected by an offshore reef. Beyond Carrillo are other extraordinary beaches: isolated, lonely places, sometimes with fresh water available, sometimes not. **Playa Caletas**, just a little way south of Carrillo on unpaved, almost non-existent roads, has large surf with offshore breezes. And further south still is **Punta Islita**. Located in the heart of a picturesque valley, Hotel Punta Islita Resort and Spa (tel: 661 3332) has wonderful ocean views, a beautiful blue-tile infinity pool, and private porches with picture windows and hammocks. Most guests arrive at this ultra-luxurious hotel by small plane but you can drive by car in the dry season from Sámara.

Parque Nacional Barra Honda

About 21 km (13 miles) east of the town of Nicoya is **Barra Honda National Park** ㉙, a vast network of caves. Along the road to the new Taiwan Friendship Bridge that spans the Río Tempisque are national park signs showing the way to this seldom-visited place. On the flat ridgeline, 300 meters (1,000 ft) above the caves, is a *mirador* (look-out point) that can be reached via marked paths. Standing there along the high ridge, with the sounds of an enormous waterfall, amongst screeching tropical birds, scary-sounding howler monkeys and iguanas in the trees, looking out across the vast Nicoya peninsula, can be a humbling experience.

You don't have to be a dedicated spelunker to enjoy Barra Honda, though some of the caves are quite deep and require steep vertical drops to enter. With names such as *La Trampa* (The Trap), and *Terciopelo* (Fer-de-Lance viper), they may not sound inviting, but the formations are dazzling. One such formation, called The Organ, produces melodic tones when gently touched.

Ancient human remains, blind salamanders, vampire bats and strange birds share the world of darkness in the Barra Honda caves, which have escaped vandalism and exploitation because they lack an easily accessible horizontal entrance. A community group has the exclusive right to lead cave tours. Basic lodging and good *campesina* food (try Las Delicias) are also available. In the dry season (Dec–Apr) it gets extremely hot, so be sure to bring a wide-brimmed hat and water.

It is another 185 km (115 miles) down the coast and up through the mountains back to San José. Along the highway, dozens of fruit stands offer an opportunity to load up on supplies of tropical fruit, honey and homemade candies before returning to the hustle and bustle of the capital.

Monteverde Cloud Forest

Atop the Continental Divide, some 180 km (110 miles) northwest of San José is the **Reserva Biológica del Bosque Nuboso de Monteverde** ③⓪. Despite some recent road improvements, it is still a difficult place to get to and you should allow 4 hours' driving time from San José. After the turn-off for Puntarenas on the Interamerican Highway, continue along the Interamericana to the Rancho Grande turning on the right. Follow this road through Sardinal. It's paved for the first 3 km (2 miles) or so, then becomes a gravel road, meeting up with the old, more pot-holed dirt road at Guacimal. Count on an hour to make the 37-km (21-mile) ascent from the main highway to Monteverde.

Despite the ordeal to get here, every year tens of thousands of people visit the preserve. In order to protect the flora and fauna and the trails themselves, visitors are now limited to 100 at any given time – which means you may have to wait your turn. You should book at least one night's accommodation in advance; to get the best out of the area you need to stay three days.

More visitors are attracted to Monteverde Cloud Forest than to any other forest reserve in Costa Rica, and usually for one purpose only: to sight the resplendent quetzal, the most colorful and spectacular bird in the tropics. Though listed as an endangered species throughout Central America, it is estimated that nearly 1,000 quetzals make their home in Monteverde. Be warned, however, it is a difficult bird to spot. With the exception of their almost luminous crimson breast, they are cloaked in radiant green plumage and easily disappear among the rich colors of the cloud forest. The best time to spot them is January to September and especially during the mating season, which runs from March through June.

Map on page 178–79

BELOW: with around 760 cm (300 inches) of rain per year, there are plenty of waterfalls in Monteverde.

The Resplendent Quetzal

The resplendent quetzal is rightly acclaimed as the most magnificent bird in the western hemisphere. Some 40 species inhabit the tropics worldwide and 10 are found in Costa Rica. It is one of the country's greatest natural treasures.

The pigeon-sized male owes his elegance to the intensity and brilliant contrasts of his colors, the sheen and glitter of his plumage, the beauty of his adornments and the great dignity of his posture. The rich crimson of his underparts contrasts with the shining, irides- cent green of his head, chest and upper parts. His head is crowned with a narrow crest of upstanding feathers that extends from his small yellow bill to his nape. The pointed tips of the long, loose-barbed coverts of his wings project over the crimson of his sides in beautiful contrast. Most notable are his central tail coverts, which stretch far

beyond his tail and, like two slender green pendants, undulate gracefully when he flies.

As may be seen on many an ancient sculp- ture and modern painting, the long tail coverts were highly valued as personal adornments by the Aztec and Maya nobility. As Guatemala's national bird, the peaceful quetzal contrasts with the fierce predators and firebreathing monsters that other nations have chosen for their emblems. Guatemalans once believed that their symbol of liberty would die if deprived of freedom, but modern aviculturists have learned how to keep them alive in captivity – a hard negation of a beautiful myth.

The quetzal's song is eminently worthy of a bird so splendidly attired. Fuller and deeper than those of any other trogon, their songs are not distinctly separated but slurred and fused into a flow of soft and mellow sound that is unforgettably beautiful.

Monogamous pairs of quetzals nest in the holes of trees located in mountain forests or in nearby clearings. The hole, like that of a woodpecker, extends straight downwards from the opening at the top. Usually it is deep enough to conceal all of the sitting birds ex- cept the ends of the male's train. On the unlined bottom of the chamber, the female lays two light blue eggs. She incubates through the night and the middle of the day. The male takes a turn on the eggs in the morning and again in the afternoon. His train arches over his back and projects through the doorway, fluttering in the breeze. On an epiphyte-burdened trunk, the ends might be mistaken for two green fern fronds.

Sometimes, when his partner arrives to relieve him of his spell in the nest, he soars straight upward, right above the treetops, loudly shouting a phrase that sounds almost like "very-good very-good." At the summit of his ascent he circles, then dives into shel- tering foliage. These "joy flights" seem to express the bird's great vitality.

Resplendent quetzals are still abundant in the tracts of unspoiled mountain forests. So long as such forests are preserved, they are in no danger of becoming extinct, but if they are destroyed, then Central America will lose its most magnificent bird. ❏

LEFT: the quetzal with its favorite food, *aguacatillo*, a type of small avocado.

Monteverde is much more than an opportunity to spot a quetzal, however. This misty verdant high-altitude cloud forest is home to a multitude of diverse creatures: 400 species of birds, 490 species of butterflies, 2,500 species of plants and 100 species of mammals. Pick up a checklist and map at the Visitors' Center. Guided tours are available. Before leaving the forest, visit the **Hummingbird Gallery**, across the road from the entrance. Owners Michael and Patricia Fogden, biologists and pre-eminent nature photographers, have spent two decades recording the fauna of Monteverde and their remarkable work is shown here.

Map on page 178–79

Monteverde's Quaker community

The community of **Monteverde** ❸ was established by a group of Quakers who, to escape the obligations of US military service, moved here from Alabama in 1951. To support themselves the Quakers began making cheese from milk brought to their primitive processing plant each morning by *Tico* dairy farmers. Today the Quakers produce tons of cheese daily: Monteverde cheese has become a proud Costa Rican specialty and can be found in markets throughout Central America. En route to the reserve, stop in at their cheese processing plant, **La Fábrica de Queso** (The Cheese Factory), for a tour (open Mon–Sat, Sun am; entrance fee), or watch the production through windows in the plant. Don't expect to see too many Quakers elsewhere in Monteverde, however. They keep themselves to themselves on their farms and generally avoid the commercialized town that Monteverde has now become.

Just north of here look in at CASEM (Comité de Artesanías Santa Elena-Monteverde), an arts and crafts cooperative founded by eight women in 1982.

ABOVE: Monteverde flora.
BELOW: sunrise mist rises above the forest canopy.

Today, more than 140 artisans contribute their work, which is on sale at less-than-downtown prices at the CASEM shop. Across the road is the popular coffee shop, Stella's Bakery, and Meg's Stables (tel: 645 5419), which offers horse-back-riding tours.

Other Monteverde attractions

Adjacent to Monteverde Cloud Forest preserve are two much smaller private reserves. There is usually good wildlife viewing at the 200-acre (81-hectare) **Reserva Sendero Tranquilo** (Quiet Path Reserve), which is open for small-group guided tours, led by expert, bilingual nature guides, operating only from December through August. You must book ahead by contacting the Hotel El Sapo Dorado (tel: 645 5010).

Opposite the Hotel Heliconia, on the road to Santa Elena, turn off left (heading west) to **El Jardín de las Mariposas** (Butterfly Garden ; tel: 645 5512), which exhibits all the butterfly species of the region (open daily 7am–4pm; entrance fee). Guided tours take you through the various stages of a butterfly's life and into a screened garden where hundreds of species flutter freely. The best time for a visit is when the sun is shining. There is also a leaf-cutter ant colony exhibition. Adjacent to the Butterfly Garden is the **Santuario Ecológico** (tel: 645 5869), which is a small private reserve with four loop trails. The longest only takes 2½ hours at a leisurely pace so is quite accessible to all visitors. Agoutis, coatis and sloths are often spotted, and porcupines and monkeys are also frequent visitors. The birdwatching is good, too – quetzals are seen here. The sanctuary also offers popular night-time walks; contact them by telephone to reserve your place.

Mayan kings prized the iridescent green tail feathers of the quetzal more than gold itself. They also believed the bird could not live in captivity, and it was therefore the supreme symbol of freedom.

BELOW: a tapir, rarely seen in the wild.

Map on page 178–79

Another Monteverde attraction is **The Sky Walk** (tel: 645 5238/479 9944), a 2.5-km (1½-mile) series of trails and six hanging bridges suspended Indiana Jones-style from platforms in the tree canopy. It's a wonderful way of getting a bird's-eye view of the forest, up to 151 feet (46 m) above the ground. For the truly adventurous the same company also offers Sky Trek, a high-speed, high-adrenaline canopy tour that involves donning mountain-climbing harnesses and zipping through the trees suspended on strong cables.

Monteverde is also famous for its artistic community, with many resident wildlife painters, sculptors and textile artists. An international music festival is held every February to March. Both local musicians and international guest artists perform programs ranging from jazz to classical to Latino. Proceeds from the festival benefit local school music programs.

Santa Elena Reserve and around

Around 5 km (3 miles) northeast of Monteverde village is an outstanding local initiative, the **Reserva Santa Elena** �32, or Santa Elena Rainforest Reserve. Comprising some 766 acres (310 hectares) of mixed montane and elfin forest, the reserve was created in 1992 as a local high-school project and includes several kilometers of well-kept paths and a visitor center. On clear days, you are treated to views of magnificent Arenal Volcano to the north. Tours are well-organized and cheaper than Monteverde, yet the flora and fauna (including quetzals, jaguars and howler monkeys) is every bit as impressive as that of its famous neighbor. There are four principal trails, all short enough to be done in a day. You also avoid the crowds here, plus you'll feel good that a proportion of your admission charge will go toward the funding of Monteverde's schools.

ABOVE: visitor and resident at Monteverde's Serpentario.
BELOW: false eyes ward off predators.

The most exciting way of exploring the nearby forests is by joining a Canopy Tour (tel: 645 5390). You are winched up to the treetops by pulleys, then go from platform to platform on horizontal cables. Selvatura (tel: 645 5929) and SkyTrek (tel: 645 5238) both offer transportation from area hotels to their canopy tours bordering the reserve.

A little farther out, on the Atlantic slope, east of Monteverde Cloud Forest, is the **Children's Eternal Forest** (El Bosque Eterno de los Niños, tel: 645 5003). Back in 1987, a group of Swedish schoolchildren raised and donated enough money to purchase 6 hectares (15 acres) of forest. Now, with support from young people from all over the world, they have bought over 22,000 hectares (54,000 acres), covering a range of cloud-, rain- and seasonal evergreen forest. A small section of the forest is open to the public, with several kilometers of nature trails as well as an education center.

Bordering the forest is the unspoiled and highly recommended **Ecolodge San Luis and Biological Station**. An integrated ecotourism and scientific research station run by tropical biologists, San Luis offers visitors many hands-on activities such as trails, farming, reforestation, cloud forest photography, birdwatching with expert guides, and Spanish language workshops plus the opportunity to experience Costa Rican rural life first-hand (tel: 645 8049). ❏

COSTA RICA'S WINGS OF WONDER

With more than 850 species of birds, Costa Rica is one of the world's foremost destinations for professional ornithologists and amateur birders

Despite its small size, Costa Rica has roughly the same number of birds as the whole of North America, and significantly more than Europe or Australia. This tremendous diversity is explained partly by the fact that the country is in the tropics, and partly by its position on one of the world's great bird migration routes, which links North and South America.

For most birders Costa Rica's resident species – rather than its migrants – are the ones that hold the most interest. The most sought-after sighting of all is undoubtedly the resplendent quetzal, a high-altitude fruit-eater that lives in the cloud forests of the Central Highlands. Quetzals are generally shy and quiet, and it takes patience to locate them. Toucans are much more vocal, while the scarlet macaw is garrulous and noisy, skimming over the treetops in fast-flying raucous pairs.

NECTAR FEEDERS

Costa Rica boasts about 50 species of tiny but pugnacious hummingbirds, which feed largely on a diet of sugary nectar and insects. They are often lured to artificial feeders and make an unmissable spectacle of color and whirring wings.

▷ **MID-AIR REFUELING**
A hummingbird, which can be surprisingly pugnacious for its size, feeds on a "hotlips" flower at Monteverde. Although hummingbirds live largely on nectar, they also catch insects to feed their young.

▽ **RESPLENDENT QUETZAL**
Rich and lustrous when seen in the open, the quetzal's iridescent green plumage provides effective camouflage against a background of leaves. The male's tail streamers are up to 1 meter (3 ft) long, and have to be folded around the body when the bird enters its nesting hole.

△ **OUTSIZE BEAK**
Although it looks unwieldy, a toucan's beak is very delicate. Internal air-spaces help to reduce its weight.

▷ **HANGING NESTS**
Montezuma oropendolas hang their long, bag-like nests from the branches of tall, isolated trees.

△ **WATCHING ON WATER**
Open waterways – such as
the canals at Tortuguero –
make good places to see
birds when they set off at
dawn to find food, or settle
down to roost at dusk.

▽ **SUBMERSIBLE SWIMMER**
An anhinga or darter with its
catch. Anhingas feed in lakes
and coastal lagoons, and
often swim with just their
head and neck visible.

△ **INSECT-EATER**
The blue-crowned motmot
lives in forests and coffee
plantations, and spends
most of its time watching
for food from its perch.
Its diet consists mainly of
insects.

ENDANGERED SPECIES

Despite Costa Rica's efforts
to protect its forests,
habitat destruction has had
a serious effect on some of
its birds. The quetzal is
particularly vulnerable
because it depends on
undisturbed cloud forest for
survival. The three-wattled
bellbird shares this habitat,
and is equally threatened
by its conversion to pasture.
Great green macaws are
the most threatened
species of macaw.
Conservation efforts on the
Caribbean coast, where
they exclusively live,
include honoring farmers
who maintain the *dipteryx*
trees the macaws feed on.
Numbers of green macaws
have now stabilized at
around 150 to 200.
National parks and private
reserves, such as
Monteverde, are a lifeline
to survival.
  Even higher on the
critical list is Costa Rica's
biggest flying predator, the
American harpy eagle.
This giant monkey-eating
bird is known to breed in
the forests of the Osa
Peninsula, but sightings of
it have become extremely
rare. A handful of species,
such as the cattle egret and
roadside hawk, have
actually benefited from
man-made changes to the
environment, because
they need open ground
to feed.

THE NORTHEAST

Volcán Arenal is the star of the region, though the Sarapiquí River and the lodges of Rara Avis and La Selva are also popular with more environmentally conscious visitors

The region to the northeast of San José corresponds roughly to the area known as the Northern Zone. The landscape is lush and agricultural for the most part. The main attractions for visitors are spectacular Arenal volcano, hot springs and spas, and some remote rainforest reserves.

Around Ciudad Quesada (San Carlos)

At the foot of the Cordillera Central, **Ciudad Quesada** ㉝, often called by its former name San Carlos, is the gateway to the north. The agricultural and commercial heart of the region, its chief products are cattle, citrus and sugar cane. It's a bustling town of around 40,000 people with several good places to stay nearby.

Some 15 km (9 miles) north of Ciudad Quesada just beyond Platanar, and overlooking the Platanar River, is La Garza (tel: 475 5222), a large working cattle and horse ranch, which has charming *cabinas* set among beautifully landscaped gardens. Guests can go horseback riding, tubing, swimming or fishing for *guapote* on the river, and they can learn about ranch life.

The Tilajari Hotel Resort (tel: 469 9091), near Muelle, around 22 km (14 miles) north of Ciudad Quesada, is a luxurious spread, set on several acres of rolling lawns overlooking the wide, muddy San Carlos River. It makes a good base for exploring this region, and offers tennis, swimming, racquetball, horseback riding and hiking in 300 hectares (750 acres) of rainforest. Further afield you can take fishing trips, and jungle river tours to Caño Negro Wildlife Reserve *(see page 220)*.

The Tilajari is also one of the lift-off points for an enchanting hot-air balloon ride over the **San Carlos Valley** with Serendipity Adventures. (Rides are also available at other sites; tel: 558 1000.) Standing in a traditional wicker balloon basket, under a multi-colored balloon just after dawn, you rise up, as if in a dream, over a forest preserve and look down into the tree tops at the howler monkeys and toucans who are just waking up. Moving on, over pasture lands, sugar cane and pineapple fields, over grazing cattle and horses, the sun rises and the countryside comes alive.

La Fortuna

From Muelle it's around 25 km (16 miles) west to **La Fortuna** ㉞ (also known as Fortuna de San Carlos). It's a busy, sun-baked village located near the base of Arenal Volcano, and functions as a gateway to the volcano with all sorts of tours, accommodations and eateries available.

Some 5 km (3 miles) east of La Fortuna is the turn-off to the **Cataratas del Río Fortuna**. These falls are accessible in an hour's easy horseback ride from La Fortuna through pastures and fields of ginger, corn,

PRECEDING PAGES: Volcán Arenal. **LEFT:** Sarapiquí waterfall. **BELOW:** white ibises.

bananas and peppers. The ride requires a four-wheel drive vehicle. Once at the falls, a muddy hike down a slippery slope to the swimming area at the base of the falls makes the clear, fresh water all the sweeter.

Tabacón Hot Springs

Moving ever closer to the volcano, between La Fortuna and Lake Arenal, is the **Tabacón Hot Springs Resort and Spa** ③⑤, one of Costa Rica's most popular tourist destinations. From here you can look directly up the small valley to the slopes of the volcano, and to cascades of glowing hot boulders. It appears dangerously close, yet the volcano also has a benign effect. Arenal heats Tabacón's therapeutic waters to a perfect temperature. Tiled slides, waterfalls and pools of varying temperatures are surrounded by tumbling warm-water creeks and lush gardens. You can even have a jacuzzi or a massage. Enjoy a meal in Tabacón's dining room and watch the erupting volcano from a quiet pool under the starry sky. And should you be there when the full moon waxes over Arenal, then that single experience is worth the trip to Costa Rica in itself.

Just west of La Fortuna, you can luxuriate in the warm mineral waters of the more affordable Baldi Termae. For about US$25, you can enjoy a bath and a view of the volcano (tel: 479 9651).

Down the highway, past the Tabacón Hot Springs Resort, is a dirt road going to the left and the **Arenal Observatory Lodge** (tel: 290 7011), formerly a research facility for the Smithsonian Institution and Costa Rica's Universidad Nacional. It is the only lodge in the national park, located on its own huge estate with primary and secondary forest, waterfalls, hiking and horseback trails. To get to the lodge follow the gravel road for 9 km (6 miles), crossing two rivers

TIP

Tabacón Springs is pricey and often crowded, especially on weekends. So try to choose an off-season weekday to visit.

BELOW:
an active Volcán Arenal is an unforgettable sight.

on the way. From here Arenal is only 1 km (⅔ mile) away and by night the air is rich with the sounds of howling monkeys and the glow of fireflies.

Map on page 178–79

Arenal Volcano

Until early July 1968, Arenal was a heavily wooded low hill, similar to many others in the area, near the village of La Fortuna. Then one morning the people there began feeling a few earth tremors. Suddenly, the forest started smoking and steaming. Women washing their clothes marveled at the sudden warm water which flowed in the creeks. Then, on July 29, **Volcán Arenal ❸❻** exploded. Rolling clouds of gas and fountains of red-hot boulders and molten lava hit the countryside. Official estimates put the death toll at 62, but local people claim that more than 80 people were killed. Over 5 sq. km (2 sq. miles) of land near the volcano was abruptly changed from pastoral farmland to a landscape out of Dante's *Inferno*. Since then, Arenal has been continuously active. It is everyone's preconception of a volcano: conical, rising abruptly out of flatland vegetation. But do not attempt to climb it. The molten lava running down her western slope has a temperature of 926°C (1,699°F), and an unpredictable spew of rocks, intense heat and poison gases. Sadly, every couple of years there is a visitor who disregards the warning signs and then the volcano claims another life.

A sign at the base of Arenal Volcano reads "Volcano influence area. If you notice abnormal activity, run away from the area and report it to the nearest authority."

The road west to **Nuevo Arenal** is perennially dreadful and a four-wheel drive vehicle is recommended. This New Arenal is a town reborn from the old village of Arenal, which was flooded in 1973 to create the lake. Nuevo Arenal has a good number of friendly and inexpensive restaurants and small hotels – and a variety of pleasant accommodations are available along the road to Tilarán. A few kilometers east is the **Jardín Botánico Arenal ❸❼** (open daily Nov–May 9am–

BELOW: beautifully landscaped grounds of the Tabacón Hot Springs Resort.

5pm, closed Sun May–Oct; entrance fee), the work of Michael Le May, an inde-fatigable amateur horticulturist. It features over 1,000 native and exotic species and is a magnet to hummingbirds and butterflies. Late afternoon is the best time to visit, though visitor numbers are limited, so the gardens are never too busy.

Lake Arenal

Laguna de Arenal ❸ offers some of Costa Rica's most challenging freshwater fishing. The *guapote* is the favorite of fishermen there *(see page 105)*. Whether or not you choose to fish, charter a boat and guide to take you sightseeing on the lake. It is best to go in the early morning, when, for much of the year, the lake's surface is like glass and the volcano can be viewed as a crystalline reflection. A few local fishermen will probably be out on the lake, sitting on chairs perched on a pair of floating balsa logs, fishing for *guapote* with simple handlines.

From December through March, usually in the afternoons, northeasterly winds blow almost daily, and the lake is anything but calm and glassy. Between 40 and 50 knots of sustained breeze is not uncommon and whips Arenal into a sea of whitecaps. Latterly, it has become a favorite destination for experienced windsurfers attracted by these conditions. Tico Wind (tel: 692 2002) in Nuevo Arenal, rents a full range of windsurfing equipment and also offers lessons. It is open from December 1 through mid-April.

The west end of the lake is the best for short board sailing and a number of windsurfing resorts have opened near **Tilarán** (pop. 8,500), an old-time Costa Rican town, whose name comes from the Chorotega words for "wind and rain." Another popular choice is the Hotel Tilawa (tel: 695 5050), an arresting replica of an ancient Cretan palace, located 9 km (6 miles) north of Tilarán, with its

ABOVE: cattle at La Fortuna.
BELOW: naturalists on a bridge over the Sarapiquí near Selva Verde.

well-equipped windsurfing school and easy access to the lake. Whether or not you are a windsurfer, it is a good place to spend the night as it is situated in the hills above the Guanacaste lowlands and is refreshingly cool. The countryside around the town is pastoral, the upland meadows spotted with dairy cattle. Villagers will arrange for boats and fishing guides on Lake Arenal.

Map on page 178–79

It is perhaps predictable that such a myth-inspiring lake as Arenal would find a resident monster. A few years ago, some local fishermen were out on their raft early one evening and felt a strange rumbling in the water. Suddenly, right in front of them an enormous, hairy serpent with horns broke through the surface with a belching roar and a stench. Moments later it slid back into the depths, trailing a tail over 2 meters (6 ft) long. The fishermen scurried back to town and told the tale. The story went around and, amplified by time and accounts of half-eaten horse carcasses found floating on the lake, the Monster of Lake Arenal is entrenched in local folklore. Above Lake Arenal is placid Lake Coter and the excellent Lake Coter Ecolodge, where you can hike miles of trails, ride horses over hills with views of Lake Arenal or zip along cables on a Canopy Tour through primary forest (tel: 289 6060).

Tourism is booming around the Arenal area and no one wants to be left out: in its own local leaflet, Tilarán proclaims itself as "the city of broad streets, fertile rains, and healthful winds in which friendship and progress is cultivated."

To Arenal via San Ramón

An alternative route to Arenal from San José is via **San Ramón**. It's a good idea to spend the night here at Villa Blanca Cloud Forest Hotel (tel: 461 0300), set in the 800-hectare (2,000-acre) **Los Angeles Cloud Forest** with miles of nature trails. The cozy cabins are elegantly furnished and each has its own fireplace.

From San Ramón continue north through San Lorenzo to La Tigra. On the gravel and dirt road between La Tigra and Chachagua is the Hotel Los Bosques de Chachagua (tel: 468 1010) cattle and horse ranch with 22 guest cabins. Elegant long-necked *paso criollo* horses are put through their paces by the trainer. Guests with riding experience can take these powerful creatures on any of the ranch's many trails.

BELOW: having fun on the Sarapiquí.

North to Caño Negro

Head northeast from San Carlos, crossing the Río Platanar and on to Aguas Zarcas and the luxurious Hotel El Tucano Occidental. Here guests enjoy natural hot springs and de-luxe accommodations, including an Olympic-size swimming pool, and jacuzzis fed with thermal waters. El Tucano has tennis courts, a mini-golf course and a natural steam sauna made of stone. The pools are also open to non-guests, for a small fee. Next door is the less expensive Hotel Termales del Bosque (tel: 460 1354). The attraction here is the enchanting experience of bathing in the riverside hot springs in a more natural setting than Tabacón. North of Aguas Zarcas outside of Pital is **La Laguna del Lagarto**, a remote lodge that offers accommodations, hiking, horseback riding, canoeing, and boat trips up the Río San Carlos to the Nicaraguan border. This is an excellent bird-watching destination. A four-wheel drive vehicle and rubber boots are recommended.

North of Arenal, toward the Nicaraguan border, is the magnificent and still uncrowded **Refugio Nacional de Vida Silvestre Caño Negro ❸⁹** (Caño Negro

Wildlife Reserve). It provides excellent bird-watching opportunities, including extremely large flocks of anhinga, roseate spoonbill, white ibis and Jabirú stork. The latter is the largest bird of the region and, in great danger of extinction. There are also several species of mammals here, including large cats. In the heart of this vast area is **Lago Caño Negro**. This lake covers around 800 hectares (2,000 acres) during the wet season, but almost dries up completely during the dry season.

Access to Caño Negro is from La Fortuna, Los Chiles or Upala, on good roads northwest of Cañas. The best way to see its myriad species of bird and animal life, particularly during the wet season, is by boat. Basic accommodations are available in Los Chiles and the village of Caño Negro boasts two upscale hotels, one a fishing lodge and the other a luxurious hotel. Several tour agencies in La Fortuna, including Sunset Tours, offer day trips to Caño Negro.

Rara Avis offers accommodations in treehouses, where guests with no fear of heights can spend the night on a platform 33 meters (100 ft) above the ground. The ascent, accompanied by a guide, is made with a rope and harness.

The Sarapiquí region

The lush, tropical jungles along the **Río Sarapiquí** region, on the Caribbean side of the Cordillera Central, are less than 100 km (60 miles) east of San José, yet once you are there it seems as though it is another continent. La Selva Biological Station, Selva Verde Lodge and Rara Avis, private reserves with lodging *(see below)*, are all accessible via a paved circuitous highway which begins and ends in San José.

The entire circuit, departing via Heredia and returning on the highway through Braulio Carrillo Park, requires approximately 5 hours of driving. A recommended stop along the route for budget travelers is Rancho Leona (tel: 761 1019) in La Virgen. Set right in the jungle, it offers good food, inexpensive lodging, and kayaking on the Río Sarapiquí.

BELOW: the jungle trail to Rara Avis.

From San José drive to Heredia. Here the highway winds up the slope of Poás Volcano to Varablanca, where the short entry road to Poás intersects the main highway. For something completely different, break your journey here at Albergue Colbert (tel: 482 2776), a genuinely French, mountain *auberge* with fireplace, fresh-baked croissants and excellent omelets. If you depart early there will be more than adequate time for a visit to the volcano, before crossing the ridge and heading down through heavily forested mountain slopes, past a spectacular waterfall, to the lowland rainforest of the Caribbean seaboard.

An alternative route to Sarapiquí which is easier and just as scenic is to take the Braulio Carillo Highway east of San José, through the Parque Nacional Braulio Carillo. Beware of driving after sunset, however, as thick night fog blankets this route

Puerto Viejo de Sarapiquí and Rara Avis

Puerto Viejo de Sarapiquí 🐵 is a small port town from which river boats depart for otherwise inaccessible settlements along these jungle waterways. Motor-driven dugout canoes laden with passengers and cargo depart regularly for the full-day trip up the Sarapiquí to the **Río San Juan**, on the Nicaraguan border, and then east to Barra del Colorado and the Caribbean.

Rara Avis (tel: 764 3131) is a pristine, 600-hectare (1,500-acre) rainforest reserve in the mountains above Las Horquetas. The main office and departure point for the reserve is in Las Horquetas, 17 km (11 miles) south of Puerto Viejo de Sarapiquí. From here, whether you are continuing by horseback or tractor-drawn cart, travel to Rara Avis is extremely difficult and can only be recommended for those who are both physically and mentally fit: the grueling 4-hour journey encounters ruts, bogs, and rivers. On the road, the transition from cattle ranches to deep jungle illustrates the devastating effects of deforestation more dramatically than any textbook or film. The tractor and cart lurch along an eroded path, through cattle ranches littered with fallen and unused timber. Even cattle are few and far between. The open land is hot, dry, dusty and inhospitable. The soil is baked crisp by the tropical sun.

Deforested land ends at El Plástico Lodge, the last stop before the final 6-km (4-mile) trip to Waterfall Lodge, high in the forest. This former prison colony gets its incongruous name from the plastic sheets under which the inmates slept. From El Plástico, the road plunges into a dark, cool cathedral-like forest, which teems with life. The sun-starved earth is a dense tangle of roots, tree trunks, and leaves, soaked in water and bathed in mud. Because it is such a rarified and isolated place, you should always arrange transportation in advance. Access is difficult, but most people feel that the mud and almost non-existent roads into the area are just part of the experience.

La Selva Biological Reserve

About 7 km (4 miles) south of Puerto Viejo you'll see the sign for "OTS" (the Organization for Tropical Studies) and the gravel road to La Selva. The diversity

Map on page 178–79

ABOVE: no through road.
BELOW: beware, Africanized bees can be very aggressive.

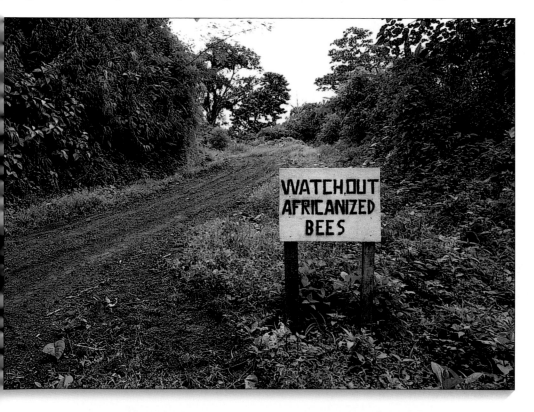

and abundance of life in the lowland tropical forest of the Sarapiquí River region attracted tropical biologists here more than 30 years ago. They subsequently founded the Organization for Tropical Studies and established the **Estación Bió-logica La Selva** ❹ (La Selva Biological Reserve and Research Station).

In 1986 the Costa Rican government also made a major commitment to rain-forest conservation by extending the boundaries of Braulio Carrillo National Park to meet the outer reaches of the 600-hectare (1,500-acre) La Selva Reserve. As a result of this decision, a total of 21,000 hectares (52,000 acres) of virgin forest now preserves the migratory pathways and large territories required for the survival of several species of Costa Rica's rare and endangered birds and mammals.

Sloths descend to the forest floor once a week to defecate – unusual behaviour that may be an attempt to move their scent away from their home.

Today, virtually all of the world's tropical biologists have spent time at La Selva as students, teachers or scientists – or at the very least they have been strongly influenced by the vast amount of scientific research that has been accomplished there over the past quarter of a century. Twice a year the Orga-nization for Tropical Studies holds an eight-week course, open to students of ecology. It's not just biologists who are taught at La Selva, either; many Sara-piquí residents who work at ecotourist lodges were also trained as naturalist guides at La Selva.

BELOW: a stream in the lowland rainforest.

The reserve is primarily a research and educational facility, but excellent, naturalist-led tours of the trails are offered daily (tel: 240 6696 or 766 6565). There is a well-developed trail system and some of the trails have boardwalks in order to give access during the wet season. Comfortable new cabins for visitors have greatly improved the accommodations here but visitors still share the cafeteria-style food with the students and researchers who live in dormitories.

Selva Verde

Map
on page
178–79

In 1986, Giovanna and Juan Holbrook, committed conservationists from Florida, bought **Selva Verde** ㊷ (tel: 766 6800), which consists of 200 hectares (500 acres) of primary and secondary tropical lowland forest, along the banks of the Sarapiquí River, in order to save the land from deforestation. They designed their beautiful river lodge specially to have a minimal impact on the environment. It rests lightly on posts above the forest floor, resembling the jungle spiders that inspired its construction.

Guests reside in tropical hardwood rooms at the end of covered corridors, which radiate from a central conference room into the forest. The lodge is also a popular lunch stop for tour groups. The jungle and its denizens are never more than a few feet away. This immersion in the lowland forest creates an extraordinary feeling of stillness, which encourages people to whisper when they speak. Selva Verde carries the Certification for Sustainable Tourism. The CST is a voluntary program that sets a standard for lodges in sustainability including environmental and community impact.

Spectacular birds are commonplace at Selva Verde: keel-billed and chestnut-mandibled toucans can be seen feeding on the fruit of the nutmeg trees near the front porch of the lodge. A stroll along the path to the main lodge building is likely to be rewarded with the iridescent colors of several species of hummingbirds. Nearby, Montezuma oropendolas utter gurgling mating calls, which harmonize with the songs of other birds and countless frogs and insects in a continual symphony. There are nearly 100 species of birds at Selva Verde. The Lodge's other main attraction is its incredibly slow-moving arboreal sloths, which have a metabolic rate of half of what is normal for an animal of its size. ❏

ABOVE keel-billed toucans are common at Selva Verde. **BELOW:** the canopy viewing system at Rara Avis.

MOUNTAINS OF FIRE

Vulcanologists are always busy in Costa Rica, which has five active volcanoes and some 112 dormant and extinct ones on the mainland

Costa Rica is a land of earthquakes and volcanoes, where time-strapped tourists, hikers and mountaineering enthusiasts can climb the Central Valley's four active cones in just two days. Visitors should remember, though, that an active volcano demands respect; proper equipment (good shoes, and in the case of Rincón de la Vieja, a compass) are essential. Taking a guided tour will ensure the greatest safety. Locals are proud of their explosive geology, and have made Poás and Irazú volcanoes the country's most visited parks.

▽ THE VIEW FROM IRAZU
On a clear day, visitors to Irazú can see both the Pacific and Caribbean. The rich soils on its slopes are excellent for growing vegetables.

The most dynamic and majestic of Costa Rica's active volcanoes is Arenal, a nearly perfect cone. The 1,633-meter (4,950-ft) high volcano rises above Alajuela's farmlands, adjacent to its own lake, and offers a spectacular show. Loud thunder-like explosions announce an eruption, and colorful clouds of gas and steam spew out of the top. While visitors to the conservation area find the explosions awe-inspiring and/or frightening, locals barely look up when Arenal thunders.

A VIOLENT PAST

Dormant until the late 1960s, Arenal was thought to be an extinct volcano until a series of earth-quakes began on July 28, 1968. Arenal blew the next morning, causing damage that stretched approximately 5 km (3 miles) west and shock waves that were felt as far away as Boulder, Colorado. More than 80 people died after being poisoned with volcanic gas and struck by rocks, and many homes were leveled. Since then, the volcano has continued to rumble and erupt on a more reduced scale, sometimes several times per day, spewing forth fiery cascades of lava and rocks the size of small houses.

POAS VOLCANO IS IN ACTIVITY
YOU ENTER UNDER YOUR OWN RISK
SPN – MIRENEM

◁ **DEADLY BEAUTY**
Arenal is most impressive at night, when incandescent rocks and lava cascade down the north slope, which is bare of vegetation most of the way down. There are explosions every few hours during the volcano's active periods, but it can rest for months without activity. The cone is often covered by clouds.

▽ **MOON WALK**
While the crater of Poás looks like the moon, the rest of the park is green: there is a dwarf cloud forest near the crater and a high-altitude wet forest also shelters the resplendent quetzal. The park has a good museum and hiking trails.

BELOW THE VOLCANOES

To observe Arenal in true luxury by day or night, pamper yourself at the Spanish colonial-style Tabacón Hot Springs Resort, built on the site of a 1975 hot avalanche deposit that provides the source of heat for the thermal waters.

Although vulcanologists feel there is a risk of future hot avalanches, this hasn't stopped the *Ticos* and tourists who flock here to exclaim excitedly over the activity of the volcano and soak their aching muscles. A dip in the waters is also supposedly beneficial for anyone suffering from skin problems and arthritis.

Twelve pools of varying depths and temperatures (the warmest is a sizzling 38°C/102°F), a jacuzzi, hot waterfall, slides and an individual tub tucked deep in the beautifully landscaped tropical gardens mean fun for everyone from kids to senior citizens.

A spa offers mud facials, and the resort has lockers, towel rental and showers. The hotel here is elegant and expensive. Book well in advance.

If you are on a tight budget, try the Baldi Termae just west of La Fortuna or the low-key but lush Termales del Bosque near San Carlos.

◁ **ACTIVE POAS**
Volcán Poás is just coming out of an active phase, and fumaroles are visible from the viewing point above the crater. However, sulfur gas emissions mean visibility is often poor.

▷ **SPRINGS OF DELIGHT**
One of the best places to view Volcán Arenal is from Tabacón Hot Springs.

THE CARIBBEAN COAST

Beautiful warm water glowing blue and turquoise, radiant sunshine and coconut palms rustling in the gentle breeze welcome you to Costa Rica's Caribbean coastline

Map on page 230

San José

T he two-hour drive from San José to the Caribbean coast is on a paved, slow-moving highway winding through the canyons, mountains, waterfalls and virgin forests of Parque Nacional Braulio Carrillo. Descending from the cool cloudiness of Braulio Carrillo into the tropical lowland forests of the Caribbean, the temperature rises and the air becomes heavy.

Puerto Limón

Puerto Limón ❶ (pop. 102,000) is pure Caribbean – with its rich, ripe jumble of sights and sounds and smells, it is a hot, steamy, laid-back place. Most middle-class *Ticos* who live in the Central Valley consider it something of a disgrace, while most young European and North American travelers are enamored with the idea of Puerto Limón, if not the place itself.

In the center of Limón you won't find the usual cathedral or soccer field facing a plaza such as you see in all the towns of the Central Valley. Instead **Parque Vargas**, named after a local governor, is filled with huge banyan trees with buttress roots that the townspeople use for bus stop seats.

Commerce began in Limón in the 17th century, when cacao plantations were worked by slaves. But pirates from Jamaica continually raided the area until production was finally abandoned in the early 1800s, and the region, which was impossibly hot, humid and swampy, was once again forgotten for several decades.

Coffee, bananas and the railroad

The growth of the coffee market meant that an Atlantic port was required for exporting to England and Europe, and in 1871, this was established on the site of "El Limón," a migrant black fishermen's village consisting of five huts. That same year, the government contracted the construction of the Atlantic railroad from San José to the Caribbean Coast. Laborers from Jamaica, Italy and China were brought in to work on the railroad and many made permanent homes in the area.

Meanwhile, Minor Keith, the North American responsible for building the railroad, had the bright idea of planting and cultivating bananas alongside the track in order to raise additional funds for the rising costs of construction of the Atlantic railroad.

Limón thus became a railroad and banana town, populated largely by Afro-Caribbean and Chinese immigrants who had come to Costa Rica looking for work. Since 1872, Limón and the banana industry have experienced great booms and busts: bumper banana crops (even exceeding the value of Costa Rica's coffee exports); labor troubles and violent strikes; and hard times of high unemployment when

PRECEDING PAGES: the road to Cahuita. **LEFT:** tributary in Barra Colorado. **BELOW:** sloth at Aviaros del Caribe.

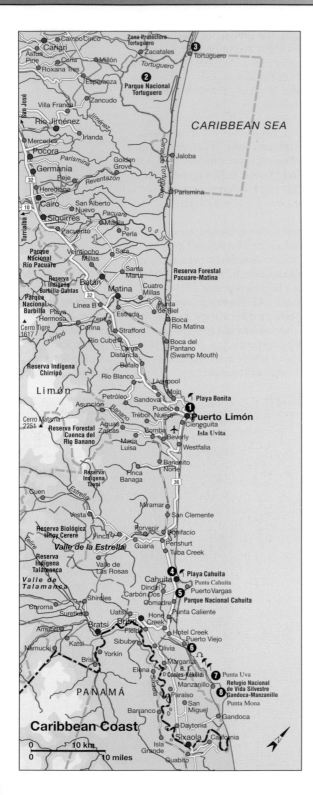

Caribbean Coast

the United Fruit Company abandoned the Caribbean Coast.

Yet Limón was effectively ignored by the Central Valley government of Costa Rica. The black workers and their families had no rights of citizenship; they were not permitted to work in the Pacific Zone nor in the Central Valley.

However, since the Civil War of 1948, living conditions have improved somewhat for the black residents of the city. Today, they are full-fledged citizens of Costa Rica, and can travel and work anywhere they wish.

Problems

There are few decent hotels in Limón. Most travelers stay at the Hotel Park or more upscale hotels north or south of the city center. Beware, however, that theft (particularly from cars) and muggings are a problem in the city and it is worth paying a little more for accommodations.

The main tourist focus here is the huge cruise-ship dock that disgorges thousands of visitors annually.

Carnaval

For many people, Puerto Limón's annual *Carnaval* (Carnival) is the best reason to visit the place. This week-long jubilant event is held every October. Carnival first began in 1949, under the leadership of a barber called Alfred Henry King, who timed the festivities to coincide with the anniversary of Christopher Columbus's landing near Limón on October 18, 1502. *El Día de la Raza,* "the Day of the People," which falls during Carnival Week and traditionally includes the participation of the indigenous peoples who live in the region, has recently been re-named *Día de las Culturas* (Day of the Cultures) in recognition of the fact that not everyone remembers Columbus with equal affection and also as a tribute to the contributions made to Costa Rica by people of all cultures.

The highlight of Carnival Week is the parade, when local people and thousands of visitors take to the streets to join in a glorious music and dance spectacle. The drums, the heat, the beat, the shining bodies of dancers and drummers in bright costumes, urge spectators to abandon their inhibitions and to surrender to the Caribbean magic. And so they do, *Limonenses* and tourists alike, filling the streets, shimmying, shaking, singing and carousing, while the irresistible rhythms of steel drums fill the warm, humid air.

Map on page 230

Tortuguero

Travel on the **Tortuguero canals**, up through the area north of Limón, has been likened to a trip on the *African Queen*, or to floating dreamily down the Amazon. It is certainly one of the most wonderfully lyrical trips to be taken anywhere. As you drift lazily amidst the fragrance of white ginger blossoms, lavender water hyacinths and the ylang ylang flower, there is a tranquility here that soothes all your cares away.

Look around and with the help of an expert naturalist guide you may catch occasional glimpses of sloths, crocodiles and basking freshwater turtles. High up in the exuberant vegetation, green macaws and multicolored parrots squawk noisily, while agile howler monkeys shake the branches. Around 19,000 hectares (47,000 acres) of the coast and hinterland have been designated as the **Parque Nacional Tortuguero** ❷ (Tortuguero National Park). There are many ways to navigate its maze of waterways, including hitching a ride on a cargo boat, or by renting a dugout canoe or speedboat. The best way to tour the canals is on a boat guided by an expert naturalist. Or you can simpy take a package tour which will include a lodge room, meals, naturalist guides, and the trip through the canals. All of the Tortuguero hotels offer guided river trips and transportation either by

ABOVE: some eating places in Costa Rica also cater for vegetarians.
BELOW: *Carnaval* revellers in Limón.

bus and boat or by small plane from San José. Launches going up Tortuguero depart from Moín, just a few miles north of Limón. NatureAir and SANSA have short flights from San José to Tortuguero and **Barra del Colorado**, which is north of Tortuguero, near the Nicaraguan border. From there you can hire a boat to travel south through the canals.

Barra del Colorado is a wildlife refuge famous for its sport fishing. Tours are available, but beware high humidity, high temperatures, and a voracious mosquito population. Much of the refuge is unexplored with few marked trails.

The green sea turtle

Tortuguero, from *tortuga*, which means turtle in Spanish, is the main nesting area in the Caribbean for green sea turtles. The turtles have been listed as endangered since the 1950s and the **Caribbean Conservation Corporation** (CCC) has been established at Tortuguero for the purpose of studying and protecting these vulnerable creatures.

The CCC runs a **Natural History Center** (www.cccturtle.org) between the village and the John H. Phipps Biological Field Station on the Tortuguero River. The center's large, colorful displays are packed with information about the region's plant and animal life, including, of course, the green sea turtle. The area has been known for its turtle-hunting grounds since at least the mid-16th century, and turtles were exploited for their meat, shells and eggs with impunity until as recently as 1970, when the area was established as a national park. Now at least the visiting green sea turtles and their leatherback cousins are afforded some degree of protection.

If possible, go to Tortuguero during the turtle-nesting season. And insist on having a knowledgeable naturalist guide to advise you of things to do (and things to avoid), in the spirit of understanding the habits and sensitivities of these magnificent creatures. Between July and October is the best time to

BELOW: Tortuga Lodge, along the Tortuguero canals.

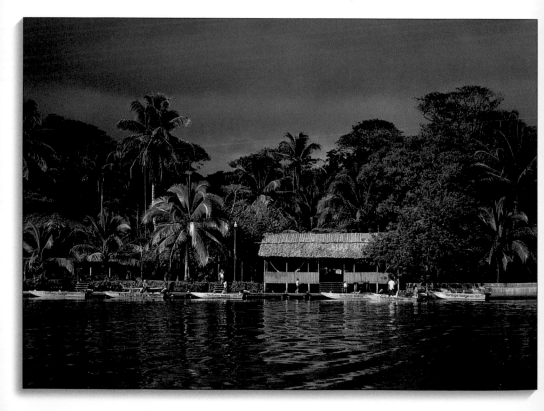

view the prehistoric ritual of the nesting of the green turtles, and between February and July is best for the leatherback turtle. The enormous tractor-tread trails, which the female turtles leave in the sand as they laboriously make their way up the beaches to dig their nests, are easily visible even at night under a thick stormy sky. And following these freshly made trails to observe the nesting of one of these turtles is an experience that affects even the most worldly traveler.

Another exciting option for turtle-watching is the beach at Parismina halfway between Tortuguero and Puerto Limón. Accessible only by boat from Siquirres or by small charter plane, this remote Caribbean village has opened a turtle hatchery to help the conservation of leatherback and green turtles. Tourists are warmly welcomed in this small community to help with the Save the Turtles of Parismina Project (www.costaricaturtles.org), and there are a few *cabinas* and rooms in the village to rent as well as an upscale fishing lodge* *(see Where to Stay, page 279–280).*

Tortuguero village

Further north, up the canals, the village of **Tortuguero** ❸ sits on a narrow spit of land bordered by the Caribbean Sea and the Tortuguero River. A brief history of Tortuguero is available at the information kiosk near the soccer field. The village has narrow paths winding through exuberant greenery. Palm trees rustle overhead. Wooden houses sit on stilts. Restaurants, shops, and *cabinas* catering to tourists have been constructed, but even so, village life seems to continue in a timeless way.

Canadian naturalist Daryl Loth, owner of Casa Marbella, in the town, can answer your questions about Tortuguero. And if you're hoping to sample Caribbean rice and beans cooked in coconut milk, you can do so in one of the village's restaurants; Miss Junie's is one of the most popular (tel: 709 8102).

ABOVE: a guided tour of Tortuguero is recommended.
BELOW: paddling up a Talamanca tributary.

Talamanca

Most travelers who come to the Caribbean coast spend only a short time in Puerto Limón, and then quickly head south to the Talamanca coast. The drive south runs parallel to the shore, with glimpses of rivers off to the right, and the sea to the left.

Somewhere near Tuba Creek begins the **Talamanca** region of Costa Rica, extending from the Caribbean coast and reaching into the mountains that run from the Central Valley southeast into Panamá. This area was the refuge of many indigenous people who fled the Spanish conquerors.

Until the 1970s, the Talamanca region was populated mainly by the Bribrí and Cabécar who lived in the mountains, and by the descendants of English-speaking black immigrants from the Caribbean islands who settled along the coast. The black settlers were farmers and fishermen following the old ways brought from Jamaica, most affectionately described in their own words in Paula Palmer's fascinating folk history, *What Happen*. They developed a local cuisine based on the foods they grew, and planted the coconut trees

TIP

Animal lovers
shouldn't miss the
**Aviarios Sloth
Sanctuary** just north
of Cahuita. The
sanctuary conducts
serious research, with
the aim of returning
orphaned and injured
sloths to the wild. A
visit here includes an
informative video
presentation, a visit
with the resident
sloths and a canoe
tour along canals to
view birds and wildlife
(tel: 750 0775).

BELOW: black beach
at Puerto Viejo.

that still line the beaches. For the little money they needed, they sold coconut oil, hawksbill turtle shells and cassava starch.

They spoke a creole English, played cricket, danced quadrilles, carved dugout canoes from local trees and recited Shakespeare for amusement. Isolated by the sea and the mountains, no roads connected these people with the rest of Spanish-speaking Costa Rica, and their life continued quite peacefully and independently. All that has changed now, with the opening of a slick new highway and other roads connecting the sleepy coastal towns of Talamanca with San José and the rest of the world.

Most black residents of the coast now speak both English and Spanish, but you'll have to listen carefully to pick up this local Caribbean patois form of English. A few of the more common expressions: "Wh'appen?" ("What's happening?") is the usual form of greeting, replacing the "Adios" of the Central Valley. "How de morning?" is "Good morning" and "Go good" is "Take care." The polite form of address is to use his or her first name preceded by Mr or Miss. For the most part, the indigenous peoples of the region now speak Spanish in addition to their own native language (of which there are several), and take part in regional political and economic life, although many maintain ancient beliefs and customs. There are three indigenous reserves in Talamanca: the large Talamanca-Bribri Reserve, the Talamanca-Cabécar Reserve and the smaller Keköldi Reserve. Access to the reserves by non-indigenous people is limited, and you usually need to obtain permission in advance. Tours in the **Keköldi Wak Ka Koneke** reserve, run by residents, focus on history and culture, medicinal plants, crafts and traditional foods, as well as bird life and mountain hikes (tel: 884 2671).

Cahuita

Local legend has it that in 1828 a turtle fisherman named William Smith (known as "Old Smith"), rowed and sailed north from his home in Panamá to fish for turtles. Finding a beautiful calm bay protected by a coral reef near Cahuita Point, he decided to settle there with his family. In those early days, green and hawksbill turtles were plentiful and, as they had not yet learned to fear man, made an easy catch. Old Smith is said to have been the first English-speaking Afro-Caribbean settler to the area, which at that time was populated with Amerindians, and frequently visited by pirates.

Map on page 230

Cahuita ❹ is a small scruffy town of faded but dignified-looking wooden houses, once painted bright colors that are now soft pastels, with a touch of Caribbean whimsy in the gingerbread details. Young travelers from Europe, Canada and the US, oblivious to more modest local sensibilities, amble along the beaches and roadways in scanty, bright beachwear.

The Snorkeling House (tel: 361 1924), next door to Miss Edith's restaurant, rents out snorkeling equipment and arranges walks in the national park. A number of guides are usually available to show visitors around the sights.

Beware that Cahuita has drug problems, and petty crime against tourists is also rife, even though the authorities crack down every so often in an attempt to keep a lid on the situation.

Cahuita National Park

To the immediate south of Cahuita is **Parque Nacional Cahuita** ❺, famous for its fine, sandy beach and coral reef. The reef extends 500 meters (1,500 ft) out to sea from **Punta Cahuita** and offers great snorkeling, although the point of the reef was severely displaced during an earthquake.

ABOVE: a bike is often a handy means of getting about on the coast.
BELOW: a sleeping red-eyed tree frog.

There are many species of tropical fish, crabs, lobsters, sea fans, anemones, sponges, seaweed and innumerable other marine creatures to observe amidst the coral formations. You can admire it all and keep your feet dry aboard a glass-bottomed boat, or you can swim from the Puerto Vargas end of the beach. Diving equipment may be rented in Cahuita town.

The main entrance to the park is at Puerto Vargas, 5 km (3 miles) south of town. Lifeguards patrol the beach and there is good snorkeling at Punta Cahuita. Camping is permitted; to get to the **Puerto Vargas** camping area enter from the south side of the park, 5 km (3 miles) from Cahuita. Coatis and raccoons frequent the campgrounds looking for fruit and other edibles, and are not above overturning a tent to get them. Fresh water, outhouses, and picnic tables are available. From Puerto Vargas you can hike along a nature trail into the jungle or explore the wreck of a British slave galleon from which cannons, cannon balls, swords, copper and bronze manacles, and arm bands have been retrieved.

North of Cahuita is a black-sand beach where the waters are gentle and good for swimming. Accommodations, some with kitchens, are available throughout town and on the beach. Reservations are essential during Christmas, Easter and during Carnival, the second week in October. The best time to visit Cahuita is from February to April, and in October. Sophisticated food is served at Cha Cha Cha in the middle of town. The other culinary hotspot is Miss Edith's. Just ask anyone where it is: the place has an enviable reputation for good, down-home Caribbean cooking. The Hotel Jaguar is also known for its innovative French-Caribbean cuisine.

Coconuts and cacao

Along the roadside look out for stands advertising "Hay Pipas." They are selling green coconuts with refreshing juice inside. The vendor will slice one open for you with a wicked-looking machete.

Heading south toward Puerto Viejo, along a pretty paved road that runs parallel to the beach, you pass houses of every style and class; but there is something magical about the Caribbean air and even the humblest shack has a picturesque quality when it is set amidst tall coconut trees. In many yards are low, wooden dryers with tin roofs, used for drying cacao and coconut. The roofs are opened to the bright sun on clear days, and closed in the rain.

Just before the turn-off to Puerto Viejo is **Hone Creek**. Hone is the name of a short palm with large roots. When the Jamaicans came to the Talamanca coast to work on the railroad in the 1890s, they began calling it "Home Creek," and today there are road signs in the area announcing both "Hone Creek" and "Home Creek." There is usually a checkpoint with a guard at Hone Creek, seeking to stem the flow of contraband goods from Panamá. To get to Puerto Viejo take the gravel road to the left. Watch for cacao trees in the now-abandoned cacao plantations along the sides of the road. The fruit grows from the trunk of the tree and turns wonderful colors as it ripens: some become a soft turquoise color, others a brilliant coral. The seeds of the ripe fruit are slightly sweet and undeniably choco-latey, even in this raw state. To experience chocolate from bean to chocolate bar, take the Chocolate Tour (tel: 750 0075), a 2-hour visit to an organic cacao plantation run by a Swiss couple. And, of course, you get to taste the finished product.

Puerto Viejo

BELOW: a beach near Punta Uva after a storm.

While Cahuita has a certain shabby dignity, **Puerto Viejo ❻** is a tumbledown community. It is a hodge-podge of dilapidated wooden houses amidst tall grass. At the entrance to the town you pass a rusted-out barge which is anchored just off the black-sand beach.

It wasn't long ago that there were no roads to Puerto Viejo: no cars, no tourists, no money. But things have changed. Puerto Viejo's beautiful undeveloped beaches and easy-going ways have been discovered. New *cabinas*, hotels, and developments throughout the area proclaim the arrival of tourism.

Puerto Viejo is famous in surfing circles for the **Salsa Brava**, a hot, fast, explosive wave that breaks over the reef from December to April and again in June and July. It attracts surfers from all over the world. At other times of the year the sea is quiet, par-ticularly inside the reef, and good for snorkeling.

North of town is the road to Chimuri Beach Cot-tages – a collection of *cabinas* constructed of thatch over bamboo in the traditional Bribrí style. Chimuri's owner, Mauricio gives guided walking tours and recently opened Chimuri Jungle Lodge (tel: 750 0506), an indigenous living experience. El Pizote Lodge (tel: 750 0088), located on the right just before town, offers lovely cabins and rooms, well-groomed grounds with trails, and even California-Tico-style meals.

Restaurant Támara and nearby Soda Miss Sam's offer Caribbean-style fish or chicken served with tasty beans and rice, and a good selection of fruit drinks. Stanford's on the beach is famous for its night-life and fish dinners. Vegetarian-friendly Chile Rojo on Main Street serves up spicey Thai and Middle Eastern food. For casual breakfasts and baked goods, try Pan Pay.

To the south of town there are *cabinas* and sophisticated new hotels along the road across from beautiful stretches of white-sand beaches edged by palm and beach almond trees; award-winning Bungalows Cariblue at Playa Cocles is renowned for service, style and gourmet Italian food (tel: 750 0035). Another Italian import is the Pecora Nera restaurant, rated as one of the best restaurants in the country (tel: 750 0257). Rivers are bridged by precarious-looking wooden structures, which become slippery in the rain. Signs advertise bicycles for rent – a great way to get around Puerto Viejo and to the nearby beaches.

If you would like to learn a bit more about the Talamanca region, the non-profit **Talamanca Association for Ecotourism and Conservation** (ATEC; tel: 750 0398) provides environmentally and culturally oriented tours led by local guides who speak Spanish and English. Choices for outings include snorkeling, fishing, birdwatching, adventure treks, visits to the Talamanca indigenous reserves and visits to the houses of local people for home-cooked meals.

Punta Uva and Manzanillo-Gandoca

To the south of Puerto Viejo is heavenly **Punta Uva ❼**, probably the best easily accessible beach along Costa Rica's Caribbean coast. Crystalline,

Map on page 230

ABOVE: there is no shortage of rest and refreshment in Puerto Viejo.
BELOW: a Mexican hairy porcupine.

aquamarine water laps quietly on palm-lined beaches, and both the air and water temperature seem fixed at a constant, perfect 27°C (80°F). You can cycle here from Puerto Viejo and there are plenty of charming and affordable accommodations all the way down the road to Punta Uva. For people who like to camp but don't want to rough it too much, there's Almonds & Corals Lodge, in the middle of a cool, shaded former cacao plantation. You'll sleep in comfortable tents nested within larger tents set on platforms and complete with electricity, hot-water showers and flush toilets (tel: 272 2024).

Further south, still on the beach, is **Manzanillo**, a tiny village which can be reached by walking along the sand for about two hours from Punta Uva, or 20 minutes from Puerto Viejo by car along the dirt and gravel road that terminates here. The two *tico* bars provide local dishes and idyllic views. Coral reefs offshore create a natural harbor. Surfers enjoy it for its fast beach break. Manzanilla is also a fisherman's haven. When news of a school of bait arrive, fishing boats appear from Puntarenas to take part in the days catch.

There is a cluster of houses, a restaurant, a bar, a grocery store, empty beaches, and very inexpensive *cabinas*. Local children play in the waves or bathe in the river, young men fish in dugout canoes, elders sit around and talk quietly in the shade, and not much more goes on around here. This is Costa Rica at its most relaxed. Local women will prepare meals for visitors in their homes if asked, and fishermen and farmers are usually happy to chat about their work and the land.

ABOVE: snacking on the street is a way of life in Costa Rica. **BELOW:** United Fruit banana train, *circa* 1916.

South of the village of Manzanillo is the **Refugio Nacional de Vida Silvestre Gandoca-Manzanillo ❽**, which protects swamplands, coral reefs, turtle nesting grounds and the only mangrove forest on Costa Rica's Caribbean coast. The Gandoca River Estuary is a nursery for tarpon. Most of the refuge is flat or has gently rolling hills, covered with forest and some farms. Hiking is limited to the coast. Bring your own supply of water since there are no facilities available in the refuge.

Map on page 230

Banana country

Sixaola is a banana town on the Panamá border. To get there continue along the paved road from Hone Creek to the south, instead of turning off to Puerto Viejo and Manzanillo. The road is paved until just outside of Bribrí: the rest of the way it is gravel, in fair condition.

In the early 1900s, the United Fruit Company expanded its successful banana plantations from across the Panamá side of the Sixaola River into Costa Rica, and although the company has long gone, the area stretching from just outside the village of Bribrí to the border at Sixaola is still very much Banana Land.

Banana-processing plants occur at intervals along the road: it's interesting to stop for a break at one of the open-air plants to watch the workers handling the large bunches, called *racimos*, pulling the dried flowers off the ends of individual bananas, cutting bunches of bananas off the stalks, sorting, washing and putting them in boxes which no longer are labeled "United Fruit" but "Chiquita."

Mountains of green bananas, which look perfectly acceptable, but don't meet the specifications of Chiquita's North American and European consumers, are formed next to the sorting area. They are used for animal feed, banana paper, fibre in baby food or mulch. And some are left to rot. The smell of fermenting bananas is a familiar one here even though the fruit is used in a number of resourceful ways, from green banana *ceviche* to banana vinegar compresses, a folk remedy for sprained muscles.   ❑

ABOVE: bananas grow in abundance. **BELOW:** banana plantations near the Panamanian border.

CARIBBEAN BANANA REPUBLIC

Banana cultivation in Costa Rica began as a by-product of the Atlantic railroad. The crop was only planted by the side of the track in order to help finance its construction. However, the easy success of the banana venture quickly attracted foreign capital and export of the fruit in huge quantities was soon under way.

In 1889 Minor Keith, the Atlantic railroad pioneer, formed the United Fruit Company and turned Costa Rica into Central America's first banana republic.

United Fruit soon became a symbol of the evils of foreign domination and control over the local economy, making huge profits for the few at the top. The company's ruthless methods and exploitation of labor were widely reviled, but it was also highly successful. By 1913 the plantations were producing 11 million bunches a year and Costa Rica was the world's top exporter.

Unfortunately, banana disease on the Caribbean coast devastated the crop and in the 1930s United Fruit pulled out of Limón province for good, leaving behind a virtually destitute region that saw little economic activity until the 1970s. Nowadays, the area is once again producing bananas on a large scale, with more than US$450 million worth exported every year.

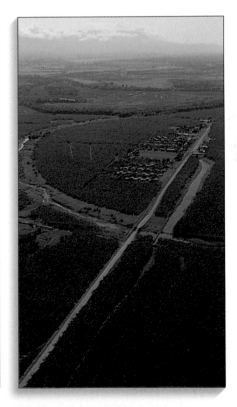

Sea Turtles

Sea turtles look more like their close but extinct relatives, the dinosaurs, than modern animals. Remarkable adaptations to life in the sea have enabled them to survive, largely unchanged, for more than 150 million years. They "fly" like birds through the water using front flippers as wings. Yet they retain terrestrial traits and must surface to breathe air and crawl ashore to nest and lay their eggs.

Costa Rica is home to five species of sea turtles: green, hawksbill, Olive Ridley, leatherback and loggerhead. They are more easily viewed here than anywhere else in the world. They nest at several well-known beaches on both Caribbean and Pacific shores. During the nesting season, if you happen to be in the right place at the right time, you may see one of the most amazing spectacles in the animal kingdom: *the arribada*, when 100,000 or more Olive Ridley turtles come ashore to nest simultaneously *(see page 202)*. Or, equally spectacular, the sight of a 680-kg (1,500-lb) leatherback hauling her massive body out of the water and up the beach to bury her clutch of eggs in the sand.

Tortuguero Beach, a 35-km (22-mile) stretch of sand on the Caribbean side of Costa Rica, is the most important nesting area for green turtles in the Western Caribbean. Here, you can see green turtles, hawksbill turtles and Ridleys.

Green turtles mate and nest several times from September through November. With the sharp hook on his front flippers, the male holds and mounts the female. If the sexually aggressive male can't locate a mate, he will eagerly clamber on top of anything that floats. Chunks of wood, other male turtles, even skin divers are not safe from a male's misguided passion.

An impregnated female waits offshore until dark before beginning her long struggle up the beach to the nesting site. During her crawl up the beach, disturbances such as noise and light will cause the female to abort the nesting procedure, and to return to the safety of the sea. But once she has begun digging the nest, nothing will distract her. Using her rear flippers, she scoops out a vase-shaped hole, approximately 1 meter (2–3 ft) deep. One hundred or more leathery, golf-ball-sized eggs covered with a mucus "fungicide" drop into the nest one or two at a time until the entire clutch is deposited. She covers the nest, tamps down the sand and begins her crawl back to the sea, leaving her progeny at the mercy of coatimundis, dogs, raccoons and human scavengers, known as *hueveros,* who steal the eggs and sell them to local bars.

In undisturbed nests, baby green turtles hatch in a couple of months. Using a temporary egg tooth, they tear open their shells. Soon the entire clutch is ready to rise to the surface. A critical mass of about 100 turtles all working together is needed to excavate the 1 meter (3 ft) of sand which is covering them. Usually before dawn, they erupt onto the beach, look for the brightest part of the horizon over the sea, and scramble for the water through a gauntlet of ghost crabs and birds, perhaps then only to be met by sharks and predatory fish once they do reach the water. Hundreds of thousands race for the sea and probably less than 3 percent survive. Those that do make it go offshore to floating rafts of Sargassum weed where they find shelter and food for their first and most difficult months at sea.

For several decades they live nomadic lives, migrating over vast distances of the open ocean to feed on turtle grass in the remote Miskito Keys off Nicaragua or at Cahuita on the Talamanca coast. Some navigate several thousand miles to the Windward Islands, using no apparent landmarks or visual cues. It is thought that crystals of magnetic iron located in the turtles' brains perhaps serve as internal compasses, guiding them across the seas, or more prosaically they may just follow a certain smell or substance.

Although no one knows for certain, marine biologists estimate that it takes 15–30 years for these turtles to reach sexual maturity, at which point they reconvene on the beaches where they were born to mate, nest and complete their incredible reproduction cycle.

To early explorers, fresh turtle meat was a welcome change from salt beef and sea biscuits. Tropical peoples still relish meat from the sea turtle. But sadly, the species is being endangered more from frivolous use than for subsistence purposes: six or seven species of sea turtle are on the brink of extinction. In bars from the Caribbean to Sri Lanka, sea turtle eggs are sucked from the shells as aphrodisiacs. Tortoiseshell has a high value when carved, polished and made into jewelry, combs and spectacle frames. Turtle skin is even being used as a substitute for alligator skin in shoes and purses.

Sea turtles remain on the endangered species list, although worldwide conservation programs are under way. Importation of turtle products into the US and other countries is strictly prohibited and carries stiff penalties. But adult turtles are accidentally caught in shrimp trawls and fishermen continue to hunt them, sometimes illegally.

Silt from unlawfully deforested land near Tortuguero washes onto the beaches, bringing weeds which grow and take valuable nesting space from the turtles. Floodlights from beachside hotels and developments frighten off females ready to nest, and disorient hatchlings trying to find the sea.

The future for many turtles is bleak, though in 1991 a new national park was created at Playa Grande on the Nicoya Peninsula and named Las Baulas, which means leatherback turtle. And the National Park authorities now take a very strict line on poaching. Perhaps this, plus the efforts of the many volunteer programs and the commercial demands of eco-tourism will yet save the turtles.

People tend to like turtles, even though they are not at first glance particularly lovable or even very attractive. In contrast to the modern way of life, the turtle's ponderous pace, non-violent nature and steady perseverance in getting from here to there seems a more reasonable way to conduct affairs.

Turtles even have a prominent place in the religious and folk histories of many cultures. Some Hindu sects venerate the turtle as a living god, the reincarnation of Shiva, creator and destroyer of all life. Myth states that a turtle brought the Buddhist world from the sea on its back. ❑

LEFT: struggling ashore to lay and bury eggs.
RIGHT: loggerheads are Caribbean dwellers.

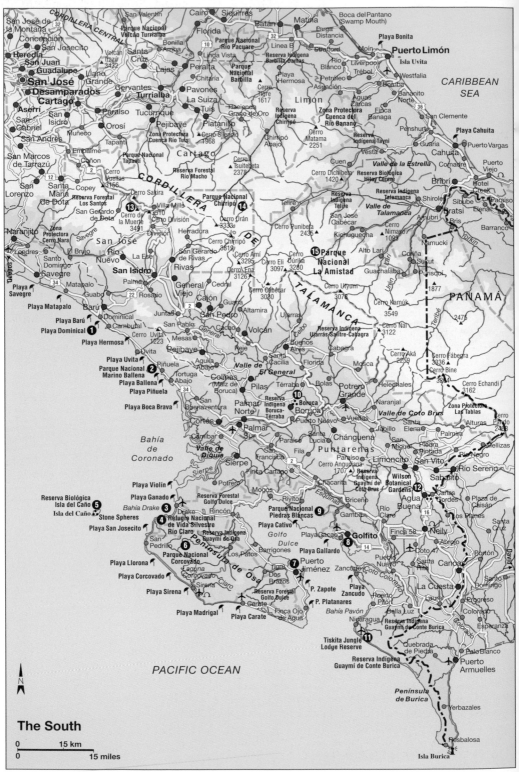

The South

Playa Savegre
Playa Matapalo
Playa Barú
Playa Dominical **1**
Playa Hermosa
Playa Uvita
Parque Nacional **2**
Marino Ballena
Playa Ballena
Playa Piñuela
Playa Boca Brava

Reserva Biológica **5**
Isla del Caño
Isla del Caño
Stone Spheres
Playa San Josecito

Playa Violín
Playa Ganado
Bahía Drake **3**
Drake
Refugio Nacional **4**
de Vida Silvestre
Río Claro
Reserva Indígena
Guaymí de Osa

Parque Nacional **6**
Corcovado
Playa Llorona
Playa Corcovado
Playa Sirena
Playa Madrigal
Playa Carate

0   15 km
0   15 miles

THE SOUTH

Map on page 246

Even by local standards, the south is a wild region. It includes the highest peak in Central America and the largest, most inaccessible national park with the most pristine tropical wet forest

The *Zona Sur,* or Southern Zone, rises in the highlands around Cerro de la Muerte, the highest point in the country, then falls away into the agricultural lands of the Valle de El General and ends in the tropical lowlands at the Panamanian border. The Interamericana Highway runs like a spine through the whole region, joining up with the Costanera coastal highway at Palmar Sur. This is an area for hikers and nature lovers with a sense of adventure, who like exploring off the beaten path.

Playa Dominical and Marino Ballena National Park

A beautiful drive of 35 km (22 miles) on a paved road from San Isidro west, through misty mountains, brings you to **Playa Dominical** ❶. (The trip from San José to Dominical via San Isidro takes about four hours, including rest stops.) Dominical can also be reached by a two-hour drive along the coast from Quepos. The coast road from Quepos, the *Costanera Sur*, has been somewhat improved, although it is still a dirt road in places. But the scenery is wonderful. Stop off for the night at secluded Pacific Edge Cabins (tel: 771 4582), high on a forested ridge with spectacular sea views. Or spend some time down at sea level at Hacienda Barú (tel: 787 0003), in the middle of a private forest reserve with miles of forest and beach trails.

PRECEDING PAGES:
Pacific breakers at
Corcovado National
Park; ox cart on the
Pacific coast.
BELOW: ancient
buttress roots.

The beach is a long stretch of brown, silty sand offering good waves for surfing, though beware dangerous currents when swimming. There are pleasant, shady places on the sand for camping. "Town" is a small, somewhat funky settlement, with a few trendy restaurants, surf shops, a health-food store and some comfortable hotels along with basic *cabinas* and hostels catering to young surfers. During the dry season Playa Dominical's weather can be impossibly hot and breezeless, and the landscape barren.

A horseback trip to **Nauyaca Falls**, also known as Santo Cristo and Barú Falls, takes about two hours. The falls consist of two cascades a total of 65 meters (210 ft) high, which tumble into a glorious warm water swimming hole. Don Lulo's Waterfall Tour arranges horseback tours to the falls; Finca Bella Vista offers sunset beach rides. Several area tour operators can book the tours for you, including Selva Mar in San Isidro de El General (tel: 771 4582).

Just south of Dominical is **Playa Dominicalito**, where there are good point-break waves for surfers. Swimming is best at low tide when beaches are exposed beyond coral rocks and there are beautiful views of the overlooking hills.

Some 17 km (11 miles) to the south of Dominical lies **Parque Nacional Marino Ballena** ❷, easily accessible along the recently widened and paved

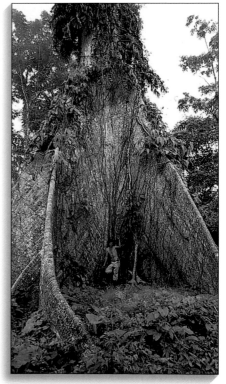

Costanera Sur. One of Costa Rica's smallest national parks, Marino Ballena offers beautiful beaches, mangroves where you can spot raccoons, lizards and caimans, and coral reefs. Dolphins and whales (in season) are common visitors.

The **Islas Ballenas**, also part of the park, provide refuge to humpback whales and their young from December through April. Two sandy beaches within the park sweep to a meeting point at Punta Uvita, and at low tide produce remarkably calm conditions for underwater exploration. Local boatmen will take visitors out to the reef for snorkeling, fishing or birdwatching, although at the north end of the park good snorkeling spots can be reached on foot at low tide.

In **Bahía Uvita**, the entry point to the park, there are a number of *cabinas* and *sodas*. Boats are available for diving, fishing and sightseeing trips. Just south of the park, on the east side of the Costanera, is a sign for Ojochal, a French-Canadian enclave with wonderful restaurants.

Farther south along the **Costanera Sur Highway** are **Playa Piñuela** and **Playa Ventanas**. Delfin Tours, right at the park entrance in the village of Bahía, can get you out onto the water for snorkeling. Mystic Dive Center (tel: 788 8636) can get you under the water. And Skyline Ultra Flight can take you above the water for a bird's-eye view from aboard an ultralight plane (tel: 743 8037).

The Osa Peninsula

Jutting out more than 50 km (30 miles) into the Pacific, the Osa Peninsula shelters the Golfo Dulce from ocean swells and creates a magnificent natural harbor. It is sculpted with picturesque beaches and rocky headlands, and is dissected by streams and rivers that cascade over volcanic cliffs on their way to the sea. The most majestic forests in all Costa Rica cover the hillsides and line

For a bird's-eye view of Marino Ballena Park, climb the hill to Cristal Ballena, a new luxury hotel with the best and biggest swimming pool on the coast. The owners are Austrian, so amongst the fresh seafood offerings in the restaurant you'll also find Wiener schnitzel.

BELOW: messing about in the bay.

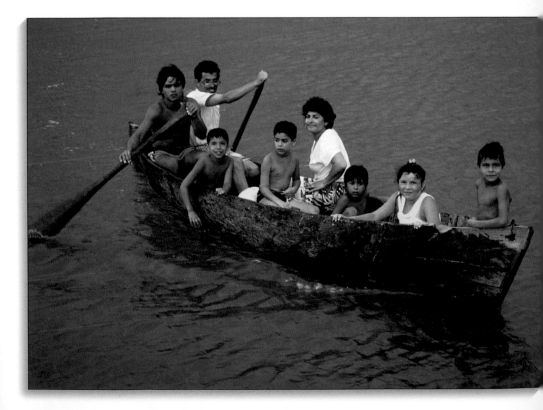

the valleys of the Osa Peninsula and, in many cases, represent the last stronghold of nature and endangered animals and plants that are endemic to southern Pacific Costa Rica. It is an imposing, impressive and wild place.

The Amerindians of the Diquis region were the first inhabitants of the peninsula, named Osa after one of their chiefs. They were accomplished goldsmiths and fashioned religious and ceremonial pieces from gold they found in the Tigre and Claro rivers. The Spanish made repeated explorations into Osa, killing the indigenous population, plundering their gold and searching for the legendary mines of Veragua. Gold continues to cause problems for the people of the Osa Peninsula. In the 1980s, the discovery of an 11-kg (25-lb) gold nugget created a gold rush and havoc in Corcovado National Park. Farmers-turned-prospectors invaded the area, tore up creeks and rivers for flakes of placer gold, hunted wildlife and burned the forest to plant crops. Gold fever destroyed many thousands of acres of parkland, and Corcovado was plagued by the usual boom-town socioeconomic ills such as alcoholism and prostitution. In response, government officials closed Corcovado National Park for years while they attempted to evict the trespassers. Then, after a minor civil war, officials reluctantly agreed to pay the miners a stipend to leave the park. Today, Corcovado is the jewel in the crown of Costa Rica's national park system. The park lodging facilities are very rustic and down-at-heel but the trails are worth the lack of comfort.

Map on page 246

ABOVE: one of the region's mysterious giant stone spheres *(see page 251).* **BELOW:** small insects often make the most noise.

Drake Bay

On the northern coast of the Osa Peninsula, **Bahía Drake ❸** is said to be the place where Sir Francis Drake, the first English navigator to sail around the world, landed in 1579. Until recently, it was only accessible on foot or by water or charter plane, but now there is a dirt road from Rincón, built by the electricity company to finally bring power to the village. It is a land of crystal-blue waters, pristine beaches and jungle. Your lodge will make your travel arrangements from San José, which can involve a flight to Palmar, transfer to Sierpe, then an exciting, open motorboat ride to the lodge. Direct flights from San José to Drake airstrip pass over Manuel Antonio Park and provide aerial perspectives of the south Pacific coast en route to Corcovado. As you land on the grass airstrip, look for scarlet macaws. You can also travel to Palmar overland, by bus or car, a 5½-hour trip, or fly to Palmar Sur and take a taxi to nearby Sierpe.

Just south of Drake Bay, along the scenic coastal footpath, is the Delfín Amor Ecolodge, an enchanting colony of hillside screened *cabinas*. Sea kayaking, snorkeling and yoga sessions are offered, along with dolphin watching (tel: 847 3131).

A little farther south is Punta Marenco Ecolodge, in the 500-hectare (1,200-acre) **Refugio Nacional de Vida Silvestre Río Claro ❹**. Guests reside in rustic but comfortable grass huts perched over the Pacific, with cool breezes, hammocks on private verandahs and views of Isla del Caño (tel: 234 1308). Bahía Drake Wilderness Camp (tel: 770 8012), just north of Marenco, is directly on the beach at Bahía Drake and offers similar programs as well as offshore fishing, canoeing, ocean kayaking and whale-watching trips

Ants in Your Plants

Should someone point out a "bull's horn acacia" to you, stop and have a close look at this thorny shrub. Measuring from between 1.5 to over 3 meters (4–10 ft) tall, along the branches are pairs of reddish spines that look like miniature replicas of a Texas steer's horns. Hence its name.

Of the many relationships that have evolved between tropical ants and plants, that of the bull's horn acacia and its stinging ants is one of the most curious. It is also one of the most dramatic examples of tropical co-evolution between species.

With some caution, shake the end of a branch. Ants burrow into the end of the spines (notice the tiny hole), excavate the inside of the branch, and set up a colony where they rear their young and go about the business of being ants. When the plant is disturbed, as in the case of your shaking the branch, the pugnacious ants charge aggressively from the spines, stingers armed and ready to defend their acacia host. It would only take one nasty sting to convince you that this unusual defense system works.

In addition to repelling would-be grazers, ranging in size from caterpillars to cattle, the ants manicure the ground around the acacia, keeping it clear of sprouts from other plants which might deprive their host of living space in a tropical forest containing 1,200 species of competing trees and countless other plants.

And the acacia is appreciative. Not only does it shelter its guardians, it also feeds them. Tiny, sausage-shaped pores hang from the ends of the leaflets. Loaded with sugar and protein, these are harvested gratefully by the ants.

On the forest floor you're almost sure to spot trails carved by leafcutter ants as they march through the jungle in search of tender leaves to attack. Their trails are veritable highways of activity. Imagine thousands of people walking home on the highway, each rushing along, carrying a 1.5 meter by 2.5 meter (4 ft by 8 ft) sheet of green plywood overhead, and you have the concept of these ants. Leafcutters are amazingly industrious insects. They can completely denude a full-grown mango tree overnight, carving circular slabs of leaf about 1 cm (½ inch) in diameter, hoisting them overhead and marching down the tree trunk back to the hive, which may be a kilometer away or more.

Several highways lead to their hive – often around the buttress roots of a large tree. Hives of over 100 sq meters, 2 meters (7 ft) deep in the forest floor, are not uncommon. In these hives, millions, perhaps billions, of ants chew the leaf fragments, mixing them with nutrient-rich saliva, into a gruel. From this gruel the ants grow and harvest mushrooms which provide their food source.

Large ant colonies can cut and process nearly 45 kg (100 lbs) of leaves a day. During the decades-long lifespan of an ant colony, tons of vegetation decomposes and is worked back into the forest floor. Constant rain and heat rapidly degrade tropical soils, and so the vast storehouse of nutrients and compost from the ant mounds create a rich oasis in the soil, without which the busy ants would be nearly sterile. ❏

LEFT: a leafcutter ant, found in the lowland forests of Costa Rica.

(during January and February). Romantic La Paloma Lodge (tel: 239 2801) is built into a hillside and offers sweeping views of the ocean; its elegant and comfortable *cabinas*, with thatched roofs and private decks, blend unobtrusively into the jungle environs. From the lodge you can arrange expeditions to fish or dive, take dreamy trips up the river in sea kayaks and visit Corcovado and Isla del Caño.

The locals of Palmar take great pride in their stone spheres and when, in the 1980s, the San José authorities tried to remove a pair of them for display in the capital, they were prevented from doing so by student demonstrations.

Isla del Caño and Parque Nacional Corcovado

The biological reserve of **Isla del Caño ❺** sits low on the horizon, 15 km (9 miles) seaward of the Corcovado coastline, and is a pleasant 1-hour boat ride from either Marenco or Bahía Drake. According to archeologists, the island was both a cemetery for indigenous peoples and a refuge for pirates. Spotted dolphins ride the boat's bow wave, and flying fish sometimes escort the traveler to the island. Between December and April, 40-ton humpback whales come from their feeding grounds in Alaska. Males sing haunting songs to attract females, and often leap high in impressive breaches during their procreative sojourn through Costa Rican waters. The island is ringed with turquoise water, tiny beaches and acres of coral-covered rock reefs. Brilliantly colored tropical fish are easily seen by skin divers within 15 meters (50 ft) of the shore at the park headquarters. Well-manicured, steep trails lead through a rich forest drooping with epiphytes and enormous philodendrons.

Covering 44,500 hectares (110,000 acres), **Parque Nacional Corcovado ❻** is an important sanctuary of biological diversity and endangered wildlife dominating the **Osa Peninsula**. It is the site of many of Costa Rica's most significant environmental conflicts. Wild animals live on the forest floor and in the

BELOW: a gift from outer space or an ancient headstone?

MYSTERY OF THE SPHERES

At the highest point on Isla del Caño, where the forest thickens and becomes silent, dried leaves crackle underfoot as you approach the pre-Columbian cemetery of the Boruca people.

Two stone spheres sit among the trees. Green with moss and highlighted by shafts of sunlight from the forest canopy, the enigmatic spheres seem impossibly symmetrical in this forest of twisted plants. Thousands of spheres like this have been found in many locations in the south of Costa Rica and a few also in northern Panamá. They pose one of the country's great riddles. Though their exact origin and significance have defied explanation, it is speculated that they were made in villages on the Osa Peninsula near Palmar Norte, brought to Caño in canoes, then possibly rolled to the cemetery at the highest point of the island.

The smaller stone spheres, which are the size of oranges, were possibly toys but the huge spheres, over 2 meters (6 ft) in diameter, may have indicated the political or social standing of the deceased. Graves with spheres as headstones, oriented to the east, had secret chambers for precious ornaments and were covered with layers of sand, coral and pebbles. Many spheres found in groups have been placed to reflect the positions of the stars.

In Corcovado Park, you are largely on your own among such dangerous wildlife as coral snakes and fer de lance vipers. Although it is rare to come across these creatures, use common sense: wear sturdy boots, long floppy pants and watch where you walk.

BELOW:
a lonely beach on Isla del Caño

tall trees that are draped with vines and lianas, supported by massive buttress roots, reaching out onto a forest floor teeming with life. Because Corcovado Park is innundated with nearly 6 meters (20 ft) of rain a year, it is technically known as a "tropical wet forest." The simplicity of that classification belies the ecological complexity of the park. Thirteen distinct habitats here are each characterized by unique assemblages of plants, animals and topography. Five hundred species of trees – one quarter of all the species in Costa Rica, 10,000 insects, hundreds of species of birds, frogs, lizards and turtles, and many of the world's most endangered and spectacular mammals live in this place.

One of Corcovado's blessings is its inaccessibility. It is a park only for those who are prepared to make a considerable commitment in time and energy. There are several different ways to sample the beauties of Corcovado and the Osa Peninsula, from charter flights and accommodations at luxury eco-lodges to days of grueling hikes, fording rivers and battling insects, and sleeping in a tent.

At one end of the scale is **Lapa Ríos**, a renowned luxury eco-resort with excellent naturalist guides and thatched-roof bungalows perched on the hillside of a 400-hectare (1,000-acre) reserve. The resort overlooks a calm and tranquil beach. Like all the lodges this far south, **Lapa Ríos** is off the electrical grid, so there is no TV and few cellular or satellite phones. You really "get away from it all" here. **Bosque del Cabo** is smaller, but just as luxurious a place, and a favorite hangout for monkeys, scarlet macaws and the odd puma. **Corcovado Lodge Tent Camp**, within earshot of the crashing surf near the park entrance at La Leona, is an exciting place to stay in comfortable tents. Guests are driven from Puerto Jiménez or flown in a small charter plane to Carate, and make the rest of the journey on foot, while their luggage travels in horse-drawn carts.

The ideal time to go hiking and camping in Corcovado is in the dry season, December through April, and might include two nights at each of the three park stations, with days spent hiking from one station to the next. (Stations are joined by trails, each of which requires from three to 10 hours of hiking time.) It is important to come well-equipped in the insect-battling department. A tent, mosquito net, insect repellent and long socks are essential. In addition to the usual camping gear, a machete is also a good idea. Make arrangements for visiting the park by contacting the park's administration office, next to the airport in Puerto Jiménez *(see page 254)*. The **Sirena Park Station** provide very basic rooms and meals, but requires at least one week's notice. Sierna Station can be reached by charter plane, by hiking or by boat. The other stations only offer camping facilities and you'll need to walk to them or arrive by boat.

The park stations

The **Sirena Station**, near the beach, has wonderful trails into the forest and along the beach. Swimming in the nearby Río Claro is refreshing, but sharks are said to frequent the ocean near the river mouth. The station itself, sadly, has been neglected and the accommodations and food here are very basic. **Los Patos Station** is an 11-km (7-mile) hike from Sirena on a wide trail that runs parallel to the El Tigre River. The trail allows relatively easy wildlife viewing. Even though it passes through thick forest, you stand a reasonably good chance of seeing at least tracks of jaguar, ocelot and tapir. Near Los Patos, there are simple accommodations available at Danta Corcovado Lodge (tel: 378 9188), an airy, all-wood lodge with dormitory-style rooms as well as a few more private rooms (no phone). It's another 8 km (5 miles) to the park entrance at Los Patos. A road to the station, accessible by four-wheel drive vehicle, is open during the dry season.

ABOVE: queen aechmea bromeliad. **BELOW:** brown pelican.

The trek to or from **San Pedrillo Station** and nearby **Llorona Waterfall** requires careful advance planning. Two rivers must be crossed at low tide during the 7–10 hour hike. Rangers at Sirena can provide estimates of transit times and tidal heights. Irish naturalist/zoologist Mike Boston specializes in multi-day hikes through the park. Call Osa Aventura (tel: 735 5670). Take a tide-table, food, water and camping gear, since you may need to use them en route. San Pedrillo is also accessible by a two-hour trail from Punta Marenco.

Of the estimated fewer than 200 jaguars remaining in the country, most are found in the forests of Corcovado, Tortuguero and the Talamanca Cordillera. An adult jaguar needs an enormous amount of land with abundant prey animals such as peccaries, deer and agouti to meet its food requirements. Since Corcovado Park was established, its jaguar population has more than tripled. Tracks are commonly seen on many of the trails, and are relatively easy to identify. The prints are wider than they are long, have three rear pads and four unequal toes showing no claw marks.

Herds of white-lipped peccaries roam the forest and root in the leaf litter for food. Evidence of their passing is easily seen: it will look like a bulldozer has gone through the forest.

TIP

Peccaries (wild pigs) have an exaggerated reputation as the forest's most ferocious animal. Nonetheless, if a group of them approaches, or worse, surrounds you, then you would do well to climb the nearest tree.

Nearly 300 species of birds live in Corcovado of which scarlet macaws are the most spectacular. They loudly announce their arrival with gravelly shrieks. If you hear a cry like a puppy, look for a toucan, with its outlandish yellow bill. The spectacular red-breasted Baird's trogon and the melodious riverside wren are also denizens of these forests. Seeds or husks dropping through the canopy will often reveal the presence of troops of squirrel monkeys or spider monkeys. To improve your chances of seeing these animals, be on the trail before dawn.

Orchids, bromeliads, philodendrons and ferns grow attached to trees high in the forest where they find abundant light, airborne nutrients and water. Rich compost created by the epiphyte gardens is often exploited by the host tree, which sprouts roots from its branches and taps into the aerial soil. The dense growth of epiphytes creates a fantastic home for tiny red and blue poison-arrow frogs, who live in pools of water caught by bromeliad leaves. Females lay their eggs on land, and later carry the developing tadpoles on their backs over a distance of 30 meters (100 ft) or more up the trees to these pools, where they lay unfertilized eggs to feed their offspring.

Mushrooms and bracket fungi with strange shapes and astounding colors stud the rotting trunks of fallen trees. Fingernail-sized frogs and tiny salamanders live in the damp hollows of logs or under moist leaf litter.

Puerto Jiménez and inland to Sierpe

BELOW: a naturalist gathers butterflies at the Golfito reserve.

Just outside Parque Nacional Corcovado to the east is **Puerto Jiménez ❼**, the main town of the Osa Peninsula and a gateway to the park. It's a friendly, funky frontier town with a burgeoning tourist infrastructure and its own Ecotourism Chamber, which will recommend guides and assist you in planning your visit around the peninsula. Inexpensive meals and lodging are available in the town, and a number of lodges and ecotourism projects in all price ranges are to be found in the surrounding area. Puerto Jiménez is accessible by car or bus. It's about a 7-hour trip from San José and most lodges will arrange transportation.

An adventurous way to leave the Osa Peninsula is to charter a boat from one of the lodges around Drake Bay and travel up the Sierpe River toward the little town of **Sierpe**. Luxurious Casa Corcovado Jungle Lodge brings all its guests to and from Sierpe by boat (tel: 256 8825). Beware, however, that the mouth (the *boca*) of the river is often very choppy. Make sure your boat is equipped with life-jackets and, as a precaution, put yours on when you near the *boca*. The shores of the river are lined with mangroves. The maze of roots of these trees is inhabited by many species of small fish. Blue herons and snowy egrets may fly from the trees as the boat passes. Even these maritime mangrove forests are not immune to deforestation. They are cut and used to make charcoal, or the bark is stripped and tannin, used to cure leather, is extracted. Damage has been minimal so far, and the Sierpe mangroves continue to provide refuge for many animals.

A wide variety of boats ply their trade on the Sierpe. Weatherbeaten dugout canoes loaded with bananas and smoking cargo boats share the river with speed-boats and naturalist tour vessels from nearby lodges. About two hours upriver in the town of Sierpe you can catch a bus to travel south to Golfito.

Golfito

On the eastern shore of the Golfo Dulce, **Golfito** ❽ is sheltered from the open sea by islands and peninsulas that form a perfect harbor within the gulf. In 1938, the United Fruit Company *(see page 239)* realized Golfito's potential, and built a

Map on page 246

ABOVE: raccoons *(mapaches)* are often eager for a human hand-out. **BELOW:** butterflies in the act of mating.

Wild Cats of Costa Rica

Costa Rica is home to half a dozen kinds of wild cat. Secretive and nocturnal, they include some of the most endangered and elusive of the country's animals.

Costa Rica's wild cats – both big and small – are extremely wary of humans, and few visitors to the country are lucky enough to see them. Although they are now fully protected, their fear of people is understandable: over the years, hunting and deforestation have reduced their numbers to a fraction of their former level.

Like all cats, these animals are elegant and efficient predators. Most hunt on their own, and most hide away by day, camouflaged by beautiful spotted coats that, ironically, have made them such valuable quarry. They range in size from the jaguar – commonly known as *el tigre* – which can tip the scales at over 100 kg (220 lb) to the little spotted cat, which is smaller than many of the domestic cats that people keep as pets.

For a cat, the jaguar shows an unusual liking for water. Its preferred habitats include mangrove swamps and the forested banks of rivers, and it seems to enjoy swimming. One of its favorite foods is peccary (a kind of wild pig), but it also catches fish and even turtles, breaking open their shells with its powerful teeth. Unfortunately, it also attacks cattle, particularly where new pasture has been created out of the former forest. As a result, many Costa Rican farmers view *el tigre* not as a national asset, but as a dangerous marauder. At one time, the jaguar was found throughout the entire country, but today its strongholds are in the national parks, particularly Santa Rosa, Tortuguero and Corcovado. You may not see a jaguar in the flesh, but you stand a chance of at least being shown its tracks.

Almost as large as the jaguar is the puma or mountain lion, one of the two Costa Rican cats that do not have spotted coats. It is a truly Pan-American animal, ranging from Canada as far south as Patagonia. The other unspotted cat, the jaguarundi, is much smaller, and has short legs and a curiously flattened forehead. Jaguarundis live in a range of habitats, but unlike pumas, they are most common in low-lying parts of the country.

The last three species have all paid a heavy price for the beauty of their coats but, with changing fashions and a ban on the trade in pelts, their future prospects look brighter than they once did. The ocelot – perhaps the most beautiful of them all – hunts mainly on the ground, although it climbs and swims well. The margay, which looks like a miniature long-tailed ocelot, is an extremely agile climber, and catches most of its food off the ground. It is the only cat that can climb head-first down a tree, instead of having to back down while holding on with its claws.

The little spotted cat is also a forest animal, sometimes living at altitudes of over 3,000 meters (9,850 ft). Although it was once widely hunted, relatively little is known about its habits in the wild. What is certain is that, despite its small size, it packs a punch: in encounters with domestic cats, the little spotted cat often comes out on top. ❑

LEFT: a young watchful puma (cougar) at Las Pumas Refuge near Cañas.

Map on page 246

major shipping port here. By 1955 over 90 percent of the bananas shipped from Costa Rica departed on banana boats from Golfito. Boatloads of crewmen and 15,000 *Guanacasteco* immigrants came to work the plantations. They turned Golfito into a boomtown of brothels, smugglers and drunks. United Fruit or "Mamita Yunai," was seen to be funneling profits out of Costa Rica and into the pockets of rich North American stockholders and became the symbol for hated Yankee imperialism. Following crippling strikes and conflicts with labor, United Fruit decided to close down and leave Golfito in 1985. Economic depression set in and former employees of the company found themselves leaving town or searching for work as fishermen or farmers. The population today is only 12,000. Recently, Golfito has begun to make a slow comeback and the old town, referred to as the **Pueblo Civil**, is regaining a touch of its boomtown atmosphere. Bars and prostitutes do business on the side streets; lively outdoor cafes overlooking the pier have taken over the main street. And in the "duty-free zone" on the waterfront, known as *El Depósito*, consumer durables sell at about 40 percent off the San José price. If you're searching for bargains, try the huge outdoor mall with air-conditioned shops. (But you must stay in Golfito at least 24 hours in order to shop here.) The **American Zone** of Golfito has a sleepy, suburban atmosphere. This former United Fruit Company neighborhood comprises large wooden plantation-style homes on stilts, with screened porches and hipped roofs.

TIP

If you would like to learn more about the harsh conditions of the banana plantations, read the exuberant *Mamita Yunai*, written by pioneer labor organizer Carlos Luis Fallas and set in the 1930s and 1940s in Limón province.

Before leaving Golfito, drive to the top of **Reserva Forestal Golfito**. A sign marks the road in Barrio Invu across from the Plaza Deportes soccer stadium. Watch for toucans and sloths in the trees beside the steep, winding gravel road. At the top, the panoramic views of **Golfo Dulce** are spectacular. Parque Nacional Piedras Blancas and the Refugio Nacional de Vida Silvestre Golfito lie just north of town; they are important wildlife corridors where birders and nature lovers can roam along miles of trails. There are regular flights to Golfito; check with the airline offices for their current schedules. For the more patient traveler, the very scenic 7-hour bus ride from San José to Golfito is a memorable experience.

BELOW: giant philodendrons.

North of Golfito

Beside the Golfo Dulce, accessible only by boat, are beautiful pebbled beaches, and dense jungle that starts almost at the water's edge. A 20-minute speedboat ride from Golfito brings you to luxurious Playa Nicuesa Rainforest Lodge (tel: 735 5237), handcrafted with more than eight kinds of tropical wood. Secluded cabins are scattered around a lush tropical garden. There is kayaking, snorkeling, fishing and dolphin-watching out the front door of the lodge, and hiking, bird-watching and waterfalls in the mountain forest just steps behind the back door. In the next cove over is **Casa Orquideas**, a beautiful landscaped garden of ginger, cacao, papaya, orchids and tropical plants. Tours last one hour (open daily; entrance fee; tel: 775 1614).

In 1991, 1,200 hectares (3,000 acres) of rainforest on the west side of Golfo Dulce was declared the **Parque Nacional Piedras Blancas** ❾. However, as the government didn't have the funds to compensate the landowners, the possibility remained that title could

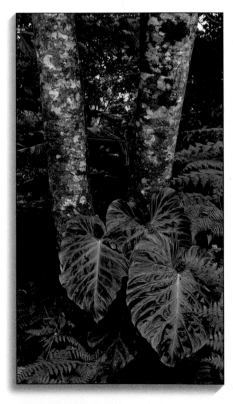

revert to the former owners and that the logging operations which had been under way could resume. Michael Schnitzler, an Austrian violinist and Golfito homeowner, solicited contributions from his countrymen and women, and with additional funds contributed by national and international groups, the money was raised to pay the landowners and ensure the continuation of Piedras Blancas as a national park. It is incorporated into Parque Nacional Corcovado, and appears under this name on maps. It is also known as Parque Nacional Esquinas, for the river that flows through it, and it has also been given the nickname of "Rainforest of the Austrians." A biological station owned and operated by the University of Vienna houses students and scientists from around the world. More luxurious accommodation is available at Esquinas Rainforest Lodge (tel: 775 0901). Guides for park exploration are available and are strongly recommended since the trails are sometimes hard to follow.

If you continue on the Interamericana Highway north past Palmar Norte, and just past Puerto Nuevo, a rough track leads to **Boruca** ⑩, a small village in a valley near Buenos Aires, where life moves at a leisurely pace. Over the New Year's holiday, Borucas celebrate the *Fiesta de los Diablitos* (Celebration of the Little Devils), a re-enactment of the war between the Spanish and indigenous population – only this time the Amerindians win.

South of Golfito

Between the mouth of the Río Coto Colorado (which lies just south of Golfito), to Punta Banco, the last major point of land before the Panamanian border, lie some of Costa Rica's most inaccessible and remote beaches. Take the old cable ferry across the river. Then, in Pueblo Nuevo, turn right for **Playa Zancudo**, an 8-km (5-mile) long, sandy crescent with excellent swimming and surfing, and several nice places to stay. Cabinas & Restaurant Sol y Mar (tel: 776 0014) is friendly and serves good food. Continue on the road parallel to the coast to **Pavones**, just before Río Claro. The beach is not suitable for swimming, but this is a renowned surfing spot. Basic lodging is available, along with more comfortable rooms at Cabinas La Ponderosa (tel: 824 4145). Some funky new restaurants have been set up by surfers who settled here, notably Café de la Suerte, a delightful vegetarian restaurant.

After the seemingly endless potholes, bogs and washboard bumps in the road, continue on for another 30 minutes to **Punta Banco**. Wide intertidal flats of volcanic and sedimentary rock, riddled with tide-pools full of marine life and battered by continual surf characterize Punta Banco.

At the end of the point, a pasture and gate on the left mark the entrance to **Tiskita Jungle Lodge** ⑪ (tel: 296 8125), Peter Aspinall's private rainforest reserve, experimental tropical fruit farm and ecolodge. The tortuous drive (a four-wheel drive vehicle is essential) can be avoided by booking a package tour, which includes a private airplane charter that sets down on a grass airstrip near the lodge. Isolated cabins with ocean views are a short walk from the main lodge. Well-designed trails lead to waterfalls, idyllic swimming holes and various points of natural history interest in Tiskita's 162-hectare (400-acre) forest. More than 100 species of fruit trees from around the tropical world are under cultivation here, attracting legions of monkeys and flocks of birds.

Map on page 246

Wilson Botanical Gardens

For the ultimate experience in tropical botany, visit **Wilson Botanical Gardens** ⑫ in Las Cruces, some 6 km (4 miles) south of San Vito on Highway 16. The gardens are operated by the Organization for Tropical Studies (OTS) as a center for research, scientific training and public education (open daily 8am–4pm; entrance fee). Designed by an Italian landscape architect, trails wind through extensive collections of "lobster claw" heliconias, bromeliads, tree ferns, orchids and palms, and lead into the wild forest reserve behind the gardens. This offers splendid mountain vistas and hiking to rocky pools around the Río Jaba. The gardens offer simple, dormitory-style accommodations, as well as comfortable private rooms in cabins with verandahs for bird-watching. You can talk with visiting scientists in residence or attend seminars by horticultural societies from around the world.

The **Villa Neilly-San Vito Road** was built in 1945 by the USA as a strategic protection point, due west of the Panamá Canal. The paved road rises sharply into the cool mountains that lead to **San Vito** at 960 meters (3,150 ft) above sea level. San Vito was founded by immigrants from post-war Italy, who were encouraged by the Costa Rican government to settle there. It's a clean, modern town of 18,000 inhabitants (including the surrounding area), high in a mountain valley, where you can get a good Italian meal and hear Italian spoken on the streets. Pizzería Liliana, in the center of town, is the most popular restaurant.

ABOVE: giant bromeliad at Wilson Botanical Gardens.
BELOW: a moment of jungle quietude.

Valle de El General

Since colonial times, people had attempted to find a pass through the Talamanca Mountains to join the Central Valley with the unknown lands on the other side of the Dota Mountains. But it was not until the end of the 1860s that Don Pedro Calderón, responding to a prize offered by the government, found a way through. The opening of the road led to the colonization of the **Valle de El General**, and later, to the building of the Interamericana Highway, which connects San José and the Central Valley with the southern Pacific zone of Costa Rica. If you are traveling south to the Valle de El General, start early to avoid the fog and rain that often appear later in the day. From San José take the Interamericana Highway toward Cartago, veering right to take the road to San Isidro.

The route to the Valle de El General passes over the spectacular **Cerro de la Muerte** ⑬ (Death Mountain), which rises to 3,491 meters (11,520 ft). Named for early foot travelers who died here from exposure, today the mountain is not as inhospitable as its name suggests. Still, it is not difficult to imagine the hardships the early pioneers endured on the week-long journey. Rain, cold and fog can make the first half of the drive miserable, but the road quickly rises above the clouds to cool, crisp sunshine, fields of flowers and hillside farms. Foxglove, azalea, hydrangea and white cala lily grow wild. Clouds swirl through the valleys and over peaks.

For almost-guaranteed quetzal sightings, visit the affordable Albergue Mirador de Quetzales, just off the main highway at Km 70. Lodging here is in quaint, A-frame cottages with hot-water showers and hot-water bottles to warm beds for the chilly nights. Miles of trails are great for both hikers and birdwatchers. Camping sites are also available (tel: 381 8456).

The country estate of former president Don Pepe (José) Figueres lies just off the highway as you start to climb Cerro de la Muerte. The house is called La Lucha Sin Fin *(the Endless Struggle) since it was here that he formulated many of the political views that led to the Civil War.*

BELOW: Mount Chirripó, the tallest peak in southern-Central America.

Villages of the Valley

Down the road to the right from Empalme is **Santa María de Dota**, a traditional small town with a beautiful little park. The paved road, which continues toward San Marcos de Tarrazú, San Pablo de Léon Cortes and San Cristóbal Sur, is called **La Ruta de Los Santos** (The Route of the Saints), since all the picturesque coffee towns here are named after saints, and is best tackled in a four-wheel drive vehicle. In **Copey**, a village in the mountains above Santa María, you can rest at a waterfall and lake, fish for trout at one of the many local trout farms or lodge comfortably at El Toucanet Lodge (tel: 541 1435). Continuing on the Interamericana Highway, about half an hour from Empalme is a sign for San Gerardo. This is the turn-off for **San Gerardo de Dota**, 9 km (6 miles) down a good, partially paved road that runs parallel to the Río Savegre. In the midst of the valley, Don Efráin Chacón and his family offer comfortable *cabinas* and delicious homemade meals at the Albergue Montaña de Savegre. Look for a bridge and some clean white buildings painted with bright red apples on the left just above the river. The area is known for its cloud forests and offers one of the best opportunities in the world to see the resplendent quetzal. The quetzals feed in aquacatillo trees almost in Don Efráin's backyard.

There are miles of challenging trails here, including a hike to a magnificent waterfall. Bring plenty of warm clothing as it becomes surprisingly chilly at night. The drive to **San Isidro de El General** is beautiful once the fog clears from Cerro de la Muerte. San Isidro is the commercial center for this agricultural area, a busy town with a large central park and lots of noisy traffic. Explore the numerous plant nurseries, coffee and cattle farms that are sprinkled on its slopes.

Map on page 246

Along the Route of the Saints, stop in at Coopedota Santa Maria (tel: 541 2828; fee) for a tour of the coffee co-operative; you can buy coffee at wholesale prices in their shop. For a taste of superlative Tarrazú coffee, stop in at La Ruta del Café on the main highway at Empalme.

BELOW: pineapple plantation in Valle de El General.

Map on page 246

ABOVE: close to nature, but with creature comforts.
BELOW: mist-clad foliage in Cerro de la Muerte.

Parque Nacional Chirripó

Situated 150 km (94 miles) south of San José, **Parque Nacional Chirripó** ⑭ covers 43,700 hectares (108,000 acres). Its main attraction is its diversity of landscapes, including páramos – flatlands with stunted growth; oak forests; fern groves; cloud forests; swamps; crystal-clear glacial lakes; and the highest peak (3,800 meters/12,500 ft) in southern Central America. Only those willing to brave a long day of hiking in the cold, and quite possibly rain, make the ascent to the top of **Mount Chirripó**. A lodge and several trails, which are regularly maintained, make the ascent at least possible. Daytime temperatures reach 27°C (80°F) but at night-time they can drop to almost freezing. The best months to attempt Chirripó are February and March, the driest time of year, but during the rainy months the flora is splendid. Visits to Chirripó require advance reservations, which you can make through the office in **San Isidro de El General** (tel: 771 3155) or by going to the ranger station near the village of **San Gerardo** in the low season. The hike to the top of Chirripó, including a day on the summit, takes at least four days. It costs $10 to enter the park and $10 for each day you are there.

You can spend the first night in the national park in San Gerardo at any number of inexpensive *cabinas*. The owner of Posada del Descanso is very knowledgeable about the area. Before entering the park, check in at park headquarters in San Gerardo. Park maps are available there, but they are basic and abbreviated, and rangers often do not have the information hikers request. Good, large-scale topographical maps are available in San José. Rangers can put you in touch with locals with horses who will haul your pack to the hut ahead of you. Río Chirripó Retreat has cozy cabins within sound of the rushing Río Chirripó (tel: 771 7065). Río Chirripo's natural setting is inspirational for yoga and meditation workshops. The area around San Gerardo is well worth visiting, even if you do not attempt to climb Chirripó. Birdwatching is good, with frequent sightings of quetzals, and hiking is very satisfying, with beautiful lush scenery, natural hot springs to relax your sore muscles and waterfalls.

Parque Nacional La Amistad

Covering approximately 12 percent of Costa Rica's total territory is the protected area of **Parque Nacional La Amistad** ⑮. Adjacent to Chirripó, in the interior of the Reserva de la Biosfera La Amistad, the park is for the most part inaccessible. La Amistad (which means "Friendship") has been declared a Biosphere Reserve and a World Patrimony site because of the diversity of its flora and fauna, and because of its great scientific value. There are over 20 species of hummingbird and you'll find 7-cm (3-inch) grasshoppers. More than half of La Amistad has yet to be explored. Hiking near **Reserva Forestal Las Tablas** is safe and rewarding, but only experienced tropical trekkers should venture into the interior. There is a ranger station with camping facilities at the Altamira park entrance (tel: 200 5355). Day trips are possible from San Isidro or San Vito, or you can stay at the eco-friendly, comfortable Hacienda La Amistad Lodge (tel: 200 5037), above San Vito. The lodge has extensive hiking trails, with the option of camping out in the forest. ❏

Isla del Coco

Isla del Coco is the most remote of Costa Rica's territories, adrift in the Pacific Ocean nearly 600 km (over 360 miles) southwest of the mainland, on the same latitude as Colombia. Because of this isolation it only counts its visitors in the hundreds, yet millions have seen it on film, in the opening moments of *Jurassic Park*. In all senses, this is a place of high drama.

At its crown is a thick coniferous forest full of springs and rivers. The cliffs that tower over 100 meters (300 ft) around the entire island are covered with incredibly thick tropical vegetation with magnificent waterfalls plummeting straight down to the sea. In all, there are 200 waterfalls on the island. Lionel Wafer, a pirate physician who visited over 300 years ago wrote "what most contributes to the loveliness of the place is the number of clear, freshwater springs that fill the entire lower part of the island." And there are rocky crags and wondrously formed islets that have been shaped by the wind and water. No wonder then that it inspired Steven Spielberg, to whom it was "Isla Nebular."

Measuring roughly 12 km by 5 km (8 miles by 3 miles), Isla del Coco is the largest uninhabited island in the world. It is now a National Park and the richest in endemic species belonging to Costa Rica.

As if these facts were not sufficiently alluring, the island's history is also full of pirate stories. Many insist that there is treasure hidden here still, yet in more than 500 expeditions none has ever been found.

Two bays, Wafer Bay and Chatham Bay, offer a way to tie up and gain entry to explore the island. Chatham Bay is small, with a rocky beach. Here, the ghosts of past explorers, and of pirates, are almost tangible. Today's visitors are mostly treasure hunters, divers and environmentalists.

Most visitors consider Wafer Bay to be the best access route to the island. From here, ancient natural paths follow steep cliffs all the way to the highest part of the humid forest. There are bountiful bromeliads, giant ferns, orchids, unnamed flowering plants, mosses and ferns covering almost everything. And from a high peak there are views of an unbelievably blue sea above an impossibly green landscape, with white, angel-like doves moving gently, hovering and fluttering in the air. Every natural path, every river, every waterfall, every beach has some rare treasure. The peace is astounding and deafening. And the views of the coral reef, the crisp clarity of the water, the lushness of the landscape, all somehow contribute to an atmosphere where the mysterious legends of the past come alive.

Camping is not permitted on the island: you must sleep on your boat. There is drinkable water, however; and hiking, although the trails are not marked. Contact the National Parks Service for information and permission to enter. Specialist tour companies operate out of Puntarenas but be warned: the price of a trip is very high. For the majority of people, Isla del Coco remains just a dream – and perhaps that is no bad thing. ❑

RIGHT: the dense, deep, little-known jungle interior of Isla del Coco.

COSTA RICA

TRAVEL TIPS

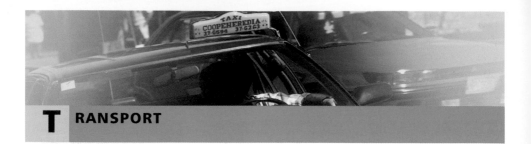

T RANSPORT

GETTING THERE AND GETTING AROUND

GETTING THERE

By Air

Most international flights arrive in Costa Rica at Juan Santamaría Airport, located in the Central Valley about 16 km (10 miles) from San José, the capital city. See www.alterra.co.cr for flight arrival and departure information for Juan Santamaría. (In Spanish only, click on *Información de Vuelos* for flight status: *estimado de salida* (estimated departure time), *demorado* (delayed), *salió* (departed).

To the airport: It is a 20-minute ride (about US$12 by taxi) to San José from the airport. Prices are standardized; pay at a kiosk at the airport, not the taxi driver. A bus into town is available for under US$1.

Five commercial airlines also fly to Daniel Oduber International Airport in Liberia: American Airlines, Continental, Delta, Northwest and US Airways. Air Canada runs direct charter flights from Toronto. The main terminal for North Pacific beach vacations, Daniel Oduber is also a hub for several charter companies.

From the US: Miami has the most direct flights, but you can also get to Costa Rica from the US in one hop from Atlanta, Charlotte, Chicago, Dallas, Houston, Los Angeles, New York, Phoenix and Washington DC. TACA and Air Canada offer direct flights from Toronto and Montreal; Vancouver trips generally go through Houston or Dallas. The best bets for flights from Australia or New Zealand are via Los Angeles and Miami.

From Europe: Iberia and Air Madrid

offer direct flights from Madrid and KLM operates a direct service from Amsterdam. Travelers from the UK may also connect in the US via Newark (the fastest route), New York or Miami.

On departure: line-ups to check in can be horrendous, so observe the recommended two-hours-before-departure airport arrival on your way home. Confirm flights the day before in case there are changes, but most airlines do not require it.

Baggage allowance: weight limits per checked bag are usually 23 kg (50 lbs), two maximum. If necessary, determine how the airline is equipped to handle surfboards, bicycles, etc. Have your luggage well tagged and identified. Be prepared in case your luggage is lost.

As of this writing, limited amounts of liquids and gels were allowed in carry on baggage (containers 100 ml or less, all items must fit in a quart-size zip lock bag). However, to get the most up-to-date policies, see www.catsa.com (Canada), www.tsa.gov (US) or www.baa.co.uk (UK).

Ticket deals: while it still pays to check newspapers for good deals, most cheap tickets are now found on a variety of budget-travel websites. Tried-and-true www.expedia.com is a good resource for travelers from North America. Try www.cheapestflights.co.uk in the UK. The site www3.travel.com.au caters to Australian travelers and www.travelonline.co.nz to those from New Zealand.

Make reservations as far ahead as possible, especially from December to February, as these flights are usually booked well in advance.

Tax: there is a departure tax for foreign visitors, of around US$26, payable in US dollars, or colones (not travelers' checks).

Airlines

Air Canada, tel: 888-247 2262 (US and Canada), 0871 220 1111 (UK), 243 1860 (Costa Rica); www.aircanada.ca

American, tel: 257 1266, 800-433 7300 (US and Canada), 0207-365 0777 (UK); www.aa.com

Condor Airlines, tel: 243 1818, 1-800-364 1667 (US and Canada), +49 (0) 180 570 7202 (Europe), 243 1818 (Costa Rica); www.condor.com

Continental Airlines, tel: 800-231 0856 (US and Canada), 0845-607 6760 (UK), 0800-044 0005 (Costa Rica); www.continental.com

Delta, tel: 0800-056 2002, 800-221 1212 (US and Canada), UK 0845-600 0950; www.delta.com

Iberia, tel: 800-772 4642 (Canada and the US), 870-609 0500 (UK) 431 5633 (Costa Rica); www.iberia.com

Martinair, tel: 232 3246, 800-627 8462 (US); www.martinair.com

Mexicana, tel: 295 6969, 800-531 7921 (US), 866-281 3049 (Canada); www.mexicana.com

TACA Costa Rica, US and Canada: tel: 800-722 8222, 299 8222, 800-400 8222 (US), 800-722 8222 (Canada), 0870-241 0340 (UK); www.taca.com

United Airlines; www.united.com

US Airways, tel: 800-622 1015 (US and Canada), 0-800-011 0793 (Costa Rica); www.usairways.com

By Bus

There are bus services to Costa Rica from Panama or Nicaragua.

Tica Bus, Paseo Colón, 200 meters N / 100 meters W of Torre Mercedes, tel: 221 0006; www.ticabus.com provides a comfortable, reliable service throughout Central America. Daily

buses from Nicaragua and Panamá.
Trans Nica, Ca 22, Av 3, tel: 223
4920; www.transnica.com
Nicaragua, tel: 505-278 2090;
El Salvador, tel: 503-240 1212.

By Car

The most common route for the
popular car journey from the US to
Costa Rica runs along the Pacific
coast of Mexico, Guatemala, El
Salvador, Honduras and Nicaragua.
Along the Nicaraguan border, the
only vehicle crossing is at Peñas
Blancas, on the Pacific side. From
the south, the main overland
vehicle crossing is also on the
Pacific side, at Paso Canoas,
although a small post at Sixaola on
the Caribbean side allows vehicles
to pass over the bridge that joins
the countries.
Driving license: Drivers will have to
show their driver's license, an
original copy of certified ownership
(or a notarized authorization from
the owner if the car is someone
else's), and a *hoja de salida* (exit
permit) from either Nicaragua or
Panama (whichever country from
which you're arriving).
Customs will mark in your
passport that you have entered with
a car, and the car is given a three-
month permit. You can exit the
country once to renew the permit;
after six months the vehicle is
subject to heavy import taxes.
There are two recommended
books available, which have reliable
information to help you navigate the
roads and border crossings: *You
Can Drive to Costa Rica in 8 Days*,
by Dawn Rae Wessler (Harmony
Gardens Publishing, US, 1998) and
*Driving the Pan-American Highway to
Mexico and Central America*, by
Raymond and Audrey Pritchard
(Costa Rica Books, US, 1997). The
website www.drivemeloco.com is also
helpful.
It is advisable to confirm border
information before travel because it
can change without notice. For
information on major driving
regulations, *see Car Rental page 271.*
Car insurance: Costa Rica
requires motorists to pay
approximately $10 for insurance
upon entry, for the three-month
period. The car is also fumigated
(approximately $5).
Sanborn's Insurance (tel: 800-
222-0158; www.sanbornsinsurance.com)
in McAllen, Texas, is an excellent
resource for insurance and
information you'll need for the trip.
They will provide you with tips and an
itinerary.

By Sea

Cruise ships come into Puerto Limón
on the Caribbean coast and Puerto
Caldera and Golfito on the Pacific.
Check with a travel agent about which
companies currently sail to Costa
Rica. Private yachts are popular as a
means to visit. The main point of
entry is Playas del Coco, although
immigration and customs services
are also available at Caldera and
Golfito, all on the Pacific side. It is
possible to go through these
procedures on the Caribbean side at
Limón, but impractical as there are no
yacht facilities. You will need the
original and one copy each of crew
member and passenger's passports,
the crew list, the boat's documents,
and the departure document from the
last port you visited. All other
international shipping protocol applies
(quarantine flag, etc). Wait until
boarded and cleared by both
immigration and customs before
going ashore.

GETTING AROUND

Finding Your Way

San José uses a grid system for its
streets. North–south-running streets
are *calles*, east–west-running streets
are *avenidas*. Avenida Central (Av Ctl)
divides the city north and south; it
becomes Paseo Colón west of
Hospital San Juan de Díos. Calle
Central (Ca Ctl) divides San José
east and west. The southern avenues
and western streets are numbered
evenly. The northern avenues and
eastern streets have odd numbers.
Avenida Central passes through
the downtown core as a wide
pedestrian walkway, passing by many
of the major attractions and
shopping, making walking a viable
way of getting around. On most other
streets, you'll often have to squeeze
through the narrow patches of
sidewalk left by *chinamos* (streetside
stands), and even with the streetlight
in your favor, crossing can be a
challenge. Taking common-sense
safety precautions, a walking tour of
San José can be a pleasant way of
seeing the sights.
Abbreviations used for addresses:
Av = avenida, Ca = Calle, Ctl =
central, Apto or Apdo = apartado
(post office box, for mailing
addresses). When an address is
given using the street and avenues,
the first part is the street or avenue
on which the building is located, and

the second part of the address
indicates the streets or avenues the
building is between. For example: the
location of the Metropolitan
Cathedral is Ca Ctl, Av 2–4. That is,
the Cathedral is on Calle Central
between Avenidas 2 and 4. *(See San
José city map, page 130.)*
For the most part, there are no
addresses nor are there street
names in Costa Rica. Although
downtown San José has numbered
avenues and streets, Costa Ricans
do not refer to them. Homes and
buildings are not numbered. Usually
an address is given as the distance
in meters *(metros)* north, east,
south, or west from a known
landmark. When it comes to walking,
remember that cars have the right of
way, not pedestrians, so look twice
before crossing the street.

By Air

Domestic flights *(vuelos locales)* are
fairly inexpensive and can provide a
comfortable alternative to many
hours on bad roads.
If you're criss-crossing the country
and are short on time, consider an air
pass that covers travel to the
commercial destinations of the
country's main domestic airlines.
Sansa offers the Costa Rica Air Pass;
$249 for one week, $299 for two
weeks. Nature Air's Adventure Pass,
available in low season only (end of
April to end of November), is $249 for
one week, $349 for two weeks.
Sansa
Tel: 290 4100
Fax: 290 3543
www.flysansa.com
Offers service to Coto 47, Golfito,
Puerto Jimenéz, Palmar Sur,
Tortuguero, Barra del Colorado,
Nosara, Sámara, Tamarindo, Punta
Islita, Quepos, Tambor, Liberia,
Limón and Drake Bay. Credit card
payment for phone reservations must
be confirmed by fax.
Nature Air
Tel: 299 6000, 800-235 9272 (US
and Canada)
Fax: 220 0413
www.natureair.com
Flies to Liberia, Tamarindo, Nosara,
Tambor, Quepos, Palmar Sur, Puerto
Jiménez, Barra del Colorado, Limón,
Drake Bay, Punta Islita, Tortuguero,
Bocas del Toro, Panama and Granada,
Nicaragua. Surf boards accepted if
there is space available, with an extra
charge. Slightly more expensive than
Sansa but worth it. Also offers a
number of interdestination flights.
Aerotaxi Alfa Romeo
Tel: 735 5178
E-mail: aerocorcovado@racsa.co.cr

Air taxi from Puerto Jiménez into Serena Ranger Station in Corcovado National Park.
Paradise Air
Tel: 296 3600
Fax: 296 1429
www.flywithparadise.com
Pavas Airport. Charter flights and flights to other Central American destinations.
Flying Crocodile
Tel: 656 8048
Fax: 656 8049
www.flying-crocodiles.com
Operates from Crocodile Lodge in Sámara. Scenic flights in an ultralight plane over sea, beaches, and tropical forests. Lessons on how to fly ultralights.
Skyline Ultra-Light Flights
Tel: 743 8037
www.flyultralight.com
Individual flights around southern Pacific and Sierpe; flying lessons.

By Bus

You can go virtually anywhere by bus in Costa Rica; it is the way most Ticos travel.
Around San José: the Sabana Cementerio bus cuts across town in both directions, just north and south of the center; ask for the stop closest to you (¿Dónde está la parada para el Sabana Cementerio?). All other buses leave to the suburbs from their respective quadrants; for example, those heading west (Rohrmoser, Escazú, Santa Ana) leave from the Coca Cola area; ones heading east (Los Yoses, San Pedro, Curridabat) leave from near the east end of the pedestrian walkway.
Further afield: San José has no central terminal for long-distance buses, each bus hub handles travel to a certain region. Major ones include the "Coca Cola", near a former bottling plant at Ca 16, Av 1–3, the departure point for the Central Pacific; the Caribbean bus terminal, Ca Ctrl, Av 11 (just east of the Children's Museum); and MUSOC, Ca Ctrl, Av 30, to San Isidro (the hub for buses to the Southern Zone). Pick up a schedule at the Costa Rican Tourist Institute (ICT) office in the Gold Museum (www.visitcostarica.com).

Airports

Juan Santamaría (international flights), tel: 437 2626
Daniel Oduber, Liberia (international flights), tel: 668 1010
Tobias Bolaños, Pavas (domestic flights), tel: 232 2820

Buy tickets a day in advance for popular routes and several days in advance for Easter week travel. Companies often only sell one way at a time; buy your return ticket upon arrival to ensure a seat. Watch your belongings closely.
Grayline Fantasy Bus and **Interbus** provide reasonably priced (between $25 and $55) shuttle transport. Air-conditioned, less crowded and hotel-to-hotel service make this a good option for those who want to enjoy the scenery of a road trip with an upgrade in comfort.
Grayline Fantasy Bus
Tel: 232 3681
www.graylinecostarica.com
Interbus
Tel: 283 5573
www.interbusonline.com
The Costa Rican Tourist Institute (ICT) office located below the Plaza de la Cultura has a list of bus companies' names and telephone numbers, tel: 222 1090.

By Taxi

Taxis are by far the easiest way of getting around San José; they are widely used and inexpensive. You'll rarely have to wait long, although it is sometimes difficult to catch a cab during rainy rush hour. All should have operational meters (marías); be sure the drivers use them. If not, negotiate before getting in. If you are greatly overcharged, write down the driver's name and license number, and call the taxi company number marked on the outside of the cab.
Arrangements can be made to take trips by taxi to places outside San José. Beware – taxi drivers who are parked in front of major hotels will always charge more, and most will charge fixed rates. Taxis are red and have a "Taxi" sign on the roof of the car. If they are not red and have no numbered yellow triangle on the door, then they are pirate taxis, or piratas, and are unlicensed.

Taxi Companies

Alfaro, tel: 221 8466.
Coopetaxi, tel: 235 9966
Coopetico, tel: 224 7979
Coopeirazu, tel: 254 3211
Coopeguarla, tel: 226 1366
San José Taxis, tel: 221 3434
Taxis Unidos, tel: 221 6865

By Train

San José's recently revived train service across town takes you within a hair's breadth of some buildings, but isn't particularly convenient. The central station is near the Clínica Bíblica on the south side of town, with a commuter-oriented schedule sending trains west to Pavas and east to San Pedro at 5am, 6.15am, 7.20am, 4.20pm and 5.30pm, returning from both sides of town approximately 40 minutes later, weekdays only. A full cross-town trip takes 75 minutes, much longer than a taxi unless it's rush hour. Tickets cost approximately $0.30.

By Ferry

Most travelers to the southern Nicoya coast will arrive via the Puntarenas-Paquera ferry route (approximately 90 minutes), served by two companies. There is not much difference between the two services; the Tambor option is owned by the Hotel Barceló and is slightly snazzier, but at certain times can be packed with hotel guests. Avoid Friday and Sunday afternoons and evenings; you could be stuck waiting for hours.
Most travelers won't need to use the Puntarenas-Naranjo ferry, but it is an option if you are heading further north on the peninsula. Generally though, those sites are better served by bus or car via the Tempisque bridge. Drivers must leave the car to purchase tickets; any vehicle passengers must purchase tickets separately, and embark and disembark on foot.
Peninsula de Nicoya
de Coonatramar R.L.
Tel: 661 1069
www.coonatramar.com.
Puntarenas to Playa Naranjo
Departs 6am, 10am, 2.20pm, and 7pm
Playa Naranjo to Puntarenas
Departs 7.30am, 12.30pm, 5pm, and 9pm
Paquera to Puntarenas
Tel: 641 0118
Departs 4.30am, 8.30am, 12.30pm, 4.30pm and 8.30pm
Puntarenas to Paquera
Departs 6.30am, 10.30am, 2.30pm, 6.30pm, 10.30pm
Tambor
Tel: 661 2084

By Bicycle

Mountain bikes are a good way to see Costa Rica's back country, especially on the lightly traveled dirt roads which crisscross the rural areas. Bicycle riding can be dangerous on the roads as they have no shoulders. Consider installing KEVLAR inner tube protectors (such as Mr Tuffy). Bring a good lock. Check with your airline about shipping.

ABOVE: watch out for wildlife.

While it is possible to go on your own, armed with decent Spanish skills and maps, your best bet is to book with a good biking company that knows the safest routes and can take care of logistics.

By Car

Pothole-filled, unlit roads, careless (to put it mildly) drivers and poor signage conspire to make driving in Costa Rica a definite challenge. But it can be done – extremely defensively.

Seatbelts are compulsory, and drink-driving laws are enforced. The law defines drink driving as blood-alcohol levels of higher than 0.099 percent (in which case the driver is fined and loses his or her license and the car is confiscated). However, blood-alcohol levels between 0.049 percent and 0.099 percent qualify a driver as "pre-drunk" and will earn you a fine. Current monetary penalties are low, approximately $25 for driving without a seat belt, $30 for drink driving.

Car Rental
Renting a car makes sense for off-the-beaten-path trips outside San José. Reserve a car well in advance and get written confirmation. Pre-payment is advised, especially during high season. Rates generally start around US$60 per day, including insurance. Four-wheel drive vehicles start around US$80 per day. Most insurance is deductible for the first US$750–$1,000, although for an extra fee many companies offer a non-deductible policy. The following agencies all accept American Express, MasterCard, and Visa. Most agencies insist that the driver is over

21 years of age, they hold a valid passport and driver's license, and have a valid credit card for a deposit (not cash).
Alamo Rent a Car, Ca 11–13, Av 18, tel: 233 7733; US toll-free: 1 800-570 0671; fax: 290 0431; www.alamocostarica.com
Avis, Cruce San Antonio de Belén tel: 293 2222;fax: 293 1111; www.avis.co.cr
Budget, Paseo Colón, tel: 436 2000; fax: 436 2002; www.budget.co.cr
Dollar, Paseo Colón, Ca 34/36, tel: 443 2950, fax: 440 1401, toll-free 866-746 7765 (US); www.dollarcostarica.com
Economy: Sabana Norte, tel: 299 2000, fax: 232 7041, 877-326 7368 (US); www.economyrentacar.com
Hertz Paseo Colón, Ca 38, tel: 800 850 7576 (Canada, US), 221 1818 (Costa Rica), fax: 233 7254; www.costaricarentacar.com
National, La Uruca, shares a building with Alamo head office, tel: 290 8787; fax: 290 0431; reservations: 800-CAR RENT; www.natcar.com Bilingual drivers available.
Payless Ca 10, Av 13/15, San José, tel: 506-257 0026, fax: 221 5671; www.paylesscr.com Minimum age 25.

Private Tour Drivers
An alternative is to hire a knowledgeable bilingual driver, experienced with Costa Rican roads. Ask at your hotel or consult *The Tico Times*.

Driving: A Survival Guide
Four-wheel drive *(doble tracción)* is recommended for many areas as the roads outside the Central Valley, especially during the rainy season, are muddy and rutted. Chains work well in the mud; try letting some air out of your tires, to increase traction, if the car is stuck.
Licenses: operating a motor vehicle without a license is a serious violation of Costa Rican law and invalidates any insurance carried on the vehicle. A valid driver's license from another country can be used for three months. Always carry your passport (photocopies, including that of your entry stamp, usually suffice).
Import: foreign vehicles brought into Costa Rica for a period over 6 months must pay a large import tax. If you enter with a vehicle, you will have to leave with it or show papers proving you have sold it.
Driving habits: drivers weave all over the road to avoid the many ruts and

holes, called *huecos*. Two headlight blinks usually indicate the other driver is giving you the right of way (especially when you are making a left turn); on the highway two headlight blinks may mean that the police are ahead. Radar is often used. If waved over by the police, don't try to get away. They will radio ahead to have you stopped.
Accidents: Costa Rica has a high accident and death rate. Always drive defensively. Don't drive an uninsured vehicle. The law requires motorists to carry a set of reflecting triangles. If you are in an accident, do not move your car until the police and INS, the government insurance agency, arrive. Give no statements, but take witnesses' names.
Parking: be careful not to park illegally. A yellow curb means no stopping. Even if you are in the car, police may prevent you from leaving and call a tow truck *(grúa)*. You can ride in the car to the yard, where you will be required to pay the towing charges. It is better to park in one of the inexpensive parking lots *(parqueos)*. This will reduce the chance of theft.
Corruption: unfortunately, there are corrupt police who target foreign drivers for the purpose of extracting some colones. You may be stopped for no apparent reason. Have all necessary automobile documents in the car and be polite. It is illegal for the police to demand payment on the spot. If you are badly treated, or if the policeman solicits a bribe or asks that you pay the fine immediately, ask for the ticket ("*Deme el parte*"), then ask for the officer's identification. Write it down, and report to the *Dirección de Tránsito* as soon as possible.

Distances

When calculating travel time, take into account bad roads and slow-moving trucks. The website www.costaricamap-online.com has a fairly good list of distances and times, but the following will give you an idea.
San José–Quepos, 192 km (120 miles), 3½ hours
San José–Tamarindo, 274 km (170 miles), 5 hours
San José–Puerto Viejo, 203 km (126 miles), 4½ hours
San José–La Fortuna, 194 km (120 miles), 3½ hours
San José–Puerto Jiménez, 332 km (206 miles), 6 hours
La Fortuna–Monteverde, 136 km (85 miles), 4 hours (3 if jeep–boat–jeep)

ACCOMMODATIONS

HOTELS, YOUTH HOSTELS, BED & BREAKFAST

Where to Stay

Downtown San José is very noisy and polluted, so you may well prefer to stay out of the center. Escazú, Santa Ana, Alajuela, Heredia, and other Central Valley towns are less expensive, more enjoyable, and still give a good taste of Costa Rican life. Note that high season in Costa Rica is from November 1 to April 30, and low season is from May 1 to October 31. During the low season, room prices may be discounted by as much as 40 percent. Price categories below indicate high season rates.

Reservations made, but not paid for, especially during high season, may not be held, especially near the beaches and Monteverde. Discounts may be given for stays of more than one night. Ask at your hotel about green (wet) season discounts.

Hotels in categories $$ and up *(see price guide box)* include breakfast unless otherwise indicated. Note that rates for remote lodges in areas such as Tortuguero or the Osa Peninsula usually include meals, and often transport and a tour or two.

Tourist office: the Instituto Costarricense de Turismo (ICT) is based in central San José, beneath the Plaza de la Cultura (tel: 223 1733, www.visitcostarica.com), open 9am–5pm Mon–Fri. However, if you arrive without reservations, don't count on the ICT office to be able to help you out; at this writing it had been temporarily closed due to staff shortages.

The Tourist Institute has a system of classifications for lodging based on size and facility; however, there is a wide range of popular names used unofficially:
Apartotel Apartments with cooking facilities and living area in a hotel-style complex. Weekly and monthly rates.
Cabina Usually a one-room cabin with a shower and bath, often close to the beach in coastal resorts. *Cabinas* vary widely in quality and price.
Bed & Breakfast Price and quality vary widely, from a modest room in someone's own house to elegant guest houses all to yourself with pools and tennis courts.
Lodge Popular in more remote areas, usually near parks or natural attractions. Price usually includes meals. Stays at lodges are almost always linked with some outdoors activity: birdwatching, guided hikes or tours on horseback.
Villa or Chalet Often indistinguishable from a hotel.
Inn Often a B&B, but with more extensive amenities.
Resort Usually a luxurious, self-contained hotel complex.
Hotel Anything with more than 10 rooms.
Hostel In Costa Rica there is a small youth hostel system. Prices vary.
Albergue/Pensión Modest, small hotels.

Most agencies dealing with Costa Rica handle combined hotel and tour packages. However, a handful of organizations deal specifically with certain kinds of lodging.

Homestays

If you would like a better understanding of the people and culture of Costa Rica, try a Homestay Service. It is designed to offer a cross-cultural experience to both visitors and Costa Ricans. Visitors are lodged in the guest room of a host family and participate in as much (or as little) of the family activities as they wish. Families have been chosen on the basis of the quality of their homes and their hospitality, and most speak English. Most are in the San José area, close to public transportation, and are quite inexpensive.

Your options are best through language schools who can help make homestay arrangements *(see page 303)*.

Visitors receive an information pack with their reservation, including data on Costa Rica, a map with directions to the host residence and an introduction to the host family. Airport and hotel pick-up service is available.

A good homestay agency in San José is **Bells' Home Hospitality**, tel: 225 4752, fax: 224 5884, www.homestay.thebells.org

Local families sometimes rent rooms at a price including meals and laundry. Check around the university and the bulletin board at the Costa Rican/North American Cultural Center, see the *Tico Times* or the local papers.

Useful Websites

Costa Rican Hotel Association
Tel: 248 0990
www.costaricanhotels.com
A good resource for hotel information.
Costa Rica Innkeepers
Tel: 441 1157
www.costaricainnkeepers.com
Association of smaller-scale and B&B lodging.
Costa Rican Vacations
Tel: 296 7715 (Costa Rica),
800-606 1860 (US and Canada)
www.vacationscostarica.com
Specializes in apartment, condo and villa rentals.

ACCOMMODATIONS LISTINGS

SAN JOSÉ

Gran Hotel
Plaza de la Cultura
Tel: 221 4000
Fax: 221 3501
www.granhotelcostarica.com
An architectural heritage landmark, right across the plaza from the National Theater. A plethora of amenities make it a good option for those who want everything at their fingertips. Has the city's best sidewalk café.
$$$–$$$$
Hotel Grano de Oro
Ca 30, Av 2–4
San José
Tel: 255 3322
Fax: 221 2782
www.hotelgranodeoro.com
There's nothing cookie-cutter about this blend of two heritage houses (one from the turn of the 20th century, the other from the 1950s). Beautiful views, excellent restaurant. $$$
Le Bergerac
Barrio Los Yoses
Ca 35, Av Ctrl
Tel: 234 7850
Fax: 225 9103
www.bergerachotel.com

Upscale elegance with minimal pretension, this French inn is a true favorite. The restaurant is a draw in its own right, serving up gourmet Gallic delicacies. $$$
Hotel 1492 – Jade y Oro
Barrio Escalante
Av 1, Ca 31/33
Tel: 256 5913
Fax: 280 6206
www.hotel1492.com
Pre-Columbian-style murals brighten the walls of this 10-room boutique hotel. A lush garden courtyard provides the setting for tropical breakfasts. Complimentary evening glass of wine and cheese is a nice touch. $$–$$$
Hotel Don Carlos
Barrio Amón
Ca 9, Av 9
Tel: 221 6707
Fax: 258 1152
www.doncarloshotel.com
This heritage building was once home to two presidential families. Art-adorned corridors, quiet gardens and classic rooms provide an elegant

environment in a central location. The gift shop is one of the city's best. Good value. $$–$$$
B & B Cinco Hormigas Rojas
Ca 15 Av 9–11bis
San José
Tel: 255 3412
Tel/fax: 257 8581
www.cincohormigasrojas.com
Funky, verdant hideaway owned by artist. $–$$
Hotel la Amistad
Barrio Otoya
Av 11, Ca 15
Tel: 258 0021
Fax: 258 4900
www.hotelamistad.com
Inside this sprawling orange building, German efficiency reigns. All 40 rooms have direct-dial phones with voice mail; deluxe rooms and studio apartments have air conditioning. Wireless connections and in-house internet café. $–$$
Posada del Museo
Av 2, Ca 17
Tel: 258 1027
Fax: 257 9414
www.hotelposadadelmuseo.com

A wide range of colonial-style rooms fill this Victorian house kitty-corner to the National Museum, right on pedestrian boulevard. Ground-floor café is a good spot to get cultural information and Argentine pastries. $–$$
Casa Ridgeway
Av 6 bis, Ca 15,
San José
Tel: 222 1400
fax: 233 6168
www.amigosparalapaz.org
Small *pensión* managed by the Society of Friends (Quakers). A pleasant, welcoming place, with comfy lounge and cable TV. Use of kitchen and laundry. $ (breakfast included)
Hotel Aranjuez
Ca 19, Av 11–13
San José
Tel: 256 1825
Fax: 223 3528
www.hotelaranjuez.com
A labyrinth-like historic building in the older part of town. The balance of economy, comfort and character is among the best you'll find in the capital. $

CENTRAL VALLEY

Alajuela

Orquídeas Inn
Tel: 433 7128
Fax: 433 9740
www.orquideasinn.com
This Spanish hacienda-style hotel offers spacious rooms, suites and a two-bedroom geodesic dome for groups, all awash in tropical colors. Restaurant serves up inventive international and vegetarian cuisine; renowned Marilyn Monroe bar. $$$–$$$$
Xandari Resort and Spa
Alajuela
Tel: 443 2020
Fax: 442 4847
www.xandari.com
An exclusive oasis with fantastic Central Valley

views, designed with an artist's eye. Spacious villas and intimate *jalapas* for the full-service spa are perfect for romance. Excellent restaurant serves gourmet dishes with healthy focus. Also runs Xandari by the Pacific (tel: 778 7070) in Esterillos Este on the Central Pacific. $$$$
Hotel Airport Inn
Tel: 441 7569
Fax: 431 0572
E-mail: larrycastillo1@hotmail.com
Good first- or last-night option. Rooms with cable TV and a balcony cost the same as other rooms – ask for one when reserving. No pool, but local waterpark Ojo de Agua is close by. $$

Hotel II Millenium
Tel: 430 5050
Fax: 441 2365
www.bbmilleniumcr.com
Bed and breakfast, 1 km (⅔ mile) from Juan Santamaría International Airport and close to the bus stop. English-speaking owner, well-run and friendly atmosphere. Monthly rates on request. $$
Hotel La Guaria Inn
Tel: 440 2948
Fax: 441 9573
E-mail: laguariahotel@netscape.net
Downtown Alajuela hotel has 21 standard rooms and four junior suites. Prices include taxes if you pay in cash. All have cable TV. Close to airport. $–$$

Heredia

Finca Rosa Blanca Country Inn
Near Heredía
Tel: 269 9392
Fax: 269 9555
www.fincarosablanca.com
Lovely boutique hotel in the foothills of Heredia, one of only two accommodations to earn the ICT's top sustainability rating. Bright,

PRICE CATEGORIES

Price categories are for a double room without breakfast:

$$$$	$150 and up
$$$	$70–150
$$	$40–70
$	up to $40

decadent tower suite with rainforest-themed bathroom generally causes a sensation. **$$$$**

Hotel Bougainvillea
Santo Domingo de Heredia
Tel: 244 1414
Fax: 244 1313
www.hb.co.cr
This is a perfect setting for nature lovers who like tranquility. 5 hectares (12 acres) of tropical gardens with reading area, heated pool, sauna, and lit tennis courts. Eighty tastefully decorated rooms. **$$–$$$**

Hotel Chalet Tirol
Tel: 267 6228
Fax: 267 6373
www.tirolcr.com
Tyrolean-style A-frame cottages in the cloud forest above Heredia, bordering Braulio Carrillo National Park. **$$–$$$**

Hotel & Villas La Condesa
San Rafael de Heredia
Tel: 267 6001
Fax: 267 6200
www.hotellacondesa.com
Mountain hotel with luxury rooms, conference center, pool, good restaurants;

hiking and nearby horseback riding trails. **$$$–$$$$**

Naranjo

Vista del Valle Plantation Inn
Naranjo, near Grecia
Tel: 450 0800
Fax: 451 1165
www.vistadelvalle.com
Simple Japanese architectural lines fit richly into the chaotic exuberance of the surrounding forest. Rooms with outdoor shower and private sunbathing patios are a particular treat. The property's 91-meter (300-ft) waterfall is a short hike away. **$$$**

Orosí

Orosí Lodge
Tel/fax: 533 3578
www.orosilodge.com
Established lodge on the edge of town. Second-floor rooms have valley and volcano views. Funky coffee shop/art gallery serves up tasty European pastries. **$$**

Santa Ana/Escazú

Hotel Alta
Santa Ana
Tel: 282 4160
Fax: 282 4162
www.thealtahotel.com
For style and views, this Spanish-inspired hotel overlooking the Central Valley is one of the area's best. The gourmet restaurant also has one of the most varied menus. **$$$$**

Casa de las Tías
Escazú
Tel: 289 5517
Fax: 289 7353
www.hotels.co.cr/casatias.html
Surprisingly peaceful, homey Victorian-style bed and breakfast. All four rooms and the suite are airy; gourmet breakfasts. Extremely knowledgeable and helpful owners. **$$**

Turrialba

Casa Turire
Tel: 531 1111
Fax: 531 1075
www.hotelcasaturire.com

Luxurious plantation-style hotel surrounded by sugar cane, coffee and macadamia fields. Pool. A center of peaceful elegance at the gateway to some of the country's best white-water rafting. The Turrialba Mountains form a dramatic backdrop. **$$$–$$$$**

Turrialtico
Turrialba
Tel: 538 1111
Fax: 538 1575
www.turrialtico.com
Top-of-the-line location, with a budget price tag. Rooms in the wood structure are simple but comfortable. The restaurant, around which the hotel was based, serves traditional food with spectacular views of the Turralba valley. **$$**

Volcán Turrialba Lodge
20 km (12½ miles) above Turrialba
Tel: 273 4335
Fax: 273 0703
www.volcanturrialbalodge.com
Cabins with wood stoves; lofty setting; horseback rides and hiking to extinct crater. Rates include three meals. **$**

CENTRAL PACIFIC

Jacó and area

Villa Caletas
Near Jacó
Tel: 637 0505
Fax: 637 0404
www.villacaletas.com
A luxurious Victorian tropical fantasy retreat on a mountain top overlooking the Pacific. Lovely pool. Amphitheater with regular cultural performances. **$$$$**

Hotel Club del Mar Resort
south end of beach
Tel: 643 3194 (Costa Rica)
Tel: 866-978 5669 (US)
Fax: 643 3550
www.clubdelmarcostarica.com
The area's highest-end lodging keeps itself at a peaceful arm's length from the mêlée. Offers a range of lodging options; the condos are the best value. Good restaurant. **$$$$**

Hotel Villa Lapas
Near Carara National Park
Tel: 637 0232
Fax: 637 0227

www.villalapas.com
The secluded hotel itself is nothing to write home about, but the lush rainforest setting will wow nature lovers. Activities include a suspension-bridge hike and canopy tour. **$$$**

Hotel Punta Leona
Punta Leona
Tel: 231 3131
Toll-free: 800-231 3131
Fax: 232 0791
www.hotelpuntaleona.com
Sprawling self-contained residential/resort community with access to good beaches in a rainforest setting. Several restaurants, a church, and standard tourist activities can all be found on the 300-hectare (740-acre) private reserve property. **$$$–$$$$**

AparHotel Vista Pacífico
Jacó
Tel: 643 3261
Fax: 643 2046
www.vistapacifico.com

Ocean views from most of the studios, equipped apartments and pool. Two rooms adapted for visitors with disabilities. Two km (1 mile) from beach. Excellent choice for families. Canadian-owned. **$$–$$$**

Encantada Hotel (formerly Bacara Beach Resort)
Esterillos
Tel: 778 7048
www.encantadacostarica.com
Two basic rooms, four larger cabins and equipped oceanfront apartment, all air conditioned, just a few hundred meters from the beach. Pool; surfboard and bike rentals. **$–$$**

Cabinas Las Olas
Playa Hermosa (near Jacó)
Tel: 652 9315
Fax: 652 9331
www.cabinaslasolashotel.com
Rooms have private baths, heated water, ceiling fans, and kitchens. Pool. Friendly surfers' hang-out. **$**

La Felicidad Country Inn
Esterillos Beach
Tel: 778 6824
Fax: 779 9960
Toll-free: 800-290 9463
www.lafelicidad.com
South-facing location gives this comfortable budget option excellent sunrise and sunset views. **$–$$**

Manuel Antonio

Gaia Hotel y Reserva
Tel: 777 9797
Fax: 777 9196
www.gaiahr.com
Belongs to "Small Luxury Hotels of the World." Accommodations, set on a 5.7-hectare (14-acre) reserve, range from a 32.5-sq meter (350-sq-ft) studio to the 186-sq meter (2,000-sq ft) villa; rates include personal valet service. Gourmet La Luna restaurant. **$$$$**

La Mariposa
Manuel Antonio

Tel: 777 0355
Fax: 777 0050
www.lamariposa.com
A view to beat all, spacious accommodations and an excellent staff make this an area favorite. Free transportation provided to the beach. **$$$$**

Makanda by the Sea
Tel: 777 0442
Fax: 777 1032
www.makanda.com
Romantic adults-only resort that merges luxury into the jungle. Vaulted-ceiling villas come with spectacular views, equipped kitchens and Japanese gardens. Gourmet restaurant highly recommended. **$$$$**

Sí Como No
Tel: 777 0777
Fax: 777 1093
www.sicomono.com
A favorite venue for weddings. Luxury rooms with rainforest and ocean views; attractions range from nearby howler monkeys and a jungle spa to a private movie theater. **$$$$**

Costa Verde
Tel: 777 0584
Fax: 777 0560
www.costaverde.com
On the forested bluffs above the area's crescent beach, this hotel advertises "More monkeys than people." Good range of equipped studios, efficient apartments and houses

with great views. Two hill-side pools. Breakfast not included. **$$$–$$$$**

Mango Moon
Tel: 777 5323
Fax: 777 5128
www.mangomoon.net
Luxury without pretension. Sliding glass doors open up to balconies, ocean views and breezes in almost all of these rooms and suites. Secluded trail leads down to beautiful Biesanz Beach. **$$$–$$$$**

Villas Nicolás
Tel: 777 0481
Fax: 777 0451
www.villasnicolas.com
Terraces with beautiful views. **$$$$**

Hotel Karahé
Tel: 777 0170
Fax: 777 1075
www.karahe.com
Nine air-conditioned bungalows surrounded by 600 hectares (1,500 acres) of grounds. Swimming pool, restaurant. Outdoor pursuits. **$$$**

El Mono Azul
Near Manuel Antonio
Tel: 777 2572
Tel: 800-381-3578 (US)
Fax: 777 1954
www.monoazul.com
Funky, family-friendly hotel with rooms and equipped villas. The gift shop was inspired by the owner's conservation-minded young

daughter. **$$–$$$**

Nature's Beachfront Apartments
Tel: 777 1473
Fax: 777 1475
www.maqbeach.com/natures.html
Equipped beach-front studio apartments, suites and a villa, just a 15-minute walk from the national park. **$$–$$$**

Didi's Charming House
Tel: 777 0069
Fax: 777 2863
www.didiscr.com
All three themed rooms are tastefully artistic. Dinner available on request. Ask about boat tours. Italian owners. **$$**

Hotel Vela Bar
Tel: 777 0413
Fax: 777 1071
www.velabar.com
The jungle almost seems to creep into the rooms here. Rooms and kitchenette-equipped apartments have air conditioning and private baths. Popular restaurant. **$–$$**

Cabinas Pedro Miguel
Quepos
Tel: 777 0035
Fax: 777 2200
www.cabinaspedromiguel.com
Comfortable rooms, some with air conditioning and TV, "eco-cabins" for four (no air conditioning or TV); rooms higher on the hill have an ocean view. Excellent value for the area. Friendly,

helpful Tico owners. **$**

Cabinas Piscis
Tel/fax: 777 0046
E-mail: piscisjf@racsa.co.cr
Simple rooms with private or shared bathrooms on large property just 600 meters/yards from the national park and 150 meters/yards from the beach; one equipped house with air conditioning. **$–$$**

Quepos

Rafiki Safari Lodge
Quepos (30 km/18 miles south)
Tel: 777 2250
Fax: 777 5327
www.rafikisafari.com
Ten luxury safari tents (complete with bathroom) on hardwood decks. Rafting, kayaking and floats on the Savegre river, hikes on 283 hectares (700 acres) of private rainforest, horseback riding and birding. **$$$$**

Cabinas Doña Alicia
Tel: 777 0419
Clean and friendly. The larger rooms have air conditioning, two have hot water; all rooms have private baths. **$**

Hotel Ceciliano
Quepos
Tel/Fax: 777 0192
Well kept and pleasant. Rooms with shared/private bathrooms, ceiling fans and air conditioning. **$**

THE NORTHWEST

Flamingo Area

Bahía Esmeralda
Potrero
Tel: 654 4480
Fax: 654 4479
www.hotelbahiaesmeralda.com
Quiet, Italian-run garden hotel offers comfortable rooms with and without kitchenettes, equipped villas and suites close to a selection of uncrowded beaches. Green-season rates include breakfast. **$$**

Hotel Brasilito
Playa Brasilito
Tel: 654 4237
Fax: 654 4247
www.brasilito.com

Wooden hotel on the beach with great views. Largely no frills, with the exception of stand-out Gecko's Restaurant, which occupies the downstairs lobby. **$**

Inland

Hotel Hacienda Guachipelín
Rincón de la Vieja
Tel: 666 8075
Fax: 665 2178
www.guachipelin.com
A working cattle ranch and adventure center. All-inclusive packages offer the best value. Excellent canopy, tubing and volcano tours. **$$**

Rancho Curubandé
Rincón de la Vieja
Tel: 665 0375
Fax: 665 6331
www.rancho-curubande.com
A 134-hectare (330-acre) working ranch; scaled-back version of Hacienda Guachipelín with added back-to-the-land feel (including horse-and-buggy tour to an old-fashioned swimming hole). **$–$$**

Casa Vieja
Liberia
Tel: 665 5826
Friendly staff, tiled floors, well-kept rooms and a small kitchen area make this an excellent budget option just off the historic Calle Real. **$**

La Ensenada Lodge
Palo Verde
Tel: 289 6655
Fax: 289 5281
www.laensenada.net
Breezy cabinas overlooking the Gulf of Nicoya. Meals, horseback rides and boat tours included. **$**

Rinconcito Lodge
Rincón de la Vieja

PRICE CATEGORIES

Price categories are for a double room without breakfast:
$$$$ $150 and up
$$$ $70–150
$$ $40–70
$ up to $40

Tel: 666 2764
Fax: 666 9178
www.rinconcitolodge.com
Rustic mountain lodge within visiting distance of Rincón de la Vieja National Park and the less touristy but also impressive Miravalles volcano and area. $

Monteverde

Monteverde Lodge
8 km (5 miles) north of Santa Elena
Tel: 645 5057
Fax: 645 5126
This comfortable woodsy lodge is the area's highest-end option. Earth-toned, ample rooms complement the nature outside the picture windows. Relax in the jacuzzi, set in a stone floor facing a floor-to-vaulted-ceiling glass wall, or the renowned gardens. $$$–$$$$

Heliconia Hotel
Monteverde
Tel: 240 7311
Fax: 240 7331
www.hotelheliconia.com
Rustic luxury in wooden lodge; relaxing spa and excellent restaurant. $$$–$$$$

Belmar
Monteverde
Tel: 645 5201
Fax: 645 5135
www.hotelbelmarcostarica.com
Chalet style and homey. Views. $$$

El Sol
4 km (3 miles) south of Santa Elena
Tel: 645 5838
www.elsolnuestro.com
Two cozy log cabins equipped with kitchens and tubs. Reserve a massage with owner Elizabeth, and savor Ignacio's Mediterranean, German and Central American gourmet dishes. Breakfast not included. $$$

Arco Iris Lodge
Monteverde
Tel: 645 5067
Fax: 645 5022
www.arcoirislodge.com
Small lodge near Monteverde cloud forest. Rooms with hot water and private bathrooms. Great breakfast buffet. Laundry. Tours offered. $$

Manakin Lodge

Santa Elena
Tel: 645 5080
Fax: 645 5517
www.manakinlodge.com
Basic rooms with mountain views – ask for one with a balcony. Common room on the second floor has a nice view. Breakfast included. $

Hotel & Restaurante El Atardecer
Santa Elena
Tel: 645 5685
Fax: 645 5462
E-mail:
hotelatardecermonteverde@hotmail.com
Budget rooms, most with views of the cloud forest and the Gulf of Nicoya. Restaurant serves Costa Rican fare. Breakfast included. $

Pensión Santa Elena
Santa Elena
Tel: 645 5051
Fax: 645 6240
www.pensionsantaelena.com
Best budget digs in the area, ranging from camping (bring your own equipment) to rooms with shared baths and cabins. A favorite of backpackers and groups. $

Nosara-Sámara

Harbor Reef Lodge
Playa Guiones, Nosara
Tel: 682 1000
Fax: 682 0060
www.harborreef.com
Comfortable rooms in garden property, perfect for surfers with good breaks nearby; two pools, restaurant. $$$–$$$$

Luna Azul
Ostional
Tel: 821 0075
www.hotellunaazul.com
Excellent base for experiencing the arribadas (nesting of thousands of sea turtles). Swiss-run, stylish boutique hotel with brightly colored and private cabins, with air conditioning and open showers. Ocean-view restaurant, infinity pool and natural health center. $$$

Café de Paris Residence
Playa Guiones
Tel: 682 0087
Fax: 682 0089
www.cafedeparis.net
Available weekly or monthly. Ocean-view air-conditioned rooms, some with equipped

kitchens, bungalows and villas offer breezy accommodations high above Nosara's coastline. Excellent bakery produces delicious bread and authentic French pastries. $$–$$$$

Hotel Giada
Playa Sámara
Tel: 656 0132
Fax: 656 0131
www.hotelgiada.net
Easily the pick of Sámara's boutique hotels. The design and creativity of the Italian owners infuse the space with a Mediterranean feel; the Pizza & Pasta a Go Go restaurant is worth a visit. $$

Lagarta Lodge Biological Reserve
Nosara
Tel: 682 0035
Fax: 682 0135
www.lagarta.com
The place to go for birdwatching, with excellent views of Ostional National Wildlife Refuge and private nature preserve. Just 10 minutes from Playa Guiones (steep trail). Exceptional breakfast buffet. $$

Casa del Mar
Sámara
Tel: 656 0264
Fax: 656 0129
www.casadelmarsamara.net
Homey rooms with a/c in the center of town, close to the beach. Shared and private baths. Cool-water backyard jacuzzi. $–$$

Hotel Belvedere
Sámara
Tel: 656 0213
Fax: 682 1047
www.belvederesamara.net
Well-kept rooms and equipped apartments with air-conditioning and a European touch; second-floor digs have small balconies. The shady gardens and sizeable pool are refreshing. Jacuzzi. Breakfast on the ocean-view terrace is included. $–$$

Papagayo to Ocotal

El Ocotal Resort
Playa Ocotal
Tel: 670 0321
Fax: 670 0083
www.ocotalresort.com
Elegant and secluded hotel overlooking the beach; two

restaurants, tennis, pools, sportfishing. $$$$

Four Seasons Resort Costa Rica
Papagayo Peninsula
Tel: 696 0000
Fax: 696 0500
www.fourseasons.com/costarica
Often referred to as the first hotel of its class in Costa Rica, this ultra-high end chain hotel welcomes guests with its trademark luxury and pomp. $$$$

Occidental Grand Papagayo
Playa Panamá
Tel: 672 0193
Fax: 672 0191
www.occidentalhoteles.com
Luxurious all-inclusive hotel-village on the hills above the Papagayo Gulf. Colonial Spanish decor. On-site transport carts shuttle you around the sprawling grounds, which include a full spa, gym, tennis court and gourmet restaurants. $$$$

Hotel El Velero
Playa Hermosa
Tel: 672 1017
Fax: 672 0016
www.costaricahotel.net
Breezy beachfront hotel and hub for expats; great base for sunset cruises and fishing. $$$

Hotel Playa Hermosa Bosque de Mar
Playa Hermosa (Guanacaste)
Tel: 672 0046
Fax: 672 0019
www.hotelplayahermosa.com
On the beach, with a good seafood restaurant. *Cabinas* have private bathrooms, heated water, and ceiling fans or air conditioning. $$$

Villa Casa Blanca
Playa Ocotal
Tel/fax: 670 0448
www.hotelvillacasablanca.com
Ultra-romantic Victorian-style suites embedded in thick tropical gardens. Hillside location, just past gates for El Ocotal Beach Resort. The breakfasts at this B&B also rank among the best in the region. $$$

La Puerta del Sol
Playas del Coco
Tel: 670 0195
Fax: 670 0650
The area's best luxury option, the hotel is a cluster of air-conditioned

private rooms and one suite in precisely landscaped gardens with an inviting pool. Rooms have an airy Mediterranean feel. Restaurant El Sol y La Luna is highly recommended. **$$–$$$**

Villa Huetares
Playa Hermosa
Tel: 672 0052
Fax: 672 0051
www.villahuetares.com
You won't get a better deal in town with these family-oriented two-bedroom equipped bungalows and 16 spacious rooms. Newer rooms have air conditioning and cable TV. Restaurant serves local food. **$–$$**

Southern Nicoya Peninsula

Hotel Flor Blanca Resort
Santa Teresa
Tel: 640 0232
Fax: 640 0226
www.florblanca.com
Gorgeous, ultra-luxurious, and romantic. Private outdoor tub, shower, yoga, gourmet restaurant, and art studio. **$$$$**

Punta Islita Hotel
Punta Islita
Tel: 231 6122
Fax: 231 0715
www.hotelpuntaislita.com
Truly secluded luxury hotel with gorgeous Pacific views; most guests arrive by plane. Lodgings, amenities and spa services provide the ultimate indulgence. The hotel is renowned for extensive community involvement. **$$$$**

Ylang Ylang Beach Resort
Montezuma
Tel: 642 0636
Fax: 642 0068
www.ylangylangresort.com
Ten-minute beach walk north of town, romantic bungalows and suites, beautiful gardens. Run by the folks at Sano Banano Village Hotel in town. **$$$–$$$$**

Blue Jay Eco-Lodge
Mal País
Tel: 640 0089
Fax: 640 0141
www.bluejaylodgecostarica.com
Ten hillside cabins set in the jungle just 200 meters/

yards from the beach; ask for a higher one to get an ocean view. The greenery spills veritably spills into the rooms, restaurant and pool area. **$$$**

Hotel El Jardín
Montezuma
Tel: 642 0548
Fax: 642 0074
www.hoteleljardin.com
The ambience of a resort in a boutique-hotel setting near the beach. Fifteen rooms and two villas, some with simple but beautiful stone and wood architectural details. Breakfast not included. **$$$**

Hotel Milarepa
Santa Teresa
Tel: 640 0023
Fax: 640 0663
www.milarepahotel.com
A craggy coastline and antique four-poster beds draped with gauzy mosquito nets evoke a tropical dream. The Asian-style hotel is designed to blend into the environment, with partly open bungalows that rise up with bamboo-striped walls; two are right on the beach. **$$$**

Hotel Amor de Mar
Montezuma
Tel/fax: 642 0262
www.amordemar.com
Just south of town; located on a rocky point overlooking the Pacific. **$$–$$$**

Sano Banano Village Hotel
Montezuma
Tel: 642 0638
Fax: 642 0636
www.elbanano.com
Downtown hotel above health-conscious restaurant of the same name. Air-conditioned rooms are decent, and relatively buffered from street and restaurant hubbub. **$$**

Hotel & Restaurante La Cascada
Montezuma
Tel/fax: 642 0057
www.playamontezuma.net/cascada.php
Budget lodgings, three nicer rooms with a/c, all have private baths. Rooms on both floors have ocean views, 400 meters from downtown Montezuma. Nice second-floor balcony. **$–$$**

Hotel Ancla de Oro

Cabuya de Cobano
Tel: 642 0369
www.caboblancopark.com/ancla
Secluded "jungalows" (A-frame cabins on stilts) near Cabo Blanco Reserve with a variety of beaches nearby. Recommended restaurant. **$–$$**

Cabinas Playa El Carmen
Santa Teresa
Tel: 640 0179
Eleven budget rooms, two with private toilets, all shared cold-water showers, just 50 meters/yards from the beach. Shared kitchen and fridge. **$**

Hotel Lucy
Montezuma
Tel: 642 0273
This two-story converted house is the best of the budget options in this area. Accommodations are basic but comfortable, some shared baths, and a restaurant serves up local food – the big draw is the location, just south of town and close to the beach. **$**

Tamarindo to Junquillal

Capitán Suizo
Tamarindo
Tel: 653 0075
Fax: 653 0292
www.hotelcapitansuizo.com
The height of small-scale luxury. Beachfront hotel with two-level rooms and bungalows and elegant equipped apartment. Shaded pool and recommended restaurant. **$$$$**

Sueño del Mar
Playa Langosta
Tel: 653 0284
Fax: 653 0558
www.sueno-del-mar.com
You'll never tire of looking around this artsy beachfront B&B. Richly decorated double rooms with showers open to the sky, equipped casitas and a honeymoon suite. Excellent breakfasts served in the garden patio. **$$$$**

Guacamaya Lodge
Playa Junquillal
Tel: 658 8431
Fax: 658 8164
www.guacamayalodge.com
Poolside rooms, studio apartments with ocean view and equipped villa, all

with air conditioning, close to one of the country's best beaches. Golf course just 20 minutes away. **$$–$$$**

Hotel Las Tortugas
Playa Grande
Tel: 653 0423
Fax: 653 0458
www.lastortugashotel.com
Turtle-friendly hotel on a long, wide beautiful beach. Conservationist management. Good restaurant. Pool. Excellent surfing directly in front of hotel. **$$–$$$**

Hotel Pasatiempo
Tamarindo
Tel: 653 0096
Fax: 653 0278
www.hotelpasatiempo.com
Popular Tamarindo institution and hang-out. Each air-conditioned room has its own hand-painted mural. At night, the bar and restaurant fill up and the place comes alive with music. Breakfast not included. **$$–$$$**

Iguanazul
Playa Junquillal
Tel: 658 8123
Fax: 658 8124
www.hoteliguanazul.com
Cliffside complex with 24 cabins (10 with air conditioning); also condos and a beach house. Popular gathering place for "Happy Hour". International restaurant, sand volleyball court and entertainment room. **$$–$$$**

Hotel Playa Negra
Playa Negra
Tel: 658 8034
Fax: 658 8035
www.playanegra.com
Across from the hotel is the surf break made famous in the Endless Summer II movie. Non-surfers can stick to the white-sand beach 100 meters/yds south. Round, thatched-roof bungalows are bright and breezy. Breakfast not included. **$$**

PRICE CATEGORIES

Price categories are for a double room without breakfast:

$$$$	$150 and up
$$$	$70–150
$$	$40–70
$	up to $40

TRANSPORT

ACCOMMODATIONS

EATING OUT

ACTIVITIES

A – Z

LANGUAGE

THE NORTHEAST

Arenal Area

Hotel Tilawa
Lake Arenal
Tel: 695 5050
Fax: 695 5766
www.tilawa.com
Columned hotel modeled after a Cretan palace overlooks Lake Arenal, favorite base for kite- and windsurfing aficionados. Hot springs, jungle trails and animals delight the whole family; kid-friendly skate park is also a hit. Rooms, suites and apartments available with lake or garden views. Breakfast not included. **$$–$$$**

Montaña de Fuego Hotel & Spa
La Fortuna
Tel: 479 1220
Fax: 479 1455
www.montanadefuego.com
All 66 air-conditioned rooms and 18 suites in the bungalows have picture-window views of the volcano. Pool, spa, jacuzzi and sauna. An excellent luxury base for exploring the Arenal area. **$$$–$$$$**

Tabacón Grand Spa & Thermal Resort
Lake Arenal
Tel: 519 1999
Fax: 519 1940
www.tabacon.com
Luxury resort famous for hot springs in landscaped gardens with views of Arenal Volcano. **$$$**

Arenal Observatory Lodge
La Fortuna area
Tel: 290 7011
Fax: 290 8427
www.arenalobservatorylodge.com
Best site for volcano viewing. The more expensive rooms have views of the volcano. Lots of observation decks. Pool, jacuzzi, trails. Includes breakfast. **$$–$$$**

Las Cabanitas
La Fortuna
Tel: 479 9400
Fax: 479 9408
www.hotelcabanita.com
One of La Fortuna's nicest places to stay. Comfortable, traditional tile-roofed cabinas. **$$–$$$**

La Catarata Lodge
La Fortuna area
Tel: 479 9522
Tel: 888-250 6472 (US and Canada)
Fax: 479 9168
www.cataratalodge.com
Run by a local sustainable-development association. Excellent volcano views, butterfly garden, and internet access. **$$**

Hotel/Restaurante La Pradera del Arenal
La Fortuna (2 km/1 mile west)
Tel: 479 9597
Fax: 479 9167
www.lapraderadelarenal.com
For a few dollars more it's worth choosing the individual wood cabins, but the concrete rooms are comfortable as well. All have air conditioning and volcano views. Pool, jacuzzi. **$$**

Cabinas Oriuma
La Fortuna
Tel/Fax: 479 9111
E-mail: oriuma@racsa.co.cr
Central budget option popular with backpackers. Almost all rooms have air conditioning, balcony, communal balcony with volcano view. **$**

Hotel Las Colinas
La Fortuna
Tel: 479 9305
Fax: 479 9160
www.lascolinasarenal.com
While not much to look at from the outside, this central hotel offers a step above what you'd expect in this price range, particularly with the spectacular volcano views in rooms 33 and 27. Breakfast included. **$**

Hotel Jungla y Senderos Los Lagos.
Tel: 479 1000
Fax: 479 1001
www.hotelloslagos.com
Moderate hotel with pool and restaurant on the lower slopes of Volcán Arenal just a few kilometers northwest

of La Fortuna; also offers campground and park. Feel the volcano rumble as you drop off to sleep. Camping price includes access to pool and hot springs. Crowded on weekends. Breakfast included. **$$$**

Central Plains

Hotel Occidental El Tucano
San Carlos area
Tel: 248 2323
Fax: 460 1692
Resort built around natural hot springs. Olympic-size swimming pool, jacuzzi. **$$$–$$$$**

Hotel Tilajari Resort
Near Muelle
Tel: 291 4081
Fax: 291 4082
www.tilajari.com
Spacious rooms and acres of rolling lawns on the San Carlos River. Tennis, spa, swimming, horses, pool. **$$$**

Termales del Bosque
Aguas Zarcas
Tel/Fax: 460 1356
www.termalesdelbosque.com
Luxuriate in natural rainforest hot springs, stay the night and enjoy breakfast for less than the entrance fee to better-known hot springs elsewhere in the country. Eco-hikes through private reserve and nearby Juan Castro Blanco national park. **$$**

La Laguna del Lagarto
San Carlos area
Tel: 289 8163
Fax: 289 5295
www.lagarto-lodge-costa-rica.com
Remote lodge on a hill with views, with comfortable rooms. Hiking, horseback riding, boat trips on the Río San Carlos. **$$**

Chachagua Rainforest Hotel
San Rafael de Peñas Blancos
Tel: 468 1010
Fax: 468 1020
www.chachaguarainforesthotel.com
Pleasant cabins on a working 150-hectare (380-acre) cattle and horse ranch. Reflective-glass showers offer a unique bird-watching experience. **$$–$$$**

Heliconias Lodge
3 km/2 miles north of Bijagua
Tel/Fax: 466 8483
Part of a rural tourism initiative, this hotel offers new rustic equipped cabins with jacuzzi and balcony and budget rooms on the skirts of the Tenorio Volcano. Excellent base for tours to the national park and iridescent Río Celeste. **$–$$**

Nuevo Arenal

Villa Decary
Nuevo Arenal area
Tel: 383 3012
Tel/fax: 694 4330
www.villadecary.com
Large rooms and bungalows in a lovely country inn with a lake view. Great birding, hearty breakfasts and excellent service. **$$$–$$$$**

La Ceiba Tree Lodge
Nuevo Arenal area
Tel/fax: 692 8050
Lovely B&B on a hill top, with an organic garden. Named for majestic, 500-year-old ceiba tree on property. Views of Lake Arenal, five homey rooms. **$$–$$$**

Lake Coter Eco-Lodge
Tel: 289 6060
Fax: 288 0123
www.ecolodgecostarica.com
Comfortable cabins with Lake Arenal views, grand fireplace in lodge; great hiking, horseback riding, kayaking, and canopy tour. **$$**

Chalet Nicholas
Tel: 694 4041
www.chaletnicholas.com
Three immaculate rooms in a large house with lake and volcano views. More than 100 orchid species flourish in the tropical gardens. You're likely to come across the three resident Great Danes – no worries, they're gentle giants. No credit cards. **$$**

San Ramón

Villa Blanca
Near San Ramón
Tel: 461 0301
Fax: 461 0302

www.villablancacr.com
Well-appointed *casitas* modeled after colonial-era workers' homes. Fireplaces, generous bathtubs. Located adjacent to Los Angeles Cloud Forest Reserve. **$$$$**

Sarapiquí

Rara Avis
Near Las Horquetas
Tel: 764 1111
Fax: 764 1114
www.rara-avis.com
For the most intrepid birders and nature lovers only. Three-hour trip by tractor-pulled wagon to rustic lodge in spectacular forest setting. Electricity only in restaurant. Rates include all meals, tours. **$$**

Selva Verde Lodge
Near Puerto Viejo de Sarapiquí
Tel: 766 6800
Fax: 766 6011
www.selvaverde.com
Beautiful river lodge. Spectacular birdwatching, nature walks, horseback riding. Meals are included. **$$**

La Quinta de Sarapiquí Country Inn
North of La Virgen
Tel: 761 1300
Fax: 761 1395
www.laquintasarapiqui.com
Classy rooms with patios. Several in-house attractions: butterfly garden and frog garden, lush heliconia, ornamental and organic gardens, pool. **$$–$$$**

La Garza
Platanar (overlooking the Platanar River)
Tel: 475 5222
Fax: 475 5015
www.hotellagarza.com
Riverside bungalows on a large working cattle and horse ranch. Beautiful gardens. Horseback riding, fishing. **$$**

La Selva Biological Station
Puerto Viejo de Sarapiquí (4 km/3 miles south)
Tel: 524 0607
Fax: 524 0608
www.threepaths.co.cr
A birding mecca, with sightings of more than 400 resident and migratory birds. Dorms are no-frills but six new private cabins

are very comfortable. More than 50 km (30 miles) of trails take you deep into the rainforest. Rates include three meals and half-day tour. **$$**

Hotel Ara Ambigua
Puerto Viejo de Sarapiquí
Tel: 766 7101
Tel/Fax: 766 6401
www.hotelaraambigua.com
The nicest cabins have teak walls, rough-hewn wooden furniture and stone-slab floors. Concrete options are acceptable but the atmosphere pales in comparison. Large pool forms a blue clearing amidst the lush jungle gardens. Breakfast included. **$**

Hotel Mi Lindo Sarapiquí
Tel/fax: 766 6281
Small hotel in the center of town. Clean rooms, TV and hot water. Student discount. **$**

Rancho Leona
Puerto Viejo de Sarapiquí area
Tel: 761 1019
www.rancholeona.com
Basic lodging with shared bath, and sauna. Kayaking and hiking. Friendly

ambiance and good food. Recommended. **$**

Varablanca

Peace Lodge
26 km/16 miles south of San Miguel to Vara Blanca
Tel: 225 0643
Fax: 482 2720
www.waterfallgardens.com
Sensuous luxury mountain resort set on the grounds of La Paz Waterfall Gardens. Decadent stone waterfall showers and balcony jacuzzi tubs are just some of the details that make these rooms some of the country's most romantic. **$$$$**

Poás Volcano Lodge
Varablanca, Heredia
Tel: 482 2194
Fax: 482 2513
www.poasvolcanolodge.com
Rough stone walls and wooden-beamed ceilings are featured in a combination of English-cottage and Alpine resort styles. Fireplaces, bathtubs are cozy accoutrements after a day of bird-watching or hiking. **$$–$$$**

THE CARIBBEAN COAST

North

Tortuga Lodge
Tortuguero
Tel: 257 0766
Fax: 257 1665
www.costaricaexpeditions.com
Pleasant lodge 2 km (1 mile) from the village. Package deal including meals and transportation from San José available. **$$$$**

Mawamba Lodge
Tortuguero
Tel: 293 8181
Fax: 222 5463/239 7657
www.grupomawamba.com/mawambalodge
A specialty in incentive travel means you risk sharing the place with large groups, but the advantage is top-notch facilities at a reasonable price. **$$$**

Pachira
Tortuguero
Tel: 256 7080 (Costa Rica),
Fax: 223 1119

www.pachiralodge.com
Fresh rooms with wicker furniture and a turtle-shaped pool at a modern wooden lodge. In season, enjoy the turtles, the 5.6-hectare (14-acre) property, kayaks and trails. Also runs Evergreen Lodge. **$$$**

Casa Marbella
Tortuguero
Tel: 709 8011
Fax: 709 8094
http://casamarbella.tripod.com
Comfortable rooms in B&B on canal, kitchenette, porch, Canadian owner provides excellent tours. Best option for independent travelers. **$**

South

Almonds and Corals
Manzanillo
Tel: 271 3000
Tel: 888-373 9044 (US)
Fax: 759 9056
www.almondsandcorals.com

Furnished luxury tents on raised platforms in the heart of a dense jungle; magically tropical atmosphere. Rates include breakfast and dinner. **$$$$**

Samasati
Puerto Viejo
Tel: 756 8015 (Costa Rica),
Tel: 800-563 9643 (US)
Tel/fax: 224 5032
www.samasati.com
Luxury holistic retreat on 100-hectare (250-acre) private reserve. Natural spa treatments, yoga and meditation, tours include a visit to a native shaman. Transport to beaches (four miles away) available for nominal cost. Rates include vegetarian meals. **$$–$$$**

Bungalows Cariblue
Cocles
Tel: 750 0035
Tel/fax: 750 0057
www.cariblue.com
Hardwood bungalows, thatched-roof rooms and an

equipped house are comfortable, cool options for the Caribbean heat. Close to beach, upscale-funky vibe. **$$$**

Shawandha
Puerto Viejo
Tel: 750 0018
Fax: 750 0037
www.shawandhalodge.com
Thatched-room wooden bungalows with style (one of the French owners is a decorator). The chef creates Gallic and local fusion cuisine in recommended restaurant. **$$$**

El Pizote Lodge
Puerto Viejo
Tel: 750 0088
Fax: 750 0226
www.pizotelodge.com
Wooden bungalows and rooms with pleasant grounds across the road from a black-sand beach. Trails. Equipped cabins offer best family deals;

volleyball, ping-pong and pool activities keep kids occupied. **$$–$$$**

Magellan Inn
Cahuita
Tel/fax: 755 0035
www.magellaninn.com
Considered the top-category alternative in the area. Simple but elegant rooms, two with air conditioning have a covered outdoor sitting area. Sunken reef pool, restaurant serves up spicy French Creole dishes (dinner only). **$$–$$$**

B & B El Encanto
Cahuita
Tel: 755 0113
Fax: 755 0432
www.elencantobedandbreakfast.com
Affordable bungalows, one equipped apartment and a house (sleeps six); beautiful Zen garden, open-air yoga platform and a Japanese *zendo*-style meditation room facilitate tropical tranquility. Breakfast included. **$$**

Escape Caribeño
Puerto Viejo area

Tel/fax: 750 0103
www.escapecaribeno.com
Cabinas near Salsa Brava. Porches, private bath, table fans. **$$–$$$**

Hotel Park
Av. 3, Ca. 2–3
Limón
Tel: 798 0555
Fax: 758 4364
E-mail: parkhotellimon@ice.co.cr
Best option in town; ocean views, air conditioning and safe parking. **$**

La Costa de Papito
Playa Cocles
Tel: 750 0704
Fax: 750 0080
www.lacostadepapito.com
Private, airy bungalows, one with wheelchair access and open-air bathroom, jungle gardens, kid-friendly, just across from the beach. Pure Jungle Spa provides reasonably priced, all-natural pampering. Breakfast not included. **$$**

Cabinas Casa Verde
Puerto Viejo
Tel: 750 0015
Fax: 750 0047
www.cabinascasaverde.com

Bright mosaics highlight the laid-back structure created by the artistic owners. Cabins have private baths, rooms don't. Enjoy the frog garden, beautiful pool with waterfall and therapeutic hut for massage, Reiki and other alternative therapies. Discounts when you pay cash. **$–$$**

Alby Lodge
Cahuita
Tel/fax: 755 0031
www.albylodge.com
The owners strove to use natural materials whenever possible to build these four rustic thatched-roof cabins. Rooms have fans, mosquito nets, veranda hammocks and hot water showers. Communal kitchen/dining room available. Surrounded by lush vegetation. No credit cards. **$**

Cabinas Arrecife
Cahuita
Tel/fax: 755 0081
Diagonal to Restaurant Edith, with clean rooms and shared verandah with hammocks. **$**

Cabinas Iguana
Cahuita
Tel: 755 0005
Fax: 755 0054
www.cabinas-iguana.com
Pleasant *cabinas* and two equipped houses; three rooms with shared bath. Organic fruit garden, pool with waterfall and bookshop. Good value.

Casas Wal-Aba
Punta Uva
Tel: 750 0147
Friendly budget lodging. Two cabins, one for a couple and one sleeping four, and two houses, which sleep six and 12. Communal kitchen. Same low per-person price for all options. **$**

Chimuri Beach Cottage
Playa Negra
Tel/fax: 750 0119
www.greencoast.com/chimuribeach.htm
Three pretty Caribbean cottages on black-sand beach, equipped and with hammocks on the porch. Two-night minimum stay. Good option for those looking for privacy. **$$**

SOUTHERN ZONE

Cerro de la Muerte

Savegre Hotel de Montaña
San Gerardo de Dota
Tel: 740 1028
Fax: 740 1027
www.savegre.co.cr
Remodeled rooms in the cool mountains near Cerro de la Muerte. Spot quetzals and enjoy fresh trout. Set in 600 hectares (1,482 acres); restaurant. Meals included. **$$$$**

Dantica Lodge and Gallery
4 km (2 miles) off Interamerican Highway on road to San Gerardo de Dota.
Tel: 740 1067
www.dantica.com
Ultra-stylish, ultra-comfortable private cabins with Jacuzzi baths, electric heaters, kitchenettes, satellite TV and picture-window views of majestic mountain valley. Perfect for bird-watching, romance and browsing in tasteful Latin American artisan gallery. **$$$**

Albergue Mirador de Quetzales
Tel: 381 8456
Fax: 710 1095
High-altitude, rustic A-frame cabins with hot water; great hiking trails and birdwatching for Resplendent Quetzal; meals included. **$$–$$$**

La Georgina
Cerro de la Muerte (Km 95)
Tel: 770 8043
Tel/fax: 279 9511
Four cabins, five basic rooms in hotel. All come with electric blankets, one large cabin with fireplace, and kitchen. Excellent Tico food, hummingbirds, trout pond, orchids. **$**

Corcovado (Drake Bay)

Casa Corcovado Jungle Lodge
Corcovado
Tel: 256 3181
Fax: 256 7409
www.casacorcovado.com

Sumptuous luxury bordering the country's most remote and vibrant national park. Guests want for nothing, with first-class food and guides, spectacular views and a plethora of activities. Minimum two-night stay, but it's a better deal (and worth it) to stay three. **$$$$**

Drake Bay Wilderness Resort
Drake Bay
Tel/fax: 770 8012
Fax: 250 1145
www.drakebay.com
Slightly more rustic atmosphere than other area options. "Cabinettes" with shared baths are a bit cheaper, but you won't regret spending a little more on the bright, airy standard cabins. Beautiful views. **$$$$**

La Paloma Lodge
Drake Bay
Tel: 239 7502
Fax: 239 0954
www.lapalomalodge.com
On a hill side with sweeping

views, this eco-lodge is an area favorite. Elegant and open rooms and ranchos with hardwood floors provide jungle eco-luxury. Excellent guides. **$$$$**

Corcovado Lodge Tent Camp
Corcovado
Tel: 257 0766
Fax: 257 1665
www.costaricaexpeditions.com
Large, walk-in tents on wooden platforms, with comfy camp-style beds and sea-view deck. Beautiful location on the beach, with range of tours, horseback riding organized. Price for half-board, excellent food. **$$**

PRICE CATEGORIES

Price categories are for a double room without breakfast:

$$$$	$150 and up
$$$	$70–150
$$	$40–70
$	up to $40

Delfín Amor EcoLodge
Drake Bay
Tel: 847 3131
www.divinedolphin.com
Pretty hillside cabins with dolphin-themed décor; all meals included; yoga, dolphin-watching, sea kayaking from beach at bottom of hill. **$$$**

Hotel Jinetes de Osa
Drake Bay
Tel: 231 5806
Tel: 866-553 7073 (US)
Tel/fax: 236 5637
www.jinetesdeosa.com
Simple, comfortable rooms. Comprehensive dive center makes this a great base for scuba enthusiasts. Reasonable per-night rates as well as packages. Price ranges are full-board. **$$$-$$$$**

Poor Man's Paradise
San Josecito
Tel: 771 4582
Fax: 771 8841
www.mypoormansparadise.com
Book through Selva Mar. Equipped tents, including meals. The best deal near Drake; also more expensive cabins. Camping, restaurant, helpful owner. **$–$$$**

Corcovado (Puerto Jiménez)

Lapa Ríos
Puerto Jiménez/ Corcovado
Tel: 735 5130
Fax: 735 5179
www.laparios.com
Luxurious thatched-roof bungalows built on the hillside of a large reserve. Resident nature guides. One of two hotels with the ICT's highest environmental sustainability rating. Among the country's cream of the crop. **$$$$**

El Remanso
Matapalo
Tel: 735 5569
Fax: 735 5569
www.elremanso.com
Serenity and natural beauty abound at this all-inclusive, elegantly rustic lodge sandwiched between beach and forest. Waterfall rappelling, hiking and bird watching keep visitors busy. **$$$–$$$$**

Bosque del Cabo
Puerto Jiménez/Corcovado
Tel/fax: 735 5206

www.bosquedelcabo.com
Remote conservation-minded inn on 243-hectare (600-acre) reserve. Luxurious cabins with garden showers, three equipped houses and a solar-powered pool and excellent restaurant. Great birding. **$$$**

Iguana Lodge
4 km (3 miles) from Puerto Jiménez
Tel: 829 5865
www.iguanalodge.com
Two-story cabins with ample verandas, some with verdant outdoor showers. The candlelit dining rancho pulls out the stops for romance. Also runs Pearl de Osa, with lower-budget rooms and equipped beachfront Villa Kula Kula. **$$$**

Lookout Inn
Carate
Tel: 644 5967
www.lookout-inn.com
Choose from tent-like cabins on 3-meter (10-ft) platforms, screened-in cabins and luxurious rooms at this funky hillside hotel just up from the beach. Expect steep stairs. The kitchen serves seafood and Asian flavors on breezy terraces with gorgeous ocean views. **$$$**

Cabinas Marcelina
Puerto Jiménez

Tel: 735 5007
Fax: 735 5286
E-mail: cabmace@hotmail.com
Eight safe, basic rooms, four with air conditioning, all private baths. Buffet breakfast in garden is $4. **$**

Dominical Area

Hacienda Barú
North of Dominical
Tel: 787 0003
Fax: 787 0057
www.haciendabaru.com
Renowned eco-lodge on 330 hectares (815 acres). Excellent base for activities. Six simple, equipped, two-bedroom cabins, great for families. **$$**

Cabinas San Clemente
Dominical
Tel: 787 0026
Fax: 787 0158
E-mail: sanclemente@dominical.com
Lively surfer and backpacker hangout with three houses right on the beach. Dorms with shared bath, or private rooms. **$**

Posada del Sol
Dominical
Tel/Fax: 787 0085
e-mail: posadadelsol@racsa.co.cr
Comfortable, basic lodging. **$**

Dos Brazos

Bosque del Río Tigre Lodge

Dos Brazos del Tigre
Tel: 735 5725 (Costa Rica)
Tel: 888-875 9543 (US)
Fax: 735 5717
www.osaadventures.com
Rustic lodge set in a remote birdwatching paradise on a 12-hectare (31-acre) private reserve. Four comfortable open rooms (shared bath) and one cabin. Energetic hosts are fountains of hospitality and nature knowledge. Rates include three gourmet meals. Great value. **$$$**

Golfito

Playa Nicuesa Rainforest Lodge
Golfo Dulce
Tel: 258 8250
www.nicuesalodge.com
New, palatial tree-house lodge; secluded cabins. Accessible only by boat. Trails, tours, water-sports. **$$$$**

Las Esquinas Rainforest Lodge
Golfito area
Tel: 775 0140
Tel/fax: 741 8001
www.esquinaslodge.com
Rainforest jungle lodge with *cabinas*, pool, and large, comfortable common areas. Excursions and activities. Profits are used to finance projects in the nearby village of La Gamba. **$$**

BELOW: breathtaking ocean views from the Lapa Ríos bungalows.

Complejo Turístico Samoa del Sur
Golfito
Tel: 775 0233
Fax: 775 0573
www.samoadelsur.com
Air-conditioned rooms on the water, restaurant, craft and shell museum, yacht club. **$$**

Hotel Las Gaviotas
Golfito
Tel: 775 0062
Fax: 775 0544
www.lasgaviotasresort.com
While showing signs of wear, this is a solid choice if you find yourself in Golfito for the night. Pool, restaurant. Arranges sportfishing tours. **$**

Inland

Wilson Botanical Gardens
San Vito
Tel: 773 4004/524 0628
Fax: 524 0629
www.esintro.co.cr
Set on Las Cruces Biological Station, spacious but simple cabins with balconies and views to the botanical gardens. A favorite with birders. Student rates. **$$$**

Pavones

Tiskita Jungle Lodge
Near Pavones
Tel: 296 8125
Fax: 296 8133
www.tiskita.com
Rustic and comfortable *cabinas* with great ocean views. Over 100 varieties of tropical fruit trees attract many birds and monkeys. Trails and waterfalls. Cabins, made from mahogany and rosewood, have screened windows and hammocks in porches. Meals included. **$$$$**

Zancudo

Cabinas Sol y Mar
Playa Zancudo
Tel: 776 0014
www.zancudo.com
Tranquil *cabinas*, private bathrooms, and fans. **$**

PRICE CATEGORIES

Price categories are for a double room without breakfast:
$$$$ $150 and up
$$$ $70–150
$$ $40–70
$ up to $40

CAMPSITES AND HOSTELS

CAMPING

There are few established campsites with facilities in Costa Rica, and those that do exist are not generally very well advertised. Property owners in rural areas are often willing to permit visitors to use their land for camping.

Sometimes rural hotels, for a small fee, will permit campers to stay on their grounds. While campers face little risk of prosecution if they bunk down on the beach, conflicts between campers and resorts have thrust beach camping into the public spotlight.

The country's best camping, ie, immersed in nature, is had at the national parks (www.costarica-nationalparks.com), also you can contact the Fundación de Parques Nacionales in San José, tel: 257 2239. Prices usually range from $3 to $6 per person, plus any applicable national-park entry fee.

Antorchas
Dominical (South)
Tel: 78/ 0307
www.campingantorchas.net
Just 25 meters/yards from the beach, includes tent rental if required. Shared bathrooms (cold water) and kitchen. Also has rooms with private baths. Active surfer vibe.

Camping Arrecife
Punta Uva (Caribbean)
Tel: 759 9200
E-mail: yes@miagenciavirtual.com
Sandy sites facing the beach, near nature refuge. Shared bathrooms, communal kitchen.

Camping Don Alex
Barra de Parismina (Caribbean, close to Tortuguero)
Tel: 710 1892
Extensive beach front, shared kitchen. Take a boat from Puerto Caño Blanco dock ($2). Also rents small cabins.

HOSTELS

Cheap cabins have always been fairly easy to come by, so the hostelling culture is not as developed here as in more expensive destinations. A handful of accommodations are affiliated with Hostelling International (www.hihostels.com).

Bekuo Hostel
San José, 100 meters/yards east of Hotel Don Fadrique
Tel: 234 1091
www.hostelbekuo.com
Small rooms make for slightly cramped dorms in this large house, but otherwise this is one of the more homely hostels. Private rooms are available. Kitchen, internet, breakfast included. Provides free long-term storage. **$**

Gaudy's Backpackers
San José
Av 5, between Ca 36/38,
Tel/fax: 258 2937
www.backpacker.co.cr
Spacious rooms, with kitchen facilities and common areas in residential house close to downtown. Free tea, coffee and internet. **$**

Kabáta Hostel
San Pedro
100 Sur y 175 Este
Tel: 283 2000
www.kabatahostel.com
Art deco style house in the quieter part of town. Shared bathroom, kitchen and dining area. Includes hot breakfast. Internet access. Walking distance to malls and nightlife. Ten minute bus ride to downtown San José. **$**

Hostal Toruma
Av Central, Ca 29/31,
San José
Tel: 234 8186
Fax: 224 4085
www.hicr.org
International hostel in a mansion near downtown. Shared baths, hot water, Internet service. **$**

Hotel Costa Linda
Manuel Antonio
Tel: 777 0304
E-mail:costalinda@gmail.com
Closest backpacker lodgings to the beach; dorm, private rooms with shared baths and one apartment, private bath. Restaurant serves breakfast and dinner. **$–$$**

Mango Verde
Alajuela
Av 3, Ca 2/4
Tel: 441 6330
Fax: 443 5074
www.hostelmangoverde.com
The bright green entrance beckons to the vibrant-hearted. Most of the 11 rooms have private baths. Communal TV room, kitchen and hammocks. Good option for first or last night. **$**

Playa Tamarindo Beach Hostel
Tamarindo
Tel: 653 0944
Fax: 653 1003
www.tamarindobeachhostel.com
Dorm-style lodging, large communal kitchen, big-screen TV, surf racks, lockers.

Tranquilo Backpackers
San José
C. 7, between Avdas. 9 and 11,
Tel: 222 2493
www.tranquilobackpackers.com
Ultra-funky décor and vibe at the San José location, with rooms or cheap beds in dorms, along with live music and open mic nights. Also runs Tranquilo Backpackers in Mal País (tel: 640 0589) just steps from the beach, camping. **$**

Wide Mouth Frog
Quepos
Tel: 777 2798
www.widemouthfrog.org
With internet access and a pool. Private rooms are among the best value in town. **$**

E ATING OUT

RECOMMENDED RESTAURANTS, CAFES & BARS

Eating Out

While still catching up with the tourism boom, Costa Rica's culinary offerings have improved significantly over the past few years. Gourmet Indian, European, South American, Asian and fusion cuisine as well as (or in innovative combinations with) local fare *(see Tico Cooking, pages 108–111)*. San José and Escazú have the best offerings, but Tamarindo, on the Pacific coast, and the Puerto Viejo area, on the southern Caribbean coast, are building up a decent cluster of tasty options.

Reservations are a good idea at upscale eateries, but not necessary as a general rule. Menus are supposed to indicate whether tax and tip (total 23 percent) is included in the price, although some do not – ask if it is not clear. Unless the

service is truly excellent, an extra tip is not necessary. Some restaurants close between 3pm and 6pm; in San José many close Monday.

Vegetarians beware – *sin carne*, while it does mean "without meat", is often understood as "without beef", so you may get a dish with ham, chicken or fish. Specify *sólo vegetales* if you want to be sure.

Weekly markets are a bonanza of tropical fruits and vegetables at farm prices. They're also good places for quick traditional breakfasts, as vendors of *gallo pinto*, corn pancakes and fresh juices set up around the action. Most areas have a market on Saturday or Sunday; the one by the old bullring in Zapote, south east of downtown San José (Sundays), and the one near the Gothic church in Coronado (Sundays) are two of the best. Get there before 9am for the best picks.

Drinking Notes

There are several beers made in Costa Rica: Imperial, Pilsen, Rock Ice, Bavaria, and Heineken. All are good, but none is exceptional.

Guaro, the local sugar cane based firewater, is cheap and can strip paint.

Opening Times

From Monday to Saturday, most bar/restaurants open any time from 8.30am to 11am, and stay open until around midnight or 2am. On Sunday, some may close earlier, others do not bother to open at all. Friday and Saturday nights are busy, but earlier in the week you may find happy hours and other attractive offers.

Legalities

You must be 18 years of age to drink alcohol in Costa Rica. Some bars may require you to show identification.

RESTAURANTS LISTINGS

SAN JOSÉ AND ENVIRONS

Bakea (Mediterranean)
300 meters/yards north of Parque Morazán, Barrio Amón
Tel: 221 1051
Upscale local favorite in restored mansion. Creative, well-executed gourmet fare. Closed Sun. Mon lunch only. **$$$**
Grano de Oro (international)
Calle 30, Ave 2–4, Paseo Colón
Tel: 255 3322
Friendly service and good food served in the covered

garden of an elegant, restored mansion. **$$$**
Ile de France (French)
Hotel Le Bergerac, Ca 35, Los Yoses
Tel: 283 5812
Intimate and consistent, this is the city's best French restaurant by far. Reservations advised. Closed Sun. **$$$**
Tin Jo (Asian)
Ca 11, Av 6/8
Tel: 221 7605
Wide selection, vegetarian

menu, creative Pan-Asian cuisine, classy ambiance. Long-time local favorite. **$$$**
Café Mundo (international)
Ca 15, Av 9, Barrio Amón
Tel: 222 6190
New fusion cuisine in an attractive old house in this historic district. Closed Sun. **$$**
Il Pomodoro (Italian)
Two blocks north of San Pedro church, also in Escazú and Calle Amargura

Tel: 224 0966
Good pizzas (try the *panzanella* which is topped with cubes of mozzarella cheese and fresh tomato). **$$**

PRICE CATEGORIES

Prices are for dinner for two, including wine:
Expensive: US$50 plus
Moderate: US$25–50
Budget: US$25 or less

Lubnán (Lebanese)
Paseo Colón, Ca 22/24
Tel: 257 6071
Excellent Middle Eastern
food, and a hopping
tapestried bar in the back.
Thursday-night belly
dancing show is great, but
arrive early to order. Closed
Mon. **$$**
Olio (Mediterranean)
200 meters/yards north of
Bagelmen's, Barrio Escalante
Tel: 281 0541
Upscale bohemian
atmosphere; tapas; popular
with university crowd. **$$**
Café del Teatro Nacional
Café del Teatro Nacional
(Café/international)
Av 2, Ca 3
Tel: 221 1329, ext. 250

Cultured, central spot for
light lunches in the lavish
lobby of the National
Theater. **$**
Cafe Ruiseñor
(international)
150 meters/yards west of Mall San
Pedro, Los Yoses
Tel: 225 2562
A casual place for lunch,
dessert, or a snack.
Closed Sun. **$**
Delicias del Perú (Peruvian)
Ca. 3 between Av. 7–9,
across from Hotel Santo Tomás.
Tel: 222 9249
Tasty fare at bargain prices,
lunch only from 11am to
4pm, closed Sun. The
signature dish of
chicharrón de calamar is a
generous plate of the

juiciest fried squid you will
ever eat. **$**
La Criollito (Costa Rican)
Near INS, downtown San José.
Tel: 256 6511
Hearty local fare; breakfast
specialties. **$**
Manolo's (Café/Costa
Rican)
Av Central, 2
Tel: 221 2041
Good place to grab a cup of
coffee or sandwich;
outdoor tables are the
best. Try the famed *churro*
(fried dough) with chocolate
sauce. Open 24 hours. **$$**
Rosti Pollo
(Nicaraguan-style chicken
roasted over coffee wood)
Several locations around town.
Casual, good and fast. Take

out or eat in. **$**
Shakti (vegetarian)
Av 8, Ca 13
Tel: 222 4475
Healthy burgers, soups
and platters in a slightly
diner-like atmosphere.
$
Whapin' (Caribbean)
200 meters/yards east of El
Farolito, Barrio Escalante
Tel: 283 1480
Authentic dishes.
Occasional live music. **$**

For good, inexpensive
food, try the areas around
the university in San Pedro
and the *sodas* (diners) in
the Central Market, down-
town San José and
Heredia.

CENTRAL VALLEY

Alajuela

Xandari (international)
Tel: 443 2020
Excellent open-air
restaurant with valley view
serves a range of gourmet
fare, including vegetarian
and healthy options.
Excellent salads. **$$$**
La Fiesta del Maiz
(Costa Rican)
La Garita, Alajuela
Tel: 487 5757
More corn-based dishes
than you've ever seen in
one place. Always packed,
family restaurant. Good
stop on the way back from
the Central Pacific. **$**
Princesa Marina (seafood)
On the north side of the Catholic
church in Barrio San José de
Alajuela (and in Curridabat,
Moravia and La Sabana).
Tel: 296 7667
Fresh fish and mixed
rice served in a casual
atmosphere. Eat in or
take away. **$**

Cartago

Restaurante 1910
(Costa Rican)
Irazú, Cartago
Tel: 536 6063
Brimming with historical
memorabilia on the
namesake earthquake, a
good stop for a hearty
lunch after exploring Irazú

Volcano. **$$**
Gecko's (international)
Orosí, Cartago
Tel: 533 3640
Light café fare in bright,
funky backpacker's hangout
with games and tourism
info center. **$**
La Casona del Cafetal
(Costa Rican/international)
Cachí, Cartago
Tel: 577 1414
Popular stop on the Orosí
loop, with nice view of the
reservoir. Huge buffet with
a panoply of coffee-flavored
desserts. **$**
Sanchirí Mirador (Costa
Rican/international)
Paraíso, Cartago
Tel: 574 5454
Simple local dishes, lots of
meat options, with great
views of the Orosí valley. **$**

Escazú

Le Monastère (French)
Escazú mountains
Tel: 228 8515
www.monastere-restaurant.com
Gorgeous view of the
Central Valley. Elegant
French cuisine upstairs
(**$$$**); *boca*-sampling at the
casual downstairs La Cava
Grill (**$$**) is what we
recommend. **$$–$$$**
Mirador Valle Azul
(international)
San Antonio de Escazú
Tel: 254 6281

One of the best views of
the Central Valley. Decent,
albeit pricey, fare and good
service. Reservations
recommended. **$$–$$$**
Caffé Torrino
Tel: 288 4476
Great salads and deli-style
fare. The best chocolate
cake in town. Closed
Sunday. **$**
Sale e Pepe (Italian)
San Rafael de Escazú, El Cruce
Tel: 289 5750
Great pizza. Local favorite.
Closed Tues. **$$**
Wall Street
Tel: 289 6440
Bright deli-style restaurant
with great sandwiches,
soups, pastas and
desserts. **$$**

Heredia

Baalbek (Costa Rican/
Middle Eastern)
Los Angeles de San Rafael de
Heredia
Tel: 267 6482
Great views, good
Lebanese food, belly
dancing Friday nights. **$$**
La Casa de Doña Lela
(Costa Rican)
2 km/1 mile past Ricardo Saprissa
stadium, road to Guápiles
Tel: 240 2228
Popular roadside restaurant
with traditional fare and
atmosphere; branches in
Escazú, Alajuela, San

Antonio de Belén, Curri-
dabat and Puntarenas. **$**

Santa Ana

Bacchus (Mediterranean)
Tel: 282 5441
Excellent Italian fare in an
elegant, friendly
environment. Excellent
desserts. Reservations
recommended. Closed
Mon. **$$$**
Taj Mahal (Indian)
1 km (⅔ mile) west of Centro
Comercial Paco, old road
to Santa Ana
Tel: 228 0980
The only exclusively Indian
restaurant in the country.
Remodeled mansion with
indoor and outdoor seating.
Will spice up dishes on
request. Closed Mon. **$$$**
Rancho del Macho
(Costa Rican)
Tel: 282 9295
Good grilled meats, excellent
view. Hopping on the
weekends. Closed Mon. **$**

Turrialba

Posada de la Luna
(Costa Rican)
Cervantes, 10 km/6 miles
northeast of Paraíso
Tel: 534 8330
Good place to stop for
breakfast, light entrées, or
grab a snack at the
adjoining bakery. **$**

CENTRAL PACIFIC

Jacó Area

El Pelícano (Costa Rican/seafood)
Playa Herradura
Tel: 637 8910
Simple beachfront restaurant that stands out from comparable offerings in the area. Excellent fresh seafood. **$$**

Poseidon (seafood grill)
Hotel Poseidon
Downtown Jacó
Tel: 643 1642
Limited but first-class surf and turf offerings. Open kitchen. **$$**

Rioasis (Mexican/Italian)
Jacó
Tel: 643 3354

Popular surf hang-out. Great wood-fired pizzas. **$–$$**

Jungle Surf Café (Tex-Mex/Costa Rican)
Playa Hermosa
Tel: 643 1495
Tex-Mex, sandwiches, and burgers, lively surfer crowd. Closed Wed. **$**

Manuel Antonio

Sunspot Grill (international)
Hotel Makanda by the Sea
Tel: 777 0442
Elegant open-air restaurant in adults-only hotel. Top-notch dishes, but the real draw is the romantic atmosphere. **$$$**

The Rico Tico (Costa Rican and Tex-Mex)
Sí Como No Hotel,
Tel: 777 0777
Casual outdoor dining surrounded by jungle gardens and with ocean view. Buffet breakfast. Fresh fish and lobster. **$$$**

Barba Roja (international)
Tel: 777 0331
Popular gathering place for locals, serves up good fresh fish. **$$**

Mar Luna (Costa Rican/seafood)
Manuel Antonio
Tel: 777 5107
Hill-side restaurant with simple but reasonable seafood. **$$**

Vela Bar (vegetarian)
Vela Bar/Hotel
Tel: 777 0413
Wooden bungalow with palm roof. Seafood, vegetarian, and Costa Rican dishes. Fresh fruit juices. **$**

El Gran Escape (seafood)
Entrance to Quepos
Tel: 777 0395
Good value, good sushi, generous portions, popular hangout. Closed Tues. **$$$**

El Patio Bistro Latino (international)
Quepos
Tel: 777 4982
Inventive fusion cuisine. Owners also run popular Café Milagro next door. **$$**

NORTHWEST PACIFIC

Flamingo Area

Gecko's at the Beach (international)
Hotel Brasilito, Brasilito
Tel: 654 5463
Popular eatery that recently moved from Tamarindo. Excellent varied fare influenced by the owner's travels. Lunch and dinner menu. Closed Wed. **$$**

Marie's Restaurant (Costa Rican/seafood)
Playa Flamingo
Tel: 654 4136
An old favorite with traditional *casados*, fresh fish and some Mexican dishes. **$$**

Mar y Sol Restaurant and Bar (French/Mediterranean)
Playa Flamingo
Tel: 654 5222
Scrumptious southwest French fare with a tropical touch, served on a terrace with an unbeatable view of sky and sea. **$$–$$$**

Inland

Café Liberia (international)
Liberia
Tel: 665 1660
Small portions and slightly overpriced, but delicious quiches, bagels and salads are worth It if you want a break from pasta, rice and

beans. Closed Sun. **$**

Coope-tortillas (Costa Rican)
Santa Cruz
Tel: 680 0688
Women's cooperative, handmade tortillas, traditional Guanacaste favorites. **$**

Monteverde

El Sapo Dorado (international)
Tel: 645 5010
Longstanding, popular restaurant with great pizza, pastas, fresh fish and vegetarian dishes. **$$$**

Restaurante de Lucia (international/steakhouse)
Tel: 645 6659
Hearty, simple meals with a Chilean accent. Choose your own cut of meat or fresh fish to be cooked to order. **$$**

Sofia (new Latino)
Tel: 645 7017
Innovative fare served in stylish restaurant with two dining rooms. Ask for a table with a jungle view. Try squash and plantain soup. **$$**

El Márquez (seafood)
Tel: 645 5918
Best place to get fresh seafood in the mountains. Casual atmosphere, good value. **$**

Flor de Vida (international/vegetarian)
Monteverde
Tel: 645 6328
Delicious homefries, desserts, excellent meal selection. Good place to lounge when it rains. **$**

Nosara to Sámara

Café de Paris (international)
Guiones Beach, Nosara
Tel: 682 0007
Fresh bread baked daily. French and North American-style breakfasts. Lunch and dinner choices include pizza, paella, beef filet and fish. **$$**

Giardino Tropicale (Italian)
Playa Guiones
Tel: 682 0002
Great brick oven pizzas and seafood. Not the fastest service, but worth the wait. **$$**

Pizza & Pasta a Go Go
Hotel Giada, Sámara
Tel: 656 0132
Dozens of pizzas and pastas to choose from, and an extensive wine list to match. Best tiramisú in the country. **$$**

Papagayo to Ocotal

Ginger (Tapas/Fusion)
Playa Hermosa
Tel: 672 0041
Inventive, fun appetizers in modern hill-side restaurant. One side of the menu is Mediterranean, the other Asian. There's nothing like it anywhere else in the country. Closed Mon. **$$**

Picante (international)
Bahía Pez Vela, Ocotal
Tel: 670 0901
Open-air oceanfront restaurant serves up good seafood and burgers, as well as creative, spicy specials. **$$**

Sol y Luna (Italian)
Hotel La Puerta del Sol
Playas del Coco
Tel: 670 0195
Al-fresco dining, authentic Italian fare. Closed Tues. **$$**

Villa del Sueño (Mediterranean)
Playa Hermosa
Tel: 672 0026
Elegant French-leaning restaurant, best option in the area. Excellent gourmet meat and seafood dishes. **$$**

PRICE CATEGORIES

Prices are for dinner for two, including wine:
Expensive: US$50 plus
Moderate: US$25–50
Budget: US$25 or less

ABOVE: rich fish soup (*sopas de mariscos*).

Puntarenas

Restaurante La Yunta
(seafood)
Tel: 661 3216
Good option on ocean drive, breezy verandah; classic surf and turf. **$$**
Restaurante y Marisquería La Leda (seafood)
Mata Limón (near Caldera)
Tel: 634 4087
Fresh, flavorful *ceviches* and garlicky *chuchecas* –

black clams only found around Puntarenas. **$–$$**

Southern Nicoya Peninsula

Néctar (international)
Florblanca Resort, Santa Teresa
Tel: 640 0232
Gourmet al fresco restaurant with Classic French/Pacific Rim influences in beautiful luxury resort setting. Daily

sunset sushi bar. **$$$**
Playa de Artistas
(Mediterranean)
Montezuma
Tel: 642 0920
Arguably the country's most romantic eatery. Dramatically rustic, excellent food and service. Closed Sun. **$$$**
El Sano Banano Village Café (café/international)
Montezuma
Tel: 642 0638
Popular hangout with delicious vegetarian, fish and chicken dishes. Nightly movie screening. **$$**

Tamarindo to Junquilla

Puesta del Sol (Italian)
Junquillal
Tel: 658 8442
Four tables, intimate upscale Italian home flavor. Fresh pasta and authentic ingredients. Reservations required. **$$$**
Dragonfly Bar & Grill
(international)
Tamarindo
Tel: 653 1506
Ample portions of creative seafood and meat dishes

with splashes of Asian influences. Reservations recommended on weekends. **$$**
Etcetera (international)
Tamarindo
Tel: 653 0100
Lively al fresco restaurant serving wonderfully eclectic menu, from Vietnamese noodle dishes to Moroccan couscous to Italian soups and sandwiches. Don't pass up the garlicky, gratinéed oysters or the sublime home-made fries served with garlic mayonnaise. **$$**
Lola's (international)
Playa Avellanas
Tel: 658 8097
Great beach restaurant with lots of vegetarian options, named for owner's pet pig. Lunch only. Closed Mon, and Oct to mid-Nov. **$$**
Pachanga (Mediterranean)
Tamarindo
Tel: 368 6983
Cordon Bleu-trained chef serves up excellent fresh Mediterranean creations. Garden tables a good romantic option. Dinner only. Closed Sun and two weeks in May. **$$**

NORTHEAST

Alajuela

El Mirador (Costa Rican)
On the road to Zarcero, Alajuela
Tel: 441 9347
The meats and seafood are fine, but the real draw is the view. **$$**
La Princesa Marina
(seafood)
Barrio San José, across from the church, Alajuela
Tel: 433 7117
Vast seafood menu with over 70 fish dishes. Decor is minimal, so prices stay low. Also serve pasta and rice dishes. **$**

Arenal Lake

Gingerbread (international)
Nuevo Arenal
Tel: 694 0039
Selected local beef and pork make up delicious dishes. Fish includes tuna, jumbo shrimp, red snapper

and sea bass. Homemade desserts range from chocolate to fresh fruit concoctions. **$$**
Mystica (Italian)
Nuevo Arenal
Tel: 692 1001
Pleasant eatery with nice views of Lake Arenal. Excellent thin-crust pizzas. **$$**
Toad Hall (natural foods)
Arenal Lake
Tel: 692 8001
Gorgeous lake views, wide selection of natural juices, fresh food. Quality Costa Rican art displayed in gallery. Macadamia nut brownies popular. **$**
Willy's Caballo Negro
(German/vegetarian)
3 km (2 miles) outside Nuevo Arenal
Tel: 694 4515
Schnitzels, sausages, and good vegetarian food. Extensive art gallery. **$**

La Fortuna

La Choza de Laurel
(Costa Rican)
100m northwest of church
Tel: 479 9231
Opens early, ideal for breakfast. Chicken rotisserie a popular dish. **$$**
Don Rufino (international)
Tel: 479 9997
Relaxed atmosphere in the town's most elegant restaurant; bar area is a popular hangout. **$$**
El Vagabundo (Italian)
Tel: 479 9565
Best place around for thin-crust pizzas and pasta dishes, funky vibe. **$$**
Lava Rocks Café (Costa Rican/international)
Tel: 479 8039
A trendy upgrade from a *soda*, serving fruit smoothies and plates of rice, beans and meat. **$**

Sarapiquí

Restaurant El Río
(Costa Rican)
La Vírgen, Sarapiquí
Tel: 841 6724
Good, cheap traditional food. **$**

Varablanca

Restaurant Colbert
(French)
Varablanca
Tel: 482 2776
Fantastic food, decadent pastries. Perfect stop when visiting Volcán Poás or La Paz Waterfall Gardens. **$$**

PRICE CATEGORIES

Prices are for dinner for two, including wine:
Expensive: US$50 plus
Moderate: US$25–50
Budget: US$25 or less

THE CARIBBEAN COAST

Cahuita

Cha Cha Cha (international)
Tel: 394 4153
Interesting Mediterranean
and Thai mix. Laid-back vibe,
excellent service. Closed
Mon. **$$**
Hotel Jaguar (Costa Rican/
Italian)
Tel: 755 0238
Good mix of pizzas, pastas,
Caribbean and Costa Rican
fare. Closed Tues. **$**
Miss Edith's
(Caribbean/Costa Rican)
Cahuita
Tel: 755 0248
Local institution and local
cuisine worth the wait. **$**

Cocles

La Pecora Nera (Italian)
Playa Cocles
Tel: 750 0490
Top Italian restaurant on
the Caribbean coast; good
service, fresh pasta,
creative chef. Also runs
nearby Galta Ci Cova. **$$$**

Puerto Viejo

Amimodo (Italian)
Puerto Viejo
Tel: 750 0257
Creative Italian-by-the-sea
cuisine, including
specialties such as lobster
ravioli. **$$**

Chile Rojo
(Thai/Middle Eastern)
No phone
An unexpected range of
exotic flavors, including
hummus, samosas,
Thai-grilled tuna and
more. **$$**
Pan Pay (bakery)
Tel: 750 0081
Great quick stop to stock
up on snacks for the
beach. Sandwiches,
croissants, empanadas.
Breakfast, lunch only. **$**
Restaurant Tamara
(Caribbean)
Downtown Puerto Viejo
Tel: 750 0148
Delicious Caribbean dishes

and seafood. Small, friendly
restaurant that plays
reggae. Closed Wed. **$**
Soda Miss Sam
(Costa Rican/Caribbean)
No Phone
Popular eatery for simple
Caribbean staples. **$**

Tortuguero

Miss Junie's
(Caribbean)
Tel: 709 8102
An institution in
Tortuguero, Miss Junie
serves up inexpensive,
stick-to-your-ribs fare
in her simple open-air
restaurant. **$**

SOUTHERN ZONE

Dominical

La Parcela (international)
4 km/2½ miles south of Dominical
Tel: 787 0016
Dramatic seaside setting
on rocky point. Excellent
seafood dishes with a
variety of international
influences. **$$$**
Coconut Spice (Thai)
Tel: 829 8397
The best place in the area
for spicy South Asian fare,
with riverside views. In green
season, dinner only. **$$**
Villas Gaia (international)
35 km/22 miles south of Dominical
Tel: 786 5044/363 3928
Excellent, eclectic dining in
boutique hotel. One of the
few places to truly take
advantage of the culinary
possibilities of bananas. **$$**
ConFusione (Italian)
Hotel Domilocos, south end of
Dominical beach
Tel: 7870244
Sophisticated, earth-toned
terrace restaurant serving
up authentic Italian flavors
in wood-fired pizzas,
creative pastas, fresh
seafood and all the classic
veal dishes, using tender
local pork instead of veal. **$**

Ojochal

Restaurant Exótica
(French/international)
Tel: 786 5050

Acclaimed cuisine served
on airy patio; limited vege-
tarian options. Save room
for dessert. Closed Sun. **$$**

Pavones

Café de la Suerte
(vegetarian)
No phone
An oasis of hearty, inventive
vegetarian cuisine in Costa
Rica's outback. Delicious
homemade yogurt and
hummus. **$**

Puerto Jiménez

Restaurant Jade Luna
(international)
Tel: 735 5739
Unexpectedly sophisticated
cuisine. Chef is renowned
for ice creams, sorbets,
and inventive chalkboard
menu. Dinner only. Closed
Sun. No credit cards. **$$**

San Vito

Pizzería Liliana (Italian)
Tel: 773 3080
Lovely hillside restaurant.
Great pizza and pasta
dishes, nice terrace. **$**

Santa María de Dota

Café de los Santos
San Marcos de Tarrazú
(Ruta de los Santos)
Lovely spot to take a break

on the Saint's route.
Choose from dozens of
coffee specialties and light
pastries. Closed Sun. **$**

Stopovers on the Mountain of Death

The drive south from San
José on the Interamerican
Highway over Cerro de la
Muerte (mountain of death,
so named because of its
death-dealing chilly weather)
is one of the most
spectacular, scenic drives in
the country – when the
weather is clear. But when
the fog rolls in or you get
stuck behind a lumbering
truck – there's only one
lane in each direction over
these steep mountains –
you'll want to take a break.
There are plenty of roadside
stops along the 100 or so
kilometers of winding
mountain road. Most cater
to weary bus passengers
and hungry truckers, with
24-hour buffets and
capacious toilet facilities.
  The most famous trio of
rest stops is the homey,
friendly **Los Chespiritos**
chain. The original
restaurant is at Km 51, with
two branches at Km 61 and
78. Join the buffet line and
try some inexpensive local
fare, such as fried plátano

(sweet plantain), green
beans fried in eggy batter or
chorreadas, cheesy fried
corn tortillas.
  The most historic road
stop is **Restaurant and
Cabinas La Georgina**, at Km
95. The white wooden
building, festooned with
giant painted quetzals, has
been here since 1947,
when the highway was being
built. Along with typical Tico
buffet fare there's a bonus
here: you can eat at a long
window counter and go
nose to beak with swarms
of wild hummingbirds
coming for a sip of sugar
water at the feeders hung
outside the window.
  For a more substantial
lunch, stop in at **Mirador
Vista del Valle** (tel: 384
4685) at Km 119, famous
for its whole fried rainbow
trout (from a nearby lake)
and bird feeders that attract
exquisite birds to the
restaurant's garden. If you
plan to visit as a large
group, phone ahead to
arrange a special menu and
a group price.
  If you want to do a little
souvenir shopping, stop at
Charlie's Coffee Shop at
Km 65. Along with coffee
and home-made cake,
there's a vast emporium of
trinkets and a sea of
colorful hammocks for sale.

A CTIVITIES

FESTIVALS, THE ARTS, NIGHTLIFE, SHOPPING, SPORTS, AND HIKING

FESTIVALS

(PH = public holiday)
January 1 Culmination of week-long festivities in San José and other locations *(Fiestas del Fin del Año)*. Celebrations continue on the following day. PH
Mid-January Fiestas in Santa Cruz (Nicoya Peninsula), and rodeos, bullfights, music, and dancing in Palmares (Alajuela).
February/March Annual Orchid Show; also the best time to see orchids in bloom at Lankester Gardens, Cartago. San José National Theater Symphony season begins in March. Rodeos in San José. The Caribbean and Monteverde have impressive music festivals in March.
Mid-March National Handicraft Fair, downtown San José. Feast of San José (St Joseph), patron saint of San José. *Día del Boyero* (Day of the Ox-cart Driver) parade and blessing of the ox-carts *(carretas)*, San Antonio de Escazú.
March/April *Semana Santa*, Holy Week: banks, post offices, and government offices, as well as most shops and restaurants, are closed Thursday and Friday. *Jueves Santo*, Holy Thursday. PH; start of Holy Week ceremonies. *Viernes Santo*, Good Friday: religious processions at 1am and 4pm. PH. "Roman soldiers," biblical personages, and black-clad mourners; San Joaquín de Flores, Heredia, has one of the most impressive processions.
April 11 Juan Santamaría Day; hero of Costa Rica, died in the Battle of Rivas in action against William Walker in 1856; celebrated especially in Alajuela. PH

May 1 Labor Day: Worker's March in San José. Election of the President of Congress. PH
May/June Feast of Corpus Christi on the Thursday after Trinity Sunday.
June 29 Feast of Saints Peter and Paul.
July 25 *Anexión de Guanacaste*. The President and his cabinet commemorate the "*Partido de Nicoya*." Horseback parades and concerts. PH
August 2 *Nuestra Señora de los Angeles*, Feast of Patroness of Costa Rica, at the Basilica in Cartago. The pilgramage of thousands the days before is impressive. PH
August 15 Feast of the Assumption and Mother's Day. PH
September 15 Independence Day. Independence from Spain since 1821 is celebrated nationwide. At 6pm on the 14th, everyone sings the national anthem. PH
October 12 Columbus Day, *El Día de la Raza* (also called *El Día de las Culturas*). Week-long Carnival in Puerto Limón with floats, dance

What's On

The *Tico Times* newspaper (in English) publishes a calendar of activities and shows in its weekly edition (Fridays), as well as a daily brief with selected events on its Daily News Page (www.ticotimes.net/daily.htm). The Spanish-language daily *La Nación* publishes an extensive events calendar in its Friday Tiempo Libre section (www.nacion.com/tiempolibre, click "Agenda") in Spanish, as well as daily theater and music ads.

AM Costa Rica (www.amcostarica.com/calendar.htm) has fairly comprehensive online listings.

contests, and an elaborate parade. PH
Mid-December: Festival of Lights: gigantic Christmas parade, fireworks throughout the month.
December 25/last week of year Christmas Day. PH. *Festejos Populares,* with fireworks and activities in Zapote. Parade of horses *(tope)* on the 26th; San José Carnival on the 27th.

THE ARTS

Art & Galleries

While San José's status as Ibero-America's Cultural Capital for 2006 (bestowed by the Union of Capital Cities of Ibero-America) may have raised eyebrows, an active community in the city keeps the scene alive.

Works such as the gigantic, marble-smooth sculptures by Jorge Jiménez Deredia, whose Saint Marcellin Champagnat statue graces St Peter's Basilica at the Vatican, have garnered considerable national and international acclaim.

More than 30 galleries showcase creativity that runs the gamut from an in-depth survey of Costa Rican art from colonial through modern periods (the Museo de Arte Costarricense) and indigenous masks from the country's southern Boruca region (Galería Namú) to local and traveling experimental and multimedia installations (Jakob Karpio, TEORética).

The **Costa Rica Art Tour** (tel: 359 5571, www.costaricaarttour.com) showcases several artist-run studios; reservations are recommended for this day tour of five studios/galleries.

Music

No description of the Costa Rican music scene would be complete without a mention of Editus, the jazzy fusion trio that has won two Grammies for its work with Panamanian singer-songwriter Rubén Blades, and Manuel Obregón, an internationally renowned pianist. Vibrant music festivals in Monteverde and the Caribbean, as well as the International Music Festival *(see Festivals)*, showcase musicians in venues ranging from the rainforest itself to the National Theater.

Local *mariachis* serenade diners in some traditional restaurants and the warm sounds of the marimba (a large, wooden xylophone) can be enjoyed in city squares and at many hotels. While best known for its reggae, the jewel of the Caribbean music scene is Walter Ferguson, a calypso legend.

The National Orchestra season runs March–November. Costa Rica-based Papaya Music captures many local sounds in its wide selection of recordings *(see Shopping, page 290)*.

Dance

Costa Rica's modern dance scene is one of the best in Central America. The **National Dance Company** performs both classical and modern works, some by Central American choreographers. The **Teatro Melico Salazar** on Av 2, Ca Ctrl in San José stages productions several times a month; another regular venue for this company is the **Teatro Nacional** on the Plaza de la Cultura. Tickets can be bought at very reasonable prices.

Theater

Spanish-language offerings at the several small-scale venues lean towards bawdy humor, peppered with thoughtful dramas and political pieces. Most recently, the long-running *El Nica* (The Nicaraguan) by César Meléndez, a one-man portrait of a Nicaraguan immigrant in Costa Rica, became a runaway hit, making a splash as far away as the United States. The expatriate-driven **Little Theatre Group** is Costa Rica's oldest theatrical troupe and puts on four English-language productions a year. Ticket prices are very cheap, tel: 289 3910; www.littletheatregroup.org

San José has a lively theater scene with shows both in English and Spanish. The **National Theater** and **Melico Salazar Theater** publish their schedules online in Spanish *(see Getting Tickets above)*.

Movies

San José, Escazú, San Pedro and Curridabat have multiple cinemas, most in malls, showing films that are usually several months behind releases in North America. Tickets are $4 or less; Wednesdays at most theaters are 2 for 1. Animated features or other films for children are usually dubbed in Spanish, with subtitled screenings at the largest cinemas.

Venues are popping up around the country: you can catch a film screening in Heredia, Liberia, San Ramón, San Carlos and San Isidro de El General. Check the *Tico Times* for English descriptions of movies and theater information; *La Nación* provides a more detailed grid of times and locations, along with ads (useful if you don't recognize the Spanish titles).

Libraries & Bookstores

7th Street Books, Ca 7, Av Central 1, tel: 256 8251.
Best-known English-language bookstore in San José. Has a large selection of travel guides, Latin American studies, reference books and posters. Helpful owners.
Librería Internacional, Multiplaza, Escazú; Barrio Dent; Mall Internacional, Alajuela; Zapote and Rohrmoser, tel: 253 9553. English and Spanish books.
Libromax, several stores around the Central Valley, tel: 800 542 7662. Low-priced books, large English stock.
Mora Books, Omni Bldg, San José, tel: 255 4136.
Popular with travelers. Used English books, magazines, and comics.
Universal, Av Ctrl, Ca 1–Ctrl, tel: 222 2222.
Large selection of English books.

Latin Dance Classes

Learning a few salsa, *merengue* or energetic *cumbia* steps adds a kinetic joy to your trip, and will come in handy if you plan on hitting the town at night. Your best bet is well-established Merecumbé, which offers group and private classes at several studios around the country. Most language schools offer an optional dance component.
Centro Merecumbé, tel/fax: 224 3531; e-mail: merecumbe@racsa.co.cr. Has studios in San Pedro, Guadalupe, Rohrmoser, Heredia, Alajuela, Escazú and Cartago. The most popular classes are from 7–9pm, and it's a great way to meet people.

Getting Tickets

Major international headliners are often sponsored by the credit-card company Credomatic, and sometimes early sales are restricted to Credomatic card holders. There is no major central ticket agency in Costa Rica; points of sale, usually stores, vary according to sponsors; *La Nación* ads generally list the ticket outlets. Tickets for local theater and musical presentations can be purchased by phone at major theaters, in person at the box office, or, in the case of the National Theater, online.

Mundo Ticket, tel: 207 2025, www.mundoticket.com
Limited listings of sports, theater, music and other events for online purchase (in Spanish).
National Theater, tel: 221 5341, www.teatronacional.go.cr (in Spanish)
Melico Salazar Theater, tel: 233 5424 or 257 6005, www.teatro melicosalazar.go.cr (in Spanish)

NIGHTLIFE

Nightclubs & Dancing

San José's nightlife offers up a decent variety for the slim offerings. Karaoke, Latin dance clubs, techno, reggae, US-style classic rock and gay-friendly establishments can all be sniffed out.

The **Centro Commercial El Pueblo**, near Villa Tournón on the northeast side of town, a complex full of boutiques, galleries and a variety of restaurants and nightclubs, is a favorite, especially since some bars are open until 4am.

Calle de la Amargura (Street of Bitterness), a boisterous street of restaurants and bars near the University of Costa Rica in San Pedro, is popular with a younger crowd. Both places have been the sites of violence (not involving tourists), but are generally safe – for partiers alert enough to keep an eye on their drinks and belongings, and take cabs.

Outside of the capital options are generally limited to bar/restaurants, but Tamarindo, Manuel Antonio (Quepos), Jacó and Puerto Viejo offer up a handful of hopping nightclubs.

San José

Café Expresivo
Barrio Escalante
Tel: 224 1202

Artsy vibe; electronic music on Fri/Sat. Closed Sun.
Castro's
Av 13, Ca 22
Tel: 256 8789.
Crowded. Good place to practice Latin dance moves. While the bar is safe, the area is not so hot – take a taxi.
Club Oh!
Ca 2, Av 14-16
Tel: 248 1500
Formerly Dejá Vu, still gay-friendly but more varied crowd now. Electronic music.
El Cuartel de la Boca del Monte
Av 1, Ca 21–23
Tel: 221 0327.
Situated downtown, close to Cine Magaly, this is a popular singles bar. Good live music, packed on Mondays.

Jacó
Murphy's Monkey Bar
Tel: 643 2357
Roots, hip hop and more.

Puerto Viejo
Stanford's Restaurant & Disco
Tel: 750 0608
Latin music and reggae until 2.30am. Closed Tues.

Quepos
El Arco Iris
The only disco in town, packed weekends.

Tamarindo
Mambobar
Tel: 653 0929
Open-air nightspot. Closed Thurs.
Tamarindo Beach Cigar Lounge and Factory
Tel: 653 0862
Laid-back cigar lounge; wine bar. Closed Wed.

Escazú
Trejos Montealegre shopping center
Several bars, most popular with young, upscale crowd.

Bars

In San José try the following:
Henry's Beach Café and Grill, San Rafael de Escazú, tel: 289 6250. Good mix of locals and expatriates; sophisticated crowd, and a popular venue.
Jazz Café, next to the Banco Popular, San Pedro, tel: 253 8933. Best live music venue, varied menu.
Calle de la Amargura, near the University of Costa Rica, is lined with a variety of spots, from cheap college drinking holes to outdoor bar/restaurants. Extremely popular.

Gay Spots

La Avispa
Ca 1, Av 8–10, tel: 223 5343.
Salsa/Merengue. Three dance floors and pool tables. Women only last Wednesday of the month.
El Bochinche
Ca 11, Av 10–12, tel: 221 0500.
Pop music.

Casinos

Herradura
Cariari
Next to the Hotel Cariari on the highway to the airport
Tel: 239 0033
Gran Hotel Costa Rica
Downtown San José
Tel: 221 4000
24-hour casino.
Hotel Fiesta
Puntarenas
Tel: 663 0808
Hotel Irazú
San José
General Cañas Highway
Tel: 232 4811
24 hours.
Hotel San José Palacio
San José
Tel: 220 2034
Hotel Corobicí
Sabana Norte
Tel: 232 8122
Club Colonial
Downtown San José
Tel: 258 2807
24 hours.

SHOPPING

What to Buy

Costa Rica's selection of souvenirs has been increasing slowly but steadily over the past few years. The traditional classics – ox carts, wood products, indigenous masks and coffee – are now sold alongside options such as locally produced CDs that rival any world-music offering. It's also worth checking out conservation organizations, such as ANAI *(see Conservation page 295)*, which raise money by selling beautiful souvenirs. Bartering is low key, but even in malls you can usually get a discount off the ticket price for paying cash.

The following products can be found just about everywhere.

Ceramics

Be skeptical of much of the "indigenous" ceramics you see for

What to Avoid

Visitors **should not** purchase any of the following:
• Coral
• Tortoiseshell items
• Furs (such as ocelot or jaguar)
• Items made from tropical hardwoods (such as mahogany, laurel, and purple heart – if in doubt, ask the seller what kind of wood has been used)
• Anything made from crocodile, cayman, or lizard skins

sale. The best are made in the northern Pacific area – Guaitil and Santa Cruz – where artisans still use the pre-Columbian pottery techniques of the Chorotega tribe.

Coffee

Costa Rican coffee is excellent and relatively inexpensive. Café Britt stands out for its wide variety of top-quality coffee in flashy packages – great for gifts, and available in grocery stores and gift shops. If it is just what's inside that counts, Café Rey and Café Volio are good, inexpensive alternatives.

Woodwork

Wooden items, including bowls, plates, cutting boards, and boxes, are widely available. Most gift shops carry them. The mountain town of Sarchí is known for its woodwork. The finest quality wooden boxes and bowls are made by Barry Biesanz of Biesanz Woodworks. He welcomes visitors to his beautiful, light-filled studio in Bello Horizonte, near Escazú: www.biesanz.com. He creates small high quality pieces such as jewelry boxes, trays and bowls.

Leatherwork

Leather bags, wallets, and briefcases are a good choice. They are available in many stores throughout the Central Valley. While a bit bulkier, fold-up leather rocking chairs, sold in Sarchí, are a great deal.

Woven Bags

Look for interesting woven bags coloured with natural dyes by the indigenous Bribri; these are available at many locations.

Jewelry

Inexpensive handmade earrings and jewelry are sold at street artisans' stalls in San José.

Music

Papaya Music offers a number of releases and at 7th Street Books, Universal, Lehman's and many other stores, featuring local legends and traditional tunes. The great sounds, funky art and English liner notes for tourists make the CDs a great souvenir.

Paper
Beautiful handmade papers, made from recycled plant materials and and using natural dyes, are sold in many gift stores.

Camping Equipment
Alumicamping, Moravia, tel: 225 1532. Purchase, rental, and repair of tents and other equipment.
Centro de Aventura, North side of the former Guadalupe rotunda, tel: 257 0253, www.centrodeaventura.com. One of the best-equipped stores.

Other Items
There is the usual array of tourist souvenir goods: T-shirts, painted feathers, watercolors of country life.

Where to Shop

After weaving through shelf after shelf of decorative miniature ox carts and polished wooden placemats you may decide it's worth a trip further afield. In Sarchí, famed for the aforementioned carts *(carreta)* and wood products, there are other craft products that will catch your eye and you can watch the artisans at work.

Shops outside San José are more likely to have unique offerings from local craftspeople. But if you're looking for convenience, the following are some of the best places to find the above items in the Central Valley.

BELOW: woven and embroidered textiles for sale.

San José
There are craft stalls in the **Plaza de la Democracia**, next to the national museum, at **La Casona**, Ca Central, Av Central–1, and at the **central market**. At **Plaza Esmeralda** in Pavas, tel: 296 0312, browse through a number of stalls and watch artisans at work.
Galería Namú, Av 7, Ca 5/7, tel: 256 3412, has an excellent selection of local art and indigenous crafts.
Annemarie Boutique, in Hotel Don Carlos, Av 9, Ca 9, tel: 221 6707, sells ceramics, wood souvenirs, and jewelry.

Moravia
100 meters/yards south of the Red Cross (Cruz Roja). Souvenir shops and arts and crafts galleries line two city blocks in the center of town. Look out for hand-painted wall mirrors.

Alajuela
The Green Turtle Souvenir Outlet, (tel: 430 0211); also at Tamarindo (tel: 653 1606), www.greenturtlesouvenirs.com, has a great selection and its Alajuela location near the airport is a good last-minute stop.

SPORT

Birdwatching

Costa Rica has more than 850 species of birds, including macaws, hummingbirds, kingfishers, toucans, trogons, and the rather shy,

resplendent quetzal. The following offer birdwatching trips:
Albergue Mirador de Quetzales (Finca Eddie Serrano) Tel: 381 8456 www.exploringcostarica.com/mirador/quetzales At Km 70 on the Interamericana heading south, a favorite for spotting quetzals.
Costa Rica Birding Journeys Tel: 889-8815 (Costa Rica), 643-1983 (international) www.costaricabirdingjourneys.org Experienced guide, focusing on trips in Carara National Park. Tours for beginners as well.
Costa Rica Expeditions, tel: 257 0766.
Horizontes, tel: 222 2022.
Keköldi Wak Ka Koneke Tel: 756 8033 Indigenous group gives migratory bird tours in the southern Caribbean (best Feb to April).
Organization for Tropical Studies, tel 524 0607, www.ots.ac.cr, arranges bilingual group birding trips and runs La Selva Biological Station.
Savegre Hotel de Montaña, tel: 740 1029, www.savegre.co.cr, has excellent birding guides.

Bungee Jumping

The 80-meter (265-ft) gorge below the Río Colorado bridge will pass before your eyes (if you can keep them open) on these plunges. Both companies listed below are based approximately one hour northwest of San José, in Grecia.

Costa Rica Bungee and Rappel Adventures, tel/fax: 494 5102 www.bungeecostarica.com
Tropical Bungee, tel: 248 2212 www.bungee.co.cr

Cycling

You can rent a bicycle from bike shops around the country. Road biking tours are available, but this is more mountain-bike territory. Favorite routes include the trails around Lake Arenal in the Northern Zone, the rolling hills of Orosí or, for the hard-core, a Caribbean-to-Pacific trek. Most companies specializing in cycling tours provide excellent equipment, but you are welcome to bring your own (check with airlines on their bicycle policy). For Sunday-style riders, most towns and many hotels have bike rentals, although the equipment quality tends to be a bit more wobbly.
Bi.Costa Rica, tel/fax: 446 7585; www.bruncas.com/bicostarica.html. Knowledgeable owner; variety of tours around the country.

Coast to Coast Adventures
Tel: 280 8054
www.ctocadventures.com
Combination adventure trips (biking, trekking, rafting, kayaking). Known for two-week coast-to-coast trip. No motor vehicles.
Lava Tours
Tel: 278 2558 or 888-862 2424 (US and Canada)
www.lava-tours.com
Mountain biking and adventure sport tours.
Norman List
Tel: 692 2062
www.rockriverlodge.com

Diving

Underwater visibility is best during the dry season (Nov–April). October is usually the best month on the Caribbean. Northern Guanacaste, the west side of the Osa Peninsula and the Southern Caribbean have the best diving.
Costa Rica Adventure Divers
In Hotel Jinetes de Osa, Drake Bay
Tel: 236 5637
www.costaricadiving.com
Also offers underwater cameras.
Diving Safaris, Playa Hermosa, Guanacaste, tel: 672 1259, fax: 672 0231, www.costaricadiving.net. Costa Rica's largest and oldest operation. Diving expeditions, equipment rental, and diver certification classes.
Ocotal Beach Resort
Playa Ocotal
Tel: 670 0321
www.ocotalresort.com
Has full-service diving operation.
Reef Runner Divers
Puerto Viejo
Tel: 750 0480
www.reefrunnerdivers.com
South Caribbean coast diving.

Fishing

Fishing permits are required and are usually taken care of by fishing guides. On the Pacific, permits are paid for just before boarding the boat. On the Caribbean, they're bought at lodges; some lodges provide all-inclusive deals. Freshwater permits are more expensive than saltwater permits, generally because these areas are often found in national parks. If you encounter rangers while fishing, they will ask you to present your permit and your passport (a copy of which may suffice).

Good sources of information on fishing in Costa Rica are:
Carlos Barrantes, La Casa del Pescador, a tackle shop at Ca 2, Av 16–18, tel: 222 1470.

Deportes Keko, Calle 20, Ave 4–6, tel: 223 4142.
Costa Rica Outdoors, a fountain of fishing information (tel: 231 0306/800-308 3394, www.costaricaoutdoors.com, publishes fishing columns bimonthly in *Costa Rica Outdoors* and arranges fishing expeditions around the country.

Golf

If you're looking to tee off between eco-tours, your options outside of the Central Valley are concentrated in major hotels along the Pacific. Most are open to the public, and equipment is available for rent.
Costa Rica Golf Adventures,
tel: 239 5176 or 877-258 2688, www.golfcr.com, is a great one-stop information source for golfing in Costa Rica.
Los Delfines Golf and Country Club, tel: 683 0333, Tambor. 9-hole course.
Cariari Country Club, tel: 293 3211, Cariari, northwest of San José. 18-hole course. Open to members and guests of the Ramada Inn.
Four Seasons Resort, tel: 696 0000, Papagayo, on the Northern Pacific coast. 18-hole Arnold Palmer-designed course.
Hacienda Pinilla, tel: 680 7000, outside of Tamarindo. 18-hole course, wide fairways.
Los Reyes Country Club, tel: 438 0004, Guácima, Alajuela. 9-hole course, open to the public Mon–Fri.
Marriott Los Sueños Golf Resort, tel: 630 9000, Playa Herradura on the Central Pacific. 18-hole Ted Robinson-designed golf course.
Paradisus Playa Conchal, tel: 654 4123, Playa Conchal. 18-hole course. Guests only.
Parque Valle del Sol, tel: 282 9222, Santa Ana. 18-hole course.
Tango Mar Resort, tel: 683 0001, Nicoya Peninsula near Tambor. 9-hole course.

Hiking

Hiking is an inherent part of most visits to Costa Rica, whether it's wandering through a national park spotting sloths or getting to the next hanging bridge to admire the canopy. Chirripó (3,820 meters/12,533 ft) is Costa Rica's highest peak. While a small number of walk-ins are accepted, traffic for the two-day trip is capped at 35 people per day, so make a reservation a month ahead of time. Fit and experienced hikers can also ranger-station hop across Corcovado National Park, a three-day trip. In addition to the following

resources, most adventure tour operators can arrange hiking and trekking trips according to your ability.
Corcovado National Park
Tel: 735 5649
www.pncorcovado.org
In charge of reservations to hike Corcovado; the website has lots of information in English.
Selva Mar
Tel: 771 4582
www.chirripo.com
Tour company specializing in the Southern Zone; arranges Chirripó trips.

Horseback Riding

Horseback riding is widely available in Costa Rica, from hour-long rides on the beach to a riding break on a working cattle ranch. The following offer interesting options:
Caballeriza El Rodeo, book through Desafío Adventures, tel: 479 9464, www.desafiocostarica.com. Horse-friendly option for Monteverde-La Fortuna ride.
Centro Ecuestre Valle de YOS-OY
Tel: 282 6934
Horseback tours around Santa Ana, in the western Central Valley.
Finca Los Caballos, Montezuma, tel/fax: 642 0124. Four-hour trail rides through beautiful scenery.
La Garza, Planatar, tel: 475 5222, fax: 475 5015, www.hotellagarza.com. Large working ranch with *cabinas*.

Hot-Air Ballooning

Available through **Serendipity Adventures**, tel: 558 1000, fax: 558 1010. Balloon trips originate from Turrialba and near Ciudad Quesada.

Kite Surfing

New to Costa Rica, kite-surfing is really only found on the North Pacific.
Kitesurfing Center and School
Playa Papaturo, near Playa Copal
Tel: 826 5221
www.suntoursandfun.com/kitesurfing.htm
Instructor Nicola Bertoldi gets you up in the air with lessons and equipment. Associated Blue Dream Hotel and Spa has 10 cabins and a restaurant.

Mountaineering

Costa Rica is not known for its climbing, the most challenging spots are excessively difficult to get to. If you're looking for a little bouldering and some climbing, Cachí, near Cartago, is the place to go.
Mundo Aventura, tel: 221 6934,

www.maventura.com. Tours, gathering spot for fledgling climbing culture, climbing wall.
Tropical Bungee
Tel: 248 2212
www.bungee.co.cr
Offers climbing tours to Cachí.

Rafting & Kayaking

Plentiful rainfall and steep topography provides ideal conditions for rafting, with the Pacuare, Reventazón, Savegre and Sarapiquí among the top draws. If you are traveling as a family, check age limits – some trips are for 12 years and older only.
Costa Rica Expeditions, tel: 257 0766, www.costasricaexpeditions.com.
Costa Sol Rafting, tel: 431 1183, fax: 431 1185 , www.costasolrafting.com.
Desafío Adventures, tel: 479 9464, www.desafiocostarica.com. Focus on Northern Zone waters.
Ríos Tropicales, tel: 233 6455, www.riostropicales.com. Rafting and sea kayaking.
An ideal river for beginners is the Corobocí (Guanacaste).

Sailing

Sailing tours tend to be focused on sunset dinner cruises and are, not surprisingly then, only offered on the Pacific coast. Most are concentrated in Guanacaste – where you might catch the famed green flash as the sun dips below the horizon – but the Central Pacific also has operators.
Hotel El Velero, Playa Hermosa, tel/fax: 672 0016, www.costarica hotel.net. Beachfront house/hotel with sailboat.
Sunset Sails
Tel: 777 1304
www.sunsetsailstours.com
The name speaks for itself; in Manuel Antonio.
The Samonique III
Tel: 388 7870
www.costarica-sailing.com
Offers a variety of sailing tours out of Flamingo.
Varso Travel, tel: 395 6090, www.costarica-realestate.com. Pacific sunset cruises.

Island Cruises

Calypso Tours, tel: 256 2727; fax: 256 6767, www.calypsocruises.com
Catamaran cruises from Puntarenas to Isla Tortuga, or the private reserve of Punta Coral.
Bay Island Cruises, tel/: 258 3536; fax: 257 4344; www.bayislandcruises.com. One day tour to Isla Tortuga. Departs from San José by bus.

Swimming & Surfing

There is good swimming and surfing on both the Caribbean and Pacific coasts, although some beaches may not be suitable all year round. Dangers include rip tides (see below) and large waves, caused by heavy swells, that may hit you when leaving the water. Always ask the locals before entering the sea.
The following are good surfing beaches:
Pacific coast: Boca Barranca near Puntarenas, Tamarindo, Jacó, Hermosa, Dominical, and Pavones.
Caribbean coast: Puerto Viejo, Punta Uva, Salsa Brava, Black Beach.
For up-to-date information on surfing conditions, call **Alacrán Surf**: tel: 201 7139, 888-427 7760 (US); toll free; 1 888 427 7769, or see www.alacransurf.com.
Rip tides: several beaches throughout Costa Rica are known for their strong rip tides. Rip tides or rip currents are forceful ocean currents that travel 5–10 km (3–6 miles) an hour, faster than even very strong swimmers. If you are unfortunate enough to get caught in a strong ocean current, relax and don't fight it. Let it carry you. Its strength will eventually diminish. Once it does, swim parallel to the beach, toward the incoming waves, and let them carry you ashore. The following beaches are famous for their rip tides:
On the **Pacific** coast: Jacó, Esterillos, Junquillal, Dominical, Manuel Antonio's North Espadilla. On the **Caribbean** coast: Cahuita, Playa Bonita.

Tennis

The big tennis sporting event, the Copa del Café (junior pro) is held at the Costa Rica Country Club in Escazú in January. Many upscale resorts have a court or two for guests, but public spaces are scarce. San José and Tamarindo are your best bets.
Academia de Tennis Valle del Sol, Near Santa Ana, tel: 282 9222, www.vallesol.com. The 10 exceptionally good courts are open to the public.
Parque La Sabana, 4 courts open to the public.

Children's Activities

From active volcanoes and white-water rapids to clouds of butterflies and prankster monkeys, just about every corner of Costa Rica has something to capture young imaginations. While it's a safe country for any age, many tour operators suggest that the offerings appeal most to kids aged five and up. The San José area has any number of kid-focused activities, but two of the best are the interactive exhibits at the **Museo de Niños** (Children's Museum), housed in a former prison, and at **INBioParque** in Heredia (tel: 507 8107, www.inbioparque.com) with snakes, butterflies, bullet-ant colonies and a few funny role-playing guides.
Kids are usually impressed by **La Paz Waterfall Gardens** (tel: 255 0643, www.waterfallgardens.com) in Varablanca, about an hour north of San José, with its chain of impressive waterfalls, snake exhibit and butterfly gardens.
The rumbling, steam-belching **Arenal Volcano** is always a hit – especially when conditions are right and you can see the glowing red lava.
It's not hard to convince anyone to spend a day immersed in a world of chocolate. On the Caribbean coast, try the **Chocolate Tour** (tel: 750 0075), or in the Southern Zone, near Puerto Jiménez, **Finca Köbö** (tel: 351 8576) gives tours of its organic chocolate process.
For beach fun, **Tamarindo** on the North Pacific is a good beginner's beach for fledgling surfers, **Punta Uva** on the southern Caribbean coast and sheltered **Playa Manuel Antonio** on the central Pacific coast provide kid-friendly snorkeling and swimming.
Night insect tours with **The Bug Lady** (www.thenighttour.com) add a touch of eerie fun – the website itself is worth a visit. Older kids may want to stay up for the mystical spectacle of giant sea **turtles laying eggs** at Tamarindo, Tortuguero or Ostional.

BELOW: the capuchin monkey always steals the show.

TRANSPORT

ACCOMMODATIONS

EATING OUT

ACTIVITIES

A – Z

LANGUAGE

A – Z

A HANDY SUMMARY OF PRACTICAL INFORMATION, ARRANGED ALPHABETICALLY

A dmission Charges

Like many developing countries, you'll come across several attractions in Costa Rica that charge two prices: one for tourists, and a lower one for Costa Ricans. Many of the smaller museums are free; the rest range from less than $1 to $6 (for the Gold Museum), usually with student and child rates. Most art galleries don't charge admission; an exception is the Museum of Costa Rican Art ($5), but Sundays are free. National park admission fees vary, but are usually around $7.

Airport Taxes

Tourists must pay a $26 exit tax upon leaving Costa Rica by air. This can be paid upon arrival, or at the airport prior to leaving (in US$ or colones, not traveler's checks). Leave extra time, as line-ups at the payment wicket can be long. Guests at some luxury hotels can pay the tax along with their bill.

B udgeting for your Trip

Many visitors find Costa Rica more expensive than they expected.

However, it still can be an economic destination (see Money Saving Tips, page 5). Much of Costa Rica can be enjoyed independently, allowing you to keep costs down. However, a tour operator-organized itinerary can be worth the extra cost in efficient time savings. Even as an independent traveler costs spike with guided tours (from $30 to $80, generally) but it's worth splurging for at least one or two – particularly if you want to get the most out of a nature hike.

Shoestring travelers can get away with $50 or less per day, for just sun, sea and self-guided hikes. An extensive public bus system gets you almost anywhere in the country from San José for less than $6 a pop. Cheap cabins (usually cold or shared showers and less privacy) for under $25 per night (double occupancy) abound, especially at the beach – but they fill up fast In the high season and on weekends. If you stick to the local sodas (small eateries), full plates of rice, meat and beans that stick to your ribs are rarely more than $3. And you still have enough for a few sunset beers (about $1).

To upgrade the comfort level, expect to pay $50 to $70 a night (double occupancy) for moderate

lodging (private baths, hot water, some views, parking, extra amenities). Air-conditioned, minivan door-to-door hotel transport costs between $30 and $55 per person one way from San José. A dinner for two with a glass of wine can be easily had for $25 or less.

No matter what your budget, you'll be taking cabs somewhere along the line. Taxis charge $0.65 for the first kilometer and $0.60 for each kilometer afterwards, but outside of San José taxi drivers tend to use their own flat rates, although it is illegal.

Business Hours

Business hours are generally 9am to 5pm, often with a lunch break between noon and 1pm. State banks are usually open from 8.30am until 4.30pm.

C limate

Costa Rica has two seasons; the rainy or green season, which Costa Ricans call winter (invierno), and the dry season or summer (verano). In the Central Valley, the rainy season lasts from May to November and the dry season from December through April. Even during the rainy season,

CLIMATE CHART

- ☐ Maximum temperature
- ■ Minimum temperature
- — Rainfall

most mornings are bright and sunny.

Many people visit during the rainy season and take advantage of green-season discounts in hotels and fewer tourists.

Rain can fall at any time on the Caribbean coast; October being the driest month to vist. It is generally more humid on the Caribbean.

The average temperature in San José is 24°C (75°F). In the highlands, temperatures drop approximately 0.6°C for each 100 meters (500 ft) of elevation. The temperature on the coasts varies from the mid 20s°C (70s°F) to the 30s°C (low 90s°F).

Conservation

Costa Rica is heralded worldwide for its progressive conservationist policies. This reputation and its renowned biodiversity have made it a hotspot for ecotourism, a term that started out closely linked to conservation, but now is used to describe just about any activity or lodging in a nature setting.

Costa Rica tries very hard to do a great deal with few resources. The following are some of the more popular environmental organizations that are actively involved in saving and protecting Costa Rica's natural resources.

APREFLOFAS (Association for the Preservation of Wild Flora and Fauna) is a private, non-profit, non-governmental organization for nature conservation. Tel: 240 6087, fax: 236 3210, www.preserveplanet.org.

Asociación ANAI: Projects include a marine turtle conservation program and bird conservation. Tel: 224 3570 (828-524 8369 in Franklin, North Carolina), fax: 253 7524, www.anaicr.org.

Caribbean Conservation Corporation: this group runs the green turtle tagging project at Tortuguero Beach on the Caribbean coast. Tel: 352 373 6441 (Florida), www.cccturtle.org. Or tel: 297 5510 (Costa Rica).

CEDARENA (Environmental and Natural Resource Legal Center): this center educates the public and government officials on the use of the law to protect the environment. Contact: CEDARENA, tel: 283 7080, www.cedarena.org.

Conservation International: Tel: 202-912 1000; www.conservation.org.

Fundación de Parques Nacionales (National Parks Foundation): the leading organization devoted to protecting and expanding Costa Rica's reserves. Tel: 257 2239, www.fpncostarica.org

Fundación Neotrópica (Neotropic Foundation): this group works to foster "sustainable development" in communities near Costa Rica's wildlife preserves, parks, forest reserves, and other protected areas. Tel: 253 2130, fax: 253 4210. www.neotropica.org.

INBio (National Biodiversity Institute): this private non-profit organization runs the 5.5 hectare (14-acre) INBioparque in Santo Domingo de Heredia. Tel: 507 8107, fax: 507 8139, www.inbio.ac.cr

Kids Saving The Rainforest: based in Manuel Antonio, runs child-oriented conservation projects including an adopt-a-tree program ($20 to sponsor a planting), and Titi monkey bridges. Tel: 777 2592, fax 777 1954, www.kidssavingtherainforest.org

Rainforest Concern: an organization that buys and protects virgin forest, and also works with local people developing responsible ecotourism. Tel: 020 7229 2093 (UK); fax: 020-7221 4094; e-mail: c.fernandez@turtleprotection.org www.rainforestconcern.org

World Society for the Protection of Animals: animal welfare watchdogs. Provides local mobilization and support for international campaigns, including whale conservation and Farm Watch. For more information tel: 508-879 8350 (US), or 262 6129 (Costa Rica).
The headquarters are in London, tel: 020-7587 5000, www.wspainternational.org

Crime and Safety

Theft is a growing problem in Costa Rica. Pickpocketing, chain and watch snatching, backpack grabbing, and other kinds of theft are becoming more common, especially in downtown San José. It is, for the most part, non-violent, snatch-and-run thievery. Do not become paranoid and frightened, but do be vigilant.

- Do not take valuables with you when you walk on the streets of San José. Carry only as much cash as you will need. Leave your backpack, passport and jewelry. Keep an eye on wallets and shoulder bags. If you buy valuable items, make your return trip by taxi.
- While walking on the street, be aware of who is around you, and act confidently.
- When driving through the city by car, keep your windows rolled up high enough that no one can reach inside.
- Avoid the streets at night.
- Avoid walking in isolated areas.
- Be especially watchful in the following areas: the pedestrian walkway near the Coca Cola bus terminal; the Plaza de la Cultura; Parque Central; Av 4 and Av Central; and Ca 12 from Av 10 to Av 5.
- Thefts from rental cars are common in all parts of the country. Do not leave anything unattended in your car. Do not assume items in a locked trunk are safe: they are not. Whenever possible, park in a guarded area.
- Do not leave things unattended on the beach. This includes towels, clothing, tents, and camping gear.

Most importantly, if you are mugged, don't resist. Ask for the Fuerza Pública if you need a street police officer. For emergencies, call 911. English-speaking officers are few and far between, and it could take hours to get a translator – try to arrange your own. Report theft immediately to the Judicial Investigative Police (OIJ, pronounced oh-ee-ho-ta) if your passport is stolen or you require a police report to collect insurance on a valuable item. Otherwise, sadly, this is a time-consuming process that will likely result in no more than a file collecting dust.

Customs and Entry

Personal effects may be taken into the country and up to six rolls of film, 500g (18 oz) of tobacco, 2 kg (4 lbs) of candy, and 5 liters (170 fl oz) of wine or liquor (if over 21). Carry prescription drugs in original containers. Anyone caught with illegal drugs can face 8–20 years in jail and no bail.

Visas & Passports

US, Canadian and UK citizens
To enter Costa Rica, you need a passport valid for at least six months past the date of entry. Travelers may remain for 90 days. If you leave the country for 72 hours, when you return you will be given another 90-day visa. Immigration is cracking down on "perpetual tourists,"

however, so multiple exits and entries are not advisable.

Identification: always carry a photocopy of your passport and the page that contains your entry stamp in case of immigration authorities' spot checks. Report lost identification to the police immediately.

Travelers from other nations
Contact the nearest Costa Rican consulate or embassy, or try the website: www.rree.go.cr.

Exit Regulations

Costa Rica, like many other Latin American countries, does not permit minors (up to and including 17 years of age) born in Costa Rica or living in Costa Rica for extended periods of time to leave the country unaccompanied without the permission of Immigration. These restrictions do not apply to foreign tourists

D isabled Travelers

Much of Costa Rica's claim-to-fame is based around rugged nature, and the country's buckled and potholed roads and sidewalks (where they exist) can be difficult to navigate at the best of times.

By no means, however, should people with mobility difficulties write off the idea of a rainforest vacation. Tourism establishments have probably made the most efforts to open up the country's treasures, although definitions of "accessible" vary widely – call ahead with specific questions to avoid disappointment.

A variety of attractions, including Poás volcano, are set up to facilitate travelers in wheelchairs. Check international agencies for full-service tour arrangements; a handful of local companies organize customized excursions or arrange transport.
Accessible Journeys
Tel: 800-846 4537 or 610-521 0339 (US)
www.disabilitytravel.com

Useful Numbers

Local collect calls: **110**
Information: **113**
International information: **124**
Operator assistance
(international calls): **116**
Airport information: **437 2626**
Tourist information: **222 1090**
Rate of exchange: **243 4143**
Time: **112**
Fire, police, ambulance: **911**
National Parks: **192**

Organizes tours September to May.
International Institute for Creative Development
Tel: 771 7482
www.empowermentaccess.com
Personalized itineraries for accessible vacations.
Vaya con Silla de Ruedas
Tel: 454 2810
www.gowithwheelchairs.com
Arranges tours and transport.

E lectricity

110 volts, 60-cycle current. Two- and three-prong flat and round plugs. Most accommodations have equipment to convert power.

Embassies and Consulates

Embassies Abroad

Australia: Honorary Consulate, Sydney, tel: 006 12 9 969 0578.
Canada: 325 Dalhousie Street Suite 407, Ottawa, Ontario, K1N 7G2. Tel: 1-613-562 2855.
www.costaricaembassy.com.
South Africa: Honorary Consulate, Johannesburg, tel: 0027 11 705 3434.
UK: 14 Lancaster Gate, London W2 3LH, tel: 0044 207 706 8844.
US: 2114/S Street, NW, Washington DC 20008, tel: 202-234 2945.
www.costarica-embassy.org

Consulates

The Canadian Consulate has an agreement to assist **Australian** nationals. The UK embassy can help nationals of **Ireland** with emergency passports (not good for the US), but any other assistance must be handled by the Irish Embassy in Mexico (tel: 0052 5555 205803).
Canada
Oficentro La Sabana, Building 5
San Jose
Tel: 242 4400
Fax: 242 4410
www.sanjose.gc.ca
South Africa (Honorary Consulate): 150 meters west of the entrance to the Pacific Rail Terminal, downtown San José, tel: 222 1470.
UK
11th Floor
Edificio Centro Colón
San José
Tel: 258 2025
Fax: 233 9938
www.britishembassy.com
US
Ca 120, Av 0
Pavas
San José
Tel: 519 2000
Fax: 519 2305
www.usembassy.or.cr

Emergencies

Dial 911 anywhere in Costa Rica for emergency assistance.
Car Accidents: tel: 800-872 6748 (the Transit Police in San José) and 800-800 8000 (National Insurance Institute in San José.
Reporting a crime: tel: 295 3272 (OIJ in San José, 24 hours).
24-hour Pharmacy: Farmacia Clínica Bíblica (tel: 257 5252, downtown San José), Farmacia CIMA (tel: 208 1080, Escazú).
Stolen Visa Card: tel: 0-800-011 0030.
Stolen MasterCard: tel: 0-800 011 0184.
Embassy Assistance: *see Embassies.*

Entry Requirements

To get into Costa Rica, most citizens of Western countries, including Australia, Canada, Ireland, New Zealand, South Africa, the United Kingdom and the United States require only a passport valid for at least six months from the date of entry. Travelers are permitted to stay 90 days; this can be extended another 90 days by leaving the country for 72 hours and returning, but multiple entries and exits could attract the attention of immigration officials.

Etiquette

Ticos are infinitely hospitable – so always accept a bite to eat and a drink if invited over to a private home.

Preceding any request with *Me puede hacer el favor de...* (Could you do me the favor of...) even if you're just ordering a drink will go a long way to ensuring the best service. While you'll see Costa Ricans snapping their fingers at wait staff and calling out *muchacha* or *muchacho* (girl or boy), foreigners should stick to the more respectful *Disculpe, señor/a* (Excuse me sir/ma'am).

Greeting: people shake hands when first introduced. Women usually greet each other with a kiss on the cheek and say goodbye in the same fashion; this also applies when a friendly relationship exists, and men and women often greet in the same way. Children are very affectionate and greet their elders with a kiss. However, among adults, excessive displays of affection in public are not well received, as attested to by the occasional *No se permite escenas amorosas* (No public displays of affection) sign in some

Pets Permits

To bring in pet cats or dogs into the country, an import permit is required, and can be obtained at the airport. Bring with you updated health and vaccination certificates. For more information, contact:
Vigilancia de la Salud, Ministerio de Salud, Costa Rica. Tel: 255 1427. Fax: 221 1167.

establishments. Having said that, such displays are quite common.

Elderly Costa Ricans are commonly addressed by Don (men) or Doña (women) followed by their first name, an honorific now considered an archaism in most Spanish-speaking countries.
Nude bathing: there are no nudist beaches in Costa Rica and topless bathing is not acceptable to Costa Ricans; nor is the wearing of bathing suits on the streets.
Prostitution: the sex trade is legal in Costa Rica, but pimping is not. With no official medical records kept for prostitutes however, the health risks are high. Some beautiful "women" are in fact transvestites. Aids is a formidable reality in Costa Rica and safe sex is encouraged. Sex with a minor is illegal and punishable by imprisonment. The children's rights group Casa Alianza, led by Bruce Harris, has kept consistent pressure on the government to crack down on pedophiles, with some success.

G ay and Lesbian Travelers

Relatively free of active oppression and intolerance, Costa Rica has become a favorite spot for gay and lesbian travelers from around the region. It now even has its own Gay-Pride Parade (in June).

The atmosphere is distinctly "don't ask, don't tell", and the general public tends to be uncomfortable with same-sex displays of affection – this also applies to straight couples in many areas (see Etiquette, above).

San José and Manuel Antonio both have clusters of gay-only and gay-friendly hotels, restaurants and bars.
The Gay and Lesbian Guide to Costa Rica (www.hometown.aol.com/gaycrica/guide.html) has tourism information.
Tiquicia Travel (tel: 256 6429, www.tiquiciatravel.com), **Aventuras Yemaya** (tel: 294 5907) and **Gaytours Costa Rica** (tel: 777 1910, www.gaytourscr.com) specialize in gay and lesbian travel around Costa Rica; the latter also operates the Gaybus

from San José to Manuel Antonio.

The free bimonthly magazines *Playita Circuit* (Manuel Antonio) and *Urbano Circuit* (San José) can be picked up at gay-friendly outlets, or checked out on a link on the Gaytours site (see above).

Guides and Tours/ Travel Agents

With high levels of English spoken in an established tourism circuit and extensive, inexpensive transport, visitors to Costa Rica will find the country fairly easy to navigate as independent travelers.

Booking with a local tour company can save transport time – and hair-raising driving experiences – and most are valuable resources if a wrench is thrown into your plans. In some remote areas, such as Tortuguero and the Osa Peninsula, options are largely, but not completely, restricted to a two-to-three day package, including meals, tours and often transport, even if you book directly with a hotel.

Drive-yourself tours, such as those offered by Vesatours, balance well-planned itineraries and in-country support with independence, and rural tours are among the best ways to immerse yourself in Costa Rica and its culture while directly benefiting local communities.

Regardless of how independent you'd like to make the trip, hiring a good guide is essential to spotting wildlife. The Costa Rican Tourism Institute has been pushing a highly criticized guide-certification program for a few years, but a better yardstick is a recommendation from your hotel or established tour agency.

The **Association of Costa Rican Tourism Professionals** (ACOPROT) has a list of tourism chambers on its website (www.acoprot.org/links/camaras.htm). The

page is in Spanish, but you can generally reach an English speaker at any of the listed phone numbers.
Costa Rica Temptations
Tel: 239 9999
www.crtinfo.com
Well known for "The Big Five" highlights tour of coffee farm, Poás Volcano, Sarapiquí River, La Paz Waterfall, as well as a variety of one- and multi-day tours.
Desafio Adventure Center
Tel: 479 9464
www.desafiocostarica.com
Solid operator specializing in Northern Zone activities: rafting, caving, extreme hiking and more.
Selva Mar
Tel: 771 4582
www.exploringcostarica.com
Southern Zone experts.
Vesatours
Tel: 239 6767
www.vesatours.com
Well-organized adventure and family trips, self-drive itineraries and rural tourism.

H ealth and Medical Care

Costa Rica ranks near the United States, Canada, and other Western nations in health-care standards.
Inoculations: no inoculations are required for visiting Costa Rica.
Water: in San José and the Central Valley, water is treated. It is, with some exceptions, potable throughout the country. If you have persistent intestinal problems, take a stool sample to the Clínica Bíblica (tel: 522 1000, results in minutes) to be analyzed (about US$12).
Illness: malaria is not generally a problem in Costa Rica, except in the remote regions of Talamanca. Cholera is not usually a problem, either, due to Costa Rica's strong public health efforts. There have

Snake Bites

Although snake bites are rare, to avoid being bitten follow these suggestions:
• When walking in the countryside, wear closed, preferably high-top shoes or boots.
• Walk with a stick in hand. Use it where visibility of the ground is blocked to probe before you step.
• Try to choose paths clear of high grass and debris.
• Never reach into areas you can't see into.
• If you encounter a snake, remain calm and retreat immediately. Never chase a retreating snake. Snakes attack people only when

they perceive a threat. If, despite all these precautions, you are bitten:
• Remain calm and try to immobilize the area of the bite.
• Do not apply ice to the affected area; it can worsen the wound.
• Do not cut the wound or attempt to suck the venom out with your mouth.
• Go immediately to the nearest clinic, hospital, or Red Cross agency for an injection of antivenin. It is not necessary to know what kind of snake bit you. Doctors can tell by the wound which kind of antivenin to give.

been incidences of dengue fever, however. Dengue symptoms include the sudden onset of fever, headache, severe joint and muscle pains followed in most cases by a rash which starts on the trunk of the body and spreads to the limbs and face. The fever subsides in a few days and recovery begins, usually with no serious side effects. Dengue is spread by the *Aedes aegypti* mosquito, which bites principally at dusk. There is presently no prophylactic treatment available for dengue, but medical attention can significantly reduce the effects.

Medical Services

Costa Rica has an excellent health care system, much less expensive than in the US. Many doctors are trained in the US or Europe and speak English, especially those at private clinics.

Public Medical Centers

Hospital Dr Calderón Guardia
Tel: 257 7922.
Hospital de los Niños
Tel: 222 0122 (for children).
Hospital México
Tel: 232 6122.
Hospital San Juan de Díos
Tel: 257 6282.

Private Medical Centers

Clínica Bíblica
Central San José
Tel: 522 1000.
Clínica Católica
Guadalupe
Tel: 246 3000.
Hospital San José CIMA
Escazú
Tel: 208 1000
Fax: 208 1001.
Also has a clinic in Los Yoses (CIMA del Este).
Hospital Cristiano Jerusalem
Guadalupe
Tel: 216 9191.

Dentists

Costa Rican dentists provide competent and inexpensive cosmetic as well as general dentistry. The *Tico Times* contains ads placed by English-speaking dentists.

Insurance

It is essential to have comprehensive insurance when traveling to Costa Rica. Some bank and credit cards may include insurance, but this may not provide adequate medical cover for your trip. In Costa Rica, you need a minimum of US$2 million of cover for medical

expenses and repatriation.
Insure yourself against theft of personal items and loss of passport and money.
Certain sporting activities may necessitate paying an additional insurance premium – always read the small print to make sure that you are adequately covered for any accidents.

Internet

Internet cafés with high-speed connections abound in San José, making it easy and cheap (less than $1 per hour) to stay dialed in. With the latest in internet telephony, the quality of computer-based calls has improved dramatically and internet cafés have essentially replaced public international call centers.
Once you leave the capital, you'll be able to find public internet access in just about any town of any size, but service becomes slower and more expensive – up to $5 per hour in beach towns. If you really need to keep in touch in the most remote places, expect to pay astronomical amounts for satellite internet.
Most upscale hotels offer a computer with internet service, WiFi, or both. Eateries such as Bagelmen's outlets in San José and Denny's at the Hotel Irazú are popular wireless hotspots, but be extra careful when taking advantage of the service; reports of laptop theft near these centers have increased.

Left Luggage

Neither international airport has an area for left luggage. However, most hotels and some tour companies will allow you to store extra gear and luggage for a few days for free or for a low price.

Maps

The ICT tourist info center under the Gold Museum in downtown San José and in the airport hand out decent free road maps, but is often out of copies. A better bet is 7th Street books or Lehman's *(see Bookstores)*.
If you're renting a car, it is useful to buy a road map; otherwise, the maps in this guide book and/or the free ICT map should be quite adequate.
For comprehensiveness, you can't beat *Insight Map Costa Rica*. The *Rough Guide Map to Costa Rica and Panama* is waterproof – a worthwhile investment. Check your local travel store or the web; the regional

Amazon.com sites have a wide selection. Travelers from New Zealand can try Fishpond (www.fishpond.co.nz), Australians Less10 (www.less10.com). Check Maptak for detailed topographic and political maps of Costa Rica's provinces, national parks and more. For simple maps, directions and driving distances, www.costaricamap-online.com is a good pre-trip reference.

Media

Radio

Radio stations in English include 107.5 FM, which plays classic rock and has news and other information in English, and Radio Dos (99.5 FM), a Spanish-language station that plays pop and rock classics, has a morning show in English and news in English, every other hour.

Television

There are more than 70 cable TV channels listed in the local TV guide; more are available. Programming includes approximately 30 channels in English, one in German, one in French, and one in Chinese. There are also programs in Hindi, Japanese, and Tagalog, as well as selections from many Latin American countries.

Newspapers & Magazines

Available in English, Spanish, and other languages, at bookstores, supermarkets, newsstands, and hotel outlets.
Weekly English-language publications include:
The Tico Times (tel: 258 1558 www.ticotimes.net), published weekly every Friday. Widely available at most newsstands in metro San José, Cartago, Heredia and Alajuela. For the week's news in Costa Rica, up-to-date listings of what's happening, and where. Also provides online news.
An annual *Exploring Costa Rica* guidebook gives an overview of the country.
Costa Rica Outdoors (tel: 231 0306, www.costaricaoutdoors.com). Bimonthly magazine featuring fishing, birding and Tico Culture.
Beach Times (tel: 654 4436), weekly community newspaper distributed along the Northern Pacific Coast.
Daily Spanish-language newspapers include: *La Nación*, *La Prensa Libre*, *La República*, and *Al Día*.

Money Matters

The currency unit is the colón. The current rate of exchange can be found in the English-language *Tico Times*

TRANSPORT

ACCOMMODATIONS

ACTIVITIES

EATING OUT

A–Z

LANGUAGE

business pages; the daily *La Nación* publishes a daily list of the rates offered at each bank. Or call a private bank for the current rate.

State Banks: the main ones are Banco Nacional (tel: 222 2000) and Banco de Costa Rica (tel: 287 9000), with offices throughout the country. If you need an early bank stop, the latter has a branch near the Clínica Bíblica in downtown San José that opens at 7.30am, or on the east side of town in Curridabat at 7am.

Private banks: the main ones are Banco Banex (tel: 287 1000) and BAC San José (tel: 295 9595). Other private banks include Bancrecen, Interfin, Scotiabank, and Citibank. Many of these are open until 7pm. BAC San José's Rápido Bancos in most Central Valley malls are even open Sundays for basic transactions, including exchange.

Traveler's checks: while the tourism industry has become more familiar with traveler's checks, high fraud rates have led some businesses to axe this payment mode. For safety, it's a good idea to bring some money in this form, which can always be changed in banks, but check with stores or hotels before trying to pay this way.

Cash: you may not be able to break 5,000 colón notes when paying for taxis and such. US dollars in small denominations are often accepted in taxis and shops, particularly in towns and cities. Counterfeiting has made many businesses highly suspicious of US$100 bills – better to bring smaller denominations.

Credit cards: American Express, Visa, and MasterCard are widely accepted in the Central Valley area. Their telephone calls are handled by local credit card firm **Credomatic**, tel: 295 9000.

Access numbers for international credit card calls are:
AT&T: 0-8000-114114
MCI: 0-8000-122222
Sprint: 0-8000-130123
Canada Direct: 0-8000-151161
British Telecom: 0-800-0441044
Bank Machines: ATMs have increased dramatically in the past few years, although it is still best to get your cash in the regional urban centers. Machines marked ATH are the best bets for foreign cards. The ATH company posts machine locations on www.ath.fi.cr; it's in Spanish, but if you click on Cajeros Automáticos, then Búsqueda de Cajeros you can easily find out if and where your destination has a machine. Those marked local dispense only colones, those marked

ambas also give dollars. Some banks accept either Visa or MasterCard but not both; check www.mastercard.com/atmlocator/index.jsp or www.visalatam.com/e_index.jsp to see where you can get cash advances in machines. Look for machines during the day, especially ones with nearby guards.

Changing money: exchange rates vary slightly between banks, and day-to-day rates go up and down. The fluctuation is generally no more than a cent per dollar, and most banks are within a cent of each other in rates. Private banks (particularly BAC San José) are the best place to exchange money if you want to avoid long line-ups. Your hotel may also change money for you. Most banks now handle euros as well as dollars.

Money can be exchanged at the airport (BAC San José) from 5am to 10pm – if you have colones, it's best to change them to euros or dollars before you get on the plane. Avoid the Casa de Cambio Global Exchange; as of this writing, its rates were consistently 10 percent less than the average. The Central Bank posts a page with the daily rates of the country's institutions at www.bccr.fi.cr/flat/bccr_flat.htm; these rates are also listed in the business pages of *La Nación* newspaper.

Taxes and Tipping: restaurants and hotels add 13 percent tax to the bill. Hotels also charge a 3 percent tourism tax on room charges and restaurants add a 10 percent service charge.

Hotel bellboys should be tipped. In restaurants tipping is not expected.

P hotography

Bring a range of film; 400 ASA generally works in the jungle, and 100 is better for the bright beach shots. Film is more expensive here; best bring a good supply – the six-roll limit customs imposes is rarely enforced. Pack it in your carry-on bag to protect it from the much stronger X-rays used on checked baggage. Wait until you get home to develop film; quality is hit and miss in San José.

Whether you've gone digital or are still using film, you won't regret packing along a telephoto lens to capture wildlife sightings.

Water damage and theft are two very real threats to your photo equipment. Consider a dry bag, or at the least a waterproof case or plastic bag, and, depending on the value of your camera, you may want to make sure it is insured.

It is possible to upload and burn

photos from your camera onto a CD or hard-drive key in most internet cafés; some even have a universal cable lying around if you forget yours.

Postal Services

Airmail between the US or Europe and Costa Rica should take about five days, but a wait of two or more weeks is not uncommon. The Central post office is located at Calle 2, Av 1–3, tel: 223 9766. Mail can be received there in the general delivery section *(Lista de Correos)*. Outgoing mail should be posted at either a hotel desk or a post office. It is usually difficult, time-consuming, and expensive to receive packages in the mail. Outrageous duties are sometimes applied and you can spend days trying to deal with numerous officials. A receipt showing a low value may help if included with the package. There are agents *(agencias de aduana)* listed in the phone book who will handle the hassles of customs clearances for a fee.

Couriers: there are many international courier services. The most popular are FedEx and DHL. Consult the *Yellow Pages* for numbers.

Public Holidays

Costa Rica moves certain public holidays to the following Monday if it falls on a weekend. When some holidays, such as Columbus Day, fall within the week, government offices and some businesses will push the holiday to the following Monday, while other businesses will close the day itself.

For a list of Public Holidays, see festivals marked with PH (there are 11) on page 288.

Public Toilets

Two of the most important pieces of tourist information relate to bathrooms. One: always carry a small supply of toilet paper. Regardless of the establishment, facilities are notoriously tissue-free. The second, which will often be emphasized on stall-door signs, is that all toilet paper goes in the garbage next to the toilet, NOT the toilet bowl, even in many upscale places.

There are very few public toilets in towns, but in the capital it's easy to slip into a fast-food restaurant, and outside of the Central Valley many restaurants and road stops allow you to use the facilities, sometimes for a 100-colón fee.

R eligious Services

Costa Rica's official religion is visibly Catholic, but a rich variety of faiths enjoy full freedom of religion. Visitors are welcome to sit in on Spanish-speaking services in the cathedrals, of course showing common-sense courtesy and dressing appropriately.

The Central Valley has active Anglican, Baha'i, Jewish, Baptist, Jehovah's Witness, and Quaker communities, among others, and approximately 25 houses of worship offer services in English. Check the *The Tico Times* weekly newspaper's calendar section for an extensive list.

S tudent Travelers

An international student ID card will get discounts on some attractions, airfares to Costa Rica and most museums, but it's the proliferation of cheap *cabinas*, dirt-cheap transport and affordable plates of rice and beans that make Costa Rica a student-friendly destination. It never hurts to ask if a student discount is available.

Many conservation organizations charge low rates to take on student volunteers for a true immersion experience *(see Conservation)*. The Association of Volunteers Working in Protected Areas (ASVO, 258 4430, www.asvocr.org) is a good bet for short-term volunteering stints maintaining trails, monitoring marine turtle conservation or teaching English, requiring only basic Spanish.

Youth-oriented hostels are springing up around the country – *see hostels in Accommodation section for details.*

T elecommunications

Costa Rica has one of the best telecommunications systems in Central America. Fax machines are popular, with public access from most post offices around the country.

For written telecommunications contact:
Radiográfica Costarricense, S.A. (RACSA), Ave 5, Calle 1, tel: 287 0087, www.racsa.co.cr. Services include telegraph, and e-mail.

Making Telephone Calls

Most telephones work with telephone cards, which can be bought at many small shops, pharmacies or supermarkets.

Ten or 20 colón coins, and the public phones that use them, are being phased out but can still be found. Place the coin(s) in the slot on top of the phone, then dial the number; the coin will drop down when

New Telephone Numbers

Can't get through? In March, 2008, all telephone numbers in Costa Rica will become 8-digit: land lines will begin with an extra 2, and all cell lines will begin with an extra 8. For example, a number currently listed here as 299-8000 will become 2299-8000. Check first, however, before trying the new system - target dates are often postponed.

the connection has been made. Extra coins placed in the slot will fall automatically, only as needed.

International Calls

Dial 124 for the codes for various countries. International phone cards are available at various locations. If you do not have access to a telephone, international calls can be made from any internet café.

Time Zone

Costa Rica is on North America's Central Standard Time which means it is six hours behind GMT. It does not observe Daylight Savings, so this time difference increases one hour during the northern summer months. Costa Rica is close to the Equator, the number of daylight hours does not vary from season to season as greatly in the more northern or southern regions of the hemisphere.

Tourist Offices

With its airport office sporadically closed due to personnel shortages and the central headquarters inconvenient for anyone except Best Western Irazú guests, the **Costa Rican Tourism Institute's (ICT)** only useful office – and it is useful – is at the Gold Museum.

The flip side is that any number of private tour agencies around the country provide just about everything you need to know. The following are particularly good:
Café Net El Sol, tel: 735 5719, www.soldeosa.com. Southern Zone information, bulletin board, gathering place in Puerto Jiménez.
ICT, open 8am–4pm, staffed by bilingual operators, tel: 1-800 343 6332 (from the US) or 506-299 5800 (outside USA), fax: 223 5452, www.visitcostarica.com. Don't miss the ICT office in the Gold Musem on the pedestrian walkway (tel: 222 1090) open Mon–Fri 9am–1pm and 2–5pm; good information and maps.
National Parks Information, tel: 257

2239 or 192, fax: 222 4732, www.fpncostarica.org. Fundación de Parques Nacionales; extensive information on all national parks.
Talamanca Ecotourism & Conservation Association (ATEC), tel: 750 0398, www.greencoast.com/atec.htm. A good option for community and tourism information around Puerto Viejo.
Tamarindo Tourist Info Center, tel: 653 0981, www.crparadise.com. A friendly resource with tourism and transport info.

Tour Operators

Eco-tourism is still the buzz word in Costa Rica and hotels can provide or recommend excellent guides. A fledgling organized rural tourism network is the latest way of guaranteeing a vacation that minimizes impact on the environment and maximizes benefits to those working in tourism. The new bilingual (English/Spanish) Rural Community Tourism Guide put out by COOPRENA, a national ecotourism network, lists several of these rural tourism projects. Tel: 290 8667, www.turismoruralcr.com
The following are some options:
Active and Progressive Women's Association of Costa de Pájaros
Gulf of Nicoya
Tel/fax: 678 8054
Women's group that has developed tourism alternatives to the fishing economy. Butterfly garden, tours of mangroves and the Gulf of Nicoya, medicinal gardens, traditional fishing tours.
Finca Educativa Lodge
Shiroles, Talamanca
Tel: 711 1598, tel/fax: 711 1600
Lodge and meals in an indigenous Dri Bri Carlbbean-slope community. Natural healing talks, traditional dances and plays, guided hikes through reserve.
Keköldi Wa Ka Koneke
Puerto Viejo de Talamanca
Tel: 756 8033, fax: 756 8133
www.corredortalamanca.org
Association focusing on natural resource conservation and development of Keköldi Indigenous Territory. Bilingual guides offer tours to observation platform, noted as the third best place in the world to observe migrant predatory birds.
Rural El Encanto de Piedra Blanca
Tel: 228 0183, www.codece.org. A good day-tour option from San José. Traditional sugar mill, dances, food in the hills of San Antonio Escazú.
Rural Tourism Association (ACTUAR), Tel: 248 9470, www.actuarcostarica.com. Well-established community tourism

with extensive network of rural lodges.
Simbiosis Tours, tel: 290-8646,
www.turismorural.cr
The tourism branch of COOPRENA,
an environmental organization.
Works with co-operative lodges.

Websites

AM Costa Rica: daily online tabloid
www.amcostarica.com
Chamber of Tourism (CANATUR):
www.canatur.org
**Costa Rican Foreign Relations
Ministry**: information on Costa Rican
consulates and embassies; official
translators. In Spanish
www.rree.go.cr
Costa Rica General Guide: blogs,
Costa Rican recipes, culture, real
estate information
www.costarica.com or www.costarica.net
Costa Rican Tourist Board (ICT):
comprehensive tourism information
and news
www.visitcostarica.com
Info Costa Rica: online forums,
articles on a wide variety of topics,
links
www.infocostarica.com
Inside Costa Rica: daily summary of
news in English
www.insidecostarica.com.
La Nación Newspaper: summarizes
news of the week in English on
Fridays
www.nacion.co.cr
Residents' Association of Costa Rica:
helpful tourism and community
information
www.arcr.net
Sustainable Tourism Certification:
overview of program and detailed list
of certified establishments
www.turismo-sostenible.co.cr
The Tico Times: weekly and daily
news and general information
www.ticotimes.net
US Embassy: comprehensive
information and links
www.arcr.net

Weights and Measures

Costa Rica uses the metric system.
When asking for directions,
remember that 100 meters usually
means one block, regardless of how
long the block is. While most real-
estate information will speak of
square meters and hectares, the
manzana (7,000 sq meters, or about
1.75 acres) is still widely used as a
unit of measurement.

What to Bring

Clothing and footwear: plan to dress
in layers. Sweaters and jackets are
needed for activities in the

mountains and cool evenings,
particularly in the Central Valley in
December. Shorts are worn for
athletic activities or at the beaches,
not normally in the cities. Bring
weatherproof gear and boots if you
plan to do much hiking. Have a
comfortable pair of walking shoes
that are already broken in. Sidewalks
are non-existent in many areas, and
uneven at best.
  Costa Rican women are always
well groomed, even the poor majority
who can be seen emerging perfectly
made-up from one-room shacks.
Bring dressy clothes for upmarket
San José restaurants and nightlife.
  Personal items: a folding umbrella
will often be welcome. Bring what
medications and specialty film you
need. It is a good idea to bring insect
repellent, sunscreen, and
contraceptives with you: they are
often expensive and difficult to find
outside San José. A very limited
selection of tampons is sold, and
many places just don't carry them.
Automercado stores usually have

some, but best to bring your own
supply from home.
  Repellent, natural brands
included, is easily available in San
José.

Women Travelers

In 2006, Costa Rica was ranked third
in a *USA Today* article on the top five
safest destinations for women, but
best to take precautions.
  Rarely will women face persistent
or physical harassment, but expect
plenty of vocal male appreciation.
Travelers of both sexes are advised
to walk in pairs or groups, and
take cabs at night. Always sit in
the back seat.
  Women-only surf camps, such as
Del Mar Surf Camp (tel: 385 8535,
www.costaricasurfingchicas.com) in Playa
Hermosa (on the Central Pacific) or
private surf lessons geared towards
women, offered by Sirena Surf (tel:
879 3799, www.sirenasurf.com) in
Dominical are great places to build
up confidence.

Specialist Tour Operators

Diving Safaris
Playa Hermosa
Tel: 672 1259
Fax: 672 0231
www.costaricadiving.net.
Long-established dive and
adventure operator. Comprehensive
website.
Costa Rica Expeditions
Tel: 257 0766
Fax: 257 1665
www.costaricaexpeditions.com.
The original whitewater rafting
company. Offers nature tours to
Tortuguero, Corcovado, and
Monteverde, with knowledgeable,
bilingual guides.
Coast to Coast Adventures
Tel: 280 8054
Fax: 225 6055
www.coasttocoastadventures.com.
Adventure tourism and races;
cycling tours.
Costa Rica Sun Tours
Tel: 296 7757
Fax: 296 4307
www.crsuntours.com.
Off-the-beaten-track tours with a
naturalist focus. Volcanoes,
national parks, cloud forests,
rainforests, beaches. Turtle-
watching tours. Whitewater rafting,
hiking, biking, and horseback riding
tours.
Costa Rican Trails
Tel: 225-6000
Fax: 225-4049
From US: 888 803 3344

From Canada: 866-865 7013
www.costaricantrails.com
Friendly company that offers a
variety of nature, family, and
adventure tours including
motor-cycling.
Discovery Costa Rica
Tel: 228-9261
Fax: 289 7124
www.discoverycostarica.com.
Design your own package from a
large range of tours.
Horizontes
Tel: 222 2022
Fax: 255 4513
www.horizontes.com.
Customized nature tours
of all types throughout Costa
Rica, including tours for
families. Day trips in the Central
Valley.
Ríos Tropicales
Tel: 233 6455
Fax: 255 4354
www.riostropicales.com
Leading tour company for rafting
and kayaking.
Serendipity Adventures
Tel: 558 1000
Fax: 558 1010.
From US: 877 507 1358
www.serendipityadventures.com.
Specialists in hot-air ballooning.
Swiss Travel
Tel: 282 4898
Fax: 282 4890
www.swisstravelcr.com.
Upscale ecotourism and adventure.

L ANGUAGE

UNDERSTANDING THE LANGUAGE

Survival Spanish

Spanish is Costa Rica's principal language so learn some phrases before you arrive, if only the simple courtesies: "Good morning," "How are you?" "I'm well, thanks." These seemingly inconsequential phrases are an important part of daily life in Costa Rica. English is spoken by many people in San José and in the larger hotels, and one can always get by without Spanish; but if your idea of a good trip includes some contact with local people, then speaking a bit of Spanish is the ticket.

If you are going on an extended trip, consider spending the first week enrolled in one of the many language schools. Tailored programs and schedules of all kinds, many with excursions and cultural programs, are available.

A pocket-sized English-Spanish dictionary is a good idea, and small electronic dictionaries are also available.

Numbers

1 *uno*
2 *dos*
3 *tres*
4 *cuatro*
5 *cinco*
6 *seis*
7 *siete*
8 *ocho*
9 *nueve*
10 *diez*
11 *once*
12 *doce*
13 *trece*
14 *catorce*
15 *quince*
16 *dieciseis*
17 *diecisiete*
18 *dieciocho*
19 *diecinueve*
20 *veinte*
21 *veinte y uno*
30 *treinta*
40 *cuarenta*
50 *cincuenta*
60 *sesenta*
70 *setenta*
80 *ochenta*
90 *noventa*
100 *cien*
101 *ciento uno*
200 *doscientos*
300 *trescientos*
400 *cuatrocientos*
500 *quinientos*
600 *seiscientos*
700 *setecientos*
800 *ochocientos*
900 *novecientos*
1,000 *mil*
2,000 *dos mil*
10,000 *diez mil*
100,000 *cien mil*
1,000,000 *un millón*

Common Expressions

Good morning *Buenos días*
Good afternoon *Buenas tardes*
Good evening *Buenas noches*
Goodbye *Hasta luego/Adios*
How are you? *¿Cómo está Usted?*
I'm well, thanks *Muy bien, gracias*
And you? *¿Y Usted?*
Please *Por favor*
Thank you *Gracias*
No, thank you *No, gracias*
You're welcome *Con mucho gusto*
How kind of you *Usted es muy amable*
I am sorry *Lo siento*
Excuse me *Disculpe* (when apologizing). *Con permiso* (when leaving the table or passing in front of someone)
Yes *Sí*
No *No*

Do you speak English? *¿Habla Usted inglés?*
Do you understand me? *¿Me entiende?*
Does anyone here speak English? *¿Hay alguien aquí que hable inglés?*
Just a moment, please *Un momentito, por favor*
This is good *Está bueno*
This is bad *Está malo*

Shopping and Eating

What is the price? *¿Cuánto cuesta?* or *¿Cuánto es?*
It's too expensive *Es muy caro*
Can you give me a discount? *¿Puede darme un descuento?*
Do you have ...? *¿Tiene Usted ...?*
I will buy this *Voy a comprar esto*
Please show me another *Muéstreme otro, por favor*
Please bring me ... *Tráigame por favor ...*
coffee with milk *café con leche*
black coffee *café negro*
tea *té*
a beer *una cerveza*
cold water *agua fría*
a soft drink *una gaseosa*
the menu *el menú*
the daily special *el plato del día*
May I have another beer? *Puede darme una cerveza más, por favor*
May I have the bill? *La cuenta, por favor*
[To get the attention of the waiter/waitress] *Disculpe Señor/Señora/Señorita*
Where is the dining room? *¿Dónde está el comedor?*
the pharmacy *la farmacia*
the gas station *la bomba* (the pump)
key *la llave*
manager *el gerente* (male)/*la gerente* (female)
owner, proprietor *el dueño* (male)/*la dueña* (female)

Can you cash a travelers' check? *Se puede cambiar un cheque de viajero?*
money *dinero or plata*
credit card *tarjeta de crédito*
tax *impuesto*
letter *carta*
postcard *tarjeta postal*
envelope *sobre*
stamp *estampilla/sello*

Getting Around

Please call a taxi for me *Pídame un taxi, por favor*
How many kilometers is ... from here? *¿Cuántos kilómetros hay de aquí a ...?*
How long does it take to go there? *¿Cuánto se tarda en llegar?*
What will you charge to take me to ...? *¿Cuánto cobra para llevarme a ...?*
How much is a ticket to ...? *¿Cuánto cuesta un billete a ...?*
I want a ticket to ... *Quiero un billete a ..., por favor*
Where does this bus go? *¿Adónde va este bus?*
Stop (on a bus) *¡Parada!*
Please stop here *Pare aquí, por favor*
Please go straight ahead *Vaya recto, por favor*
right *a la derecha*
left *a la izquierda*
What is this place called? *¿Cómo se llama este lugar?*
I'm going to ... *Me voy a ...*
bus stop *parada del bus*
reserved seat *asiento reservado*
reservation *reservación*
airplane *avión*
train *tren*
bus *bus*
Where is there an inexpensive hotel? *¿Dónde hay un hotel económico?*
Do you have a room with... *¿Hay un cuarto con ...?*
bath *baño*
fan *abanico/ventilador*
air-conditioning *aire-climatización*
Where is ...? *¿Dónde está ...?*
the exit *la salida*
the entrance *la entrada*
the airport *el aeropuerto*
a taxi *un taxi*
the police station *la delegación de policía*
the embassy *la embajada*
the post office *la oficina de correos*
the telegraph office *la oficina de telégrafos*
a public telephone *un teléfono público*
a bank *un banco*
a hotel *un hotel*
a restaurant *un restaurante*
a restroom *un servicio*
a private bathroom *el baño*
the ticket office *la oficina de billetes*
a department store *una tienda*
the market *el mercado*

Driving

Fill it up, please *Lleno, por favor*
Please check the oil *Vea el aceite, por favor*
Please fill the radiator *Favor de llenar el radiador*
the battery *la batería*
I need ... *Necesito ...*
a jack *un gato*
a towtruck *una grúa*
a mechanic *un mecánico*
a tire *una llanta*
Help me, please *Ayúdeme, por favor*
Call a doctor quickly! *¡Llame a un médico de prisa!*

Speaking Tico: Tiquismos

If you already speak some Spanish, learn a few *Tiquismos*, uniquely Costa Rican expressions. Tico (Costa Rican) Spanish is rich with them.

The familiar "*tú*" (you) is not used in Costa Rica, even with children. They often use an archaic form, "*vos*." The rules regarding the use of "*vos*" are tricky and elude even advanced students of Spanish: best to stick with "*Usted*," which is always correct.

When walking in areas outside of San José, people passing on the street greet one another with "*Adios*," or " '*dios*." "*Hasta luego*" is used to say "goodbye."

Costa Ricans love to use *sobrenombres*, nicknames. More often than not, the nicknames used have to do with a person's physical appearance: *Macho/Macha* if he or she is ever-so-slightly fair-skinned or fair-haired (not to be confused with *machismo*, an attribute of Latin males, used in Mexico); *China* if she has a slight slant to the eyes, or is actually Oriental; *Negro* if his skin is dark; *Gordito* for someone even slightly overweight; *Moreno* if the person is slightly dark-complexioned, and so on.

If someone asks, "*¿Cómo está Usted?*" it's always correct to reply, "*Muy bien, gracias a Dios*" ("Very well, thanks to God") or "*Muy bien, por dicho*" (Very well, fortunately") but you might want to try something a little more zippy and informal, such as: "*Pura vida*" ("Great") or "*Con toda la pata*" ("Terrific" – literally, "with all the paw") or "*Tranquilo*" ("Relaxed, or cool").

Spanish Language Schools

Whatever a student's language needs, whether merely conversational, for business, or to master the structure of Spanish, an appropriate language school exists in Costa Rica. Listed below are some of the better-known schools. Consult *The Tico Times* for others.

Centro Cultural Costarricense Norteamericano
San José, Costa Rica
Tel: 207 7500
Fax: 224 1480.
www.cccncr.com
Standard, intensive classes in Los Yoses, Cartago, La Sabana, Alajuela, Palmares, Ciudad Quesada and Liberia. Special courses and individual tutoring. Conversation club. The center sponsors plays and concerts. Homestays. Academic credit available.

COSI
Tel: 234 1001
Fax: 253 2117
Toll free: 1-800-771-5184
www.cosi.co.cr
Intensive classes for groups and private tutition. Programs from 1–16 weeks. Classes start every Monday in San José and Manuel Antonio. Homestays.

CPI
Tel. 265 6306
UFax: 265 6866
www.cpi-edu.com
Classes, group and private, in Heredia, Monteverde, and Flamingo. Academic credit offered. Homestays.

Instituto de Español Costa Rica
Tel/fax: 283 4733
www.professionalspanish.com
Role playing, discussions, listening exercises, and videos are part of the classes. Courses at all levels for individuals or in groups. Also cultural programs such as Costa Rican cooking or Latin American dance workshops.

ILISA
San José
Tel: 280 0700
Toll-free: 1-800 ILISA
Fax: 225 4665
www.ilisa.com
Courses with a maximum of four students. Also one-to-one programs. Spanish for professionals available. ILISA uses a communicative approach rather than a method. Homestay and hotels. Free email and computer access.

Mesoamerica Language Institute
San Pedro
Tel: 253 3195
www.mesoamericaonline.com.
A department of the Institute for Central America Studies which is dedicated to the causes of peace, justice, and the well-being of the people and land of Central America. Offers a one-day survival Spanish class for tourists.

FURTHER READING

Books

Because reference books are often unavailable or expensive in Costa Rica, consider purchasing books before leaving home. The ones listed below give a good insight into Costa Rican life.

The Birds of Costa Rica: A Field Guide, by Richard Garrigues, ill. by Robert Dean. San José, Costa Rica: Zona Tropical Publications, 2007. Extraordinary, up-to-date reference with 116 original color plates.

Butterfly in the City: A Good Life in Costa Rica, by Jo Stuart. San José, Costa Rica: Litografía y Imprente LIL S.A., 2006. Musings by a long-term resident.

The Children of Mariplata, by Miguel Benavides. London: Forest Books, 1992. Eleven fables from Costa Rica with local color and deep on human feelings. Translated into English.

Costa Rica: National Parks, by Mario Boza. Madrid: Incafo S.A., 2006. Lavish bilingual coffee-table book by one of the founders of the national park system.

Costa Rica Nature Atlas, by Wilberth Herrera. Heredia: Editorial Incafo S.A. Notes, maps, and pictures of diverse sites, from mountains peaks and volcanoes to rivers and valleys.

The Costa Rican Indigenous People, by Rodrigo Salazar. San José: Editorial Tecnológico de Costa Rica, 2006. Bilingual overview of the country's indigenous history.

Costa Rican Natural History, ed. Daniel H. Janzen. University of Chicago Press, 1983.

Costa Rica: A Traveler's Literary Companion, by Barbara Ras (editor). San Francisco: Whereabouts Press, 1993. A collection of 26 short stories by Costa Rican writers, skillfully translated into English.

Costa Rica: Wildlife of the National Parks and Reserves, by Michael and Patricia Fogden, for the Fundación Neotrópica, 1997. Gorgeous coffee-table book with easy-to-read, fascinating text.

A Guide to the Birds of Costa Rica, by Gary F. Stiles and A.F. Skutch. Cornell University Press, 1990. The bible for birders in Costa Rica; indispensable.

A Guide to Tropical Plants of Costa Rica, by Willow Zuchowski. San José, Costa Rica: Zona Tropical Publications, 2005. Highly recommended guide by expert botanist.

The Green Republic: A Conservation History of Costa Rica, by Sterling Evans. University of Texas Press, 1999. History of conservation ethic in Costa Rica.

A Guide to Amphibians and Reptiles of Costa Rica, by Twan Leenders. Distribuidores Zona Tropical, S.A., 2001.

The History of Costa Rica, by Iván Molina and Steven Palmer. University of Costa Rica, 2001. Complete overview of the country's history.

Hostile Acts: US Policy in Costa Rica in the 1980s, by Martha Honey. Gainesville, Florida: University of Florida Press, 1994.

INBio Pocket Guides: Various easy-to-carry and complete guides on native ornamental plants, mammals, insects, butterflies, and mushrooms. Contact INBio (www.inbio.co.cr).

Monkeys are Made of Chocolate, by Jack Ewing. Colorado: Pixy Jack Press, 2005. A collection of stories from a long-time conservationist on the southern Pacific Coast of Costa Rica.

The New Costa Rican Cuisine, by Isabel Campabadal. San José: Santillana, 1999. Coffee-table book full of beautiful photos, history, and natural information about Costa Rica's Caribbean coast and its people.

The New Key to Costa Rica, by Beatrice Blake and Anne Becher. Berkeley, CA: Ulysses Press, 2004. A guide full of detailed information on bus travel, hotels, restaurants and bars, and all tourist destinations.

The Painted Oxcart, by Michael Sims. San José, Costa Rica: Impresión Comercial, Grupo Nación, 2005. Colorful picture book on the traditional artisanry of Sarchí.

Passion for the Caribbean, by Yazmín Ross. San José: Santillana, 2003. Coffee-table book full of beautiful photos, history, and natural information about Costa Rica's Caribbean coast and its people.

Potholes to Paradise, by Tessa Borner. Silvio Mattachione, 2001. Personal account and advice about moving to Costa Rica.

Pura Vida: The Waterfalls and Hot Springs of Costa Rica, by Sam Mitchell. Menasha Ridge Press, 1995. A self-published guide to 25 waterfalls, seven hot springs, and camping sites. Includes a variety of suggested excursions.

The Surfer's Guide to Costa Rica, by Mike Parise. Los Angeles: SurfPress Publishing, 2004. Low-budget but comprehensive surfing guide.

The Ticos: Culture and Social Change in Costa Rica, by Mavis Biesanz, Richard Biesanz, and Karen Biesanz. Colorado: Lynne Rienner Publishers, 1998. A fluent, well-researched analysis of Costa Rican culture.

The Tico Times Restaurant Guide to Costa Rica, by Eliot Greenspan, San José, Costa Rica: The Tico Times, 2006. Comprehensive bilingual guide to the country's culinary hotspots.

What Happen, by Paula Palmer. San José, Costa Rica: Zona Tropical Publications, 2005. A history of the Talamanca Coast.

Other Insight Guides

Other *Insight Guides* that highlight destinations in this region include:
Insight Guide: Belize offers a full portrait of one of the world's leading eco-tourism destinations, including its rainforests and coral reefs.

Insight Pocket Guide: Cancún & Yucatán Peninsula sifts through Maya history and Spanish heritage to unveil the mysteries of southern Mexico.

Insight Fleximap Costa Rica is a fully laminated pocket-size map (scale 1:730 000), with handy practical data and illustrated highlights of top tourist attractions.

Insight Compact Guide Costa Rica is a handy little guide, with Top 10 Sights and Star-rating to help you plan your visit; fully illustrated, with maps.

Berlitz Compact Guide Costa Rica is a small but well-packed guide, with comprehensive information on where to go and what to do, including hotel and restaurant listings.

ART & PHOTO CREDITS

Glyn Genin/Apa all small cover pictures, 6TL, 6BR, 7CR, 7BL, 7BR, 8CR, 8BR, 9CL, 9BR, 17, 25, 27L, 45, 82/83, 90, 96, 135T, 138, 139, 139T, 140, 140T, 147T, 149T, 151, 151T, 155, 155T, 156T, 159, 159T, 161T, 166/167, 171T, 172, 174T, 183T, 184, 187T, 188, 189T, 193T, 196, 197T, 198, 199, 201, 209T, 216, 217, 218T, 221T, 223T, 229, 231T, 233T, 234, 235, 235T, 238T, 239T, 254T, 253T, 255T, 259T, 260, 262T, 263
Martin Bache/Alamy 291
André Bårtschi 12/13, 88, 148, 190, 208, 237, 239, 242/243, 254, 255, 259
Suzy Bennett/Alamy 271
Gary Braasch 85, 202, 228, 232, 233, 247
John Coletti/Jon Arnold 141
Reinhard D/Robert Harding 6TR
John Elleston 98
Michael & Patricia Fogden 1, 10/11, 78/79, 80/81, 86, 87, 147, 175, 206, 207, 209, 222, 223, 258
Henry C Genthe 14, 20/21, 24, 28, 31R, 31L, 33R, 33L, 36, 37, 43, 44, 49, 56/57, 59, 60, 68, 74R, 104, 110, 111, 112, 113, 114, 115, 117, 118/119, 122/123, 124, 136, 137, 142/143, 149, 152, 153, 154, 158, 161, 169, 171, 173, 182, 192, 194, 200, 218, 220, 221, 226/227, 249, 250, 251, 252, 264
Cozzi Guldo/4Corners Images 135
Genthe/Haber 23, 32, 35, 40, 41, 42
Lode Greven/Free Lens 150

Harvey Haber 16, 22, 34R, 34L, 38, 39, 69, 73
Harvey Haber Collection 46/47, 48, 52/53, 61, 238
Heeb/laif 191
Chip and Jill Isenhart 18, 54, 74L, 84, 89, 120/121, 180, 181, 214, 254, 257, 262
Carlos Jinesta 76, 156, 157, 186, 231
Julio Lainez 62/63, 64/65, 174
Lapa Rios Eco Lodge 281
Miriam Lefkowitz 99
Yadid Levy/Alamy 108L, 108R
Neil P Lucas/Nature Picture Library 212/213
Luiz Claudio Marigo/Bruce Coleman Ltd 241
Buddy Mays 8T, 9TR, 26, 58, 67, 70, 72, 77, 91, 97, 100, 102L, 109, 183, 187, 195, 203, 205, 248, 286, 293
Carl Purcell 66, 71, 145
Jose Fuste Raga/Corbis 134
Schmid Reinhard/SIME/4Corners Images 6BL, 160
Reuters/Corbis 132
R H Productions/Robert Harding 8BL
Orlando Sierra/AFP/Getty Images 55
John Skiffington 27R, 29, 30, 50/51, 75, 94/95, 101, 102R, 103, 105, 106/7, 116, 128/129, 133, 162, 163, 168, 176/177, 185, 189, 192, 193, 197, 215, 219, 236, 240, 253
Marco T Saborio 19
Dave & Sigrun Tollerton/Alamy 261
Mary Steinbacher/Pictures Colour Library 7TR
Carlos M Uribe 204

PICTURE SPREADS

Pages 92/93
Top row from left to right: Michael & Patricia Fogden, Michael & Patricia Fogden, Michael & Patricia Fogden, Buddy Mays
Center row: Arco Images/Alamy, Michael & Patricia Fogden
Bottom row: Buddy Mays, Buddy Mays, Buddy Mays, Glyn Genin.
Pages 164/165
Top row from left to right: Glyn Genin, Glyn Genin, Buddy Mays
Center row: Glyn Genin, Glyn Genin, Marco T Saborio
Bottom row: all by Glyn Genin
Pages 210/211
Top row from left to right: Buddy Mays, Michael & Patricia Fogden, Peter Oxford/Nature Picture Library
Center row: Michael & Patricia Fogden, Gerry Ellis/Nature Picture Library, Michael & Patricia Fogden
Bottom row: Michael & Patricia Fogden, Jeff Foott/Nature Picture Library
Pages 224/225
Top row from left to right: Marco T Saborio, Marco T Saborio, Marco T Saborio, Glyn Genin
Center row: Glyn Genin, Buddy Mays
Bottom row: all by Glyn Genin

Map Production
Colourmap Scanning Ltd

© 2007 Apa Publications GmbH & Co.
Verlag KG (Singapore branch)

COSTA RICA

Cartographic Editor **Zoë Goodwin**
Production **Linton Donaldson**
Design Consultants
Klaus Geisler, Graham Mitchener
Picture Research **Hilary Genin**

INDEX

Numbers in italics refer to photographs

Lago de
Nicaragua

Islas
Solentiname

Punta
Pizote

Punta
Guacalito

Refugio Nacional de
Fauna Silvestre Isla Bolaños

La Cruz

Los Chiles

Golfo de
Santa Elena

Parque Nacional
Guanacaste

Cabo
Santa Elena

Península
Santa Elena

Upala

Refugio Nacional
de Vida Silvestre
Caño Negro

Islas
Murciélagos

Parque Nacional
Santa Rosa

Parque Nacional
Rincón de la Vieja

Zona Protectora
Miravalles

Alajuela

Golfo
de
Papagayo

Liberia

Guanacaste

Zona
Protectora
Tehorio

Punta
Zapotal

Reserva Biológica
Lomas Barbudal

Bagaces

Aguacate

Laguna de
Arenal

Sardinal

Cañas

Parque Nacional
Volcán Arenal

Ciud
Quesa
(San Carl

Cabo Velas

Valle de
Tempisque

Reserva
Santa
Elena

Reserva Biológica
del Bosque Nuboso
de Monteverde

CORDILLERA DE TILARÁN

Parque Nacional
Marino Las Baulas

Ref. Nac. de Fauna
Silvestre Tamarindo

Parque Nacional
Palo Verde

R. F.
Taboga

Zona Protector
de San Ramón

P. N. Barra
Honda

Refugio de
Vida Silvestre
Peñas Blancas

San
Ramón

Bosque
Nacional Diriá

Nicoya

PENÍNSULA DE NICOYA

Reserva
Biológica
Isla Pájaros

Puntarenas

Z. P. F
Gran

Refugio Nacional
de Fauna Silvestre Ostional

Reserva Biológica
Isla Guayabo

Z. P. C
Att

Punta Guiones

Puntarenas

Zona Protectora
Tivives

Z. P. Cerro
de Turruba

Reserva Biológica
Islas Negritos

Parque Nacional
Carara

Punta Coyote

Refugio Nacional
De Vida
Silvestre Curú

Zona Protect
La Cang

Punta Conejo

Reserva Natural Absoluta Cabo Blanco

Cabo Blanco

Isla Cabo
Blanco

Punta Judas

PACIFIC OCEAN

Isla del Coco

0 — 2 km

0 — 2 miles

Punta Agujas

Isla Manuelita

Isla Pájara

Bahía Chatham

Bahía Wafer

Cabo Barreto

Parque Nacional
Isla del Coco

Cerro Yglesias
634

Cabo
Atrevida

Cerro
Jesús Jiménez
430

Cabo Lionel

Isla Muela

Cabo Dampier